THE TRUTH
Israelites Identity, Wisdom And Destiny

ROBERT DENIS

http://www.israelite.net

Copyright 1987
The Israelite Network
P.O. Box 1747
NYC, NY 10101

ISBN 0-9669147-0-8

About The Author And The Book

THE TRUTH is a guidebook to understanding the deep secrets and mysteries of the Bible, human identity and destiny. Many readers claimed to have attained more understanding from reading this book than they could have gotten in a lifetime of going to church and Sunday school. **THE TRUTH** is considered by many authorities as a prerequisite to any study of the Bible.

The author, Robert Yawanathan Denis, is a modern day pioneer of the Israelite movement. The goal of the movement is to awaken, heal and unite the Afro-Asiatic descendents of the biblical twelve tribes of Israel that are scattered around the world, so that they may begin to reap the joys, benefits and dignity of their own nationality, community and culture as exemplified in the Holy Bible. From his youth, the author has been standing firmly in the Lord, contributing actively to the spread of the gospel of the kingdom of heaven to all nations. Over the past twenty years Yawanathan has sacrificed without reserve, suffering many persecutions, as he struggles to increase the world's awareness of the one true God and the identity of the original twelve tribes of Israel; through lectures, publications and Bible studies.

The author's exceptionally diversified life experiences, meekness and spiritual insight, enables him to present the truth concerning the origin and destiny of mankind in an objective manner that can be readily understood and felt. The author hopes that this book will continue to serve as an inspiration and a guideline to the many scholars, Christians and Israelites around the world in their study of the Bible.

The author has learned that there is a universal principle of reciprocal love that was enunciated by the Creator from the foundation of the universe. This principle is contained in most religious texts, mythologies and sciences, but is interpreted by each society in the context of their own environment and symbols. Over time, the original principal of love that founded the universe became polluted and corrupted, as society begins to exploit and misinterpret it to satisfy personal greed and lust by creating false religions and social systems.

The goal of this book is to present the facts concerning the identity, wisdom and destiny of the descendents of the twelve tribes of Israel; and let you the reader draw your own conclusions. The author addresses the major issues and brings to light the great mysteries concerning history and prophecy. Above all, the book reveals the genealogical and the geographical identity of the nations, including the location of the original twelve tribes of Israel. It has been called the official handbook of the Israelite movement.

The book contains a wide scope of concrete scientific evidence: historical, bibliographical and archeological, from around the world. The mysteries found in this book have not been taught in nearly 2,000 years. As the truth begins to propagate, it will bring joy, freedom and real hope to those who receive it. The physical and spiritual change has already begun.

TABLE OF CONTENTS

INTRODUCTION

True love is the meaning of life. The truth is the foundation of life, liberty, and destiny; authenticated by the Almighty. The essence of truth is spiritual, absolute, and eternal. Realization of truth is brought about by the expansion of awareness through deliberate meditation and exercises in: knowledge, wisdom, understanding, discipline, compassion, humility, sacrifice, and transformation. The truth is important because it is the foundation of love: love is the law, the meaning, the purpose, and the destiny of life!

To find the truth we must be open minded, and ready to surrender our personal ideas, prejudices, lusts, and selfishness, respecting the universal laws. All dimensions, energies, and life are one in purpose, with love as the central theme and original purpose of the universe, defined by the Creator.

Our hate, fear, ignorance, prejudices, philosophical and worldly religious fanaticism, excessive materialistic and carnal cravings, and selfish desires are like shackles binding our minds. They keep us from experiencing the exhilarating mystery and rapture of being alive: to live life with freedom, harmony, meaning, purpose, and destiny. We have to learn of our true origin and identity, and become spiritually conscious, to achieve peace within ourselves. Only then can we begin to recognize and experience at-one-ment with the Creator, and fulfill our destiny! Achieving this realization of our identity provides the keys to solving the trials of daily living, and leads to peace, freedom, and joy.

The greatest and most powerful of all truth is love. There is no truth to be found, where there is no love in the heart. This book will scientifically explore the existence of the Creator, the true origin of the universe, and the identity and destiny of mankind on the earth. This book will challenge you to scrutinize various historical, scientific, and prophetic mediums. We will also expose and obliterate the fallacies of institutionalized religion and politics; bringing to light the worlds most well kept secrets!

Now it is high time to wake up out of sleep. We are living in the time of spiritual and physical war, at the crossroads of destiny! What people are not going to hear, they will certainly feel. It is time to learn the truth concerning our origin, identity, purpose, and destiny. It is time to learn the meaning of true civilization. It is hoped that this urgent message will bring light where there is darkness, strength where there is weakness, comfort where there is pain, and unity where there is division. Where there was death and captivity, the truth can guarantee freedom and joy for you!

THE TRUTH

ORIGIN AND IDENTITY

EXISTENCE OF THE CREATOR

The existence of the Creator should be examined, because throughout history and in this generation, more people have died in the name of religion than for any other reason. Today people often find it difficult believing that the Creator exists, mainly because most institutionalized educators profess to the world that the Lord God YAHAWAH, the Almighty Creator, does not exist. The so-called authorities of this world have claimed that God did not create the universe and the living organisms. The scientists of today are telling us that it was man that created god, in his own image.

Just because you can't see something does not mean it does not exist! We can't see the wind, and neither can we see the future; however they do exist! The universe for all practical purposes is infinite; man can not know everything that exists unless he has infinite knowledge. In order for anyone to make a statement of absolute negativism, like saying there is no God, he would have to be all knowing. In fact, a person that can say that is basically saying he is god, since only a god is omniscient!

Another very important reason why some people deny the existence of the Creator is because the religions have been maliciously teaching them about a false god, and lies against the true words of the Bible, giving people a false idea of what the Bible is truly saying! Not only are most churches set up against the Bible, most of the leaders of this world have in addition been brainwashing people with lies in the westernized educational systems by misrepresenting the facts in a form of false science! What is even stranger is that many people believe in the devil, and worship Satan, but they don't believe in the Almighty God that created all things.

Like religion, the main purpose of modern institutionalized education today is not to teach the truth, but to exploit the people economically and politically, and to brainwash and colonize the minds of unsuspecting people. Organized religion, like organized crime, has forced people to idolize the picture of a man instead of God, creating many atheists in the process, when the people begin to recognize that they are being bombarded with false and malicious interpretations of the Bible.

People believe in evolutionism rather than creationism because they were never taught both sides of the story fairly. Maliciously so, the school system has only shown the evolutionist viewpoint for the origin of the universe! These pseudo-scholars would like to deny the Lord as Creator so they can give themselves the glory, and selfishly set up their own image and gods.

Logically there has to be a first cause to all the effects that have manifested in the existing universe. Lets now prove beyond the slightest doubt that the Creator exists, and that the universe was made by him! First, according to the theory of relativity the physical laws observable in one part of the universe have to relatively apply to any other part: all frames of reference are not absolute, but relative. Therefore the universe in no way could have created itself, it had to be created by a force of absolute power outside of itself. This is very easily proven!

The first scientific law to be considered is the law of cause and effect. An effect can not cause itself. By law, every effect must have a cause. Therefore all the effects observed, including the universe itself, must have a First Cause external to themselves! What was it? By all logic and true science this could only be the work of an omnipotent, omniscient Creator.

The scientists of the world have maliciously fabricated a false story to explain the origin of the physical universe. They're teaching that twenty billion years ago, a Cosmic Egg (a ball of tremendous mass and energy), was sitting peacefully in equilibrium until one day the thing exploded. And that super hot expanding gas was supposed to have somehow condensed into the stars, planets and galaxies. They call this idea the Big Bang

THE TRUTH

Theory! And they're also teaching that to this day somewhere out in space matter is automatically creating itself out of nothingness: they call this the Steady State! Be informed that these false teachings don't have a shred of evidence to prove them, and we will see that all of the true evidence, observations, and facts definitely do disprove these lies concerning the origin of the universe!

Now, consider the First Law of Motion: an object sitting in equilibrium will remain in equilibrium unless acted upon by an external force. So it is contradictory and false to say that a Cosmic Egg sitting in equilibrium from eternity can spontaneously explode. This is impossible and unscientific, objects at rest remain at rest unless acted upon by an external force. It would require an external force to cause this thing to leave the state of equilibrium and to explode. Furthermore, those guys were not there twenty billion years ago to witness and confirm that this explosion did occur! Many complex fields and waves are observed in the universe: gravitational, nuclear, and electromagnetic. Waves need an external energy to start them vibrating and propagating; they could not have evolved by themselves in the vacuum of space. Objects at rest remain at rest unless acted upon by an external force! The universe could not have originated itself!

Secondly, according to the Law of Conservation of Matter and Energy, matter and energy can neither be created nor destroyed but only changed in form. So where did the exploding Cosmic Egg and the substance of it come from? Where did the energy that caused it to explode come from? Who initiated the explosion? The total amount of mass and energy in the universe has to be conserved! So it is impossible for this Cosmic Egg to have ever existed. Because by natural forces nothing can be created or destroyed but only changed in form; this predicts that the universe could not have created itself out of anything, and had to be of supernatural origin! The universe could only be the product of an omnipotent, omniscient Creator!

Thirdly, According to the Natural Gas Laws, a gas in a certain volume of space will continue to expand due to its kinetic energy, until it fills up that space. So the explosion of the Cosmic Egg would create a super-heated gas, expanding at thousands of miles per hour and filling up the infinite void of space. There would be nothing in the vacuum of space to cause this gas to stop expanding. It would be impossible for this expanding gas to stop expanding by itself and out of nowhere create spinning: stars, planets, galaxies, and living organisms.

This occurrence would be impossible because the First Law of motion states that an object in motion remains in motion unless acted upon by an external force! If the universe is all there is, what external force, in the vacuum of space, would cause that rapidly expanding gas to stop, and condense into complex galaxies and star systems and so on? This so-called Big Bang explosion contradicts and is opposite to every natural and man-made explosion observed, since explosions destroy order; explosions do not create order! Evolution and the Big Bang Theory are nothing but myths. The institutionalized cosmologists and evolutionists are claiming that complex order and design are the result of an explosion, instead of chaos and decay. If you believe in the Big Bang you probably believe in all the other fairy tales that were devised to enslave the mind!

And not only this, they've claimed to have detected echoes from the Big Bang explosion with a microwave antenna. This is impossible, because the microwave is a form of electromagnetic energy, like visible light, ultraviolet light, and X-rays. Now these waves travel in space at approximately 299,792,500 meters per second, away from their point of origin. And remember that according to the Theory of Relativity no object of mass in the natural universe can exceed the speed of light waves, including microwaves. When we examine the sound wave or the noise produced by an explosion, we see that the sound travel at the speed of the wave and away from the site of the explosion. Therefore if a burst of cosmic rays were produced by an explosion twenty billion years ago, they could not possibly be detect today within the boundaries of the physical universe, because the electromagnetic radiation moving away at the speed of light since the moment of the explosion would have separated itself from the material universe and would be expanding ahead of and faster than the material universe

THE TRUTH

(waves travel faster than gases), forever outward at the speed of light, away from the universe and never to return and be detected!

According to the Inverse Square Wave Propagation Theory, this Background Microwave Radiation can not be from a Primordial Big Bang explosion, because upon close examination of the Cosmic Background Radiation as measured from different parts of the sky, it is observed that the radiation readings vary randomly from one section of the sky to the next. But according to the Laws of Wave propagation the readings should be even and constant for every section of the sky compared to the next. This proves that the detected radiation could not be from a primordial Big Bang explosion!

When we observe the universe we see every system is in rotational motion: the planets rotate, the stars rotate, and galaxies rotate. Now the force of an explosion in the vacuum of space is only radial or outward, nothing rotational; so where did rotational motion come from? According to the Laws of Angular Momentum, it takes an external force to start an object spinning since the only possible motion that can be created by an explosion is radial, meaning outward expansion, this Big Bang idea also contradicts the Law of Angular Momentum. The Universe is observed to have spin to it imparted by the Creator, which would not have been there otherwise!

Furthermore, according to the Second Law of Thermal Dynamics, in any reaction the total amount of useful energy has to decrease and the total amount of entropy (randomness) have to increase. In other words, a system left to itself will tend to decay to a state from maximum order and maximum energy and to maximum disorder and minimum energy. For example, a river runs downhill, not up and a clock spring will unwind, not wind itself up.

The Second Law of Thermal Dynamics predicts decay and disorder. For example, that perfume will escape from a bottle into the air and not return back into the bottle. It also predicts that a mixture of solutions will not sort itself into separate substances. A gas is a mixture of particles of different kinetic energy, but it will never separate itself into two halves, each half of the gas a different temperature. According to the Second Law of Thermal Dynamics an explosion has to create disorder and randomness, not order!

All independent systems have to go from a state of maximum energy to minimum energy, and to disorder! The universe and all life are decaying, they are not evolving and becoming more complex with time. All things decay as they grow older. The Second Law of Thermal Dynamics confirms that the universe could not have started out as an explosion since explosions create disorder and destroy order. In addition to that it naturally has to be decaying further, and not evolving to become more complex.

Evolution and the Big Bang would not be natural or scientific. That's like the perfume finding its way out of the air and back into the bottle, or like warm water separating itself into cold and hot halves. When we look at the universe we see a highly ordered place, with physical laws and highly ordered systems, and all this could not have evolved from a simple state of maximum chaos, like an explosion! The concept of Spontaneous Evolution and the Big Bang Theory contradict the Second Law of Thermal Dynamics!

Any system left to itself will decay; that is why you can not create a Virtual Energy machine, a machine of one hundred percent efficiency as it converts energy from one form to another. In any process involving energy conversion, the total amount of energy left for useful work has to be less than the initial amount; this is the Law of Decay. The observable universe is slowly decaying. Stars and people don't grow younger, they grow older and gas clouds are observed to dissipate over time.

Upon further observation, when we apply the Second Law of Thermal Dynamics, this universe appears to be a very young creation. If the universe were twenty billion years old, there would be no star clusters left, the members of clusters are observed to be flying apart, so they would have long since flown apart! And the spiral arms of the galaxies would have pulled in and assumed the configuration of a ring or a disk, due to momentum!

THE TRUTH

The earth's magnetic field is decaying exponentially, and if the earth was even a hundred thousand years old, there would be no detectable magnetic field. The Earth has to be a very recent creation!

And according to the laws of decay (entropy and enthalpy of matter and energy), if the universe was infinitely old, it would be dead; the fact that it is not proves that it isn't infinitely old! God is not pretending to exist, He really does exist. If He did not exist the atheists would not be trying so hard to deny the facts! This universe is full of life and energy because it is the recent creation of an existing omnipotent and omniscient Creator!

THE ORIGIN OF WISDOM

The words of the Almighty God YAHAWAH are the origin of all wisdom. The prophecies of the Bible existed long before the Bible came to be in its present form. In fact the prophecies concerning world events existed before man was created to exist upon the earth. The prophecies are simply the plans, which the Creator had outlined for his creation before he formed it!

The prophecies were first revealed to mankind by way of the names of stars, and the cycles of the zodiac. In other words the very first gospel given to man was the zodiac. However, astrology is false. Astrology is the pollution of the zodiac, as man made religion is the pollution of the Bible.

Knowledge of the zodiac prophecies was conveyed to Adam, approximately six thousand years ago, directly from the Almighty Creator. Teaching Adam the stellar names, whose names are symbolic of scriptures, accomplished this. It was the Creator, not man that gave each star a spiritual prophetic name! Each original star name represents an event to be accomplished upon the earth; the names are scriptures! The Lord taught those prophetic names of stars to Adam, which he was to preserve and teach to his descendants after him.

Noah, a descendent of Adam, also preserved and taught this sacred knowledge to his three sons: Shem, Ham, and Japhet. Their ancestors thus transferred this spiritual knowledge from the pre-flood Adamic world to the people of the New World after the flood. Since Shem, Ham, and Japhet are the progenitors of all people and nations upon the earth, initially all the nations were taught the prophecies about the first and Second Coming of the Savior and Deliverer that was to redeem mankind! Glimpses of this Gospel can be found in various forms within the ancient myths and religions of all nations of antiquity: the Egyptians, the Asians, the Aztecs, and so on!

After the descendants of the three sons of Noah began to multiply and populate the world, some people started to pervert and misuse the pure knowledge contained in the prophecies of the zodiac for their own selfish political, social, and economic benefits; to gain power and exploit others. For example, they created many false religions to idolize their kings and false gods! This confusion began at Babel, a city in ancient Mesopotamia. The leaders of the nations out of their own imaginations first created the different religions and occult practices. They used perverted forms of the original zodiac gospel, in order to satisfy their selfish personal lust and greed for wealth and power. They used it to glorify themselves instead of the Creator. In fact the same problems still exist in the modern religions and political systems of this world.

The sphinx and the great pyramid, constructed at the time of the patriarchs, are the keys to solving the mysteries of the zodiac prophecies. The word Sphinx means binder, and it serves as a marker to indicate the true beginning and end of the twelve signs of the zodiac. The Sphinx consists of two parts: the head of a woman, and the body of a lion. The head of the woman represents Virgo, and the body of a lion represents Leo. Virgo the head, is the true beginning of the zodiac, and Leo is the end of the zodiac! Now we know where to begin our examination of the zodiac. More details are given in a later chapter.

In brief, Virgo is symbolic of the original Hebrew Israelite nation, the nation that would bring forth Jesus Christ, the savior! Virgo does not represent Mary, but the twelve tribes of Israel, and the seed is Jesus. Libra represents the price that Christ would come to pay, as an atonement to redeem us from sin. Scorpio represents the afflictions and the death of Christ. Sagittarius represents the triumph of Jesus over sin and death.

Capricorn is shown as half goat and half fish. The goat is representative of the fact that Christ died as a sin offering; the scapegoat that died for our sins. The lively tail of a fish, which is connected to the goat, represents life. The tail of a fish is lively. Capricorn reveals that through the death of Jesus Christ as our sin offering, comes life! Capricorn represents the resurrection.

Aquarius shows Christ as the Water Bearer, bringing to us the waters of life; which represent the gospel of truth: the word of God. Pisces represent the people in captivity within the ocean of false philosophy, religion, and materialism. Aries represents Christ as the Lamb who would come to deliver us!

Now, The second half of the zodiac deals with the Second Coming of Jesus Christ. The Milky Way divides the zodiac in two. The second half starts with Taurus, depicted by a charging bull. The raging bull is a symbol of the violent destruction, catastrophes, plagues, and the judgment against this world that is to occur in the last days; just before the Second Coming of Jesus Christ.

Gemini represents unity and victory for the people who accept the truth, and become united as one with God and Christ in the truth. The crab often represents Cancer. The hard shell of the crab protects it from the violence of the ocean around it. This sign represents the divine protection that is guaranteed by God to those that believe, obey, and accept the truth of the gospel concerning Jesus Christ. The followers of the truth will be protected and delivered from the plagues and destructions of the last days.

The last sign is Leo. Leo the Lion represents Christ at his Second Coming, as the conquering Lion, coming to subdue and bring judgment upon the head of the unrepentant sinners and the enemies of the gospel! The Lion represents Jesus Christ returning as the King of kings and the Lord of lords.

What is called Christianity today is not new. The gospel of the zodiac is the original Christianity. That is why Christ says, "In the beginning was the Word." In the Chapter called the zodiac, we will examine the detailed revelations contained in the zodiac gospel to see the prophecies pertaining to the first and Second Coming of Jesus Christ, and the destiny of mankind! You can rightly say that Adam was the first Christian!

All of the classic myths, pagan gods, religions, and occult practices of all the nations of antiquity (Egypt, Babylonian, Asia, Aztec and pre-Columbian civilizations) are polluted forms of the original zodiac gospel. All the gods of Greece and Rome were imported from Egypt, and then given Greek and Latin names. Therefore, they too are polluted versions of the zodiac gospel! This knowledge was based on the gospel of the zodiac, which Ham taught to his descendants. Ham was the progenitor of the Egyptians and all the Africans. Ham had learned the gospel from his father Noah.

The Egyptians preserved the zodiac prophecies concerning Christ as the coming Deliverer and Redeemer in the legend of Osiris. Osiris, accompanied by his disciples, performed many miracles. Later he was eventually crucified on the vernal equinox. He remained three days and nights to judge the dead, and he was then resurrected, and he ascended to heaven. As you can see, Osiris personifies the Christ that was to come!

The Egyptians also illustrated several Christian-like scenes on the walls of the temple of Luxor in which Horus is represented: The Annunciation, the Immaculate Conception, the Birth, and the Adoration. The story of Horus, Osirus, and Isis was an imitation of the ancient zodiac gospel concerning the first and Second Coming of Christ, which God had taught to Adam. Also, what we call Christianity today is nothing new. This knowledge was already prerecorded in all its details in the zodiac gospel, from the foundation of the world!

In America, a famous myth that also imitates and conceals the original gospel of Christianity is the story of Quetzalcoatl. Quetzalcoatl was described as an Asiatic man with brown-skin and wooly hair, and having supernatural powers. He practiced exorcism, healing, fasting (for forty days), and making miracles. When Quetzalcoatl resisted the temptations of the devil, he was persecuted and crucified on the vernal equinox. Here again is another perfect example of how the original gospel, handed down from ancient times, had been concealed in a polluted form, as a myth.

All the nations had inherited the original gospel from the ancient ancestors. Unfortunately they transformed and polluted it with false religion. And they replaced Jesus Christ with their own false gods, idols, and fake savior images. Images such as Apollo, Prometheus, and Zeus of the Greeks; Buddha and Krishna of India; Fuhi of the Chinese; Zaha of the Japanese; Quetzalcoatl of the Mexicans; Osiris, Isis, and Horus of the Egyptians; and so on.

Because all the false gods and religions have a common origin, deriving from the original zodiac gospel, upon close examination they are found to correspond to each other in almost every act and deed. For example the nine gods of ancient Egypt correspond to the nine lords of the night found in the Mexican legends. Kwan-Yin, the Chinese queen of heaven, called Kwannon in Japan, correspond to Isis of the Egyptians. However Jesus Christ, who is the true Savior and redeemer of mankind, fulfilled the true prophecies depicted by the zodiac.

For example, the female goddesses of the pagan religions were derived from the sign of Virgo. Virgo depicts an impregnated woman. The image of a woman is used symbolically in the Bible to represent the original nation of Israel; the nation which was to bring forth the Savior Jesus Christ to the world.

<< Revelation 12:1,2 >> [There appeared a great wonder in heaven; a woman clothed with the sun, and the moon under her feet, and upon her head a crown of twelve stars: And she being with child cried, travailing in birth, and pained to be delivered.]

If you have doubts, check your Bible! The twelve stars represent the original twelve tribes of Israel, the child of course represents Jesus Christ!

The Lord gave man a law, not a religion, and created a family of nations not churches, and cults. The only true religion is the law of the creator: to love God, and to love your neighbor. Considering the way the word religion is used today, the Bible is not a religious book. The idea of religion started with men that were greedy for power and wealth, who needed a method of controlling the minds of ignorant people, to enslave and exploit them. Among other things, religion is also a tool used in colonial societies to colonize the mind with false images of the colonizer as your god and savior.

The Lord gave man a law, not a religion. The religions have created their own laws and rejected the laws of God, found in the Bible! The word religion comes from the Greek word religlio, meaning to restrain, hold back, and bind. Modern political religion has been used as a prison, a drug to keep your mind in a trapped state, keeping you from experiencing reality, identity, consciousness, and spiritual truth!

Most people did not choose their religion, but got it by accident. Their religion is a result of environmental, cultural, and geographical factors; such as where they were born and raised. They acquired the religion because it was forced on them from youth, and they were never allowed to see alternate sides of the story.

Religion imprisons your mind; but the Bible is truth that creates freedom and joy! Unfortunately, the gospel of the kingdom as found in the Bible has not been accurately taught for about two thousand years. There is only one truth; why are there so many religions? If it had not been for all the man-made religions confusing the people, they would have seen and believed the truth that is found in the sacred scriptures of the Bible. The only purpose of man-made organized religious systems is to turn the truth into lies, and to take the glory from the Creator and give it to man and false idols!

<< Romans 1:19 to 23 >> [Because that which may be known of God is manifest in them; for God hath shewed it unto them. For the invisible things from the creation of the world are clearly seen, being understood by the things that are made, even his eternal power and Godhead; so that they are without excuse: Because that, when they knew God, they glorified him not as God, neither were thankful; but became vain in their imaginations and their foolish heart was darkened. Professing themselves to be wise, they became fools And changed

the glory of the incorruptible God into an image made like to corruptible man, and to birds, and four footed beasts, and creeping things.]

The religious leaders of today are leading the whole world into darkness, teaching lies so they can rule and be idolized. They are teaching the people lies in the scholastic and religious institutions. They are condemned to suffer in hell, for teaching lies against the Bible and for teaching others to do so!

Let's be clear about the name of the real God. There are two words in the original Hebrew text of the Bible that is translated as God. The most common is the word ALAHAYAM. ALAHAYAM has two parts, ALAH and YAM. The word ALAH means power, and YAM makes it plural: Powers. ALAHAYAM can either refer to the Almighty God, or it could also refer to an angel or group of angels representing God. The word ALAHAYAM is plural, the Powers.

The second, and the most important word in the original Hebrew text that is translated as God, is YAHAWAH. The word YAHAWAH is the proper name of God, which identifies him directly. It consists of two parts: YAH means He, HAWA means to be. YAHAWAH is often translated as meaning I AM. Although we used it, the word "God" is not the proper name for the Creator, his proper name is in the ancient Hebrew: YAHAWAH! We often use the words Lord, Creator, Most High, the Almighty, or the Father when referring to the Almighty God, the Lord YAHAWAH.

> << Exodus 3:13,14 >> [And Moses said unto God, Behold, when I come unto the children of Israel, and shall say unto them, The God of your fathers hath sent me unto you; and they shall say to me, What is his name? What shall I say unto them? <14> And God said unto Moses, I AM THAT I AM: and he said, Thus shalt thou say unto the sons of Israel, I AM hath sent you.]

The true name of Jesus Christ is the Hebrew name: MASHAYAK YAHAWASHY. MASHAYAK means the Anointed or Chosen. YAHAWASHY means Savior. Jesus is a Greek name that means savior, and Christ means anointed or chosen. Jesus Christ is our Anointed Savior, the mediator between God and man!

> << Matthew 1:21 >> [...Thou shalt call his name Jesus: for he shall save his people from their sins.]

Man did not create the Bible, it is the word of the Creator as recorded by the prophets. First of all let us not be prejudiced or racist about the true origin of the prophets of God that recorded the Bible. If you say man wrote the Bible, then ask yourself: was it the Asiatic man, or the European man that wrote the Bible? Because there was no literate European civilization in ancient history, when most of the Bible was written! Furthermore, God spake to Moses in Egypt, not Europe or to Europeans. Ancient Egyptians were of the Asiatic type, and did not resemble the people living in Egypt today: who are the descendants of Greek and Arab colonists. The truth should have priority over racism. The Bible is a record of the instructions of the Creator given to all of mankind for a blessing.

> << Second Timothy 3:16 >> [All scripture is given by the inspiration of God, and is profitable for doctrine, for reproof, for correction, for instruction in righteousness]

THE TRUTH

<< *Second Peters 1:20,21* >> *[Knowing this first, that no prophecy of the scriptures is of any private interpretation* [the Bible means exactly what it say]. *For the prophecy came not in old time by the will of man: but of holy men of the Lord spoke as they were moved by the Holy Spirit.]*

Not every person can decide to be a teacher of the Bible, and then begin to teach. To qualify, the Creator has to ordain the teacher and send the teacher:

<< *Psalms 147: 19, 20* >> *[He Sheweth his words unto Jacob, his statutes and his judgments unto Israel. He hath not dealt so with any nation]*

<< *Micah 4:2* >> *[And many nations shall come, and say, come, and let us go up to the mountain of the Lord and to the house of the Power of Jacob; and he will teach us his ways, and we will walk in his paths: for the law shall go forth of Zion, and the word of the Lord from Jerusalem.]*

And most importantly, a person can not interpret the Bible, and put their own meaning for what the Bible is saying!

<< *Second Peters 1:20,21* >> explains: *[Knowing this first, that no prophecy of the scripture is of any private interpretation. For the prophecy came not by the will of man: but of holy men of the Father spoke as they were moved by the Holy Spirit.]*

First of all to understand the Bible you have to first pray and ask the Almighty to reveal it to you. Secondly, the Bible interprets itself. It says what it says and also repeats itself in different sections. If something is not clear in one section, you'll find it in other sections. As you compare the two, the meaning becomes clearer the more you study. The mystery within the Bible is like a puzzle that has to be pieced together here and there. All of the pieces will come together and fit only in one way, and create a perfect picture! As you jump around and compare the verses, it will also become clear that the Bible interprets itself!

<< *Isaiah 28:10* >> *[For precept must be upon precept, precept upon precept; line upon line, line upon line; here a little, and there a little.]*

All the organized religions of the world originate from pagan cults. Roman Christianity is identical to the religions of ancient Babylon and Egypt, which worship false idols, and elevate the image of the woman (Mary) above Jesus Christ! The Lord gave a law for all mankind to follow; not all of these different religions, they can't all be correct because they are all in conflict and contradict each other. More people have died because of deception by false religion than any other cause!

<< *Psalms 50:16-20* >> *[But unto the wicked the Lord saith; What has thou to do to declare my statutes, or that thou shouldest take my covenant in thy mouth? Seeing thou hatest instruction, and casteth my words behind thee. When thou sawest a thief then thou consentedst with him, and has been partakers with adulterers. Thou givest thy mouth to evil, and thy tongue frameth deceit.]*

MANIFESTATION OF THE UNIVERSE.

For a person to understand himself and realize his destiny, it is imperative that he is cognizant of his identity and origin. It was earlier proven beyond doubt that the creator has to exist, the universe is his special creation, and the Bible contains the words of the Almighty Creator! We saw that the Theory of Evolution is nothing but a racist and colonialist lie. We will now confirm the origin and age of the creation, and the origin of life on the earth!

Scientists today have maliciously claimed that the universe is billions of years old. However, all the evidence confirms the opposite, that in fact this is a very young universe! Yet, these institutional scientists have chosen to reject the facts and have created a myth to glorify themselves to discredit the Bible. Those charlatans have nothing in terms of actual facts supporting their claim concerning evolution and their false assumption that the universe started from an explosion billions of years ago! They have maliciously and diabolically used their assumptions as proof; this is illogical and unscientific! The evolutionists have no true evidence at all, but a lot of misrepresentation of the facts!

Firstly, they claim that the process of radiometry can date the age of materials. Radiometric dating is based on the decay rate of radioactive elements. By observing the rate at which one radioactive element, like Uranium, decays into another element like Lead. Traces of radioactive elements and the product elements they decay into are found in rocks. By analyzing the amount of the parent element that have decayed into the end product, some scientists claim they can determine the age of rocks and their contents.

For example, Uranium 238 decays into Lead 206 plus 8 Helium atoms, the Half-life being 4.5 billion years (alpha decay method); Potassium 40 decays to Argon 40, and then into Calcium 40, having a half life of 1.3 billion years (electron capture method); Rubidium 87 decays into Strontium 87, with a half-life of 60 billion years (beta-decay). The half-life of a radioactive element is the calculation of the amount of time based on the probability that half of a given sample of radioactive atoms will undergo nuclear decay, transforming half of that sample into a different element. It is the average amount of time it takes for half of a given sample of element to decay into another element. Then again in the next half-life, half of the remaining undecayed atoms will decay, and so on, until the sample is transformed!

It is true that radioactive elements do decay, but the process can not be used as a clock to date the age of rocks because the rate of decay is not constant. It has been proven that the rate of decay can be altered by factors such as pressure, stress, concentration, temperature, magnetic and electric fields. The earth's environmental conditions were never constant, and the earth's magnetic field has never in history been constant. Therefore, it is not possible to determine how fast or how slow the radioactive elements were decaying in the past, since no one was there watching them decay and recording the rates.

The second reason why radiometric decay can not be used as a clock for dating the earth is because there is no way of determining how much of each of the substances were present in the original sample at the beginning of the decay. And also there are no closed systems in nature: traces of the radioactive elements are constantly migrating out of the rocks, and radioactive elements and radiation from outside the system are constantly contaminating the rocks. The concept of radioscopy was a hoax fabricated as an attempt by the worldly institutions to discredit the word of God!

Secondly, the laws of thermal dynamics require and confirm that the universe has to be very young! According to the Second Law of Thermal Dynamics, in any reaction the total amount of useful energy has to decrease and the total amount of entropy (randomness) has to increase. In other words, a system left to itself will tend to decay to a state of maximum disorder and minimum energy. For example, a river runs downhill, not up and a clock spring will unwind, not wind itself up. They have to go to a state of minimum energy and maximum disorder!

The Second Law of Thermal Dynamics predicts, for example that perfume will escape from a bottle into the air and not return back into the bottle. It also predicts that a mixture of solutions will not sort itself into separate substances. A gas is a mixture of particles of different kinetic energy, but it will never separate itself into two halves, each half of the gas a different temperature. According to the Second Law of Thermal Dynamics an explosion has to create disorder and randomness, not order!

Therefore, the Second Law of Thermal Dynamics implies that the universe could not have started out as an explosion since explosions create disorder and not order. In addition, any system left to itself has to be naturally decaying into simpler parts and can not be evolving to become more complex. That would not be natural; that's like the perfume finding its way out of the air and back into the bottle, or like warm water separating itself into cold and hot halves.

A complex design, comprised of simple parts requires a designer and a builder. In nature everything decays with time. Only an external force directed by an intelligent being could cause a collection of simple parts to form into a complex structure. When we look at the universe we see a highly ordered place, with physical laws and highly ordered systems, and all this could not have evolved from a simpler state! It would be unnatural. The concept of Spontaneous Evolution contradicts the Second Law of Thermal Dynamics.

Any system left to itself will decay; that is why you can not create a Virtual Energy machine, a machine of one hundred percent efficiency as it converts energy from one form to another. In any process involving energy conversion, the total amount of energy left for useful work has to be less than the initial; this is the Law of Energy Decay. The observable universe is slowly decaying. Stars and people don't grow younger, they grow older, and gas clouds are observed to dissipate over time. If the universe were ten billion years old, it would have run out of energy many times over!

Upon further observation, when we apply the Second Law of Thermal Dynamics, this universe appears to be a very young creation. If the universe were twenty billion years old, there would be no star clusters since the members of clusters are observed to be flying apart, so they would have long since flown apart! And the Spiral arms of the galaxies would have pulled in due to rotational forces.

The earth's magnetic field is decaying exponentially, and if the earth were even a hundred thousand years old, there would be no detectable magnetic field. The Earth has to be a very recent creation! And, according to this law, if the universe were billions of years old, it would be dead. The fact that it is not proves that it is not infinitely old, but is a rather recent creation of an omnipotent, omniscient Creator!

It is very important to understand the truth concerning the origin of mankind, not only for scientific reasons, but also for social and personal reasons! To know your origin is to know your identity. An identity provides a person with a frame of reference in society, a sense of purpose and destiny.

The scientists of this world have claimed that twenty million years ago, man evolved from apes; and that complex life forms evolve from simpler forms of life. They are contradicting every law of science and denying that the Lord God YAHAWAH created all creatures after its own kind. This falsehood is taught to the nations around the world, to blind and deceive the people and to keep them from worshipping the true God. The concept that life evolved from nonliving elements is impossible according to all the laws of the universe. The idea that life evolved spontaneously is contrary to all the laws of statistical science and to all the laws that govern the physical universe!

The evolutionists say that the so-called theory of evolution has its evidence in what they call the fossil record, which they say is proof of their theory of evolution. The fossil record is based on the bones of dead animals that have been found. Those bones are so arranged as to reveal an assumed pattern of one animal evolving to become another animal, over the course of millions of years.

They place one-cell animals at the bottom of that evolutionary scale, which appears out of nowhere. Then they claim that other simple life forms spontaneously evolve into complex ones, with many transitional animals in between. None of these transitional forms of animals were ever found.

And they claim that the new body parts somehow began spontaneously: bones, organs, arms, legs, and wings resulting in complex life forms with all parts perfectly complete. Evolutionist claim that eventually mankind evolved out of the monkey. All of this they claim occurred by pure chance. A cloud is about ninety-percent water and a watermelon is about ninety-percent water but that does not mean the watermelon came from the cloud. The theory of evolution is also illogical.

But in reality the fossil record reveals the opposite. All biological processes are continuous, but the fossil record does not show in any place where animals are being transformed into others. The evolutionists try to explain this by saying that they have missing links in the evolutionary chart. For years, they have been trying to find those missing links, and with all the modern technology, they have not been able to find one! Obviously, links can not be missing if they were not there in the first place.

For example: there have been no transitional animals found to prove the false assumption that protozoan evolved into metazoan invertebrates. And although there are thousands of invertebrates and thousands of vertebrates, but not one fossil has been found of any transition animal that is part vertebrate and part invertebrate! This fact proves that the evolution model is false!

Although animals might vary in kind, they do not evolve into other kinds, as predicted by the Creations! Natural selection is the process by which a specific kind of animal adapts to its environment. Those traits of variation are already built into the genetic structure of the animal; they are turned on when needed for adaptation to various environmental conditions. Natural selection does not produce new kinds, it acts in the preservation of the original kind by allowing the animal to adapt!

There has never been evidence of any sort to prove the assumption that one kind of animal has evolved from another kind. There has never been found any fossil evidence of a transitional animal that is part fish and part amphibian to prove that amphibians evolved from fish. The actual fossil record confirms the opposites: that fish are of one kind, and amphibians have always been of a separate kind. The same holds true between amphibians and reptiles, and between reptiles and mammals, and between reptiles and birds! According to the fossil record the different kinds of animals in reality did not evolve, but appear to have been created individually, after their kind!

And what is even more devastating to those evolutionists is the origin of insects, which are shown in the so-called evolution chart as appearing out of nowhere. Furthermore many animals they've claimed should have long evolved into other animals are being found alive today. Evolution is unscientific and contrary to the Second Law of Thermal Dynamics: a complex biological animal can not spontaneously evolve from a simpler animal!

The evolutionists claim that the dinosaurs walked the earth sixty-five million years before man evolved into existence. But to the contrary, archeologist studying dried river beds around the world have found footprints of dinosaurs and man's footprints that had formed together in the same rock, and sometimes they are found overlapping each other. This proves that man and the dinosaurs did not walk the earth 65 million years apart, but must have co-inhabited simultaneously. Man and the dinosaurs must have walked the earth at the same time! This finding proves that the evolutionary chart is in error by 65 million years and in actuality completely false!

The fossils could not have been formed over millions of years because either other animals would have eaten and scattered the dead carcasses, or the bodies left exposed to the environment would have decayed, and deteriorated, and scattered. The only possible way for a fossil to have been formed is if an animal got buried by a mudslide that eventually cemented into rock, or by some other catastrophe that quickly enclosed the dead body, protecting it from the environment and hungry animals. The only global event in recorded history that could have created fossils simultaneously around the world is the biblical flood of Noah!

Local floods today are observed to create major landslides, and cause the death of many humans and animals. Imagine the kind of destruction that would result from a great worldwide flood. Both geological and archeological evidence have confirmed that there was a global flood at one time on the planet. It was that flood which killed off many species of animals and created major geologic and seasonal changes on the planet.

Prior to the flood, the entire earth was populated, and the climate was tropical all over the earth. But when the flood came it covered the entire planet, killed off most of the animals, and caused a change in the global climate. It was from the sediments and the mud created by the flood that the animals were fossilized. The mud trapped the animals; the mud then cemented rapidly into rocks as it dried, causing the animals trapped inside to become preserved as fossils.

The rocks containing the fossils had to be formed quickly and not over millions of years because the rocks containing the fossils are almost pure in content. If they were formed over millions of years they would have been contaminated with all kinds of junk. Furthermore, dead bodies exposed to the environment are soon eroded, and their bones are scattered. Fossils of animals can never be formed!

The accurate record of the creation is found in the Bible! The Lord YAHAWAH created the universe in order to express and share love. Genesis chapter one gives a detailed account of the creation. We see that it took six days for the making and forming of the universe by the Lord YAHAWAH and the angels!   This   verse specifically states that the universe was a creation of the Almighty, and not the result of an accidental explosion. There is a difference between the creation of the universe, and the making of it. The Lord created the Universe supernaturally, then formed and fashioned it in six days.

<< Genesis 1:1 >> [In the beginning God created the heaven and the earth.]

In the original text, the plural word ALAHAYAM is used for God, because God orchestrated the creation. The Lord gave the orders and the instructions to Christ and the angels on what work was to be done. The angels and Christ, together with the Almighty God, made the creation. God was not alone at that time.

<< John 1:1-3 >> [In the beginning was the Word, and the Word was with God, and the Word was God. <2> The same was in the beginning with God. <3> All things were made by him; and without him was not anything made.]

The him and The Word are Jesus Christ. The "Us", in "Let us make man", is evidence that the Lord God was not alone at the Creation.

<< Genesis 1:2 >> [And the earth was without form, and void; and darkness was upon the face of the deep. And the spirit of God moved upon the face of the waters.]

This verse simply describes the condition of the earth and the elements of the universe shortly after the Almighty God had supernaturally created them. The elements had not yet been energized, and the planet earth, although created, was in a void and uninhabitable state at the time. For these events the Bible did not indicate to us a time interval, except to say that it was in the very beginning.

THE TRUTH

It should also be noted that the prophets of the Bible, for thousands of years, have always instructed that the earth is a round body suspended in space:

<< Job 26:7 >> [He stretched out the north over the empty place, and hangeth the earth upon nothing.]

<< Isaiah 40:22 >> [It is he that sitteth upon the circle of the earth...]

<< Genesis 1:3-5 >> [And God said, let there be light: and there was light. And God saw the light, that it was good: and God divided the light from the darkness. And God called the light Day, and the darkness he called night. And the evening and the morning were the first day.]

Understand that by days the Bible literally means twenty-four hours. The Most High God is omnipotent and omniscient; he has the power to do the same thing in one day that he could do in a thousand or a million years.

<< Second Peter 3:8 >> [But, beloved, be not ignorant of this one thing, that one day is with the Lord as a thousand years, and a thousand years as one day]

People often misinterpret this scripture, thinking that the days of the creation represent a thousand years each. That is the wrong reasoning. Second Peters 3:8 is simply saying that the Lord God YAHAWAH has the power to do in one day what he can do in a thousand. His power and wisdom are boundless!

The days of creation were literally days; firstly because morning and evening only come after a literal day and secondly because the Most High says he called the light day and the darkness night. Night and day constitute a twenty-four hour period.

So, the scriptures of the Bible confirm:

<< Exodus 20:11 >> [For in six days the Lord made heaven and earth, the sea, and all that in them is, and rested the seventh day] (not resting, but he rested already)

<< Exodus 31:17 >> [...for in six days the Lord made heaven and earth, and on the seventh day he rested, and was refreshed.]

Notice that "rested" is in the past tense-he did not need a thousand years to rest. The creation occurred about 6,000 years ago. Therefore, we are now living at the end of the sixth thousandth year since the creation of the universe!

<< Genesis 1:6-8 >> [And God said, let there be a firmament in the midst of the waters, and let it divide the waters from the waters. And God made the firmament, and divided the waters which were under the firmament from the waters which were above the firmament: and it was so. And God called the firmament Heaven. And the evening and the morning were the second day.]

THE TRUTH

The Chaotic atmosphere of the earth was tamed and adjusted so it could be made to support moisture and sustain life! On the second day, he formed the atmosphere and the hydrosphere, which is the ocean.

<< Genesis 1:9 >> [And God said, Let the waters under the heaven be gathered together unto one place, and let dry land appear: and it was so. And God said, Let the earth bring forth grass, the herb yielding seed, and the fruit tree yielding fruit after his kind, whose seed is in itself upon the earth: and it was so. And the earth brought forth grass, and herb yielding seed after his kind, and the tree yielding fruit, whose seed was in it, after his kind: And God saw that it was good. And the evening and the morning were the third day.]

On the third day, the Lord caused the original continent to emerge, tamed the ocean, and defined the altitude of sea level. Notice that before the flood, the earth consisted of a single landmass and a single ocean. It was the cataclysmic mechanism of the global flood that had caused the earth's tectonic plates to become unstable, resulting in continental drifts. The original continent broke off into the many continents that we have on the earth today.

Also on the third day the Lord caused vegetation to appear. Notice that each plant life was created after its own kind, it did not evolve, one kind into another; each was after its own kind and the third day, The Lord made the land (lithosphere) and the vegetation (biosphere).

<< Genesis 1:14-19 >> [And God said, Let there be lights in the firmament of the heaven to divide the day from the night; and let them be for signs, and for seasons, and for days, and years: And let them be for lights in the firmament of the heaven to give light upon the earth: and it was so. And God made two great lights; the greater light to rule the day, and the lesser light to rule the night: he made the stars also.
And God set them in the firmament of the heaven to give light upon the earth, and to rule over the day and over the night, and to divide the light from the darkness: And God saw that it was good. And the evening and the morning were the fourth day.]

On the fourth day the Lord YAHAWAH defined the zodiac: he named the stars, the planets, and all the heavenly bodies with prophetic names and defined their prophetic cycles of motion. The Lord encoded much wisdom and knowledge within the spiritual names and cycles of the heavenly bodies. The Lord also energized the universe with light. He made all the light rays that would reach the earth from the distant stars.

<< Genesis 1:20-23 >> [And God said, let the waters bring forth abundantly the moving creatures that hath life, and fowl that may fly above the earth in the open firmament of the heaven. And God created great whales, and every living creature that moveth, which the waters brought forth abundantly, after their kind, and every winged fowl after his kind: and God saw that it was good. And God blessed them, saying, Be fruitful, and multiply, and fill the waters in the seas, and let the fowl multiply in the earth. And the evening and the morning were the fifth day.]

We see that on the fifth day the Lord orchestrated the creation of all the fish, and of all the birds, each after its own kind. Each kind of animal was a unique creation, for no creature had evolved from any other creature. Each species was created with dormant genetic characteristics that could be evoked whenever needed.

Therefore, they would have the ability to evoke those traits whenever necessary, in order to variegated and adapt to various environmental conditions and survive! The various traits found within a species are not new, they are built in from the beginning, stored within the DNA molecules, and activated when the survival of the creature is challenged by environmental factors, making it necessary for the species to adapt and survive.

> *<< Genesis 1:24-31 >> [And God said, Let the earth bring forth the living creature after his kind, cattle, and creeping thing, and beast of the earth after his kind: and it was so. <25> And God made great beast of the earth after his kind, and every thing that creepeth upon the earth after his kind: and God saw that it was good.*
>
> *<26> And God said, let us make man in our image, after our likeness: and let them have dominion over the fish of the sea, and the fowl of the air, and over the cattle, and over all the earth, and over the creeping thing that creepeth upon the earth. <27> So God created man in his image, in the image of God created he him male and female created he them. <28> And God blessed them, and God said unto them, Be fruitful, and multiply, and replenish the earth, and subdue it: and have dominion over the fish of the sea, and the fowl of the air, and over every living thing that moveth upon the earth.*
>
> *<29> And God said, Behold, I have given you every herb bearing seed, which is upon the face of all the earth, and every tree, in the which is the fruit of a tree yielding seed; to you it shall be for meat. <30> And to every beast of the earth, and to every fowl of the air, and to every thing that creepeth upon the earth, wherein there is life, I have given every green herb for meat: and it was so. <31> And God saw everything that he had made, and, behold, it was very good. And the evening and the morning were the sixth day.]*

All land animals and mankind were created on the sixth day. Each kind of animal was created separately and uniquely, not by evolution! The Lord God YAHAWAH created man as a unique being, man did not evolve from apes. The so-called evolutionists have distorted the laws of science in order to fabricate a lie. Man was created in the image of God.

Mankind is a different type of creation from the other animals: we were created to be in the very image and likeness of the Almighty Creator. Granted, we are creatures too, but in the sixth day the Most High made man in his likeness by giving him the law, and understanding of spiritual principles.

Before his disobedience, the body of Adam was divine and immortal. It was covered in a glorious robe of light so that he had no need of material clothing to hide his nakedness!

Man in the image of God means that man is a microcosmic encapsulation of God. A human being consists of both physical parts, formed by God from the elements; and also an everlasting spiritual part, the breath of life, which originates directly from God! We are not just physical beings, we are also spiritual beings. Therefore, just as we strive to develop our physical selves, we also have spiritual selves and spiritual bodies that need to grow and develop, which must be nurtured and exercised.

Man was given three original commandments from God: to be fruitful, to multiply, and to have dominion! The purpose of the three blessings was to bring the kingdom of heaven on the earth. The first was to be fruitful; a tree is fruitful when it is mature. For a person to be fruitful means becoming physically and spiritually mature. In other words, and we must achieve mental and spiritual growth by seeking after wisdom, and knowledge, understanding in order to become one with God!

The second blessing was to multiply and replenish the earth; which means to establish families on the earth whose foundations are centered on the love and righteousness of the Lord God YAHAWAH. These families, one with God, would serve as the foundation for the society and the global village. We will multiply either good or evil on this earth, depending on our character. We are obligated to have children and instill good character, centered on God.

The third blessing requires us to subdue and govern the earth. Having dominion over the creation means being responsible, taking care of the environment and not abusing or polluting it. It also means mastering the sciences and technologies that govern the universe. All of these things are necessary for man to truly reflect the image of God. Adam was a perfect creation, but he was not yet fully mature. Therefore, he was open to temptations.

The organized religions have taught that Adam was the only man physically walking on the Earth at the time of creation. However, this is not the truth. The fact is, the Bible confirms that there were many other people created on the Earth on the sixth day. And God also created a special group of people in his image, which he called Adam. The word "ADAM" refers to the richest dark earth of Eden. The original people of God resembled the rich dark earth. Adam the man was not alone. The name Adam refers to a group of people collectively:

<< *Genesis 5:2* >> [*Male and female created he them; and blessed them, and called their name Adam, in the day when they were created.*]

Then God needed a caretaker to be in charge of Eden. Because he could not find anyone, he made the man Adam; an additional person to supervise the garden. This Adam was the leader of those people that were made in the image of the Lord God YAHAWAH! Adam and his people were referred to as the sons of God, and the other people were called the sons of man.

<< *Genesis 6:2* >> [*That the sons of God saw the daughters of men that they were fair...*]

There are additional clues to the fact that there were many other people in the Garden, not only Adam:

<< *Genesis 4:16,17* >> [*And Cain went out from the presence of the Lord, and dwelt in the Land of Nod, on the East of Eden. And Cain knew his wife; and she conceived.*]

Who was Nod, and where did he come from, if there weren't other people created? Where did the wife of Cain come from, if there were no other people in the garden? We should be aware that in some cases when the Bible uses the word creature, it also includes mankind:

<< *Romans 8:19-21* >> [*For the earnest expectation of the creature waiteth for manifestation of the sons of God. For the creature was made subject to vanity, not willingly, but by reason of him who hath subjected the same in hope, Because the creature itself also shall be delivered from the bondage of corruption into the glorious liberty of the children of God.*]

Mankind also is a creature. A variety of humans were created on the sixth day, but Adam and his group were the only ones made in the image and likeness of the Lord God, and given dominion over all the other creations and people!

We have to understand that there is a difference between the creation of man, and the making of man. All animals, including man were created from the elements; but the Adam was spiritually made in the image of the

THE TRUTH

Heavenly, by being given spiritual attributes: wisdom, knowledge and understanding! Although the physical man was created, but the spiritual man had to be formed and made! The difference between the family of Adam and the other people in the garden is that they were MADE IN THE IMAGE AND LIKENESS OF LORD GOD YAHAWAH, having the spirit and wisdom of God in them.

> << Genesis 1:26 >> *[And God said, Let us make man after our image, after our likeness and let them have dominion...]*

When the Most High made man in his image, this means he gave man the laws and principles of righteousness. Adam was the first man taught in these principles. For this reason, Adam and his people were called sons of God. Even today, you can say a child is the image of his father, meaning he is like his father in every way- like father like son!

> << Genesis 5:3 >> *[And Adam lived an hundred and thirty years, and begot a son in his own likeness, after his image]*

> << Genesis 2:7 >> *[And the Lord formed man from the dust of the ground* (meaning after the making of the physical man, he was in a low condition, carnal, void of spiritual truth*), and breath into his nostrils the breath of life* (the man Adam was then taught spiritual knowledge and principles, such as the law and the prophecies*); and man became a living soul.]*

Christ is the breath of life. It is the belief in the words of Christ that can change us from the animal nature, into becoming the sons of the Lord God. We are beasts without the words and the laws of Lord YAHAWAH.

> << John 20:22 >> *[And when he had said this, he breathed on them, and said unto them, Receive ye the Holy Spirit.]*

The breath of life in the Bible refers to the receiving and obeying of the knowledge and the laws of God.

> << Ezekiel 37:5 >> *[Thus saith the Lord unto these bones* (the African-Americans and American-Indians in their lost and ignorant state*); Behold, I will cause breath to enter into you* (spiritual knowledge*), and ye shall live.]*

> << Genesis 2:7 >> *[And the Lord YAHAWAH formed man of the dust of the ground, and breath into his nostrils the breath of life; and man became a living soul.]*

God made man's mind and spirit from the spiritual world, which he breathed into man, and God formed the physical man from the elements. Originally, we were given both physical and spiritual senses. Mankind is the only creation that can deal with both the physical and the spiritual world simultaneously. Mankind is the microcosmic encapsulation of the spiritual and the physical world: the image of God!

> << I CORINTHIANS 15:35-58 >> *[But some man will say, How are the dead raised up? and with what body do they come? <36> Thou fool, that which thou sowest is not quickened,*

except it die: <37> And that which thou sowest, thou sowest not that body that shall be, but bare grain, it may chance of wheat, or of some other grain: <38> But God giveth it a body as it hath pleased him, and to every seed his own body.

<39> All flesh is not the same flesh: but there is one kind of flesh of men, another flesh of beasts, another of fishes, and another of birds. <40> There are also celestial bodies, and bodies terrestrial: but the glory of the celestial is one, and the glory of the terrestrial is another. <41> There is one glory of the sun, and another glory of the moon, and another glory of the stars: for one star differeth from another star in glory.

<42> So also is the resurrection of the dead. It is sown in corruption; it is raised in incorruption: <43> It is sown in dishonor; it is raised in glory: it is sown in weakness; it is raised in power: <44> It is sown a natural body; it is raised a spiritual body. There is a natural body, and there is a spiritual body.

<45> And so it is written, The first man Adam was made a living soul; the last Adam was made a quickening spirit. <46> Howbeit that was not first which is spiritual, but that which is natural; and afterward that which is spiritual. <47> The first man is of the earth, earthy: the second man is the Lord from heaven. <48> As is the earthy, such are they also that are earthy: and as is the heavenly, such are they also that are heavenly. <49> And as we have borne the image of the earthy, we shall also bear the image of the heavenly.

<50> Now this I say, brethren, that flesh and blood cannot inherit the kingdom of God; neither doth corruption inherit incorruption. <15> Behold, I shew you a mystery; We shall not all sleep, but we shall all be changed, <15> In a moment, in the twinkling of an eye, at the last trump: for the trumpet shall sound, and the dead shall be raised incorruptible, and we shall be changed. <53> For this corruptible must put on incorruption, and this mortal must put on immortality. <54> So when this corruptible shall have put on incorruption, and this mortal shall have put on immortality, then shall be brought to pass the saying that is written, Death is swallowed up in victory.

<55> O death, where is thy sting? O grave, where is thy victory? <56> The sting of death is sin; and the strength of sin is the law. <57> But thanks be to God, which giveth us the victory through our Lord Jesus Christ. <15> Therefore, my beloved brethren, be ye steadfast, unmovable, always abounding in the work of the Lord, forasmuch as ye know that your labor is not in vain in the Lord.]

<< ECCLESIASTES 12:7 >> [Then shall the dust return to the earth as it was: and the spirit shall return unto God who gave it.]

<< II CORINTHIANS 5:1-11 >> [For we know that if our earthly house of this tabernacle were dissolved, we have a building of God, an house not made with hands, eternal in the heavens. <2> For in this we groan, earnestly desiring to be clothed upon with our house which is from heaven: <3> If so be that being clothed we shall not be found naked. <4> For we that are in this tabernacle do groan, being burdened: not for that we would be unclothed, but clothed upon, that mortality might be swallowed up of life.

<5> Now he that hath wrought us for the selfsame thing is God, who also hath given unto us the earnest of the Spirit. <6> Therefore we are always confident, knowing that, whilst we are at home in the body, we are absent from the Lord: <7> For we walk by faith, not by

sight:) <8> We are confident, I say, and willing rather to be absent from the body, and to be present with the Lord.

<9> Wherefore we labor, that, whether present or absent, we may be accepted of him. <10> For we must all appear before the judgment seat of Christ; that every one may receive the things done in his body, according to that he hath done, whether it be good or bad. <11> Knowing therefore the terror of the Lord, we persuade men; but we are made manifest unto God; and I trust also are made manifest in your consciences.]

Clearly we can see how Adam was made in the image of the God, and was called the son of the God:

<< Luke 3:38 >> [...Adam, which was the Son of God.]

<< John 1:12 >> [But as many as received Him (the real Jesus Christ), *to them gave he power to become the sons of God, even to them that believe on his name!]*

Not only was Adam a unique creation, so was Eve. Eve was custom made for Adam, to help him. Eve was made miraculously by God, from an anatomical rib of Adam.

<< Genesis 2:22 >> [And the rib which the Lord had taken from the man, made he a woman.]

Since then, the term rib has been used in referring to a person's near of kin, like we say flesh and blood today! There are many good examples of this usage in the Bible:

<< Genesis 49:14 >> [And Laban said to him, Surely thou art my bone and my flesh.]

Bone and flesh represents near of kin, a close relative. Rib in this context does not refer to the anatomical rib inside of the body at all!

<< First Chronicle 11:1 >> [Then all Israel gathered themselves unto David unto Hebron, saying, Behold, we are thy bone and thy flesh.]

A verse that is often misunderstood is:

<< Genesis 2:25 >> [And they were both naked, the man and his wife, and were not ashamed]

In this context, naked does not imply that Adam and Eve were walking around in Eden with their private parts showing. The original man when he was created was enveloped in a robe of glorious light. Adam had no need of material clothing to cover his skin. As the image of God, his entire body originally had a glow of light for a covering. Examples are found throughout the scriptures:

<< Psalm 104:1,2 >> [Blessed the Lord, O my soul. O Lord my God, thou art very great; thou art clothed with honor and majesty. Who coverest thyself with light as with a garment.]

THE TRUTH

<< I Corinthians 11:7 >> [For a man indeed ought not to cover his head, for as much as he is the image and glory of God]

It was after Adam's disobedience that the glow of glory, which covered him, was lost from his body, requiring him to find material covering to hide his nakedness!

The Location of Eden

The Bible tells us the location of the Garden of Eden:

<< Genesis 2:10-14 >> [And a river went forth out of Eden to water the Garden; and from thence it was parted into four heads. The name of the first is Pison (today called Wadi Al-Batin, a dried river bed; it flowed from the limestone of north-central Saudi Arabia*): that is it which compasseth the whole land of Havilah (today called Saudi Arabia), where there is gold; And the gold of that land is good: there is bdellium and the onyx stone.*

And the name of the second river is Gihon (today called the Nile river*): the same is it that compasseth the whole land of Ethiopia. And the name of the third river is Hiddekel* (today called the Tigris river*): that is it, which goeth toward the east of Assyria. And the fourth river is the Euphrates.]*

The key to locating the Garden of Eden is to first note that the river that went through the Garden of Eden was parted into four heads; meaning the four rivers joined together at that point before flowing into the Persian Golf. The top two sets of rivers were the Tigris and the Euphrates, and the bottom two rivers were Wadi Al-Batin and the Nile.

Notice that Palestine and Egypt are connected through the Sinai Peninsula. Recall that Genesis chapter two is describing geography the way it was before the flood. At that time the continents and all of the landmasses were connected as one major continent surrounded by one ocean. It was the global flood at the time of Noah which caused the earth to become unstable and the continents to drift apart!

Genesis 2:10-14 is telling us that these four bodies of water, the Tigris, the Euphrates, Wadi Al-Batin and the Nile, met to form one river in the Garden of Eden before flowing into the Persian Gulf. Therefore, today the Garden of Eden would be located in Hor, of Southern Iraq, where the waters of the Tigris and the Euphrates meet in the marshy Shatt-al-Arab delta.

THE ORIGIN OF EVIL

We are made in the image of the Lord God YAHAWAH. Our purpose is to reflect the character of God, and to be one with the Lord God in a relationship characterized by reciprocal love. Evil begins when a person has rationalized himself into believing that he can live independent from the Lord God YAHAWAH. That person usually creates a god in his own image, to serve his own purposes, for his own glory. Eventually this person seeks to make himself the center of all things, disregarding others, and exploiting all things as a result of irrational lust. A person whose life is not centered on the love of God will multiply evil in the world.

The first account of mankind committing evil is the temptation of Adam and Eve:

<< *Genesis 3:1-6* >>: *[Now the Serpent was more subtle than any beast of the field which the Lord God had made. And he said unto the woman, Yea, hath God said, Ye shall not eat of every tree of the garden?*

And the woman said unto the serpent, We may eat of the fruit of the trees of the garden: But of the fruit of the tree which is in the midst of the garden, God hath said, Ye shall not eat of it, and neither shall ye touch it, lest ye die (dying: to become mortal). *And the serpent said unto the woman, Ye shall not surely die: For God doth know that in the day ye eat thereof, then your eyes shall be opened, and ye shall be as gods, knowing good and evil.*

And when the woman saw that the tree was good for food, and that it was pleasant to the eyes, and a tree to be desired to make one wise, she took of the fruit thereof and did eat (the Bible never said that the fruit was an apple), *and gave also unto her husband with her; and he did eat.]*

Identity of the Serpent

It was Satan the Devil that used the snake as a medium through which he would speak to the woman. Spirits can take over the bodies of animals and act through them.

The term serpent and beasts of the field are also symbolic of people that have rebelled against God. Even Christ uses the word serpent when he addresses rebellious people:

<< *Matthew 23:33* >> *[Ye serpents, ye generation of vipers, how can ye escape the damnation of hell?]*

The word devil simply means deceiver. Any person who is deceitful can be called a devil. For example:

<< *John 6:70* >> *[Jesus answered them, Have not I chosen you twelve, and one of you is a devil?]*

<< *John 8:44* >> *[Ye are of your father the devil, and the lusts of your father ye will do. He was a murderer from the beginning* (Satan, Cain), *and abode not in the truth, because there is*

no truth in him. When he speaketh a lie, he speaketh of his own: for he is a liar, and the father of it.]

There are numerous examples, proving that beasts, according to the Bible, represent nations and people. Daniel describes the four kingdoms as beasts:

<< *Daniel 7:3* >> *[And four beasts came up from the sea, diverse one from another. The first was like to a lion, and had eagle's wings...]*

The Bible explains that the four beasts were symbolic of nations:

<< *Verse 17* >> *[These great beasts, which are four, are four kings, which shall arise out of the earth.]*

Another place where the Bible uses beasts to symbolize nations is:

<< *Revelation 12:3 and 9* >> *[And there appeared another wonder in heaven; and behold a great red dragon, having seven heads and ten horns, and seven crowns upon his heads.]*

We know that this beast or dragon (a dragon is a form of serpent) symbolizes the fourth kingdom, which is the Roman Empire, past and present. This is still the Roman Empire! The seven heads are the seven evolutions of the Roman Empire, from the Greeks to modern day America, Europe, and Russia. The nations and people are controlled today in the same way by the same old devil, Satan who existed in the Garden of Eden.

<< *Revelation 12:9* >> *[And the great dragon was cast out, that old serpent, called the Devil and Satan.]*

He is called "Old serpent" because that was the same devil found in Genesis. Satan teams up with rebellious people to work his evil devices. Satan the Devil and his agents are seeking self-glory, to create reversal of dominion, seeking to replace God.

Symbolic Trees

The history of Eden is recorded in the form of many symbols: the serpent, the beast, the trees, the fruit, the seed, and more. We must first discover the meaning of those symbols. The trees and the fruit were symbolic of people, and the serpent was not a regular snake. It was a snake that had been possessed by Satan the Devil, which he was using as a medium.

The eating of the fruit could not have been a sin; it was their disobedience. We know that the fruit is symbolic because Jesus says:

<< *Matthew 15:11* >> *[Not that which goeth into the mouth defileth a man; but that which cometh out of the mouth, this defileth a man.]*

THE TRUTH

Also it is a false interpretation to say that the fruit was an apple, because apple is not what is written in the Bible. The Bible never said that the fruit was an apple. And clearly it could not have been simply the eating of a literal fruit that caused the fall of Adam, because eating a literal fruit can never be a sin. Also there is no tree called the tree of good and evil. So if the fruit is Symbolic, the trees must also be symbolic!

It is important to realize that the trees referred to in Genesis represent people, and the fruit is their mentality and system of beliefs! To take of the fruit of those trees means to adopt a certain mentality or custom of an individual, a group, or a nation that is contrary to the word of God. Adam and Eve sinned by disobeying God, and they proceeded to follow a false religion.

If you recall, it was mentioned earlier that Adam and Eve were not the only people that were created by God. In the beginning the Lord made a multitude of people to inhabit the earth. However those groups were referred to symbolically, either as trees, serpents, sons of God, daughters of men, seeds, or beasts.

Many scriptures can confirm that in fact the other people in the garden were mentioned in symbolic ways, for example, as trees:

<< *Ezekiel 31:7-9* >> [*Thus was he fair in his greatness, in the length of his branches: for his roots were by great waters. The cedars in the garden of the Lord could not hide him: the fir trees were not like his boughs, and the chestnut trees were not like his branches; nor any tree* (nation) *in the garden of the Lord* (on earth) *was like unto him in beauty. I have made him fair by the multitude of his branches: so that all the trees of Eden, which were in the garden of the Lord, envied him.*]

Those trees are symbolic of nations. Trees can not envy other trees, it has to be symbolic of nations or people envying. Here is another good example proving that the trees of the Garden of Eden refer to people:

<< *Isaiah 14:8* >> [*Yea, the fir trees rejoice at thee, and the cedars of Lebanon, saying, since thou art laid down, no feller is come up against us.*]

Literal trees can not speak and complain about nations coming against them! Beyond the slightest doubt, trees in Genesis symbolize nations! Most importantly, it should be clear that since the trees of the garden were people, the fruits of those trees had to be the false religions and the customs of those nations. It is because the people are at times represented as trees that God can say to Adam in << Genesis 1:28 >>, " Be fruitful!"

We should study in detail what the symbolic tree of life and the tree of the knowledge of good and evil represent. The Bible explains:

<< *Proverb 13:12* >> [*Hope deferred maketh the heart sick: but when the desire cometh, it is the tree of life.*]

Basically, desire fulfilled is the tree of life, success and joy! Jesus Christ is the Tree of Life and we are the branches. Jesus Christ leads us to joy and freedom. Also the tree of life is encountered again in the book of Revelation.

<< *Revelation 22:14* >> [*Blessed are they that do his commandments, that they may have right to the tree of life, and may enter in through the gates of the city.*]

THE TRUTH

A person who has fulfilled the ideal of creation has attained the tree of life. This is people who puts God first as the center of life, accepts Jesus as Savior, and obeys the words and commandments of God.

The second tree, the tree of the knowledge of good and evil, is the tree of judgment. It represents a person who seeks to makes himself the judge of what is good and evil, instead of looking to the Lord YAHAWAH for leadership. This is an individual who creates his own standards of truth and of right and wrong. This type of Person seeks for knowledge as a way to gain personal power and live independently from God.

A person who has eaten the fruit from the tree of the knowledge of good and evil does not trust in God's words. Instead, this person trusts in his own carnal wisdom and knowledge as the source for his welfare and salvation.

This is a person who has decided to make himself god. And he replaces the real God with a false god that will serve his purposes! Even today, many people believe that science and technology are the solution to the problems of the world. If this were true there would not be so much greed, injustice, and violence in the world today. Science and technology is very helpful. They are tools that can be used for either good or evil. But because man has turned from God, and his heart is evil, the technology is being used to exploit the people and to destroy the environment. It is vanity-man can not hope to replace God! This sin is called the reversal of dominion. It is blasphemy.

A person who seeks to reverse the order that God has established has eaten of the fruit of the knowledge of good and evil. This person has become the tree of the knowledge of good and evil, capable of bringing forth good fruits or evil fruits. This person can bear children of goodness or children of evil, to either multiply good or evil in the world. Jesus said:

<< *Matthew 7:16-20* >> [*Ye shall know them by their fruits. Do men gather grapes of thorns, or figs of thistle? Even so every good tree bringeth forth good fruits; but a corrupt tree bringeth forth evil fruits. A good tree cannot bring forth evil fruit, neither can a corrupt tree bring forth good fruit. Every tree that bringeth not forth good fruit is hewn down, and cast into the fire. wherefore by their fruits ye shall know them.*]

Christ is the master, and he also uses trees to symbolize people, as they were used in Genesis!

The Edenic Rebellion

Man is the only creature that can deal simultaneously with both the physical and the spiritual world. This is because we have a twofold nature, a physical and a spiritual nature. The angels and the demons are spiritual beings only. Adam had authority both in the physical and the spiritual world. The serpent represents Satan the Devil, who was envious and jealous of Adam, because God loved Adam, and also because of the position of dominion and authority that God had given to Adam!

<< *I Corinthians 6:3* >> [*Know ye not that ye shall judge angels? How much more things that pertain to this life?*]

<< *Genesis 3:1-3* >> [*Now the serpent was more subtle than any beast of the field which the Lord had made. And he said unto the woman, Yea, hath the Lord said, Ye shall not eat of every tree of the garden?*]

THE TRUTH

We know the fruit of the tree is symbolic. It represents faith in personal knowledge rather than faith in the words, wisdom, and the laws of the Lord YAHAWAH as the source of salvation! The Bible often represents knowledge as if it were some object that can be eaten with the mouth:

<< *Revelation 10:9-11* >> [*And I went unto the angel, and said unto him, Give me the little book. And he said unto me, Take it, and eat it up; and it shall be in thy belly bitter, but it shall be in thy mouth sweet as honey.*]

The book gives wisdom and knowledge, which is always sweet to hear. It is bitter in the belly because once it is digested in the mind, it sometimes makes us sad, angry, and even bitter. Here is another example where knowledge for the mind is compared to food for the mouth:

<< *Ezekiel 3:1-3* >> [*Moreover he said unto me, son of man, eat that thou findest; eat this roll* (acquire the knowledge in the scrolls), *and go speak unto the house of Israel. So I opened my mouth, and he caused me to eat that roll. And he said unto me, Son of man, cause thy belly to eat, and fill thy bowels with this roll that I give thee. Then did I eat it; and it was in my mouth as honey for sweetness.*]

Notice that the tree of the knowledge of good and evil is mentioned as being in the midst of the garden. The tree being in the midst of the garden symbolizes the egotistical mentality of a person who seeks to make himself the center of all things. It represents a jealous person who fails to love the word of God and serve the Creator, and who seeks to replace God. The tree being in the midst of the garden represents an individual who instead of praising the Lord, seeks to make himself the center of glory, creating a reversal of dominion between God and man!

The serpent was extremely wise, and he played on Eve's intellect. Eve's only defense was to know the words of God. The serpent got technical with her, questioning the accuracy and authorship of the word of God: "Are you sure God really said that? Because you were not there, and maybe something was lost in the transmission." The reason why the serpent questioned Eve concerning the commandments of God is because he wanted to create a state of doubt and confusion in her mind, making her more vulnerable to deception!

<< *Genesis 3:2* >> [*And the woman said unto the serpent, We may eat* (freely eat) *of every fruit of the trees of the garden: But of the fruit of the tree which is in the midst of the garden, God hath said, Ye shall not eat of it, neither shall ye touch it, lest ye die* (to become mortal)!]

But God never said to Eve that they could not touch the fruit. And God had said they may freely eat of every tree. She subtracted and added to God's words. She caused God to appear ungenerous and too demanding! The serpent was successful at beguiling Eve, by making her think that God was hiding something from her; as a result Eve became resentful. He told her that the fruit would make her more mature, and that she could do her own thing. The serpent got her confused enough to make her want to change God's words. Her doubt and denial created a great delusion; she started to believe that she could become as God. It is a dangerous thing to either add or take away from God's words!

THE TRUTH

<< Genesis 3:4 >> *[And the serpent said unto the woman, ye shall not surely die: For the Lord doth know that in the day that ye eat thereof; then your eyes shall be opened, and ye shall be as gods, knowing good and evil.]*

Eve was deceived because she doubted God's words. We did become mortals, and we lost our spiritual senses and communion with God and the spirit world. The serpent told Eve that knowledge is power: power to be as a god, to decide for herself what the standards of righteousness are; to be her own judge, and to decide for herself what is good and bad! The serpent was telling Eve that knowledge would give her power to be independent from God. He told her that she could trust in her own wisdom to be her salvation. The serpent told her that she could become the center of glory, as God was! So Eve traded her innocence for conscience.

[And when the woman saw that the tree was good for food (lust of the flesh*), and that it was pleasant to the eyes* (lust of the eyes*), and a tree to be desired to make one wise* (appealing to her pride and ego)*, she took of the fruit thereof* (she adopted those ways*), and did eat, and gave also unto her husband with her; and he did eat.]*

The serpent succeeded at tempting Eve by playing on her intellect and ego. By gazing upon the forbidden fruit, Eve was inviting the temptation. The fruit was good for food, meaning it was physically appealing. It was pleasant to the eye, meaning it was emotionally appealing. The fruit was desired to make one wise, which means it was mentally appealing. The serpent had launched a simultaneous three-fold attack on Eve.

Some people say that there is no harm in looking, but Eve's gaze became lust. And her lust turned into a desire, a desire that became a decision! Finally, the serpent transformed the decision into the shackles of mankind!

<< John 8:34 >> *[Jesus answered them, Verily, verily, I say unto you, Whosoever committeth sin is the servant of sin.]*

But Adam was intellectually strong and knowledgeable. Adam loved Eve, calling her bone of his bones and flesh of his flesh. The serpent did not try to tempt Adam, but used Eve to do it, due to Adam's emotional attachment to his wife. Eve tempted Adam because after her sin, she felt alone, inferior, and jealous against Adam. In her misery, she wanted him as company. Eve the sinner turned into Eve the seducer. The serpent made Eve into his weapon to destroy Adam, and once Adam sinned, mankind was condemned.

Adam allowed his passion for the woman to rule over his logic, and did what he knew in his heart to be wrong. For the second time, by dominating Adam through his emotions, Eve was guilty of the reversal of dominion, this time against Adam as well.

<< I Timothy 2:14 >> *[And Adam was not deceived, but the woman being deceived was in the transgression.]*

Jesus Christ is called Savior because he came to make atonement for what Adam had done, in order to restore mankind to God. Recall that Satan confronted Jesus Christ with a similar three-fold attack:

<< Matthew 4:2-11 >> *[And when he had fasted forty days and forty nights, he was afterward an hungered. <3> And when the tempter came to him, he said, If thou be the Son of God, command that these stones be made bread* (physical appeal)*. <4> But he answered and*

said, It is written, Man shall not live by bread alone, but by every word that proceedeth out of the mouth of God.

<5> Then the devil taketh him up into the holy city, and setteth him on a pinnacle of the temple, <6> And saith unto him, If thou be the Son of God, cast thyself down: for it is written, He shall give his angels charge concerning thee: and in their hands they shall bear thee up, lest at any time thou dash thy foot against a stone (pride and mental appeal). *<7> Jesus said unto him, It is written again, Thou shalt not tempt the Lord thy God.*

<8> Again, the devil taketh him up into an exceeding high mountain, and sheweth him all the kingdoms of the world, and the glory of them; <9> And saith unto him, All these things will I give thee (emotional appeal), *if thou wilt fall down and worship me. <10> Then saith Jesus unto him, Get thee hence, Satan: for it is written, Thou shalt worship the Lord thy God, and him only shalt thou serve.]*

The reason why Christ was placed in a parallel situation was so that he can restore the three blessings that were lost due to the disobedience of Adam and Eve. Christ came to establish the conditions necessary to restore mankind to our original position as sons of God, by removing our sins. Christ had to establish certain foundations by offering his life as a sacrifice for our sins.

<< First Corinthians 15:20-23 >> [But now is Christ risen from the dead, and become the first fruits of them that slept. <21> For since by man came death, by man also the resurrection of the dead. For as in Adam all died, even so in Christ shall all be made alive. <23> But every man in his own order: Christ the First Fruits; afterward they that are Christ's at his coming.]

The three blessings of Eden which Christ had to restore were fruitfulness, multiplication, and dominion! By so doing Christ would bring about the kingdom of Heaven upon the earth, where man could have direct communion with God and the spirit world. When Jesus rejected the devil's temptation to turn the stone into bread, he was restoring the word of God, which makes us fruitful or mature. Jesus said to Satan that it was written that man shall live by God's words alone!

When Jesus refused to throw himself from the temple, he was restoring the second blessing, that of the multiplication of the sons of God. Our bodies are the temples of God:

<< I Corinthians 3:16,17 >> [Know ye not that ye are the temple of God, and that the spirit dwelleth in you? If any man defile the temple of God, him shall God destroy; for the temple of God is holy, which temple ye are.]

We are to multiply goodness, as the branches of Jesus Christ. When Jesus refused Satan's offer of glory and wealth in exchange for his submission, Christ was restoring the third Edenic blessing of dominion. Christ returned the glory to the Lord YAHAWAH, saying: "Thou shalt worship the Lord thy God and him only shalt thou serve!"

All of us in one way or another are being confronted with the same temptations in our lives. The scriptures alert us to guard against temptations. For example:

THE TRUTH

<< I John 2:15-17 >> [Love not the world, neither the things that are in the world. If any man love the world, the love of the Father is not in him. For all that is in the world, the lust of the flesh, and the lust of the eyes, and the pride of life, is not of the father, but is of the world. And the world passeth away, and the lust thereof: but the will of God abideth forever.]

We must be prepared and on guard against satanic attacks:

<< Ephesians 6:12-16 >> [For we wrestle not against flesh and blood, but against principalities, against powers, against the rulers of the darkness of the world, against spiritual wickedness in high places. <13> Wherefore take unto you the whole armor of God, that ye may be able to withstand in the evil day, and having done all, stand.

<14> Stand therefore, having your loins girt about with truth, and having on the breastplate of righteousness; <15> And your feet shod with the preparation of the gospel of peace; <16> Above all, taking the shield of faith, wherewith ye shall be able to quench all the fiery darts of the wicked. <17> And take the helmet of salvation, and the sword of the spirit, which is the word of God: Praying always with all prayer and supplication in the Spirit, and watching thereunto with all perseverance and supplication for all saints.]

Spiritual Nakedness

The original man was created in the image of God, and had a similar glow, an envelope of light covering his body as the angels. This robe of light made material clothing unnecessary, which is why it is said that man was naked in the beginning and felt no shame. But after sinning, mankind lost this glorious robe of light and had to improvise with material covering!

<< Genesis 3:7 >> [And the eyes of them both were opened, and they knew that they were naked; and they sewed fig leaves together, and made themselves aprons.]

The term naked is also used in the Bible to indicate a shameful condition of sin. For example, Moses said that Aaron made the people naked, because he made them worship a golden calf:

<< Exodus 32:25 >> [And when Moses saw that the people were naked; for Aaron had made them naked unto their shame among their enemies.]

This means, it was a sin for them to make and worship this false idol of gold. The garment that we must keep is righteousness and the words of the Bible, obeying the laws of God. To walk naked is to be walking in sin.

<< Revelation 16:15 >> Christ says: [Behold, I come as a thief. Blessed is he that watcheth, and keepeth his garments, less he walk naked, and they see his shame.]

<< Genesis 3:8-11 >> [And they heard the voice of the Lord walking in the cool of the day: and Adam and his wife hid themselves from the presence of the Lord among the trees of the garden (hiding among the other nations by adopting a false identity and a false truth: doing evil). <9> And the Lord called unto Adam, and said unto him, Where art thou? <10> And he said,

THE TRUTH

I heard thy voice in the garden, and I was afraid, because I was naked (in sin*); and I hid myself. <11> And he said, Who told thee that thou wast naked? Hast thou eaten of the tree, whereof I commanded thee that thou shouldest not eat?]*

God gave man the commandments because although man was made complete, he was not yet fully mature. Living beings require time in order to reach maturity. Even the physical universe wasn't made at once, it took six days to be completed. The commandments are given so as to protect us during our period of spiritual and mental development, by guarding us from unprincipled love, lust, and deception during our premature period. The reason why man was given a choice of good and evil, was so that he could develop himself through his own efforts, because man was created to be lord and to have dominion over the creation. Mankind has to fulfill his share of the responsibilities in order to qualify to inherit the lordship with God, and to be one with God!

The Judgment

<< Genesis 3:12-15 >> [And the man said, The woman whom thou gavest to be with me, she gave me of the tree (Adam tried to put the blame on God, then on the woman.*), and I did eat. <13> And the Lord God said unto the woman, What is this that thou hast done? And the woman said, The serpent beguiled me, and I did eat. <14> And the Lord God said unto the serpent, Because thou hast done this, thou art cursed above every beast of the field; upon thy belly shalt thou go, and dust shalt thou eat all the days of thy life.]*

Prophetically speaking on a national level, the seed of Adam and Eve is represented by the original Israelites. The seed that would bruise the serpent specifically refers to Jesus Christ! The serpent of course is the Roman Empire, past and present.

<15> [And I will put enmity between thee and the woman (between Israel and the Edomite*), and between thy seed and her seed* (spirits don't reproduce with seed, only plants and animals; seed pertain to nations: the devil's seed is a nation of people*); it shall bruise thy head, and thou shall bruise his heel.]*

This prophecy is a declaration of war against the serpent. The people who have adopted the fruit of the reversal of dominion are doomed from the start. By attacking Adam, the serpent outsmarted himself and sealed his own doom. Israelites, and specifically Christ, are the redeeming seed. You kill a serpent by bruising his head. At the return of Jesus Christ the wicked societies of this world, governed by Satan, will be judged and destroyed by natural disasters, super-natural disasters, and nuclear war.

This prophecy of Adam is the root of all other prophecies. It incorporates both the first and Second Coming of Jesus Christ. Christ's heel was in a way bruised at the time of his first coming, when he fell to the cross. The serpent's head will be bruised at the Second Coming of Jesus Christ. It was the Roman Empire that killed Jesus, and Christ at his return will put an end to all heathens. History itself has been the process of restoring mankind to its original glorious state, to be reunited with the Lord God!

Concerning the Israelites, the serpent bruised our heel and caused us to fall as a nation! When your heel is bruised you fall. It was the Romans in 70 AD that overthrew the original Israelites and dispersed the nation!

THE TRUTH

<< Revelation 12:4 >> [And his tail drew the third part of the stars of heaven, and did cast them to the Earth (It was the tribes of Judah, Benjamin, and Levy that was left, which the Romans defeated, and had forced to run into Africa*): And the dragon* (Romans*) stood before the woman* (Israel*) which was ready to be delivered, for to devour her child* (Herod wanted to kill Christ*) as soon as it was born. And she brought forth a man child which was to rule all nations with a rod of iron: and her child was caught up unto the Most High, and to his throne.]*

This verse confirms the identity of the seed of the serpent as the Roman Empire and the Western nations that came out of it. It also identifies the original Israelites, and specifically Jesus Christ, as the righteous seed, destined to destroy the serpent!

<< Genesis 3:16-24 >> [Unto the woman he said, I will greatly multiply thy sorrow and thy conception; in sorrow thou shalt bring forth children (hardships and difficulties in giving birth to and the raising of children*); and thy desire shall be to thy husband, and he shall rule over thee.*

>*<17> And unto Adam he said, Because thou hast hearkened unto the voice of thy wife, and hast eaten of the tree, of which I commanded thee, saying Thou shalt not eat of it: cursed is the ground for thy sake; in sorrow shalt thou eat of it all the days of thy life; <18> Thorns also and thistles shall it bring forth to thee* (hard work that will prove unrewarding, toils and terror*); and thou shalt eat the herb of the field; <19> In the sweat of thy face shalt thou eat bread, till thou return unto the ground; for out of it wast thou taken: for dust thou art, and unto dust shalt thou return.*   *<20> And Adam called his wife's name Eve; because she* (the earth) *was the mother of all living. <21> Unto Adam also and to his wife did the Lord God make coats of skins, and clothed them.]*

The blood of an animal was shed. This animal was killed instead of Adam, its skin was made into a covering for Adam. This is an example of the mercy of the Lord YAHAWAH. Also, the killing of the animal represents the fact that the blood of Jesus Christ was going to be shed for our sins, he was crucified for our redemption!

<< Genesis 3:22-24 >> [And the Lord God said, Behold, the man is become as one of us, to know good and evil: and now, lest he put forth his hand, and take also of the tree of life, and eat, and live forever.]

Eating of the tree of life would have caused them to live forever in their shameful and sinful condition, and to be in agony forever, with no hope for redemption.

<23> Therefore the Lord God sent him forth from the Garden of Eden, to till the ground from whence he was taken. <24> So he drove out the man; and he placed at the east of the Garden of Eden Cherubim, and a flaming sword which turned every way, to keep the way of the tree of life.]

Multiplication of Evil

<< *Genesis 4:1-17* >> [*And Adam knew his wife; and she conceived, and bore Cain, and said, I have gotten a man from the Lord. And she again bares his brother Abel. And Abel was a keeper of sheep, but Cain was a tiller of the ground.*

<3> And in process of time it came to pass, that Cain brought of the fruit of the ground an offering unto the Lord. <4> And Abel, he also brought of the firstlings of his flock and of the fat thereof (the difference is that Abel gave the very best from his heart to God)*, And the Lord had respect unto Abel and his offering: <5> But unto Cain and his offering he had not respect. And Cain was very wroth, and his countenance fell.*]

God rejected Cain's offering, not because of the quality of his offering, but because of the character with which it was offered. Abel gave the firstlings of his flock, but Cain did not give the best from his heart.

<< *Genesis 4:6* >> [*And the Lord said unto Cain, Why art thou wroth? And why is thy countenance fallen? If thou doest well, shalt thou not be accepted? And if thou doest not well, sin lieth at the door. And unto thee shall be his desire, and thou shalt rule over him.*

<8> And Cain talked with Abel his brother: and it came to pass, when they were in the field, that Cain rose up against Abel his brother, and slew him.

<9> And the Lord said unto Cain, Where is Abel thy brother? And he said, I know not: Am I my brother's keeper?]

Yes, we are our brother's keepers according to the Biblical law! Jesus said it himself:

<< *Matthew 22:36-39* >> [*Master, which is the great commandment in the law? <37> Jesus said unto him, Thou shalt love the Lord thy God with all thy heart, and with all thy soul, and with all thy mind. <38> This is the first and the second is like unto it, Thou shalt love thy neighbor as thyself. <40> On these two commandments hang all the laws and the prophets.*]

<< *John 15:12,13* >> [*This is my commandment, That ye love one another, as I have loved you. <13> Greater love hath no man than this, that a man lay down his life for his friends.*]

<< *Genesis 4:10*> [*And he (God) said, What hast thou done? the voice of thy brother's blood crieth unto me from the ground. <11> And now art thou cursed from the earth, which hath opened her mouth to receive thy brother's blood from thy hand; <12> When thou tillest the ground, it shall not henceforth yield unto thee her strength; a fugitive and a vagabond shalt thou be in the earth.*

<13> And Cain said unto the Lord, My punishment is greater than I can bear. <14> Behold, thou hast driven me out this day from the face of the earth; and from thy face shall I be hid; and I shall be a fugitive and a vagabond in the earth; and it shall come to pass, that every one that findeth me shall slay me.

<15> And the Lord said unto him, Therefore whosoever slayeth Cain, vengeance shall be taken on him seven fold. And the Lord set a mark upon Cain, lest any finding him should kill him. <16> And Cain went out from the Lord, and dwelt in the land of Nod, on the east of Eden.]

THE TRUTH

To teach us not to use violence as a way to resolve conflicts, the Lord allowed Cain to live.

<< Matthew 26:52 >> [Then said Jesus unto him, Put up again thy sword into his place: for all they that take the sword shall perish with the sword.]

The children of Seth, son of Adam, are referred to as the sons of God because they were keeping and preserving the customs of Adam (the Hebrew customs), which God had taught to him.

<< Genesis 6:1-20 >> [And it came to pass, when men began to multiply on the face of the earth, and daughters were born unto them, <2> That the sons of God (referring to the descendants of Seth) *saw the daughters of men* (the other people) *that they were fair; and they took them wives of all which they chose.*

<3> And the Lord said, My spirit shall not always strive with man, for that he also is flesh: yet his days shall be an hundred twenty years. <4> There were giants in the earth in those days; and also after that, when the sons of God came in unto the daughters of men, and they bare children to them, the same became mighty men which were of old, men of renown.]

<< Genesis 6:5 >> [And God saw that the wickedness of man was great in the earth, and that every imagination of the thoughts of his heart was only evil continually. <6> And it repented the Lord that he had made man on the earth, and it grieved him at his heart. <7> And the Lord said, I will destroy man whom I had created from the face of the earth; both man, and beast, and the creeping thing, and the fowls of the air; for it repenteth me that I have made them. <8> But Noah found grace in the eyes of the Lord.]

IDENTITY OF THE NATIONS

JUDAH...........Afr.Americans, Caribs.
ISRAEL...American-Indians, Hispanics.
SHEM.….....…….Mid-East, The West.
JAPHET.................…..Asians, Russia.
ELAM.................…....India, Dravidians.
ISHMAEL.….....…....…......The Arabs.
EDOMITES.….....…........The Caucasians.
HAM......…..…............The Africans.
CUSH.........…...…...…….....Ethiopia.
MIZRAIM.................Ancient Egypt.
PHUT....…........…….......North Africa.
CANAAN....…...…….......Sub-Saharan.

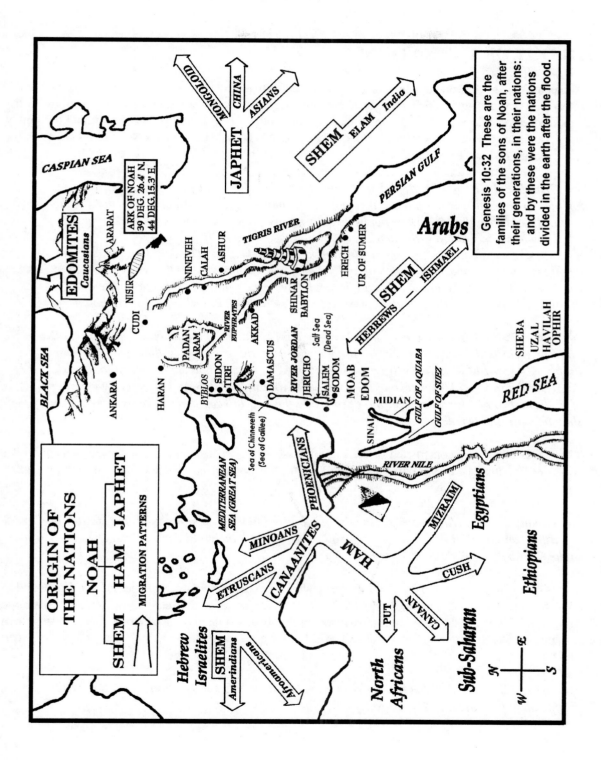

ORIGIN OF THE NATIONS

NOAH

SHEM   HAM   JAPHET

MIGRATION PATTERNS

Genesis 10:32 These are the families of the sons of Noah, after their generations, in their nations: and by these were the nations divided in the earth after the flood.

GENEALOGY OF THE NATIONS

Archeological, geological and historical evidence confirm extensively that there was a global flood, approximately 5,300 years ago, which brought about a cataclysmic worldwide destruction! According to the historical and archeological records of Mesopotamia, Asia and other ancient civilizations, Noah and his family were the only people to survive this worldwide flood. The Lord YAHAWAH instructed Noah to build an ark for his safety; in preparation for the coming flood.

> << Genesis 6:13-19 >> [And God said unto Noah, The end of all flesh is come before me; for the earth is filled with violence through them; and behold, I will destroy them with the earth. <14> Make thee an ark of gopher wood; rooms shalt thou make in the ark, and shalt pitch it within and without with pitch.
>
> <15> And this is the fashion which thou shalt make it of: The length of the ark shall be three hundred cubits, the breadth of it fifty cubits, and the height of it thirty cubits. <16> A window shalt thou make to the ark, and in a cubit shalt thou finish it above; and the door of the ark shalt thou set in the side thereof; with lower, second, and third stories shalt thou make it.
>
> <17> And, behold, I, even I, do bring a flood of waters upon the earth, to destroy all flesh, wherein is the breath of life, from under heaven; and every thing that is in the earth shall die. <18> But with thee will I establish my covenant; and thou shalt come into the ark, thou, and thy sons, and thy wife, and thy sons' wives with thee. <19> And of every living thing of all flesh, two of every sort shalt thou bring into the ark, to keep them alive with thee; they shall be male and female.]

The ark of Noah was constructed of reeds compressed together and encased in cement, similar to the arks described in Exodus 2:3, and Isaiah 18:2. This kind of construction is what the Bible means by gopher wood.

> << Exodus 2:3 >> [And when she could not longer hide him, she took for him an ark of bulrushes, and daubed it with slime and with pitch, and put the child therein; and she laid it in the flags by the river's bank.]

The Biblical cubit is equal to 20.61432 inches. When the rediscovered ark was measured it was found to be about 514 feet in length, and contained about 2,275,630 cubic feet of space, equivalent to about 900 cattle cars of a freight train! Most of the time, the animals were probably in a state of induced hibernation, causing them to require minimum attention during the voyage! The Bible gave us the location as to where the ark of Noah would be found:

> << Genesis 8:4 >> [And the ark rested in the seventh month, on the seventeenth day of the month, upon the Mountains of Ararat.]

THE TRUTH

Notice that the Bible never said that the ark of Noah was on the exact mountain peak of Ararat. It tells us that the ark is to be found in the region of the Ararat Mountains. People have gone exploring, and have successfully located and photographed Noah's ark!

The real ark was first rediscovered in May of 1948 after an earthquake caused it to surface out of the ground, where it had sunken and became fossilized in the mud left from the flood. It is possible to visit and touch the fossilized ark! It is located at 39 Degrees 26.4 minutes North Latitude, and 44 Degrees 15.3 minutes East Longitude. The ark of Noah is to be found at an altitude of 6245 feet above sea level! This region of Ararat where the ark is found is in Turkey, near the Iranian border, 11.3 kilometers east of a Turkish town called Dogubayazit. Since we now have the exact location of Noah's ark, all of this is easy to confirm.

Anchor stones originating from the ark of Noah have been recovered on land, that could not have gotten there any other way! Detailed books have been written on the rediscovered ark of Noah. However, not all of those books have the correct location! The resurfacing of the ark in 1948 is a sign of the Second Coming judgment and also the salvation from the Lord YAHAWAH!

After the flood, the three sons of Noah began to repopulate the earth. It was from these three men that all the nations of the world descended.

<< *Geneses 9:19* >> [*These are the three sons of Noah: and of them was the whole earth overspread.*]

This fact concerning the true origin of the human race, as conveyed to us in the Bible, has been proven time and time again through a variety of experiments performed by genetic scientists all over the world, and supported by several archeological facts! The Lord never divided mankind by race; he made us as a single human race, a family upon the earth. All people on this earth are related! All nations came out of the three sons of Noah: Shem, Ham, and Japheth!

<< *Genesis 10:1* >> [*Now these are the generations of the sons of Noah, Shem, Ham, and Japheth: and unto them were sons born after the flood.*]

Every person living today can be traced back to one of the three sons of Noah: Shem, Ham, or Japheth! Noah and his sons were of the Asiatic type. This is easily proven. When you look around on the planet, you notice the majority of nations are different shades of brown. The Polynesian Asians, the original American-Indians, the East Indians, the original Arabs and Egyptians were all brown-skinned people. The Africans are dark brown-skinned. When you look around on the earth and see that the majority of the nations are colored people, then you have to conclude that their father Noah had to be an Asiatic man with woolly hair! You can't get dark colored-skinned children from light-skinned Caucasian parents. Our common ancestors had to be of the Asiatic type.

The most significant key that allows us to identify the Biblical nations is the fact that the patriarchs of the Bible were given prophetic names. The giving of prophetic names has been a tradition even before the flood. For example, Methuselah's name, given at birth means, at his death the sending forth of waters. Methuselah lived 969 years, and the flood came one week after his death.

THE TRUTH

The Middle-Eastern Nations

Noah's Asiatic son Shem was the progenitor of the original Middle Eastern nations, including the Israelites!

> *<< Genesis 10:22-25 >> [The children of Shem: Elam, and Asshur, and Arphaxad, and Lud, and Aram. <23> And the children of Aram; Uz, and Hul, and Gether, and Mash. <24> And Arphaxad begat Salah, and Salah begat Beer. <25> And unto Eber were born sons: the name of one was Peleg; for in his days was the earth divided.]*

The Elamites are the people living in the regions of India today. Asshur inhabited the vicinity of Iran. From Arphaxad came the Hebrew Israelites, the Caucasians, and the Arabs. Lud inhabited the area that is Turkey today; and Aram's descendants inhabited the region of Syria! Of course, because of war and migration, those nations are all mixed with remnants from each other.

Abraham, Isaac, and Jacob were purely Asiatic people who had descended from the family line of Arphaxad! Abraham was the son of Terah, son of Nahor, son of Serug, son of Reu, son of Peleg, son of Eber, son of Salah, son of Arphaxad, the son of Shem, who was the son of Noah. And Lot, Abraham's brother's son, had two sons of whom the Moabite and Amonite nations originated. They became amalgamated among the Middle-Eastern nations.

Furthermore, we observe in << Genesis 19:37-38 >> that Abraham had two sons, Isaac and Ishmael. The Ishmaelites are the Arab nations of today. And Abraham's son Isaac also had two sons Jacob and Esau. Jacob became the father of the twelve tribes of Israel, which are the African-Americans and American-Indians. Esau was the ancestor of the Edomites (Edom means red). The Edomites are known as the Caucasians and Europeans of today!

> *<< Genesis 10:2 >> [The sons of Japheth; Gomer, Magog, and Madai, and Javan, Tubal, and Meshech, and Tiras.]*

Noah's Asiatic son Japheth was the father of the Asians: the Chinese, Japanese, Indo-Chinese, and certain tribes in Russia.

To identify the nations we will examine the prophetic meanings of the names given to the patriarchs. Also, the prophetic blessings of Noah to his three sons, who were to repopulate the earth, convey the condition and present status of their descendants. These prophetic conditions serve to identify which descendent became which nation today.

> *<< Genesis 9:19-27 >> [These are the three sons of Noah: and of them was the whole earth overspread. <20> And Noah began to be an husbandman, and he planted a vineyard: <21> And he drank of the wine, and was drunken; and he was uncovered within his tent. <22> And Ham, the father of Canaan, saw the nakedness of his father, and told his two brethren without. <23> And Shem and Japheth took a garment, and went backward, and covered the nakedness of their father; and their faces were backward, and they saw not their father's nakedness.*

THE TRUTH

<24> And Noah awoke from his wine, and knew what his younger son had done unto him. And he said, Cursed be Canaan; a servant of servants shall he be unto his brethren. <25> And he said, Blessed be the Lord God of Shem; and Canaan shall be his servant. God shall enlarge Japheth, and he shall dwell in the tents of Shem (Chinatowns are found world wide, among many nations*); and Canaan shall be his servant.]*

The Asians

Japheth was the oldest son of Noah. Japheth's blessing was that he would be enlarged, according to Genesis 10:27 above. The Asians have the most numerous populations. By the year 2,000 the world's population will be about 6.1 Billion, of which the Asians will number around 3.7 billion. China alone has a population of over 1.3 billion today; add to this the populations of Japan, Korea, Indochina, plus the number of Asians living in foreign countries. Therefore, to identify the descendants of Japheth, we simply find which groups of people are the most numerous. Obviously, no other people can compare in population to the Asians!

<< Genesis 10:2-5 >> [The sons of Japheth; Gomer, and Magog, and Madai, and Javan, and Tubal, and Meshech, and Tiras. And the sons of Gomer; Ashkenaz, and Riphath, and Togarmah. And the sons of Javan; Elishah, and Tarshish, Kitties, and Duodenum. By these were the isles of the Gentiles divided in their lands; every one after his tongue, after their families, in their nations.]

In the ancient world, the people were given names according to certain prominent social, spiritual, and prophetic characteristics. Thus, by analyzing the names of each of Japheth's sons, we will find them to be prophetic names serving to identify the people geographically in the last days! The name Japheth is derived from the Hebrew word for expansion. This meaning is prophetic, informing us that the people descended from Japheth would be identified as numerous. Gomer was the first born of Japheth, his name means addition and accumulation, again implying a multitude. Gomer had three sons: Ashkenaz, meaning bunched together; Riphath, meaning as grounded corn or wheat; and Togarmah, meaning in many pieces.

Four more of the sons of Japheth: Magog, Madai, Tubal, and Meshech, are the various tribes in the area of Russia and Asia. Javan, the son of Japheth, his name means boiling or bubbling over; implying rapid expansion, overflowing, and multiplication. The Asians have the largest population. According to Biblical prophecy, the Asians must be the descendents of Japhet.

The Africans

Noah's son Ham, was the progenitor of the Africans. Ham had to be brown-skinned like his father Noah. The complexion of the modern Africans, who had descended from Ham, proves that he had to be brown! Shem and Japheth also had to be brown like their father Noah and their brother Ham. In the beginning, the world was made only of Afro-asiatic people and from such were all other shades, darker and lighter, derived!

<< Genesis 10:6 >> [And the sons of Ham; Cush, and Mizraim, and Put, and Canaan.]

THE TRUTH

The sons of Ham were the progenitors of the African nations: Cushites are called Ethiopians today; Put, was the father of the North Africans nations, and the descendents of Canaan migrated to the southern and central parts of Africa and Mizraim is the name of the original Egyptians.

>> *Genesis 50:11* >> *[...This is a great morning to the Egyptians: Wherefore the name of it was called Abel-Mizraim.]*

It was the Romans that called the Hamites Africans, but the continent was first called the land of Ham. However, today most of North Africa is inhabited by non-Africans, which are the offspring of the Arabs, Greeks, Romans, and other imperialists that invaded and mixed among the Africans. Don't be surprised if you visit North Africa and find a great number of Caucasians and Arabs living there.

Canaan was the grandson of Noah, and is the ancestor of the Southern African nations of today. The Canaanites were cursed to be servants (Today all the nations of the earth are cursed, because we are all living in wickedness) Canaan was not cursed with leprosy or any other physical abnormality. His curse is clearly stated in the Bible: to be a servant. The curse had nothing to do with the color of his skin; as the white supremacists have maliciously claimed.

>> *Genesis 10:19-27* >> *[These are the three sons of Noah: and of them was the whole earth overspread. And Noah began to be an husbandman, and he planted a vineyard: And he drank of the wine, and was drunken; and he was uncovered within his tent. And Ham, the father of Canaan, saw the nakedness of his father, and told his two brethren without. And Shem and Japheth took a garment, and went backward, and covered the nakedness of their father; and their faces were backward, and they saw not their father's nakedness.*

And Noah awoke from his wine, and knew what his younger son had done unto him. And he said, Cursed be Canaan; a servant of servants shall he be unto his brethren. And he said, Blessed be the Lord God of Shem; and Canaan shall be his servant. God shall enlarge Japheth, and he shall dwell in the tents of Shem; and Canaan shall be his servant.]

Canaan was cursed to be a servant because Ham had looked upon the nakedness of Noah, and told it to his brothers. For the longest time, the Caucasians and Arabs had the majority of sub-Saharan African nations suffering under colonialism, slavery, and apartheid!

There is a difference between Israelites and Africans. Africans are descendents of Ham and Israelites are the descendents of Shem. There are Ethiopians who are claiming to be Jews, but according to the bible they are imposters. The Ethiopians were converted to the religion of Judaism during the time when the ten tribes of Israel were removed from the land of Samaria, at the beginning of the Babylonian captivity, about 2,720 years ago.

>> *2 Kings 17:22-28* >> *[For the children of Israel walked in all the sins of Jeroboam which he did; they departed not from them; <23> Until the LORD removed Israel out of his sight, as he had said by all his servants the prophets. So was Israel carried away out of their own land to Assyria unto this day. <24> And the king of Assyria brought men from Babylon, and from Cuthah, (Ethiopians) and from Ava, and from Hamath, and from Sepharvaim, and placed them in the cities of Samaria instead of the children of Israel: and they possessed Samaria, and dwelt in the cities thereof.*

<25> And so it was at the beginning of their dwelling there, that they feared not the

LORD: therefore the LORD sent lions among them, which slew some of them. 26 Wherefore they spake to the king of Assyria, saying, The nations which thou hast removed, and placed in the cities of Samaria, know not the manner of the God of the land: therefore he hath sent lions among them, and, behold, they slay them, because they know not the manner of the God of the land. <27> Then the king of Assyria commanded, saying, Carry thither one of the priests whom ye brought from thence; and let them go and dwell there, and let him teach them the manner of the God of the land. <28> Then one of the priests whom they had carried away from Samaria came and dwelt in Bethel, and taught them how they should fear the LORD.]

The reason why Jesus told the disciples not to go into Samaria was because the people living there were Ethiopians claiming to be Jews but were not descendents of Abraham, Isaac and Jacob. The Samaritans were not of the twelve tribes of Israel.

<< Matthew 10:5,6 >> [These twelve Jesus sent forth, and commanded them, saying, Go not into the way of the Gentiles, and into any city of the Samaritans enter ye not: <6> But go rather to the lost sheep of the house of Israel.]

Jesus encountered a Samaritan woman and explained to her that God is seeking the true Israelites to worship him at Jerusalem, not religious converts:

<< John 4:3-26 >> [He left Judaea, and departed again into Galilee, <4> And he must needs go through Samaria. <5> Then cometh he to a city of Samaria, which is called Sychar, near to the parcel of ground that Jacob gave to his son Joseph. <6> Now Jacob's well was there. Jesus therefore, being wearied with his journey, sat thus on the well: and it was about the sixth hour. <7> There cometh a woman of Samaria (Ethiopians living in Samaria) *to draw water: Jesus saith unto her, Give me to drink. <8> (For his disciples were gone away unto the city to buy meat.) <9> Then saith the woman of Samaria unto him, How is it that thou, being a Jew, askest drink of me, which am a woman of Samaria? for the Jews have no dealings with the Samaritans. <10> Jesus answered and said unto her, If thou knewest the gift of God, and who it is that saith to thee, Give me to drink; thou wouldest have asked of him, and he would have given thee living water.*

<11> The woman saith unto him, Sir, thou hast nothing to draw with, and the well is deep: from whence then hast thou that living water? <12> Art thou greater than our father Jacob (Jacob is not her father, Cush was father of the Ethiopians. She was pretending to be a Jew)*...*

<19> The woman saith unto him, Sir, I perceive that thou art a prophet. <20> Our fathers worshipped in this mountain; and ye (the real Jews) *say, that in Jerusalem is the place where men ought to worship. <21> Jesus saith unto her, Woman, believe me, the hour cometh, when ye shall neither in this mountain, nor yet at Jerusalem, worship the Father. <22>* __**Ye worship ye know not what: we know what we worship: for salvation is of the Jews**__*. 23 But the hour cometh, and now is, when the* <u>true worshippers</u> (real Israelites) *shall worship the Father in spirit and in truth: for the Father seeketh*

such to worship him. <24> God is a Spirit: and they that worship him must worship him in spirit and in truth. <25> The woman saith unto him, I know that Messias cometh, which is called Christ: when he is come, he will tell us all things. <26> Jesus saith unto her, I that speak unto thee am he.]

According to the Bible Solomon never laid with the queen of Sheba to make a child with her. This story was a myth. The Bible says she came to visit with him to hear his wisdom and counsel then returned to her own country.

> *<< 1 Kings 10:1-13 >> [And when the queen of Sheba heard of the fame of Solomon concerning the name of the LORD, she came to prove him with hard questions. <2> And she came to Jerusalem with a very great train, with camels that bare spices, and very much gold, and precious stones: and when she was come to Solomon, she communed with him of all that was in her heart. <3> And Solomon told her all her questions: there was not any thing hid from the king, which he told her not. <4> And when the queen of Sheba had seen all Solomon's wisdom, and the house that he had built, <5> And the meat of his table, and the sitting of his servants, and the attendance of his ministers, and their apparel, and his cupbearers, and his ascent by which he went up unto the house of the LORD; there was no more spirit in her.*
>
> *<6> And she said to the king, It was a true report that I heard in mine own land of thy acts and of thy wisdom. <7> Howbeit I believed not the words, until I came, and mine eyes had seen it: and, behold, the half was not told me: thy wisdom and prosperity exceedeth the fame which I heard. <8> Happy are thy men, happy are these thy servants, which stand continually before thee, and that hear thy wisdom. 9 Blessed be the LORD thy God, which delighted in thee, to set thee on the throne of Israel: because the LORD loved Israel for ever, therefore made he thee king, to do judgment and justice. <10> And she gave the king an hundred and twenty talents of gold, and of spices very great store, and precious stones: there came no more such abundance of spices as these which the queen of Sheba gave to king Solomon.*
>
> *<11> And the navy also of Hiram, that brought gold from Ophir, brought in from Ophir great plenty of almug trees, and precious stones. 12 And the king made of the almug trees pillars for the house of the LORD, and for the king's house, harps also and psalteries for singers: there came no such almug trees, nor were seen unto this day. <13> And king Solomon gave unto the queen of Sheba all her desire, whatsoever she asked, beside that which Solomon gave her of his royal bounty. So she turned and went to her own country, she and her servants.*

In addition to the Hamites who populated Africa, there is also a large number of Israelites who had fled into Africa during the Diaspora. The Israelites did set up a number of colonies and nations in the northern and western parts of Africa. Many Israelite communities can still be found amongst the African nations today, and are keeping the Hebrew Israelite customs and traditions. The History of the Israelites in Africa is well documented in the book by Rudolf Windsor: **From Babylon To Timbuktu**.

The Caucasians

THE TRUTH

The historical and genealogical origin of the Caucasians is recorded in the bible:

<< *Genesis 25:21 to 26* >> *[And Isaac entreated the Lord for his wife, because she was barren: and the Lord was entreated of him, and Rebekah his wife conceived. And the children struggled together within her; and she said, If it be so, why am I thus? And the Lord said unto her, Two nations* (Israel from Jacob, and the Caucasians from Esau) *are in thy womb, and two manner of people shall be separated from thy bowels; the one people shall be stronger than the other people; and the elder shall serve the younger.*

And when her days to be delivered were fulfilled, behold, there were twins in her womb. And the first came out Red, all over like an hairy garment and they call his name Esau (The word Esau means, "wasted away is he"). *And after that came his brother out, and his hand took hold on Esau's heel; and his name was called Jacob.]*

<< *Genesis 32:28* >>*[Thy name shall be called no more Jacob, but Israel: for a prince hast thou power with the Lord and with men, and hast prevailed.]*

Jacob's twelve sons became the original twelve tribes of Israel; and are today being called the African-Americans and the American-Indians of north, south, and Central America, as well as the Caribbean! The original name of the Caucasians is Edom, this is a Hebrew word meaning red. Caucasians are reddish in complexion because the blood shows through their skin. Caucasian Edomites are not descended from any of the twelve tribes of Israel.

<< *Genesis 36:8* >> *[Thus dwelt Esau in mount Seir: Esau is Edom* (Edomites are red or so-called white people).]

<< *Verse 15* >> *[These were the Dukes of the sons of Esau: the sons of Eliaphaz the firstborn son of Esau; Duke Teman, Duke Omar, Duke zepho, Duke kenaz.]*

The Caucasians, like all nations of the earth, descended from Asiatic ancestors. Esau, the progenitor of the Caucasians, was born red. The blood shows through his pale-skin, due to a lack of pigmentation:

<< *Numbers 12:10-12* >> *[And the cloud departed from off the tabernacle; and, behold, Miriam became leprous, white as snow: and Aaron looked upon Miriam, and, behold, she was leprous. And Aaron said unto Moses, Alas, my lord, I beseech thee, lay not the sin upon us, wherein we have sinned. Let her not be as one dead, of whom the flesh is half consumed when he cometh out of his mother's womb.]*

<< *Genesis 4:15* >> *[...The Lord set a mark upon Cain.]*

SECRET OF THE CHINESE CHARACTERS

All men on earth have a responsibility to fulfill the purpose of their creation. The purpose of mankind is to become like a mirror, reflecting the perfect character of God the Creator, whose name is Lord YAHAWAH. Therefore, we should expect that the Lord will again reveal the gospel of truth to all nations.

The Lord is not a respecter of persons. His gospel can be found all over the earth, in every nation. For thousands of years, the basic gospel has been recorded in various forms within the different nations. Each culture has something valuable to teach, and each method can be useful in revealing the ultimate biblical truth. However, the gospel is often found in a polluted state, mixed with man-made religions and other philosophies. Nevertheless, we are all responsible for our individual salvation. When the truth is presented it is our responsibility to research, prove, accept, and restore it!

What is called Christianity today is nothing new in the world. The prophecies concerning the works of Jesus Christ had been known from the foundation of the world. Christ came in fulfillment of those prophecies. What we call Christianity today is just another polluted version of the original truth. So-called Christianity existed in Asia, Africa, and in all civilizations of antiquity, thousands of years before it was known to the Western world. It was called by other names, and was in different forms, polluted by individual customs. It is also mentioned in the scriptures that there would be found among all nations evidence that would serve as witness and reminder of the gospel of truth:

> << Acts 14:16 >> [Who in times past suffered all nations to walk in their own ways. <17> Nevertheless he left not himself without witness...]

A fascinating and clear example of Christianity before Christ is found among the ancient Chinese. About five thousand years ago, the Chinese were a monotheistic people, believing in the God of heaven. They did not worship any idols, and had very moral and ethical sets of laws. China remained monotheistic for centuries because mountains, oceans, and deserts geographically isolated it. It was protected from the influence of pagan societies and remained unpolluted by idol worship for centuries.

The records of Confucius reveal that the earlier emperors of China regularly made sacrifices to the God of heaven in a ceremony known as the border sacrifices. Some of the details of the border ceremony are recorded in an ancient Chinese text called the Shu Ching (Book of History). Monotheism continued in China from the time of the Hsia, and the Shang dynasty up until the Chou dynasty about four thousand years ago. Monotheism in China was terminated during the reign of Emperor Ch'in Shih Huan-ti, who conquered and unified all of China. He built the 1,500-mile Great Wall, and placed all of China under a common standard of economy, science, and character system of writing.

The Asian civilization is one of the oldest existing societies on earth, and has always been impressive throughout history. The Lord YAHAWAH left himself a witness among the Asians, a record encoded within the writing system of the Chinese, over four thousand years ago. Within the design of the Chinese character, is recorded the history found in the Bible, many other Biblical prophecies are also recorded within the Chinese characters. To prove this point we will now decipher a few of the Chinese characters.

[GOD]

上 Above

+

帝 Emperor

[GOD AS A SPIRIT]

礻

To Proclaim
Manifest

[THE HOLY SPIRIT]

聖 Holy

+

靈 Spirit

[SPIRIT]

Heaven + Cover + Water

Rain + Three + Worker
Person   Of Magic

[CREATE]

Dust + Breath + Alive
Of Mouth

To Talk + Walking

[DEVIL]

儿 ノ ム
Man + Alive + Secretly

田
Garden

十
A River Parted
Into Four Heads

[TEMPTER]

鬼 广 林
Devil + Cover + Trees

THE TRUTH

The set of Chinese characters that represent God proves that the Chinese were originally a monotheistic society. Secondly, the design of the characters proves that they worshipped the Biblical God of heaven. There are primarily three representations for God:

[Above Emperor] [God as a Spirit] [The Holy Spirit] (Please refer to the diagram.)

The first representation for God consists of two characters: above and emperor. The Bible describes the true God as the God of heaven, the possessor of the kingdom of heaven:

> << Matthew 5:9,10 >> [...Our Father which art in heaven, hallowed be thy name. <10> Thy kingdom come. Thy will be done in earth, as it is in heaven.]

The second representation for God in the Chinese script is composed of two Characters: God and Proclaimer. The Bible describes the true God as a Proclaimer, an Exhibitor, and a Revealer:

> << John 1:1 >> [In the beginning was the Word, and the word was with God, and the Word was God.]

The third representation is of two characters: Holy and Spirit. When we dissect the character for spirit into its components, further evidence is found to confirm the fact that the Chinese preserved the knowledge of the one true God within their writing system:

[Spirit] (Please refer to the diagram.)

The consecutive brush strokes in the character for spirit represent heaven, cover, water, rain, three persons, and worker of magic. The character for spirit seems to be describing the event of creation perfectly, by the spirit of God:

> << Genesis 1:1,2 >> [In the beginning God created the heaven and the earth. <2> and the earth was without form, and void; and darkness was upon the face of the deep. and the spirit of God moved upon the face of the waters.]

The spirit of God is described as moving over the face of the waters, and causing the creation to appear in a miraculous way. And when we examine the bottom half of the character we see that it suggests some kind of trinity. Christ also describes a threefold manifestation of God, saying:

> << Matthew 28:19 >> [Go ye therefore, and teach all nations, baptizing them in the name of the father, and of the Son, and of the Holy Spirit.]

Basically the character describes a trinity working miracles under heaven upon the earth.

THE TRUTH

<< *Psalm 33:6,9* >> [*By the word of the Lord were the heavens made; and all the host of them by the breath of his mouth... For he spake, and it was done; he commanded, and it stood fast.*]

The creation of man is also recorded within the Chinese characters. The character for create depicts almost word for word the Biblical account of the creation of man:

[**Create**] (Please refer to the diagram.)

The character consists of two main sections. The first depicts the leg of a man walking. The second section means talking, and can be further split into three parts: dust, breath of mouth, and alive. The scripture describes the same account for the creation of man:

<< *Genesis 2:7* >> [*And the Lord formed man from the dust of the ground, and breathed into his nostrils the breath of life; and man became a living soul.*]

According to the Bible and also the Chinese characters, God made the physical man from the dust of the earth, and then breathed life and spirit into that body. the man then became alive, able to talk and to walk.

We can also examine the records of the temptation of Adam and Eve not only in the Bible but also through the Chinese characters. This great mystery was recorded within several of the characters. We will consider two of them: the character for devil, and also the character for tempter.

[**Devil**] (Please refer to the diagram.)

The character for devil consists of four basic parts: motion, garden divided into four parts, the symbol for man (the two legs), and the character for privately (or secretly).

This character depicts the devil as a secret man, alive in the garden. He is the secret garden man. The garden is divided into four parts. According to the Bible, the Garden of Eden was divided into four parts by rivers flowing through it:

<< *Genesis 2:10* >>. [*And a river went forth out of Eden to water the Garden; and from thence it was parted into four heads.*]

Also in the Garden of Eden the Lord YAHAWAH placed two trees: the Tree of Life and the Tree of Knowledge of Good and Evil. God warned Adam and Eve concerning those trees:

<< *Genesis 2:9,16,17* >> [*<9> And out of the ground made the Lord to grow every tree that is pleasant to the sight, and good for food; the Tree of Life also in the midst of the garden, and the Tree of knowledge of Good and Evil...*

<16> And the Lord commanded the man, saying, Of every tree of the garden thou mayest freely eat: <17> But of the tree of the knowledge of Good and Evil, thou shalt not eat of it: for in the day that thou eatest thereof thou shalt surely die.]

THE TRUTH

The Bible describes the devil as the tempter that caused Adam and Eve to violate the commandment. Similarly, when we examine the Chinese character for Tempter, it describes clearly the temptation of Adam and Eve:

[Tempter] (Please refer to the diagram.)

The character is composed of three parts: devil, two trees, and cover. The tempter is described as the devil, hiding under the cover of the trees, tempting Adam and Eve. We can read the same account in the Bible:

<< Genesis 3:1-6 >> *[Now the Serpent was more subtle than any beast of the field which the Lord God had made. And he said unto the woman, Yea, hath God said, Ye shall not eat of every tree of the garden? And the woman said unto the serpent, We may eat of the fruit of the trees of the garden: But of the fruit of the tree which is in the midst of the garden, God hath said, Ye shall not eat of it, and neither shall ye touch it, lest ye die* (dying, to become mortal). *And the serpent said unto the woman, Ye shall not surely die: For God doth know that in the day ye eat thereof, then your eyes shall be opened, and ye shall be as gods, knowing good and evil.]*

[And when the woman saw that the tree was good for food, and that it was pleasant to the eyes, and a tree to be desired to make one wise, she took of the fruit thereof and did eat (Both the fruit and the tree were symbolic), *and gave also unto her husband with her; and he did eat.]*

<< Genesis 3:7-15 >> *[And the eyes of them both were opened, and they knew that they were naked; and they sewed fig leaves together, and made themselves aprons. <8> And they heard the voice of the Lord walking in the cool of the day: and Adam and his wife hid themselves from the presence of the Lord among the trees of the garden. <9> And the Lord called unto Adam, and said unto him, Where art thou? And he said, I heard thy voice in the garden, and I was afraid, because I was naked* (in sin); *and I hid myself.*

<11> And he said, Who told thee that thou wast naked? Hast thou eaten of the tree, whereof I commanded thee that thou shouldest not eat?

<12> And the man said, The woman whom thou gavest to be with me, she gave me of the tree, and I did eat. <13> And the Lord said unto the woman, what is this that thou hast done? And the woman said, The serpent beguiled me, and I did eat.

<14> And the Lord said unto the serpent, Because thou hast done this, thou art cursed above every beast of the field; upon thy belly shalt thou go, and dust shalt thou eat all the days of thy life". <15> And I will put enmity between thee and the woman, and between thy seed and her seed (Israel and Edom); *it shall bruise thy head, and thou shall bruise his heel.]*

The account of the flood of Noah also is recorded within several of the Chinese characters. We will examine two of those characters: boat and flood:

[Boat] [Flood] (Please refer to the diagram.)

THE TRUTH

According to Biblical history, about four-thousand-three-hundred-forty years ago, there was a global flood upon the earth. All animal life on the land perished, except for those that went into the ark with Noah and his three sons and their wives, a total of eight persons.

<< Genesis 7:7,13>> [And Noah went in, and his sons, and his wife, and his sons' wives with him into the Arc, because of the waters of the flood. <13> In the selfsame day entered Noah, Shem, Ham, and Japhet, the sons of Noah, and Noah's wife, and the three wives of his sons with them, into the ark;]

The character for boat is divided into three parts: vessel, eight, and mouth (or person). According to the Biblical records only eight people survived the flood in the ark: Noah, Shem, Ham, Japhet, and also their four wives, for a total of eight.

<< Genesis 6:5-7 >> [And God saw that the wickedness of man was great in the earth, and that every imagination of the thoughts of his heart was only evil continually. <6> And it repented the Lord that he had made man on the earth, and it grieved him at his heart.

<7> And the Lord said, I will destroy man whom I had created from the face of the earth; both man, and beast, and the creeping thing, and the fowls of the air; for it repenteth me that I have made them. <8> But Noah found grace in the eyes of the Lord.]

<< Genesis 6:13-19 >> [And God said unto Noah, The end of all flesh is come before me; for the earth is filled with violence through them; and behold, I will destroy them with the earth. <14> Make thee an ark of gopher wood; rooms shalt thou make in the ark, and shalt pitch it within and without with pitch. <15> And this is the fashion which thou shalt make it of: The length of the ark shall be three hundred cubits, the breadth of it fifty cubits, and the height of it thirty cubits. <16> A window shalt thou make to the ark, and in a cubit shalt thou finish it above; and the door of the ark shalt thou set in the side thereof; with lower, second, and third stories shalt thou make it.

<17> And, behold, I, even I, do bring a flood of waters upon the earth, to destroy all flesh, wherein is the breath of life, from under heaven; and every thing that is in the earth shall die. <18> But with thee will I establish my covenant; and thou shalt come into the ark, thou, and thy sons, and thy wife, and thy sons' wives with thee. <19> And of every living thing of all flesh, two of every sort shalt thou bring into the ark, to keep them alive with thee; they shall be male and female.]

[BOAT]

VESSEL + EIGHT + MOUTH

[FLOOD]

EIGHT+UNITED+EARTH+TOTAL+WATER

THE TRUTH

The Bible also gave us the location as to where the ark of Noah would be found today:

<< Genesis 8:4 >> [And the ark rested in the seventh month, on the seventeenth day of the month, upon the Mountains of Ararat.]

The ark of Noah is located at exactly 39 degrees 26.4 minutes north latitude, and 44 degrees 15.3 minutes east longitude. The ark of Noah is to be found at an altitude of 6245 feet above sea level! This region of Ararat where the ark is found is in Turkey, near the Iranian border, 11.3 kilometers east of a Turkish town called Dogubayazit.

Several anchor stones originating from the ark of Noah have been recovered! The resurfacing of the ark is a sign of the coming judgment and salvation from the Lord YAHAWAH!

After the flood, the three sons of Noah began to repopulate the earth. It was from these three men that all the nations of the world descended.

<< Geneses 9:19 >> [These are the three sons of Noah: and of them was the whole earth overspread.]

<< Genesis Chapter 10:1 >> [Now these are the generations of the sons of Noah, Shem, Ham, and Japheth: and unto them were sons born after the flood.]

The Chinese characters cover a wide range of early Biblical history, and are a valuable source of information. The Gospel of the Lord YAHAWAH is not a secret; if we seek we shall find it in a variety of forms.

ANTIQUITY OF CIVILIZATION

My friend, do you know what time you're living in? The trumpet of truth must be sounded. The identity of the nations and the identity of the original twelve tribes of Israel must be revealed. People must learn their genuine identity and true destiny! It is the duty and the right of every human being to learn the purpose of life, which has been the world's most well-kept secret, and the greatest mystery of all time!

The first fact that must be brought out concerning the identity of the nations is that the people who are claiming to be the Jews today are not the original Jews of the Bible! The so-called Jewish people are actually the descendants of the Khazar empire (located between the Caspian and the Black Sea); who in 740 AD were under religious and political pressure from the two world powers which were at war: the Byzantine Roman Empire, and the Islamic Arabs. To stay politically neutral to both sides, the Khazars rejected both Christianity and Islam, and converted their entire nation to Judaism! The so-called Jewish people are not authentic Jews, but are originally known as the Khazars of Europe.

Some Caucasians ignorantly claim to be Jewish by religion, and also some others have been maliciously and falsely claiming to be Jews by nationality. But understand clearly that they are not the original Jews and Israelites of the Bible! Further historical evidence of this fact is neatly presented in a book called *The Thirteenth Tribe*, by Arthur Koestler! The historical and archeological evidence confirms beyond all doubt that the original Israelites, the real Jews, are Asiatic people.

The Caucasians are not descendants of Jacob at all and they did not come from Palestine and Egypt; they are originally from the Caucasus Mountains region and Europe! Some of them have conspired to steal the heritage of the Asiatic people, by calling themselves Jews, and falsely portraying themselves as Israelites and Jews. The Bible protests clearly against impostors claiming to be Jews. Jesus Christ said:

>> *<< Revelation 2:9 >> [I know thy works, and tribulation, and poverty;* (but thou art rich*) and I know the blasphemy of them which say they are Jews, and are not, but are the synagogue of Satan.]*

>> *<< Revelation 3:9 >> [Behold, I will make them of the synagogue of Satan, which say they are Jews, and are not, but do lie; behold, I will make them to come and worship before thy feet, and to know that I have loved thee.]*

THE ORIGIN OF EUROPEAN JUDAISM

The Khazars were European nomad heathens. The Khazars were converted to Judaism in 700 AD, by their king, as a way of remaining neutral in the war between Christianity and Islam. In 1016, The Russians and the Byzantines conquered and dispersed the so-called Jewish Khazars. Modern Judaism originated mainly with the Khazar converts, who were dispersed throughout Eastern Europe. Jewish Caucasians are not descendents of the Biblical twelve tribes of Israel at all.

Revelation 2:9 I know thy works, and tribulation, and poverty, (but thou art rich) and I know the blasphemy of them that say they are Jews, and are not, but are the synagogue of Satan.

Revelation 3:9 Behold, I will make them of the synagogue of Satan, which say they are Jews and are not, but do lie; behold, I will make them to come and worship before thy feet, and to know that I have loved thee.

THE TRUTH

Biblically, archaeologically, and historically, it will be proven and confirmed beyond any doubt: The Caucasians that are claiming to be Jews today are impostors, and the real Jews are Asiatic people, namely the African-Americans and American-Indians of North, South, and Central America.

For the past two thousand years, western anthropologists have been literally chiseling the broad noses and scraping the color from off of the Egyptian and other ancient statues to conceal the fact that the original civilized cultures around the world were founded by non-Caucasian, Asiatic people. Because of political, social, and economic reasons, white supremacists have conspired to destroy the image of the non-Caucasian people of the world, and to falsify history, and to steal the wisdom and philosophical contributions of Asiatic people. This was done in order to exploit people mentally, to create division, and to set up white supremacy.

Caucasian images for God and Jesus have been introduced to all the nations of the world, in order to cause everyone to look up to the Europeans as the people of the Bible and of God. The western world has also been teaching a great lie, saying that civilization started with the Greeks. In fact, the Greeks are the destroyers of civilization. The Greeks took all of their concepts of civilization from the Egyptians, the Phoenicians, and the Mesopotamians. What the Greeks and Romans could not copy or steal, they destroyed. The truth is western society has sought to conceal the truly recent origin of Caucasian society, and the antiquity of Asiatic civilization!

The teaching of ethnic and racial supremacy, saying that other people are inferior and subhuman, was devised by the colonists to justify themselves in the exploitation and the destruction of other nations and civilizations for material gain. The colonizers seek to dehumanize and to develop an inferiority complex in their victims; creating psychological barriers to keep them in a state of fear, oppression, and division. Many nations, including Caucasians, Africans, as well as Asians, have used similar tactics to exploit a weaker people or group!

Racism has been an economic and political tool for the colonizers. Their leaders have used the false idea of racial superiority to justify putting other people into slavery, exploiting and treating them as subhuman for economic gain. This grand deception has been a mental chain holding the world captive, and keeping people divided and powerless!

It was the original Asiatic inhabitants of Babylon, Palestine, Assyria, and Egypt who were the inventors of writing, science, mathematics, and the concept of a written law. The builders of the pyramids of the world, and of the Sphinx: were all originally non-Caucasian people. It is very disturbing to find that so many people are ignorant of the fact that the original Egyptians were dark in complexion, having Asiatic features! Egypt is located in Africa not Europe. This is because the leaders of western education and religion have maliciously conspired to deceive the world, with propagandistic images in support of white supremacy. Herodotus the historian in Book Two, after visiting Egypt wrote:

[The Egyptians, the Nubians, and the Ethiopians have thick lips, broad nose, woolly hair, and they are burnt of skin!]

The Europeans learned the concept of religion from Asiatic people. In *The Odyssey* Homer says Zeus and Apollo came from Ethiopia! The Greeks did not originate philosophy or anything pertaining to civilized culture. The Greeks and Romans were mostly barbarians at that time. According to historical facts, the Greeks and Romans tried to end civilization wherever they found it! Documented evidence confirms that all the so-called prominent Greek philosophers were thieves; they studied from the Egyptian and Eastern schools, temples, and libraries. They then brought back that knowledge, and several stolen Egyptian books, rewriting and falsely claiming those works to be their own ideas!

THE TRUTH

The first people to use paper on a wide scale to record were the Babylonians, Egyptians, Hebrews, and the Chinese. The original paper was papyrus, from which also the word paper is derived. The Hebrews and the Egyptians produced some of the first books in the ancient town called Byblos in the land of Canaan, from which the words book and Bible were derived!

The Greeks are not an ancient people. Civilization started with the original Hebrews, Babylonians, Asians, and Egyptians. These were all people of brown complexion! Many historians and scientists confirm this information in great detail.

However, because of censorship, great books have not been easy to find. Your best bet of finding good books is to look in the Bible section, the African-American, or the indigenous studies section of a bookstore. Check also some of the Bible bookstores or any stores with spiritual books. And also, look into the underground or revolutionary bookstores. Many of those books will help you to learn the truth and to understand the Holy Bible.

Read a book called "*The Thirteenth Tribe*", by A. Koestler. Koestler goes into a lot of scientific details to prove that the Caucasians claiming to be the Jews today are actually religious converts that are not blood descendants of the original twelve tribes of Israel. The original Hebrews were not Europeans. The Hebrew Israelites came out of Egypt with Moses. We will shortly see how the historical facts prove the true identity of every one of the original twelve tribes of Israel beyond all doubt.

The twelve tribes are not lost. Evidence will show that the African-Americans and American-Indians are the only true blood descendants of the original Hebrew Israelites! The terms African-American and American-Indian do not refer to Indians from India or the Africans in Africa; only to the indigenous inhabitants of North, South, and Central America, and the people sold into slavery, who came to America on the slave ships. James Adair wrote a very important book called: "*History Of The American Indians*", in which he presents an enormous amount of evidence confirming that the American Indians are in fact the lost ten tribes of Israel!

Unlike commercial churches and religions, the original Bible contains no man-made myths or lies. The Bible is the accurate record of the history, the laws, and the understanding of the Creators' purpose. The Bible is the only book given to man from the Most High God. All other books and religions are false. There can only be one truth! The Bible explains:

<< Isaiah 34:16 >> [Seek ye out of the book of the Lord, and read: no one of these shall fail, none shall want her mate: for my mouth it hath commanded, and his spirit it hath gathered them.]

<< Isaiah 8:20 >> [To the law and to the testimony: if they speak not according to this word, it is because there is no light in them!]

All things must be proven from the Bible! The Bible is the first and last word. Now, concerning antiquity, the Bible says Jesus Christ was brass-brown in complexion:

<< Revelation 1:15 >> [And his feet like unto fine brass, as if they burned in a furnace.]

Brass is already brown, like a doorknob; and anything burned in a furnace has to turn dark from oxidation! If Christ's feet were brown, so was the skin covering the rest of his body. The people of the world must wake up to that very important fact: Jesus was not European. Accepting the truth of the Bible would end the suffering of the world overnight. Furthermore, the Bible says the Most High God in heaven appears to have Asiatic features, including woolly textured hair:

>*<< Daniel 7:9 >> [...The Ancient of days did sit, whose garment was white as snow, and the hair of his head like the pure wool: his throne was like the fiery flame.]*

Anatomically speaking, woolly hair is not a Caucasian characteristic at all. Jesus Christ was not Caucasian, with straight yellow hair. Christ was brown, with the royal natural woolly hair, and it was fully gray!

>*<< Revelation 1:14,15 >> [His head and his hairs were white like wool, as white as snow; and his eyes were as a flame of fire; <15> And his feet like unto fine brass, as if they burned in a furnace; and his voice as the sound of many waters]*

THE IMAGE OF THE BEAST
666 THE ANTICHRIST, SATAN THE DEVIL

Michelangelo fraudulently painted Ceasar Borgia as Jesus Christ, deceiving the world

Exodus 20:3-4 Thou shalt have no other gods before me [4] Thou shalt not make unto thee any graven image, or any likeness of any thing that is in heaven above, or that is in the earth.

II THESSALONIANS 2:3,4 Let no man deceive you by any means: for that day shall not come, except there come a falling away first, and that man of sin be revealed, the son of perdition; [4] Who opposeth and exalteth himself above all that is called God, or that is worshipped; so that he as God sitteth in the temple of God, shewing himself that he is God.

THE ISRAELITE NETWORK, P.O. Box 1747 NYC 10101, 212-586-5969, http://israelite.net

If you want the TRUTH, come to our meetings, before it is too late.

THE TRUTH

Color is not important to me, but the truth is important. For this reason it is important to know the truth about the color of the Hebrew Israelites. However this book is not intended to be about color or race. It is about the truth. I am not a racist! I am a Hebrew Israelite, who believes in loving everyone that loves God. I know Asians, Caucasians, and Africans. I don't care what nation a person is from; you are my brother if you treat me like one! I love righteous people from all nations, and recognize only one race on this earth: the human race!

However, I would be racist to say that Jesus Christ was a Caucasian, when the Bible says and the historical evidence confirms that he was Asiatic! Even if color does not matter to you and in fact it does not matter to me either, the truth must matter. My point is not a point of race, but a point of truth!

The concept of racial superiority is a myth, a lie created as a tool of exploitation and colonization. According to the Bible It is the seed, the genealogy of the father that determines true nationality, not color or geography or so-called race! The historical, archeological, and Biblical evidence confirm that the family lines of the African-Americans and the American-Indians (Hispanics) originate from the twelve tribes of Israel. Hispanics here is not referring to people from Spain in Europe, but only to the Spanish-speaking American-Indian people of the west: from North, South, and Central America.

It is very important to realize that Israel pertains to a nation and not a color. In fact not all Asiatic people are Israelites. It is the seed, the genealogy along the line of the father only, that determines nationality. Regardless of your color or texture of hair, you are an original Israelite if the genealogy along your father's line goes back to the ancient twelve tribes of Israel.

Israelites have always been different shades of brown, from yellow to chocolate. From the beginning,, the phenotype of the twelve tribes displays a wide spectrum of physical features in terms of complexion, and hair texture. The majority of people from the tribes of Judah, Benjamin, and Levi resemble the Africans, while the remaining tribes resemble the Indians.

But, The modern so-called Jews of Caucasian descent are not from any of the twelve tribes of Israel. They are the Edomites of the Bible. The Caucasians who are claiming to be Jews today originated from the converts of the Khazar Empire and other medieval European tribes, who adopted the Jewish religion. Jewish or Judaism is just another false religion that is being used to colonize and teach white supremacy to the world by misrepresenting the people of the Bible as Europeans!

Keep in mind that not all Asiatic people are Israelites. The Africans are descended from Noah's son Ham, and not from Jacob; therefore the Africans are not Israelites, although there are remnants of the twelve tribes of Israel living among them!

The Israelites went to live in Africa, trying to escape political persecution from the Assyrians, the Greeks, and the Romans. During the persecution of the Israelites by the Assyrians (720B.C.E to 530B.C.E.), millions of Israelites fled mostly into coastal Africa to establish Hebrew colonies there. Also during the persecution of the Israelites by the Greeks, especially under Antiochus Epiphanies (168 BCE), Israelites fled from Palestine and sought to establish colonies in Africa and Asia.

The African-Americans of today are the original Jews who in 70 AD the Roman general Titus drove out of Palestine into Africa, the Middle East, and certain provinces of the Roman Empire. Some of the Israelites were also captured by the Romans and sold as slaves. Later on, the remaining Hebrew Israelites who were living within the Roman Empire (Asia Minor, Spain, Portugal) had to leave Europe and flee into Africa in order to escape the Roman Catholic Inquisition, which targeted to exterminate the original Hebrew Israelites.

The Turks, who were Muslims, conquered the Hebrew Israelites that were living in the Byzantine Empire of the East. They took the Hebrews and traded them as slaves in the Middle East and Africa!

THE TRUTH

The so-called African-Americans are not Africans and had no land in Africa; that is why their slave merchants captured and sold the Israelites. The Arabs and the Africans had the Israelites as slaves before the Caucasians did in America!

Secondly, the American-Indians were the other ten tribes that left Samaria about two thousand seven hundred years ago, and came to America after the king of Babylon had taken their land and evicted the inhabitants. Israelites had been traveling to so-called America since around the time of King Solomon and even earlier. The African-Americans and American-Indians are originally the same exact nation of people.

It is wrong to teach the idea that all people of dark complexion are Africans; just like there are different Asian and Caucasian nations, the Hebrew Israelites are a separate nation from the Africans. We are Shemites, and the Africans are Hamites!

There are so many internal and external obstacles preventing the Israelites from uniting as a people under their nationality as Israelites. Learning the Biblical truth is the only solution. The day the twelve tribes become conscious of their true identity and unite is the day their exploitation and suffering will come to an end. It is an insult to be called "Negro" or "Black", these words are adjectives, not proper nouns, and are used to describe a degraded condition. An adjective can not be used as an identity, it can only be used to describe.

The words Africa and America are colonial names, not true nationalities. Africa was named after an Italian General named Leos Scipio Africanus. America was named after another Italian called Amerigo Vaspuchi. So any Asiatic person who calls himself African, American, or any combination of the two is naming himself after his slave masters and oppressors. It is time to cast off these colonial labels. True nationality is determined by genealogy along the father's line only. Africa and America pertain to European colonies.

The words "Hispanic" and "Latino" pertain to Europeans from Spain, they are colonial words. It is shameful to label yourself after the colonizers and the exploiters of your land and people and to adopt their heathenish customs. A person's identity and nationality is determined by his or her genealogy. Colonial labels are derived from ignorance and hate. The Israelites and other oppressed people of the world must learn to seek truth, righteousness, and love centered on God.

No one can hold you down unless you allow them the opportunity, and no one will respect you unless you learn to respect and love yourself. If you would stop the violence, ignorance, prejudice, and self-hatred, and return to the true God, only then would all the curses and plagues be eliminated. The power to change your condition is in your hands. You simply have to abandon the materialistic mind of fear, ignorance, and hate. Then separate from the addictive colonial religions and cults. The only true religion is love. Sacrifice the time and resources to study, remove all the fear from your hearts, and have compassion toward others. Repent from evil, and seek the true God first, to obey his laws and customs!

The majority of people will not listen to reason; they only respect force. Unity under love and truth is the first priority! We must defeat the colonial policy of hate, division, and exploitation! We must realize the true Biblical identity of the nations and of the original twelve tribes of the Hebrew Israelites!

Western society and false religion have raped the true history of the world by denying the antiquity of the Asiatic civilizations! First of all there is no reason for the mockery of physical features of any person. From the beginning of time, Woolly hair has always been a symbol of divinity, and dark-skin has symbolized the mystical! All of the ancient anthropomorphisms of even the false pagan gods were given woolly hair and brown-skin, from Osiris of Egypt to Krishna of India; from the Buddha of China and India to Quetzalcoatl of Mexico; and from Isis of the pagans to the Black Madonna of Christianity! Dark-skin has always represented the mystical, and woolly hair has always been a symbol of the divine!

We see that traditionally in the ancient world, even the false gods were anthropomorphized with Asiatic features, in an attempt to make them appear more like the real God, for example: the dark-skinned and woolly-

THE TRUTH

haired Buddha, Krishna, Quetzalcoatl, Zaha, Fuhi, Horus, Osiris. Even in Europe. All of the ancient churches portray God, Jesus, the disciples, and the Israelites as Asiatic persons. The following European churches display an Asiatic Jesus and the Black Madonna: the German Cathedral of Augsburg, the Russian's Notre Dame of Khazar, and the Italian Church of San Francisco at Pisa, the Black Madonna of Czestochowa in Poland, and the Queen of Pyrenees of Nuria, Spain. You can go see with your own eyes. If the Mother is the Black Madonna, the child has to resemble her. The original Hebrew Israelites and Jews of the Bible were of purely the Asiatic type!

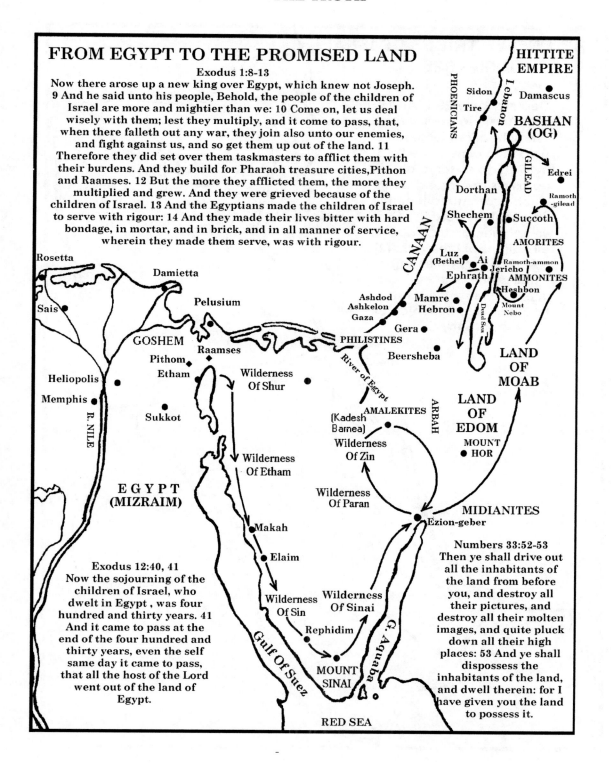

FROM EGYPT TO THE PROMISED LAND

Exodus 1:8-13

Now there arose up a new king over Egypt, which knew not Joseph. 9 And he said unto his people, Behold, the people of the children of Israel are more and mightier than we: 10 Come on, let us deal wisely with them; lest they multiply, and it come to pass, that, when there falleth out any war, they join also unto our enemies, and fight against us, and so get them up out of the land. 11 Therefore they did set over them taskmasters to afflict them with their burdens. And they build for Pharaoh treasure cities, Pithon and Raamses. 12 But the more they afflicted them, the more they multiplied and grew. And they were grieved because of the children of Israel. 13 And the Egyptians made the children of Israel to serve with rigour: 14 And they made their lives bitter with hard bondage, in mortar, and in brick, and in all manner of service, wherein they made them serve, was with rigour.

HITTITE EMPIRE

PHOENICIANS

Sidon
Tire
Damascus

Lebanon

BASHAN (OG)

GILEAD

Edrei

Ramoth-gilead

Dorthan

Shechem
Succoth

AMORITES

CANAAN

Luz (Bethel)
Ai
Jericho
Ramoth-ammon

Ephrath

AMMONITES

Heshbon

Rosetta

Damietta

Pelusium

Ashdod
Ashkelon
Gaza

Mamre
Hebron

Mount Nebo

Dead Sea

Sais

GOSHEM
Raamses

Pithom
Etham

Wilderness Of Shur

River of Egypt

Gera

PHILISTINES

Beersheba

LAND OF MOAB

Heliopolis

Memphis

R. NILE

Sukkot

Wilderness Of Etham

AMALEKITES
(Kadesh Barnea)

Wilderness Of Zin

ARBAH

LAND OF EDOM

MOUNT HOR

EGYPT (MIZRAIM)

Wilderness Of Paran

MIDIANITES

Makah

Ezion-geber

Elaim

Exodus 12:40, 41

Now the sojourning of the children of Israel, who dwelt in Egypt, was four hundred and thirty years. 41 And it came to pass at the end of the four hundred and thirty years, even the self same day it came to pass, that all the host of the Lord went out of the land of Egypt.

Gulf Of Suez

Wilderness Of Sin

Wilderness Of Sinai

Rephidim

G. Aquaba

MOUNT SINAI

Numbers 33:52-53

Then ye shall drive out all the inhabitants of the land from before you, and destroy all their pictures, and destroy all their molten images, and quite pluck down all their high places: 53 And ye shall dispossess the inhabitants of the land, and dwell therein: for I have given you the land to possess it.

RED SEA

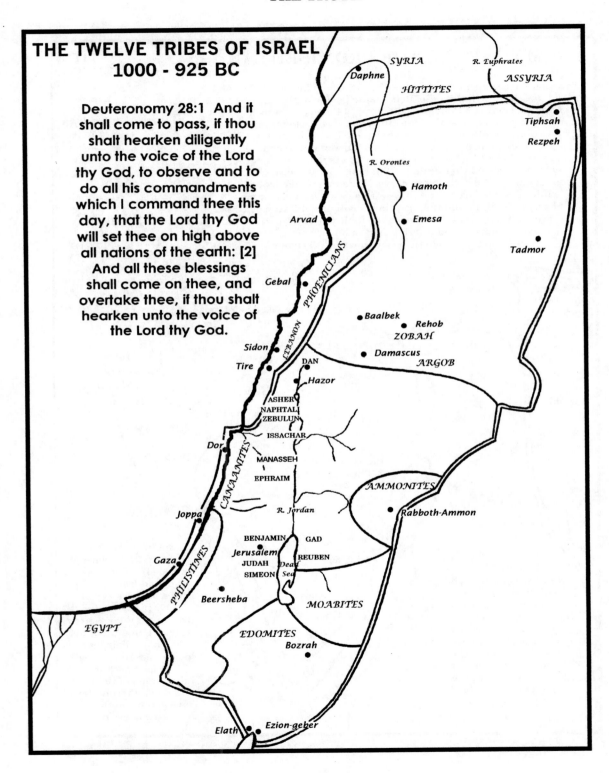

THE TWELVE TRIBES OF ISRAEL
1000 - 925 BC

Deuteronomy 28:1 And it shall come to pass, if thou shalt hearken diligently unto the voice of the Lord thy God, to observe and to do all his commandments which I command thee this day, that the Lord thy God will set thee on high above all nations of the earth: [2] And all these blessings shall come on thee, and overtake thee, if thou shalt hearken unto the voice of the Lord thy God.

THE TRUTH

Now, you should not be surprised to learn that the same truth regarding Asiatic antiquity is found recorded everywhere in the Bible because Jacob, progenitor of the Israelites, went into Egypt with his twelve sons. According to the Bible the family of Jacob was incubated among the Egyptians (in Africa, not Europe), where they multiplied into millions, to become a nation. The real Israelites have to be colored people.

<< Exodus 1:1-5 >> [...And all the souls that came out of the loins of Jacob were seventy souls: for Joseph was in Egypt already.]

By the time the Israelites had left Egypt (430 years later) they numbered over four million, with an army of about six-hundred-thousand men:

<< Exodus 12:37 >> [And the children of Israel journeyed from Rameses to Succoth, about six hundred thousand on foot that were men, besides children...]

Egypt is located in Africa, where Africans were living. If the Israelites were incubated among Africans for four hundred and thirty years, they would not resemble Europeans. Even before Jacob and his sons entered Egypt, the Bible reveals that they were non-Caucasian Asiatic people. For example, Joseph's brothers thought he was an Egyptian because of his appearance; even after he had conversations with them on many occasions.

<< Genesis 42:8; 45:4 >> [And Joseph knew his brethren, but they knew not him.]

The European images and idols displayed in the churches are not of Christ. Michelangelo, first painted the most common religious image used in deceiving the world today. It is a picture of a blue-eyes European with blond hair, who they maliciously claim to be Jesus Christ. This false image was modeled after Cesare Borgia, who was the second son of so-called Pope Alexander VI, of Rome. The real Jesus, according to all scientific and historical facts, is an Asiatic man. Most of the institutionalized religions have raped and robbed the minds, the wallets, and the spirits of innocent people around the world by deceiving them with false images and false doctrines.

<< John 10:10 >> Christ says, [The thief cometh not, but for to steal, and to kill, and to destroy: I am come that they might have life, and that they might have it more abundantly.]

Be careful whom you go to when you're looking for the truth because the devil has been very busy deceiving the world by using the major religions, churches, and other educational institutions! If your church or religion is not teaching you the true identity of the original twelve tribes of Israelites and the Biblical identity of the other nations, as well as the real name, laws and Holy Days of the true God, the Lord YAHAWAH, that organization is led by Satan, and there is no truth there.

It is a well-known fact that before the Greeks, Romans, Europeans, and Arabs went into Egypt to colonize, rape and evict the original Egyptians, and that the inhabitants were all dark-skinned Africans. In the tombs of Egypt, what color are the Egyptians and the Hebrews depicted? They are shown to be different shades of brown, not with blond hair and blue eyes! This is one of many archeological proofs! Herodotus, an ancient historian, described exactly what the ancient Egyptians looked like, which he witnessed with his own eyes. Herodotus, who visited Egypt about 457 BC, says in Book II:

THE TRUTH

[The Nubians, the Egyptians, and the Ethiopians have broad noses, thick lips, woolly hair, And they are burnt of skin.]

The Israelites did not look any different from the original Egyptians! There are many Biblical proofs to confirm the Asiatic antiquity of the Israelites! Consider the case of Moses, a Hebrew Israelite who was adopted by and concealed within the court of the pharaoh. If Moses were a Caucasian it would have been impossible to conceal his race in the presence of dark Egyptians! At first glance, Moses was even called an Egyptian, as recorded in the Bible:

<< Exodus 2:19 >> [And they said, An Egyptian (Moses) delivered us out of the hand of the shepherds, and also drew water enough for us, and watered the flock.]

<< Exodus 4:6,7 >> [And the Lord said furthermore unto him (Moses), Put now thine hand into thine bosom. And he put his hand into his bosom: and when he took it out, behold, it was leprous white as snow. And he said, Put thine hand into thine bosom again. And he put his hand into his bosom again; and plucked it out of his bosom, Behold, it was turned again as his other flesh.]

For the hand of Moses to turn white it had to have been colored in the first place; it was when he put it back into his bosom that it changed by a miracle, from white to the original brown! All the original Hebrews and their ancestors were as brown as Moses. Even if the color of a person does not matter; which it should not, the truth does matter. We must not put up those false blond-haired and blue-eyed Caucasian images, to make every historical figure appear as Europeans. This is racism, it is wrong.

Some of the so-called religious and political leaders of the western world have historically changed the race of the Israelites in order to claim credit for another person's achievements. As a result, they have maliciously made color into an important issue, as it never should have been. The patriarchs, Moses, the disciples, and all of the Israelites were of the Asiatic type, ranging in complexion from yellow to chocolate. However, don't waste your time arguing if people will not listen to you, when you try to tell them the truth. Because of their prejudice, fear, and ignorance, they will not hear you. Remember that they did not listen to the Almighty God YAHAWAH, to Christ, or to the prophets.

In the original Hebrew scriptures a person can read where it is clearly stated that the Israelites are of Asiatic descent! Furthermore, the Caucasians had no civilization when they came out of the caves of the Caucasus Mountains. The Greeks and Romans were barbarians, destroyers of civilization everywhere they went. The concept of civilization is not European in origin, it is Asiatic! Furthermore, only Asiatic people were writing at the time when most of the Bible was written. Also, there was no such place as Europe in all of classical ancient history! So how can Caucasians claim to be the people of the Bible and of antiquity? Those that teach this are liars. Historically, the Asiatic people taught the Caucasian people how to read, how to write, and how to dress decently!

A person might ignorantly say that the Jews changed color because they moved to Europe. Historically and scientifically this is not the case. First, the Israelites did not move to Europe. Secondly, the environment did not threaten their survival over a long enough time period in order to cause mutations. This idea contradicts the Genetic Law of Independent Assortment, and also the Law of Genetic Segregation! Offspring must resemble their parents.

THE TRUTH

In ancient times, after the families of the earth became dispersed and isolated by geographical factors such as mountains, oceans, and distances, each isolated group became victim of a reduced gene pool. Inbreeding within each isolated group over a long period of time produced children that began to look more and more homogeneous to that group. Certain features and characteristics became more and more emphasized in the succeeding generation; features such as shape of the eyes, nose, lips, and body, as well as the shades of the skin and the eyes! This isolation also generated cultural differences such as languages.

Look around, has the skin of the Caucasians living in Africa turned black because of the sun? Of course not, because the environment has not threatened their survival. Their descendants are still red. Have the African-Americans living in Alaska and Canada turned white? Even the original Eskimo Indians living in the Polar region are brown in complexion. People do not change color simply by moving around. Your color is determined by the genetic codes within the chromosomes in your cells; those codes are handed down from your ancestors. They are not determined by where you're living on the planet! It is a good thing that we are different colors, for it is one of the characteristics that adds variety and beauty to the human family, and allows us to survive.

The Jewish Caucasians of today are not the original Jews of the Bible. They are Europeans from the Khazar Empire and other various medieval groups that converted to the Jewish religion in 700 AD as a way of staying neutral in the war between the Christians and the Moslems. Around 740 AD, the Russians started attacking the Khazars and drove them into the Crimea. A joint Byzantine-Russian expedition in 1016 destroyed the Khazar kingdom.

The Khazarian Jewish converts were expelled to Poland. It is those same Khazarians in Palestine today that are falsely claiming to be Jews. Acting as Jews, they have taken possession of Palestine today! In Germany, Hitler was killing Khazarians claiming to be Jews, But he probably never killed a real Hebrew Israelite from the tribe of Judah in his life.

The Roman Emperor Titus overthrew the original Jews of Palestine in AD 70. Some of the Asiatic Jews were taken as captives to the colonies of the Roman Empire, and the rest were expelled and fled into Africa, where they established colonies. It was at that time when the African and Arab merchants took many of the original Jews as slaves. That is how the Israelites got to Africa, and that is why they are falsely called Africans-Americans today.

Later on in the 1600s, the remaining Asiatic Hebrew Israelites that were living in Spain, Portugal, and other parts of the Roman Empire were forced to flee for their lives due to the persecutions and murder resulting from the barbaric inquisitions of the Roman Catholic Church! The original Asiatic Jews fled into Africa and Asia to established colonies there. Many of those Asiatic Jews were captured by the Arabs and the Africans, and later sold to the Americas as slaves!

If the Israelites had run towards Europe, they would have been captured and killed. Europe was their aggressive enemy, specifically the Roman Empire, which sought to exterminate them. In a similar fashion, when America was fighting against Mexico, the Mexicans would never run north to escape, they headed towards South America for sanctuary. Jesus Christ had prophesied that the real Israelites would escape from the Roman Empire by running towards the wilderness into Africa.

<< Mark 13:14 >> [But when ye shall see the abomination of desolation, spoken of by Daniel the prophet (the Romans occupying Palestine), standing in where it ought not, let him that readeth understand, then let them that be in Judea flee to the mountains.]

THE TRUTH

IDENTITY OF CHRIST AND THE ISRAELITES

According to the Bible and all of the historical and archeological evidence, the Israelite as a nation came out of Egypt, not Europe. An Israelite is a genealogical descendent of the original twelve tribes along their father's line, going back to Abraham, Isaac and Jacob. Genealogy along the mother's line does not determine the nationality. Jacob, who is also called Israel, was the father of the twelve tribes of Israel. Jacob went into Egypt with his twelve sons. His son Joseph was already living there and had a good position working under the Pharaoh of Egypt. Among the Egyptians in Africa, the sons of Israel multiplied and became the twelve tribes of Israel.

> << Genesis 46:26-34 >> [All the souls that came with Jacob into Egypt, which came out of his loins, besides Jacob's sons' wives, all the souls were threescore and six; <27> And the sons of Joseph, which were born him in Egypt, were two souls: all the souls of the house of Jacob, which came into Egypt, were threescore and ten. <28> And he sent Judah before him unto Joseph, to direct his face unto Goshen; and they came into the land of Goshen. <29> And Joseph made ready his chariot, and went up to meet Israel his father, to Goshen, and presented himself unto him; and he fell on his neck, and wept on his neck a good while.
> <30> And Israel said unto Joseph, Now let me die, since I have seen thy face, because thou art yet alive. <31> And Joseph said unto his brethren, and unto his father's house, I will go up, and shew Pharaoh, and say unto him, My brethren, and my father's house, which were in the land of Canaan, are come unto me; <32> And the men are shepherds, for their trade hath been to feed cattle; and they have brought their flocks, and their herds, and all that they have. <33> And it shall come to pass, when Pharaoh shall call you, and shall say, What is your occupation? <34> That ye shall say, Thy servants' trade hath been about cattle from our youth even until now, both we, and also our fathers: that ye may dwell in the land of Goshen; for every shepherd is an abomination unto the Egyptians.]

We can see from Genesis 46:34 that the Egyptians were ruling Egypt and not the Hyksos, at the time the Israel and Joseph entered Egypt. The Hyksos were shepherds and Shepherd kings of Shemite origin. The Egyptians, who were now in rulership, hated shepherds because the Hyksos who had occupied their land were shepherds. The Israelites never ruled when they were in Egypt. According to the Bible the Israelites were put into slavery for four hundred years after the death of Joseph.

> << Genesis 15:13 >> [And He (YAHAWAH) said unto Abram, Know of a surety that thy seed shall be a stranger in a land that is not theirs, and shall serve them; and they shall afflict them four hundred years.]

> << Exodus 1:1-11 >> [Now these are the names of the children of Israel, which came into Egypt; every man and his household came with Jacob. <2> Reuben, Simeon, Levi, and Judah, <3> Issachar, Zebulun, and Benjamin, <4> Dan, and Naphtali, Gad, and Asher. <5> And all the souls that came out of the loins of Jacob were seventy souls: for Joseph was in Egypt already. <6> And Joseph died, and all his brethren, and all that

generation. <7> And the children of Israel were fruitful, and increased abundantly, and multiplied, and waxed exceeding mighty; and the land was filled with them.

<8> Now there arose up a new king over Egypt, which knew not Joseph. <9> And he said unto his people, Behold, the people of the children of Israel are more and mightier than we: <10> Come on, let us deal wisely with them; lest they multiply, and it come to pass, that, when there falleth out any war, they join also unto our enemies, and fight against us, and so get them up out of the land. <11> Therefore they did set over them taskmasters to afflict them with their burdens. And they built for Pharaoh treasure cities, Pithom and Raamses.]

It is obvious that the Israelites were not Europeans. The Bible proves beyond all doubt Biblically and historically that the Most High in heaven, Jesus Christ, and the angels are anthropomorphically Asiatic! Secondly, the African-Americans and the American-Indians of today, together make up the original twelve tribes of Israel! The western Asiatic people are the bulk of the original Israelites. Also, there are remnants of the original twelve tribes scattered from Africa to Asia. The Bible emphasizes the fact that the Caucasian so-called Jewish people of today are impostors:

<< Revelation 2:9 >> [...I know the Blasphemy of them which say they are Jews, and are not, but are the synagogue of Satan.]

<< Revelation 3:9 >> [Behold, I will make them of the synagogue of Satan, which say they are Jews, and are not but do lie; behold, I will make them to come and worship before thy feet, and to know that I have loved thee!]

Let's examine some principle verses in the 1611 translation of the original Bible which confirm the fact that the Israelites were a non-Caucasian people of Asiatic descent. Please be aware that many of the new versions and translations of the Bible have maliciously mistranslated the verses where the prophets are describing the complexion of the Israelites! If the Bible you're using translates the following verses differently, that translation is false. Of all the English translations, the King James 1611 translation is so far the most accurate I've seen. The 1611 version is the closest translation to the original Hebrew Bible. Use that version only, unless you can understand the original Hebrew. Do not waste your time reading those so-called new translations of the Bible. They are false.

Directly and indirectly, the following verses reveal the visual appearance of the Biblical Israelites:

<< Lamentations 4:8 >> [Their visage is blacker than a coal.]

<< Lamentations 5:10 >> [our skin was black like an oven.]

<< Job 30:30 >> [My skin is black upon me.]

<< Jeremiah 14:2 >> [Judah mourneth, and the gates thereof languish, they are black unto the ground.]

...Different shades of brown like the earth!

<< Song of Solomon 1:5, 6 >> [I am black, but comely, O ye daughters of Jerusalem, as the tents of Kedar, as the curtains of Solomon. Look not upon me because I am black.]

<< Acts 13:1 >> [Now there were in the church that was at Antioch certain prophets and teachers; as Barnabas and Simeon that was called Niger..]

The disciples were being called "Niger", a word that means black. There was an event in the Bible where a Roman policeman called Paul an Egyptian, because Paul resembled the Africans:

<< Acts 21:38,39 >> [And as Paul was to be led into the castle, he said unto the chief captain, May I speak unto thee? Who said, canst thou speak Greek? (Paul did not look European: Paul was of a dark complexion) ...Art not thou that Egyptian (African), which before these days madest an uproar, and leddest out into the wilderness four thousand men that were murderers? But Paul said, I am a man which am a Jew.]

<< Amos 9:7 >> [Are ye not as the children of the Ethiopians unto me, Oh house of Israel.]

Paul and all of the disciples where Asiatic in appearance, as were the original Egyptians and Ethiopians. They did not look like Greeks, Romans, and Germans. That is why the centurion captain asked Paul if he was an Egyptian.

All of the nations descended from Noah. According to the tenth chapter of Genesis, Noah had three sons: Shem, Ham, and Japhet. Ham is the father of the Africans. Therefore, Ham could not have been a Caucasian man. Japhet was the father of the Asian and Hawaiian nations. Therefore, Japhet had to be an Asiatic man, like his brother Ham. Shem was the father of the Middle Easterners, the Indians of India. In reality we are all one family upon the earth, with common ancestors! The nations of antiquity were all of the Asiatic type. If all three of Noah's sons gave birth to people of color, Noah himself must have been of the Asiatic type also, and going all the way back to Adam.

There is another big lie being taught against Asiatic people. Western organized religions have taught to the world that people of color look so because God cursed their skin to become brown when Ham looked upon the nakedness of Noah. This is not true! According to the Bible it was Canaan that was cursed, the other sons of Ham were not. Secondly, the curse had nothing to do with skin color. Canaan was cursed to become a servant.

<< Genesis 9:25 >> [And he said, Cursed be Canaan; a servant of servants shall he be unto his brethren.]

Now, all Africans are not Canaanites. The descendants of the Canaanites today are mostly the Sub-Saharan Africans. The South Africans had been servants under the system of apartheid and colonialism! However, the African-Americans are not Africans at all, they are not descended from Ham. The ancestor of the African-Americans is Shem!

Please note that the word Israel refers to a seed, a nationality determined by genealogy. Israelites are so, only because of birth. Israelites are descended from the twelve sons of Jacob, who multiplied to become the twelve tribes of the nation of Israel. Race, religion, or geography does not determine nationality; it is the genealogy along the father's line. The Africans and other Asiatic nations are not Israelites, because their ancestor was not Jacob. However, Israelites are found dispersed all over the world, and living among every nation on the earth. The bulk of the twelve tribes consist of the African-Americans and the American-Indians.

The Biblical, archeological, and historical facts confirm that the original Jews are not of Caucasian descent but are of Asiatic descent! But the Caucasian so-called Jews are mostly Khazarians, whose leaders have conned and fooled them and the world into accepting Khazars as the original Jews, but the fact is they are impostors!

Jesus Christ Described

To present a false image of a Caucasian as Jesus Christ is to be denying that he came in the flesh as an Asiatic man. Color should not be important, but evil people have exploited the issue. Why is the true representation of Christ important? Firstly, because the truth is important, and secondly because the western world has been selfishly exploiting the Bible by presenting a false European picture of Christ, in order to brainwash people. Thirdly, because the Bible says it's important to know his true identity.

Every living person walking around, past and present, must have flesh, and skin covering that flesh. That skin has to be a certain color. Jesus Christ was a historic person. Jesus was not invisible, he was of pure Asiatic origin, resembling an Asiatic man. It is impossible for him to have looked white, off-white, dirty white, pink, or red in complexion. Christ's ancestors came from ancient Egypt and the ancient East, not Europe.

<< I John 4:2,3 >> [Hereby know ye the Spirit of God: every Spirit that confesseth that Jesus Christ is come in the flesh is of God, (the skin on his body, and all other physical attributes) And every spirit that confesseth not that Jesus Christ is come in the flesh is not of God: and this is that spirit of an antichrist, whereof ye have heard that it should come; and even now already is it in the world.]

An Antichrist is a person that makes ignorant, false, and foolish statements such as: "Christ has no color, his true color does not matter" or say, "Christ was a Caucasian". Organized Western Religions and educational institutions have only showed the world a European picture of Christ, and never introduced an Asiatic picture of Christ. If people set up a false image of Christ, they are denying the truth that his skin was brass brown, as was accurately recorded in the Bible! They are discriminating against God and Christ. People that deny the Asiatic appearance of Jesus are called Antichrists!

We know for sure that Jesus is Asiatic because the Bible describes him in Revelation 1:15, and because historically and genealogically he descended from the seed of the original Asiatic Hebrew Israelites of the tribe of Judah.

<< Hebrews 7:14 >> [For it is evident that our Lord sprang out of Judah.]

There is no such thing as a Caucasian Jew. In fact this is a contradiction. The Caucasians are from Europe but the real Jews are from the original nation of ancient Israel who came out of Egypt and went into Palestine. This was an Asiatic nation of people. All of the historical, archeological, scientific, and Biblical evidence confirms this! People must realize that Jesus Christ was not only a spiritual being, he was also a real physical human being of flesh and blood.

<< St. John 1:14 >> [And the word was made flesh, and dwelt among us.]

77

THE TRUTH

<< *Luke 24:39* >> *Jesus said, [Behold my hands and my feet: handle me and see; for a spirit hath not flesh and bones, as ye see me have.]*

Flesh has skin on it; Christ's flesh had Asiatic skin on it! So no one should ever say that Christ has no color! To say that is to say he did not exist! The physical description of Jesus Christ is given in *Revelation 1:14,15.* It describes his hair as being fully gray, and woolly in texture, because anatomically, only Asiatic people have woolly hair. His eyes are described as reddish like fire because Christ was mournful and at times he drank wine.

<< *Genesis 49:10,11* >> *[His eyes shall be red with wine.]*

<< *Matthew 11:19* >> *[The son of man came eating and drinking, and they said, behold a man gluttonous, and a winebibber.]*

The skin of Christ is described as being dark: as if it was burned in a furnace.

<< *Revelation 1:14,15* >> *[His head and his hairs were white like wool, white as snow* (Christ suffered a lot, and went gray early in life*), and his eyes were as a flame of fire* (reddish*), and his feet like unto fine brass as if they burned in a furnace!]*

Brass is already brown, like a doorknob; anything burned has to get very dark from oxidation. And Christ's feet were the same color as the rest of his body: dark brass! Many of the new translations of the Bible have maliciously mistranslated this verse. Compare these verses in the original Hebrew Bible, with the King James 1611 translation, and with the new Bible translations; you will discover the world's conspiracy to hide the true description of Christ. If your translation does not say his skin was burnt brass, and his hair was like wool, you are using a racist version of the Bible that was falsely and maliciously mistranslated to conceal the true color of Jesus Christ, and other important Biblical truths! If you are reading the Bible in English, the old King James 1611 version is the most accurate translation. The Bible even describes the voice of Christ as very deep and strong:

<< *Revelation 1:15* >> *[and his voice as the sound of many waters.]*

<< *Isaiah 52:14* >> *[As many were astonished at thee; his visage was so marred more than any man, and his form more than the sons of men: So shall he sprinkle many nations; and kings shall shut their mouth at him.]*

This world is ignorantly expecting Christ to return as a blue-eyed and blond-haired European. When Christ returns, the world will be astonished to see he is Asiatic with woolly hair.

<< *Isaiah 52:15* >> *[So shall he sprinkle many nations; the kings shall shut their mouths at him: for that which had not been told them* (Christ is Asiatic*) shall they see; and that which they had not heard* (The real Jews are the African-Americans and American Indians*) shall they consider.]*

THE TRUTH

When the western world was making a mockery of and discriminating against Asiatic people, they never considered the fact that the Father in heaven is anthropomorphically Asiatic, with woolly hair, and so is Jesus Christ. And also they failed to see that the original twelve tribes of Israel are the people known as the African-Americans and American-Indians of today. Many people will have to pay on the day of judgment for being wicked, and for setting up false images in their homes, and going to churches that display racist images for God, Jesus Christ, the saints, the angels, and the Israelites!

> << Isaiah 53:1-3 >> [Who hath believed our report? And to whom is the arm of the Lord revealed? For he shall grow up before him as a tender plant and as a root out of a dry ground (Christ had little or no material wealth): he hath neither form nor comeliness; and when we shall see him, there is no beauty that we should desire him. He is despised and rejected of men; a man of sorrows and acquainted with grief: and we hid as it were our faces from him; he was despised, and we esteemed him not.]

Many have and will stand up to fight for and defend the interest of their colonist enemy, the same enemy who had kept them ignorant, oppressed, and enslaved. And they will worship a false image of their oppressor as god. But when were they or any of their so-called leaders ever man enough to stand up for themselves as the real Israelites, expose the Khazars who have been falsely claiming to be Jews, and defend the Asiatic antiquity of the Bible, God, and Jesus? They are hypocrites and have no sense of honor, respect, or manhood.

Some people talk about nationalism, revolution, and equality, but yet they have an image of a European man with blue eyes and blond hair in their churches, in their homes, and hanging around their necks for "God". They hang a giant picture, painted by Michelangelo, modeled after Cesar Borgia, in their houses, in front of their wives and kids; looking up to the false image as a god!

Many people claim to stand for freedom, yet they go into religions set up by their slave master and colonizer. This is a shame! Setting up false images for God, Jesus, and the Jews is a dangerous lie that will create self-hatred and an inferiority complex. It is also blasphemy, which will condemn the soul to eternal hell unless there is repentance.

The fact that the angels in heaven are anthropomorphized as Asiatic can be proven Biblically. The prophet Ezekiel describes the color of the Angels as burned brass:

> << Ezekiel 1:7 >> [...and they (the angels) sparkle like the color of burnished brass.]

The Angels looked brown to Ezekiel. Not only this, the Bible also describes God in a similar way:

> << Daniel 7:9 >> [...The Ancient of days did sit, whose garment was white as snow, And the hair of his head like the pure wool.]

The Ancient of days has no beginning and no end, this can only be the Most High God himself, the eternal Creator who was there before time began! God manifested himself with woolly hair. Europeans do not have the royal woolly hair. Woolly hair is a characteristic of Asiatic people only. Christ and the disciples testify that God in heaven looks as Asiatic as his son Jesus Christ.

THE TRUTH

<< *John 14:8,9* >> *[Philip saith unto him, Lord shew us the father, and it sufficeth us. Jesus saith unto him, Have I been so long time with you, and yet has thou not known me, Philip? He that has seen me has seen the Father.]*

If Christ appeared as an Asiatic man, his Father must look similar! The reason is that the scriptures say that the Asiatic Christ is the image of the invisible Almighty Heavenly Creator, God in heaven:

<< *Colossians 1:15* >> *[(Jesus Christ)... Who is the image of the invisible God, the first born of every creature.]*

Marks of Identity

The Bible contains the true history of the Hebrew Israelites! They are the Asiatic people that Titus, the Roman general, drove out of Palestine into Africa. The small remnants, which were scattered throughout the colonies of the Roman Empire, places like Spain and Portugal, were driven out by the persecutions and genocide resulting from the Roman Catholic Church's inquisition system. The real Jews were driven into Africa and later sold as slaves by the Arab and the African merchants. Although we are Asiatic descent, we had no land in Africa, and we were captives under the Africans and the Arabs. Then, later on, the African and the Arab merchants sold the original Israelite Jews to the Caucasians for guns and wine! This historical fact is also documented in the Bible:

<< *Joel 3:3* >> *[They have cast lots for my people; and have given a boy for an harlot, and sold a girl for wine that they might drink.]*

<< *Joel 3:6* >> *[The children of Judah and of Jerusalem have ye sold unto the Grecians* (Grecians refer to the European colonizers), *that ye might remove them far from their border.]*

The tribes of Judah, Benjamin, and Levi came over to this modern Egypt (the Americas) on slave ships:

<< *Deuteronomy 28:68* >> *[And the Lord shall bring thee into Egypt again with ships; by the way whereof I spake unto thee* (Palestine), *thou shalt see it no more again: and there ye shall be sold unto your enemies for bondmen and bondwomen, and no man shall buy you.]*

This verse can only pertain to the people that came to America on the slave ships in the sixteen hundreds, today being called African-Americans. They were mostly the tribes of Judah, Benjamin, and Levi that came over on those slave ships. The rest of the twelve tribes had already left Palestine almost three thousand years earlier, after their land had been taken by the Babylonians. This happened during the time of the Babylonian Empire; when Salmanasar king of Assyria ruled. It was at this time that the ten tribes came by boats, to settle North, South, and Central America.

Those Hebrew Israelites that came to America during the Babylonian/Assyrian Empire are the people being ignorantly called Indians and Hispanics today. But they are not from Spain, and are not related to the people in India at all. And the people in India are not Israelites. The people in India are Elamites. The American Indians, (also called Hispanics), are the remaining ten tribes of the original twelve tribes of the Biblical Hebrew Israel; namely, the tribes of Reuben, Gad, Asher, Naphtali, Manasseh, Simeon, Zebulon, Ephraim, Dan, and

THE TRUTH

Issachar. The African-Americans and the American-Indians make up the bulk of the original twelve tribes of Israel!

The historic condition of the African-Americans and American-Indians is astonishing, but there is a reason for what has occurred. It started about six thousand years ago in the Garden of Eden, when mankind rebelled against the Creator. The Lord wanted us to know the consequences of this mistake, to understand the meaning of good and evil, of our existence, and his righteous purpose! The Lord reveals this great drama to us in both a cosmic and a microcosmic scale! This great work was accomplished through Christ, and mirrored in the history of the original Israelites.

<< Genesis 3:14,15 >> [And the Lord spake and said unto the serpent, Because thou hast done this, thou art cursed above all cattle, and above every beast of the field; upon thy belly shalt thou go, and dust shalt thou eat all the days of thy life: And I will put enmity between thee and the woman, and between thy seed and her seed; it shall bruise thy head, and thou shalt bruise his heel.]

The serpent represents the people that dominate society through evil. The seed of the woman represents Christ; and in an indirect way, it also represents the Israelites and others that love God! Jesus Christ is the seed that was bruised, to make atonement for sins:

<< Isaiah 53:4,5 >> [Surely he (Jesus) hath borne our grief, and carried our sorrows: yet we did esteem him stricken, smitten of God, and afflicted. But he was wounded for our transgressions, he was bruised for our iniquities: the chastisement of our peace was upon him; and with his stripes we are healed.]

Because of sin, it was ordained that Christ, Israel, and all of mankind had to suffer. This suffering is our re-initiation into the family of God! The reason why the Israelite suffered is because they rebelled against the Lord YAHAWAH. Don't blame God, he warned us and gave us the rules of life. It is a simple principle of cause and effect: we went against the natural order of things and abandoned the love of God, therefore we must face the consequences!

African-Americans and American-Indians are exploited because the majority of them have no unity, no knowledge, and no love an respect. Many of them, follow the ways of this world, put material things before spiritual and intellectual things. The African-Americans and American-Indians can be exploited because they allow others the opportunity.

<< Jeremiah 2:12-14 >> [Be astonished, O ye heavens, at this, and be horribly afraid, be ye very desolate, saith the Lord. For my people have committed two evils; they have forsaken me the fountain of living waters, and hewed them out cisterns, broken cisterns, that can hold no water. Is Israel a servant? Is he a homeborn slave? Why is he spoiled?]

The reason Israelites are so plagued and exploited can be narrowed to a single verse:

<< Hosea 4:6,7 >> [My people are destroyed for lack of knowledge: because thou hast rejected knowledge, I will also reject thee, that thou shalt be no priest to me: seeing thou hast

THE TRUTH

forgotten the law of thy God, I will also forget thy children. As they were increased, so they sinned against me: therefore will I change their glory into shame.]

Many African-Americans and American-Indians feel like the Caucasians and other nations owe them much for the slavery that they suffered in building and making colonial America strong. And in fact it is true that the Europeans along with many other nations have stolen and exploited the identity, the history, the resources, the creativity, and the culture of the Israelites. Our stolen heritage must be reclaimed by any means necessary!

But instead of complaining and hating, why not begin with the self? Unite and start rebuilding character, honoring family structure, assuming responsibility for the community, and forming a society centered around **the love of God and your true identity as Hebrew Israelites.** Only the teachings of the Bible can restore humanity and glory back all mankind and to the Israelites. Therefore our primary goal is to learn the true word of God and teach it to the people; specifically the identity of the original Hebrew Israelites and the identity of the real God. We are all responsible for one another. Unity is strength. Surely if the good people from among the other nations see that you are trying to do something positive they will be happy to help!

But the majority of people refuse to listen to reason they are lazy, prejudiced, envious, jealous, and full of excuses, ignorance, greed, fear, and self-hatred.

<< *Jeremiah 4:22* >> *[For my people are foolish, they have not known me; they are sottish children, and they have no understanding: they are wise to do evil, but to do good they have no knowledge.]*

<< *Isaiah 42:19* >> *[Who is blind, but my servant? or death, as my messenger that I had sent? Who is blind as he that is perfect, and blind as the Lord's servant?]*

God himself became sick and tired of all the stupidity and decided to teach the Israelites a lesson:

<< *Lamentations 2:5* >> *[The Lord was as an enemy: he hath swallowed up Israel, he hath swallowed up all her palaces: he hath destroyed his strong holds, and hath increased in the daughter of Judah mourning and lamentation.]*

To be free, people must first learn about discipline, how to love and respect themselves and others, to value truth, sacrifice, and above all to put God at the center of all things! It is in vain, to blame the problem on other people, and hide under a veil of excuses, hatred, fear, and ignorance.

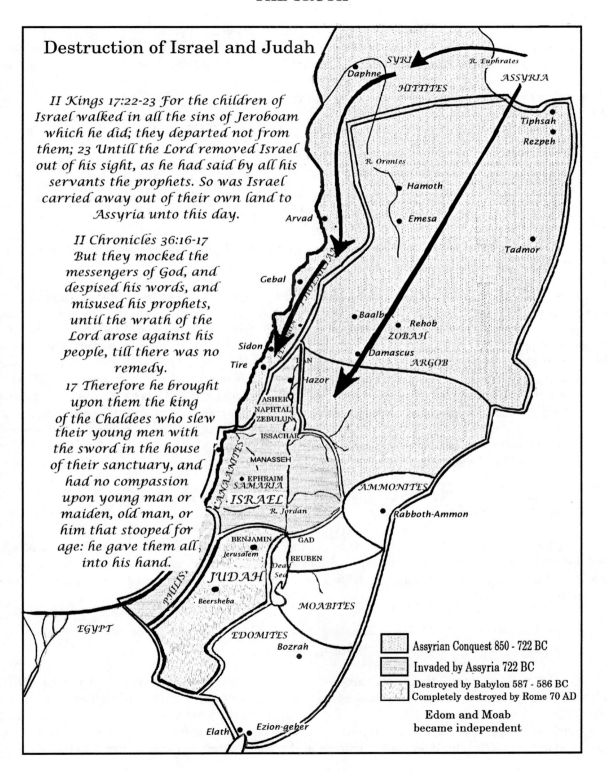

Destruction of Israel and Judah

II Kings 17:22-23 For the children of Israel walked in all the sins of Jeroboam which he did; they departed not from them; 23 Untill the Lord removed Israel out of his sight, as he had said by all his servants the prophets. So was Israel carried away out of their own land to Assyria unto this day.

II Chronicles 36:16-17 But they mocked the messengers of God, and despised his words, and misused his prophets, until the wrath of the Lord arose against his people, till there was no remedy.
17 Therefore he brought upon them the king of the Chaldees who slew their young men with the sword in the house of their sanctuary, and had no compassion upon young man or maiden, old man, or him that stooped for age: he gave them all into his hand.

SYRIA
Daphne
R. Euphrates
ASSYRIA
HITTITES
Tiphsah
Rezpeh
R. Orontes
Hamoth
Emesa
Tadmor
Arvad
Gebal
Baalb
Rehob
ZOBAH
Sidon
Damascus
ARGOB
Tire
Hazor
ASHER
NAPHTALI
ZEBULUN
ISSACHAR
MANASSEH
EPHRAIM
SAMARIA
ISRAEL
R. Jordan
AMMONITES
Rabboth-Ammon
BENJAMIN
GAD
Jerusalem
REUBEN
Dead Sea
JUDAH
Beersheba
MOABITES
EGYPT
EDOMITES
Bozrah
Elath
Ezion-geber

Assyrian Conquest 850 - 722 BC

Invaded by Assyria 722 BC

Destroyed by Babylon 587 - 586 BC
Completely destroyed by Rome 70 AD

Edom and Moab
became independent

THE TRUTH

Now there is one particular chapter, Deuteronomy twenty-eight, a pivotal chapter containing the facts that will pinpoint the true nationality of the African-Americans and American-Indians. It identifies them using specific conditions, to prove their genealogy as the original Israelites of the Bible! Deuteronomy twenty eight does this by revealing the specific social, political, economic, psychological and spiritual conditions that would as a whole pertain to no other people but to the African-Americans and American-Indian/Hispanics; and thus uniquely identifies them as the original Hebrew Israelites!

Here is the verse that classifies this chapter as the key in the identification of the original Israelites, who they are today:

> << Deuteronomy 28:15 >> *[It shall come to pass, if thou will not hearken unto the Lord thy God, to observe to do all his commandments and his statutes which I command thee this day that all these curses shall come upon thee, and overtake thee.]*

> << Deuteronomy 28:46 >> (These curses) *[...They shall be upon thee for a sign and for a wonder, and upon thy seed forever!]*

It is the sum of these particular distressful and destitute historic, economic, and social conditions that have fallen upon the African-Americans and American-Indians that serves as an identification tag, a unique fingerprint pertaining only to the true descendants of Israel! When these required Biblical conditions of the Israelites be applied as a sum, they only pertain to the African-Americans and American-Indians. The conditions described in Deuteronomy chapter twenty-eight points to no other people but to the African-Americans and American-Indians; thus, according to the Bible, they serve to identify them as the only true Hebrew Israelites!

Consequently, to identify the real Israelite, we simply look to see whom among the nations (what group of people) these conditions apply to. The fact discovered is that socially, psychologically, economically, and historically no other nation or people can entirely fit the terms described in Deuteronomy twenty eight; they apply only to the African-Americans and American-Indians, identifying them exactly as the original and only true Hebrew Israelites! Let's examine some of these conditions:

> << Deuteronomy 28:19 >> *[Cursed shall thou be when thou comest in, and cursed shalt thou be when thou goest out.]*

The bulk of African-Americans and American-Indians are born poor and suffering and they die poor and suffering. The groups of Caucasians who like to call themselves Jews or Jewish are born in wealth and they die rich. The Caucasians do not match that condition in any way. However, the African-Americans and American-Indians match them perfectly!

> << Deuteronomy. 28:43 >> *[The stranger that is within thee shall get up above thee very high; and thou shall come down very low.]*

For example, when you go to Chinatown, you see Chinese running businesses. If you go to Italian neighborhoods, you see Italians running businesses. And if you go to the East-Indian neighborhoods, you see East-Indians running businesses. But when you come to the African-American neighborhoods, you see the Asians, the Arabs, the Caucasians, and everyone else running businesses in the African-American neighborhoods except the residents! Often the other nations mistreat the Israelites in their own neighborhood and get away with

THE TRUTH

it! The other nations learn to disrespect the Israelites by seeing how they murder and disrespect each other. Act right, stand in unity, repent of evil, and put God first - then people will treat you right!

The African-Americans and American-Indians did accomplish some incredible things, for example, it was the African-Americans and American-Indians who fought and died to get the Americas open to non-Caucasians, such as the Asians and Arabs. It is for this reason that many people are astonished when they see other nationalities immigrate to the Americas and benefit from all the progress that African-Americans have fought for and achieved. Yet the African-Americans and American-Indians themselves don't get any social, economic, or political benefits, or any recognition, or any of the opportunities resulting from their struggle. Even people that come from countries that were or are enemies of America get treated better, and they are elevated above the African-Americans and the American-Indians. The same situation is found in Central and South America. The original inhabitants are the American-Indians (Hispanics) who live in poverty and oppression. The descendants of Spaniards and other foreigners are exploiting them.

The particular groups of Europeans, who are claiming to be Jews today don't match that description of being economically cursed. They run the world and don't need to be saved or delivered from anything except their own blasphemy. And in some cases the so-called Jewish people are among the ones leading in and causing the mistreatment and exploitation, because of their greed and lusts!

<< Deuteronomy 28:44 >> *[He shall lend to thee, and thou shall not lend to him: he shall be the head, and thou shall be the tail.]*

The African-Americans and American-Indians have been in this country longer than anyone else, but they constantly have to go to the Caucasians and other nations and ask to rent a house, try to receive a loan, get a job, and many other necessities. As a people, they are economically and socially oppressed and discriminated against! It is time for the Israelites to stand up in unity and take responsibility for and control of their own destiny. This economic plight of the Hebrews is another unique sign that serves to identify them as the original Israelites!

The Caucasians who are claiming to be Jews control the world's economy, and some of them are exploiting the people. It is therefore impossible for them to match that identifying condition as the historically oppressed, to claim to be the Jews and Israelites of the Bible! The conditions described in Deuteronomy twenty-eight are contrary to Caucasian history and current status, therefore those so-called European Jews cannot be the original Hebrew Israelites of the Bible!

<< Deuteronomy 28:16,17,18 >> *[Cursed shall thou be in the city, and cursed shall thou be in the field.]*

In the cities, the Israelites live in ghettos, reservations, and slums. While the so-called Jews live in the best and most expensive communities. The field refers to the rest of the world. The true Israelites would be rejected and looked down upon by all nations. But the Caucasians have set up their flags, institutions, and embassies all over the world. Again they fail to match the description of the original Jews, a rejected people.

<< Deuteronomy 28:17 >> *[Cursed shall be thy basket and thy store.]*

The basket refers to material resources and accumulated wealth. The Israelites can't seem to save any money; mainly because they don't get paid anything significant while working for others. The African-Americans and American-Indians are the last to be hired and the first to be fired at any job. Moreover, every time they start to acquire anything of value, the nations under which they are living cheats them out of it or change the laws in order to keep the Asiatic Hebrew Israelites from progressing socially, politically, and economically! The Israelites are among the worst victims of the class struggle between the rich and the poor.

According to the prophecies of the Bible, the true Israelites as a group should be in a condition of poverty and oppression as a people. Historically no one else fits this condition more accurately than the African-Americans and American-Indians! The rich Caucasians that are claiming to be Jews in Palestine today are impostors. They own and control the majority of all the gold, silver, and money in the world. According to the Bible, the real Jews will be in a state of captivity and oppression until the day of deliverance at the Second Coming of Jesus Christ.

The so-called Jewish Caucasians are descendants of the Khazars, who, in order to stay neutral in the war between the Eastern Roman Empire in Byzantine and the Islamic empire (700 AD), converted their entire nation to Judaism. Today they are falsely claiming to be Jews. But the fact is that those Caucasians did not descend from the twelve tribes of Israel, so they do not fit the description of the Israelites. They are Khazarian converts from the Caucasus Mountains of Europe: Edomites!

<< Deuteronomy 28:18 >> [Cursed shall be the fruit of thy body, and the fruit of thy land, the increase of thy kin, and the flocks of thy sheep.]

Children are the fruits of the body. The Israelite children are deprived of heritage, identity, education, skills, health care, and economic opportunity. The American-Indians and African-Americans are starving in North, South and Central America, as well as in the Caribbean Islands! However, you don't see the Caucasian world poor and starving in such large numbers. The historical description of the Israelites does not pertain to Caucasians at all!

<< Deuteronomy 28:33 >> [The fruit of thy land, and all thy labors, shall a nation which thou knowest not eat up.]

The Americas were built mainly off the blood of African-Americans and American Indians under forced slave labor. That is how America became so rich and powerful. They still have the African-Americans and American-Indians in captivity and oppression today!

[...Thou shall be only oppressed and crushed always: so that thou shalt be mad for the sight of thine eyes, which thou shalt see.]

Imperialists have driven us mad with physical, mental, economic, and spiritual oppression and exploitation. They have completely destroyed the heritage, identity, and family structure of the so-called African-Americans and American-Indians. The Caucasians that are professing to be Jewish do not fit the description of the oppressed! The fact is, in many cases, some of them are the oppressors! I don't think all Caucasians are oppressors, there are some with good intentions. But the point is that they are not the original Jews according to the facts and conditions describing the Israelites! Israelites must first be of Asiatic descent; Caucasians are from Europe!

<< Deuteronomy 28:28,29 >> [The Lord shall smite thee with blindness and astonishment of heart: And thou shall grope at noonday as the blind gropeth in darkness.]

THE TRUTH

The conditions of Israelites are shocking. The Israelites have been blind to their Biblical identity and the solution to the oppression! We are the dry bones In the Valley, which the prophet Ezekiel saw. If Ezekiel could not identify those people he saw in the valley, you should not be surprised when the world also does not recognize the true Israelites of today. But the Lord reveals who we are in the Bible:

<< Ezekiel 37:1-11 >> [The hand of the Lord was upon me, and carried me out in the spirit of the Lord, and set me down in the midst of the valley which was full of bones <2> And caused me to pass by them round about: and, behold, there were very many in the open valley; and, lo, they were very dry. <3> And he said unto me, Son of man, can these bones live? And I answered, O Lord God, thou knowest.

<11>...Then he said unto me, Son of man, these bones are the whole house of Israel!]

The valley of dry bones represents the low mental, spiritual, and social condition of the real Hebrews. They are described as dry bones, because the Israelites have been dead as far as their true identity is concerned.

For a long time the world could not realize the fact that the Caucasians are not at all the Israelites of the Bible, nor that: "Black", "Negro", "Indian", and "Hispanic" are not true identities. Also the world refuse to realize that the African-Americans and American-Indians are the original Hebrew Israelites! Those false names are colonial labels that were forced upon the Israelites during slavery times, to create inferiority complexes and self-hatred!

The word black cannot be used as a nationality, the word is an adjective. Adjectives are used to describe nouns and pronouns. The word black is not an identify, it is a byword and an insult! Even the modern terms African-American, American Indian, and Hispanic are not true identities either. The African-Americans and American-Indian/Hispanics are the only people suffering because of the lack of a true identity. Among other pivotal facts, it is this historical condition that allows us to confirm Biblically their identity as the original Jews, the Hebrew Israelites!

<< Deuteronomy 28:37 >> [Thou shalt become an astonishment, Thou shall become a proverb and a byword, among all nations whither the lord shall lead thee.]

Astonishment: other people shake their heads when they see the condition of savagery, poverty, and ignorance of the African-Americans and American-Indians. The heathens compose proverbs against the Israelites, like: "Catch a nigger by the toe, if he hollers let him go", "Black is back", "One little Indian, two little Indians". They used bywords against the Israelites, calling them by adjectives: Black, Nigger, Negro, Shine, Monkeys, Spick, Spade, and Wetback!

Asiatic features are royal features, we are not the carbon copy, but we are the originals! The Creator himself is shown as Asiatic in appearance, with brown complexion and woolly hair! So is Jesus Christ and so are the angels. This is according to the Bible and according to historical facts!

The Caucasians and the other nations must not use our Hebrew Israelite identity as their own, and they should not exploit it for religious, economic, and political vices; to do so is blasphemy! The Khazars are not Jews; everyone around the world should see their leaders and the other deceivers for what they are: liars, impostors, and blasphemers.

THE TRUTH

<< Revelation 2:9, 3:9 >> [...I know the blasphemy of them which say they are Jews, and are not, but are the Synagogue of Satan.

<< Revelation 3:9 >>...Behold, I will make them of the synagogue of Satan, which say they are Jews and are not, but do lie; Behold, I will make them to come and worship before thy feet, and to know that I have love thee.]

The Khazar and other heathen leaders have deliberately concealed the identity of the true Israelites from the world, through conspiracy:

<< Psalms 83:4-12 >> [They have said, come, and let us cut them off from being a nation; that the name of Israel be no more in remembrance. For they have consulted together with one consent: they are confederate against thee... Who said, Let us take the house of the Lord in possession.]

So it was many nations together that had conspired to blot out the history of the twelve tribes of Israel. Today most Israelites don't even know their true nationality. They are running around calling themselves by the names the slave master labeled them with, and speaking the colonial language he forced upon them. The Israelites have been raped of their history, nationality and culture. This condition serves as a mark to identify the true Israelites!

The real Jews would be lost to their identity. How can Caucasians claim to be Jews when they not only remember all of their history, culture, and language; but they have everyone on the planet Earth following their customs and speaking their languages? The Edomites advertise their history twenty-four hours a day. The Khazar Edomites do not, and cannot fit the description of the people that the Bible describes as the original Jews; a people lost to their national identity. And most importantly, the true Israelites are of Asiatic descent, not of Caucasian descent!

In addition to the miserable social conditions, the astonishing psychological conditions, and the despairing economic conditions; the incessant genocide of the African-Americans and American-Indians also serves as a mark, identifying them as the original twelve tribes of Israel!

<< Leviticus 26:17 >> [And I will set my face against you, and ye shall be slain before your enemies: they that hate you shall reign over you; and ye shall flee when none pursueth you.]

From the American colonial slavery period to now, at least ninety million African-Americans have been brutally murdered as a result of exploitation, violence, and injustice! Today, Israelites are the constant victims of police brutality, injustice, and genocide; far more often than any other ethnic group! One-third of African-American men are in Jail in America, and over forty percent of the ones that are not in jail are unemployed.

<< Deuteronomy 28:25 >> [The Lord shall cause thee to be smitten before thine enemies: Thou shall go out one way against them, and flee seven ways before them; and shalt be removed into all the kingdoms of the earth.]

Israelites have been slaves for centuries in Africa, and starting from the 1600's they were sold into slavery by the Arab and African merchants to the Caucasians. They were packed like sardines, for months at a

THE TRUTH

time on wet, rodent infested and dirty cargo ships. Many of them died due to the unsanitary conditions and the cruel treatment aboard the slave ships.

The United States Cavalry took this land from the American-Indians through mass genocide, injustice, and terrorism. These same barbaric acts of imperialism, and terrorism continue all over the world today! Other nations are revolting against injustice and exploitation. What are you African-Americans and American-Indians doing about defending your communities, your nationality, your history, and your culture, your manhood and your honor? Like Malcolm says:

"It seems you (so-called minorities) bleed for White people, fighting their wars. You bleed when the White man says bleed. But when your land, your houses are being taken, and your children are being murdered, you haven't got any blood! This is a shame."

<< Deuteronomy 28:62 >> [And ye shall be left few in number, whereas ye were as the stars of heaven for a multitude; because thou wouldest not obey the voice of the Lord.]

The colonizers murdered over two hundred million American-Indians while raping the men, women, and children. They robbed, enslaved, and stole the land and resources of North, South, and Central America! The Europeans, along with the African and the Arab merchants of slavery, exterminated thirty million Israelites during the slave trade, forcing them to build their colonies and fight their wars with sweat, blood, and tears! This long history of genocide is another distinct mark that would serve to identify the African-Americans and American-Indians as the true Israelites!

<< Deuteronomy 28:66 >> [And thy life shall hang in doubt before thee; and thou shall fear day and night, and shall have no assurance of thy life.]

Compared to the African-Americans and American-Indians, the Caucasians that are claiming to be Jews have all the assurance for their life in this world. They control the banks, the markets, the schools, and the hospitals; and they have the Israelites in captivity. They have economic power and financial security. They have the strongest military established in Palestine and America, and are controlling the economics and politics of many nations. They're more secure than any other people.

The real Israelites would have no such power, or security. Therefore, according to the Bible these Caucasians cannot be the Jews. They have nothing in common with the people that the Bible is talking about. They are the descendants of the Khazar Empire that have converted to the Judaism religion, and conspired to deceive the world!

<< Deuteronomy 28:22 >> [The Lord shall smite thee with a consumption, and with a fever, and with an inflammation, and with and extreme burning, and with the sword]

<< Deuteronomy 28: 60 >> [Moreover, he will bring upon thee all the diseases of Egypt, which thou was afraid of; and they shall cleave unto thee. Also every sickness, and every plague, which is not written in the book of this law.]

There is a terrible health crisis among the poor Israelites. Because of the oppressed and destitute condition of the African-Americans and American-Indians, they are subject to all kinds of sicknesses. The colonizers infested this land with all kinds of diseases from Europe, which were totally unknown to the Western continents, causing many American-Indians to die. Whenever possible, the colonizers would intentionally contaminate the water supply, causing many American-Indians to become infected with fevers and die. Various forms of biological warfare tactics are used against the Israelites and other underprivileged people to this day.

According to the Bible the real Israelites will be in such a desperate condition that they will turn extremely violent against each other. Today it is often called Black on Black crime:

<< *Deuteronomy 28: 53* >> *[And thou shalt eat the fruit of thine own body, the flesh of thy sons and of thy daughters, which the Lord thy God hath given thee, in the siege, and in the straightness, where with thine enemies shall distress thee in all thine gates.]*

The colonizers are holding the Israelites in a cycle of oppression, murder, and exploitation in the ghettos, slums, and reservations. However it is because there is among the people so much ignorance, wickedness and self-hatred, that is causing them to remain in this condition of oppression. They have rejected the Lord God YAHAWAH. The so-called African-Americans act like crabs in a barrel! They are constantly disrespecting, fighting, killing, and discriminating against their own kind. For example, some of the dark-skinned people have jealousy and hatred towards light-skinned people. They discriminate against light-skinned people. This occurs even within the same family.

In fact it is mostly the parents of the African-Americans and the American-Indian Hispanic children that are directly responsible for causing the destruction of the generation. Most of them have no love for their children, and will not provide their children with proper discipline, education, and support. Very often these so-called parents seek only to exploit and used their children for begging and for other scams to get money! The children are hated and do not receive any benefit or support.

Many African-Americans and Americans have no self respect, or respect for anyone else. Many have no love in their hearts! They are full of hate and bitterness. There is no excuse for bad behavior. You cannot blame everything on the Caucasians and the other nations, that is just not realistic!

The Israelites should not have rebelled against the laws of God in the first place. People cannot take advantage of you unless you provide them with an opportunity and the conditions to exploit you. Acting like a bunch of ignorant, savage fools will only make it harder for everyone. You don't deserve any respect if you don't respect yourself and others.

It is clear that the nations have decided to take advantage of the situation and conspired against the Israelites to exploit them. According to the prophecies of the Bible, the nations that have oppressed us and perverted the truth will have to pay! If God did what he did to the Israelites, can you imagine the hell he is going to send upon the heathens!

<< *Isaiah 47:6* >> *[I was wroth with my people, I have polluted mine inheritance, and given them into thine hand: thou didst shew them no mercy; upon the ancient hast thou very heavily laid thy yoke.]*

<< *Zechariah 1:15* >> *[I am sore displeased with the heathens that are at ease: for I was but a little displeased, and they help forward the affliction.]*

<< *Zechariah 2:8* >> *[For thus saith the Lord of hosts; after the glory hath he sent me unto the nations, which spoiled you: for he that toucheth you toucheth the apple of his eye.]*

THE TRUTH

So it is no accident that the African-Americans and American-Indians had to live in the ghettos, slums, and reservations for the past three-hundred years; and every foreigner that comes to our lands is automatically elevated above us. They keep on oppressing us, although we've built this hemisphere. We've fought and died in all of its wars. The African-Americans and American-Indians have to learn to act like men and not as clowns and fools by singing, dancing, fighting, and playing games for the entertainment of the oppressors. In doing this, the Asiatic people are destroying their own image and doing great damage to themselves. If you provide them the opportunity to exploit you, how can you blame them? We must learn to seek love, truth, and righteousness!

These unique identifying characteristics pertaining to the African-Americans and American-Indians serve as a reference mark that will allow them to wake up to their true nationality as Israelites in the last days! Historically, no other people have been so oppressed, for such a long time, under so many different nations. No other people can match the sum of those historical and social conditions that would to identify the real Jews and Israelites. The condition of the African-Americans and American-Indians/Hispanics of North, South, and Central America matches it exactly to identify them as the Hebrew Israelites of the Bible!

Now, the most indisputable mark that identifies the Israelites is the mark of slavery! The real Israelites, according to the Bible, were to be sold into slavery by way of slave ships away from Palestine.

<< Deuteronomy 28:32,33 >> [Thy sons and thy daughters shall be given unto another people, and thine eyes shall look and fail with longing for them all the daylong: and there shall be no might in thine hand]

<< Deuteronomy 28:41 >> [Thou shalt beget sons and daughters, but they shall go into captivity.]

In colonial slavery times, the slave owners would take the young children away from the slaves and sell them to other plantations all over the country! The slaves had no power. Even today they have effective and subtle ways of destroying our family structure. In the foster homes, the African-American and American-Indian/Hispanic children are repeatedly tortured, raped, and treated like animals. Also the immigration policy is such that the illegal aliens are made to work as slaves. However, if the Israelites would return to God and take responsibility to love and help each other, others would not be exploiting them!

Many people think that the American Civil War was fought to liberate the slaves, but this was never the case! Concerning the American Civil War of 1861, it was never fought in order to liberate the slaves. The war was a result of political struggle for power between the Democratic and the Republican parties.

The Southern slave owners were Democrats, and favored an agricultural economy. At that time, they were in control of the government. The Republican Party of the North was calling for an industrial-based economy instead of an agricultural economy. To destroy the power of the Southern Democrats, the Republicans started calling for the liberation of the slaves, which would result in the collapse of the South, both politically and economically; thus leaving Abraham Lincoln's Republican Party in control of the government.

And the Republican party told the world that the war was being fought over the issue of slavery, in order to make it sound like a moral issue, as a way of keeping England or any other country from siding with the South! The true purpose of the Civil war was never to free the slaves but to restructure the political and economic power of the country! The African-Americans and the American-Indians still could not vote after the war. And once the Republicans were confident of their power, they gave amnesty to the Southern Confederates, and returned their plantations to them. The slaves had to return to the plantations, and suffer helplessly again!

THE TRUTH

The slaves were never freed as a result of the Civil War! After the Civil War African-Americans were constantly being lynched and tortured everywhere, and the government did nothing! However, it was not until Martin Luther King and other leaders marched against the United States capital in Washington that the African-Americans were granted the right to vote. In some cases their human rights and civil rights are still lacking today!

The Caucasians who are claiming to be Jews did not go through anything comparable to the slavery of many generations that the African-Americans and American-Indian/Hispanics did:

> << *Joel 3:3* >> *[And they have cast lots for my people; and have given a boy for an harlot, and sold a girl for wine, that they might drink.]*

> << *Joel 3:6* >> *[The children of Judah and of Jerusalem have ye* (Africans, and Arabs) *sold unto the Grecians* (the Caucasians), *that ye might remove them far from their border* (Palestine).*]*

The African and the Arab merchants did not sell Europeans or Khazars; therefore they cannot claim to be the original Jews. They sold the Asiatic people (so-called African Americans) for guns and wine. Again, so-called African Americans are the only people that carry this distinctive mark: to be sold into slavery, plus all the other required conditions added. Therefore, according to the Bible, we are the real Jews! The Caucasian converts are impostors from the Khazar Empire, they were never sold into slavery in exchange for gold, wine, or money!

How can Caucasians claim to be the Jews when the Bible says the Jews are an Asiatic people, who would be sold into slavery until the last days? The African-Americans are the real Jews, and the American-Indian/Hispanics are the remaining tribes of Israel. The tribes will reunite as Hebrew Israelites... According to the Bible, this is exactly what is soon going to happen!

Now here is another pivotal verse that serves as a key to the identity of the original Jews:

> << *Deuteronomy. 28:48* >> *[And he shall put a yoke of iron upon thy neck, until he has destroyed thee.]*

No other people had yokes of iron upon their necks, coming to America as a group, except the slaves! This scripture is a definite key, an identifying mark set upon us, that proves beyond the shadow of a doubt that the African-Americans alone are the real Jews! When did any of the Europeans ever come to America with a yoke of iron around his neck? They cannot claim to be the Jews.

Now here is another powerful scripture that provides the solution beyond doubt as to the Identity of the real Israelites:

> << *Deuteronomy 28:68* >> *[And the Lord shall bring thee into Egypt again with ships, by the way whereof I spake unto thee, Thou shalt see it no more again: and there ye shall be sold unto your enemies for bondmen and bondwoman, and no man shall buy you.]*

Deuteronomy 28:68 cannot be referring to the land of Egypt in Africa, because you don't need a ship to get there from Palestine. You could walk into Egypt from there. But this modern Egypt is America, the Bible confirms this fact:

> << *Revelation 11:8* >> *[...Which spiritually is called Egypt, and Sodom.]*

THE TRUTH

The word Egypt is Greek for bondage. America is the modern Egypt where Israelites would go into a second captivity!

<< *Deuteronomy 28:68* >> *[By the way whereof I spake unto thee* (Palestine)*, Thou shalt see it no more again: and there ye shall be sold unto your enemies* (the colonizers of North, South, and Central America) *for bondmen, and bond women* (as slaves).*]*

This verse should pinpoint and identify the specific group of Asiatic people who are the real Jews beyond any doubt! They are the Asiatic people in the West that were sold into slavery by way of the slave ships to the Caucasians, who treated them as enemies. These real Israelites would not see Palestine again! All of this happened to no other group of people in history!

According to the Bible the real Jews would not see Palestine until after the return of Christ! Therefore, if the Caucasians were the real Jews, they would not be in Palestine! And these Caucasians don't pertain in any other condition to the Israelites of the Bible! The fact is that impostors who are claiming to be Jews have established themselves as a nation in Palestine. This directly contradicts the conditions and the prophecies pertaining to the real Jews. The real Israelites are to be in oppression in another land until Christ returns to deliver and re-establish them as the kingdom of heaven on earth.

Deuteronomy, chapter twenty-eight, provided us with an absolutely positive historical, social, psychological, and economic identification; a tag or fingers prints as to whom the real Jews are today.

<< *Verse 28:48* >> *[And they shall be upon thee for a sign* (identification)*, and for a wonder, and upon thy seed forever]*

According to God and the Bible those conditions would serve as an identification tag or mark to identify the real Jews! The African-Americans, (not the Africans who sold them, nor any other Afro-Asiatic people) are the only people to come to America on **slave ships, with yokes of iron upon their necks.** These are the only ones to be continually oppressed economically, socially, and mentally. These signs would serve to identify the real Jews in the last days!

It is our Savior Jesus Christ, who would come to deliver his people, the African-Americans and American-Indians: who are the original Jews and Israelites, from the tribes of Judah, Benjamin, Levi, Simeon, Zebulon, Ephraim, Manasseh, Gad, Reuben, Napthali, Asher, and Issachar.

The Modern Exodus

The Israelite nation consisted of twelve tribes and one priestly tribe. In BC 975, shortly after the death of King Solomon, the kingdom was split into two parts. The one part was called Judah (Judea), and it consisted primarily of three tribes: Judah, Benjamin, and Levi. The other division was called Israel, the bulk of which consisted of the remaining tribes: Reuben, Gad, Asher, Napthali, Manasseh, Simeon, Issachar, Dan, Zebulun and Ephraim. In BC 721 the king of Assyria carried Israel away into captivity, and it seemed to have been lost from history ever since.

Many myths have developed as to the whereabouts of the ten tribes. But the reality is that they were not heard from because they had migrated primarily to the Western Hemisphere and settled in North, South, and

Central America. This fact is documented in the Apocrypha << Second Esdras 13:39-49 >>, in the Book of Mormons, and also in James Adair's History of the American Indians, and several other sources!

In the Book of Mormons, Third Nephi 15:21, Jesus appeared to the indigenous American-Indians, and told them that they were the lost Hebrew Israelite tribes:

> *<< Third Nephi 15:21 >> [And verily I say unto you, that ye are they of whom I said: Other sheep I have which are not of this fold; them also I must bring, and they shall be one fold, and one shepherd.]*

However, the Judeo-Christian religions are maliciously saying that the Europeans are the lost tribes of Israel. This is false, and is in direct contradiction with the true history and the Biblical record! Concerning the national status of the tribes of Israel, the Bible records:

> *<< Numbers 23:9 >> [...lo, the people shall dwell alone, and shall not be reckoned among the nations!]*

According to this verse, as a people the Israelites would not be counted among the nations! But the European nations are counted; therefore, they cannot be the Israelites of the Bible! And secondly, the Bible also says in reference to the condition of the true Israelites that they would for the most part be without a leader:

> *<< Hosea 3:4,5 >> [For the children of Israel shall abide many days without a king, and without a prince... Afterward shall the children of Israel return, and seek the Lord their God, and David their king (referring to Christ); and shall fear the Lord and his goodness in the latter days.]*

The Europeans have land, nations, presidents, prime ministers, princes, and kings. It is impossible for the Europeans to be the Israelites that the Bible is referring to! And remember, the real Israelites would be under many curses:

> *<< Deuteronomy 4:26,27 >> [I call heaven and earth to witness against you this day, that ye shall soon utterly perish from off the land whereunto ye go over Jordan to possess it; ye shall not prolong your days upon it, but shall utterly be destroyed. And the Lord shall scatter you among the nations, and ye shall be left few in number among the heathen, whither the Lord shall lead you.]*

Because of this curse, today the true descendants of the real Israelites would not exist as a world power until after the return of Christ. But the Europeans have a long history of military might and economic leadership. Their conditions do not pertain in any way to the Israelites of the Bible! And the true Israelites would not at this time be in any kind of prosperous condition as a people:

> *<< Deuteronomy 28:62-65 >> [And it shall come to pass, that as the Lord rejoiced over you to do you good, and to multiply you; so the Lord will rejoice over you to destroy you, and to bring you to nought; and ye shall be plucked from off the land whither thou goest to possess it.*

THE TRUTH

And the Lord shall scatter thee among all people, from the one end of the earth even unto the other; and there thou shalt serve other gods, which neither thou nor thy fathers have known, even wood and stone. And among these nations shalt thou find no ease, neither shall the sole of thy foot have rest: but the Lord shall give thee there a trembling heart, and failing of eyes, and sorrow of mind.]

The other thing is that the Nation of so-called Jewish Caucasians, falsely called Israel today, yet consisting mostly of Europeans from Russia and Poland, clearly cannot be the Israel that the Bible is talking about. For one thing, the true kingdom of Israel will not be established until after the Second Coming of Christ. And it will be established overnight, in one day:

<< Isaiah 66:8 >> *[Who hath heard such a thing? Who hath seen such things? Shall the earth be made to bring forth in one day? Or shall a nation be born at once? for as soon as Zion travailed, she brought forth her children.]*

In that day Jesus Christ will return to deliver and to lead the African-Americans and indigenous American-Indian/Hispanic (which are together the original twelve tribes of Israelites) from the tribulations, plagues, and nuclear destruction of the last days. He is coming to establish them as Israelites, the kingdom of Heaven on earth, in the land of Palestine! This deliverance will be comparable to the time (around BC 1440) when the Israelites were delivered out of the first Egypt:

<< Jeremiah 16:14-15 >> *[Therefore, behold, the days come, saith the Lord, that it shall no more be said, The Lord liveth, that brought up the children of Israel out of the land of Egypt; But, the Lord liveth, that brought up the children of Israel from the land of the north, and from all the lands whither he had driven them: and I will bring them again into their land that I gave unto their fathers.]*

The gathering of the twelve tribes of Israel will be a direct miraculous act of the Lord YAHAWAH:

<< Ezekiel 20:34 >> *[And I will bring you out from the people, and will gather you out of the countries wherein ye are scattered, with a mighty hand, and with a stretched out arm, and with fury poured out.]*

<< Isaiah 43:3-7 >> *[For I am the Lord thy God, the Holy One of Israel, thy Savior: I gave Egypt for thy ransom, Ethiopia and Seba for thee. Since thou wast precious in my sight, thou hast been honorable, and I have loved thee: therefore will I give men for thee, and people for thy life. Fear not: for I am with thee: I will bring thy seed from the east, and gather thee from the west; I will say to the north, Give up; and to the south, Keep not back: bring my sons from far, and my daughters from the ends of the earth; Even every one that is called by my name: for I have created him for my glory, I have formed him.]*

<< Ezekiel 36:24-28 >> *[For I will take you from among the heathen, and gather you out of all countries, and will bring you into your own land. Then will I sprinkle clean water upon you, and ye shall be clean: from all your filthiness, and from all your idols... And ye shall*

THE TRUTH

dwell in the land that I gave to your fathers; and ye shall be my people, and I will be your God.]

Although there is to be some grace in the last days, the true Israelites will be in oppression right up to the moment that Christ returns to deliver them:

<< Jeremiah 30:7,8 >> [Alas! for that day is great, so that none is like it: it is even the time of Jacob's trouble; but he shall be saved out of it. For it shall come to pass in that day, saith the Lord of hosts, that I will break his yoke from off thy neck, and will burst thy bonds, and strangers shall no more serve themselves of him.]

The Khazars in Palestine acting as Jews are not serving under any other nation. Through conspiracy they have created a so-called Jewish nation, claiming it to be Israel. This is blasphemy. But the true Hebrew Israelites are to be in a state of oppression, serving under other nations. The people claiming to be Jews in Palestine today contradict every aspect of the Biblical record as it pertains to the identity of the true Israelites!

This period that we are living in is called the Times Of The Gentiles. The everlasting Kingdom that will be ruled by the true Israelites will be formed after the Times of the Gentiles. Until that time, the true Israelites of the Bible will not exist as a free people under its own identity and customs!

<< Luke 21:24 >> [And they (the Israelites) *shall fall by the edge of the sword, and shall be led away captive into all nations: and Jerusalem shall be trodden down of the Gentiles, until the times of the Gentiles be fulfilled.]*

<< Romans 11:25,26 >> [For I would not, brethren, that ye should be ignorant of this mystery, lest ye should be wise in your own conceit; that blindness in part is happened to Israel, until the fullness of the Gentiles be come in. And so all Israel shall be saved: as it is written, There shall come out of Sion the Deliverer (Christ), *and shall turn away ungodliness from Jacob.]*

When will the captivity of the Israelites end, the so-called African Americans and the American Indians? When will they learn their true identity. When will the Israelites be delivered from all the curses that they are under? According to the scriptures the Israelites would be existing under the curses and destroyed as a people for two thousand years, but in the third millenium we would be restored. In Second Peters 3:8 we learn that one prophetic day to God is one thousand years on earth.

<< Hosea 6:2 >> [After two days will he revive us: in the third day he will raise us up, and we shall live in his sight.]

The people claiming to be Jews in Palestine today are impostors! Soon, the real Israelites will wake up to their true identity, in this generation. Christ will return with power to restore the true Israelites as a nation and people:

<< Daniel 12:1 >> [And at that time shall Michael stand up, the great prince which standeth for the children of thy people: and there shall be a time of trouble, such as never was since

there was a nation even to that same time: and at that time thy people shall be delivered, everyone that shall be found written in the book.]

To deliver and to restore the original Israelites is the very purpose of the Second Coming of Jesus Christ!

<< Matthew 24:21,22,30,31 >> [For then shall be a great tribulation, such as was not since the beginning of the world to this time, no nor ever shall be. And except those days should be shortened, there should no flesh be saved: but for the elect's sake those days shall be shortened.
...And then shall appear the sign of the Son of man in heaven: then shall all the tribes of the earth mourn, and they shall see the Son of man coming in the clouds of heaven with power and great glory. And he shall send his angels with a great sound of a trumpet, and they shall gather together his elect from the four winds, from one end of heaven to the other.]

If the Caucasians were the real Jews and Israelites Christ would not have to come, because they rule the world and they don't need to be delivered from anything! This world refuses to accept the true Israelites; instead, some have conjured up new lies, saying: "Israel is destroyed and done away with forever." That is not what the Bible says! Granted, it is true the Lord did reject the Israelites, but this was only for a time.

<< Jeremiah 31:31,32 >> [Behold, the days come, saith the Lord, that I will make a new covenant with the house of Israel, and with the house of Judah: Not according to the covenant that I made with their fathers in the day that I took them by the hand to bring them out of the land of Egypt; which my covenant they break, although I was an husband unto them, saith the Lord:]

That new covenant was made through Christ by the offering of his life as the price that would cover our sins: making atonement between the LORD GOD YAHAWAH and us!

<< Luke 22:20 >> [This is the New Testament in my blood, which is shed for you!]

The apostle Paul also testifies that the Israelites are not done away with:

<< Romans 11:1 >> [I say then, Hath God cast away his people? God forbid. For I am an Israelite, of the seed of Abraham, of the tribe of Benjamin.]

The Bible explains clearly, beyond a doubt, the original Israelites are not, and can never be done away with!

<< Jeremiah 33:20-26 >> [Thus saith the Lord; if ye can break my covenant of the day, and my covenant of the night, and that there should not be day and night in their season; then may also my covenant be broken with David my servant, that he should not have a son to reign upon his throne; and with the Levites the priest my ministers. As the host of heaven cannot be numbered, neither the sand of the sea measured: so will I multiply the seed of David my servant, and the Levites that minister unto me.]

THE TRUTH

Only if you can stop the day and the night from coming, and the stars from shining, then would it be possible to eliminate the original Israelites. In other words, we are everlasting!

<< Jeremiah 33:23-26 >> *[Moreover the word of the Lord came to Jeremiah, saying, 24 Consider thou not what this people have spoken, saying, The two Families which the Lord hath chosen, he hath even cast them off? Thus they have despised my people, that they should be no more a nation before them.*

25 Thus saith the Lord; If my covenant be not with day and night, and if I have not appointed the ordinances of heaven and earth; 26 then will I cast away the seed of Jacob, and David my servant, so that I will not take any of his seed to be rulers over the seed of Abraham, Isaac, and Jacob: for I will cause their captivity to return, and have mercy on them!]

Biblically, we know that the majority of Asiatic people that came on the slave ships with chains around their necks are the real Jews. Also, the Bible reveals historically that the people being called Indians/Hispanics of the Americas are the remaining nine tribes of the original nation of Israel! Moses led twelve tribes out of Egypt, not counting Levi, the priests of Israel.

But there was a civil war after the death of Solomon, and the nation became divided. Ten of the tribes became known as the Kingdom of Israel; which eventually migrated to the Americas and are today known as the American-Indian/Hispanics. The remaining two tribes plus the Levites and some remnants of the other tribes became known as the nation of Judah today known as the African-Americans!

The reason for the division in Israel is recorded:

<< First Kings 11:31-36 >> *[Because they have forsaken me, and worshipped Astoreth... I will take the kingdom out of his son's hand, and give it unto thee, even ten tribes. And unto his son will I give one tribe, that David my servant may have a light always before me in Jerusalem, the city on which I have chosen to put my name.]*

But, those ten tribes went into idol worship. For this, the Most High caused them to be expelled from the land, and taken captive.

<< First Kings 14:15 >> *[For the Lord shall smite Israel, as a reed is shaken in the water, and he shall root up Israel out of this good land, which he gave to their fathers, and scatter them beyond the river, because they have made their groves, provoking the Lord to anger.]*

The ten tribes were taken away captive into Babylon. Only three tribes remained in Palestine: Judah, Benjamin, and Levi, plus small traces of the other tribes (together called the Jews). Today, the historians of the world claim that the ten tribes are lost, which is very silly. How can the tribes be lost? Did they go into outer space or under the ocean? It can be proven in the Bible that they are the indigenous American-Indians of North, South, and Central America!

First of all, it was recorded that the Israelites had big ships, capable of crossing the Atlantic Ocean.

<< First Kings 9:26, 27 >> *[And king Solomon made a navy of ships, ...beyond the Red sea. And Hiram sent in the navy his servants, shipmen that had knowledge of the sea.]*

THE TRUTH

<< Second Chronicles 9:21 >> [For the king's ships went to Tarshish with the servants of Huram: every three years once came the ships of Tarshish (Ships of the Atlantic*) bringing gold, and silver, ivory, and apes, and peacocks.]*

Not only did we have large ships capable of transporting heavy cargo, but we also had knowledge of the sea and navigation, which made travel to the Americas common. It took the ships three years, because they were also coming to the Americas for provisions!

In the Bible Apocrypha, it is documented specifically how ten of the twelve tribes of Israel (the indigenous American-Indians) got from the Middle East to the Americas. The Apocrypha is a collection of books that the western religious powers have conspired to remove from the original compilation of the Bible, because they feel it contradicted their teaching of white supremacy. Fortunately, you can buy those books separately if they are missing from your Bible.

<< Apocrypha, Second Esdras 13:39-48 >> [And whereas thou sawest that he gathered another peaceable multitude unto him; Those are the ten tribes, which were carried away prisoners out of their own land in the time of Osea the king, whom Salmanasar the king of Assyria led away captive, and carried them over the waters, and so came they to another land.

But they took this counsel among themselves, that they would leave the multitude of the heathen, and go forth into a further country, where never mankind dwelt (North, South, and Central America*), that they might there keep their statutes, which they never kept in their own land.*

And they entered into Euphrates by the narrow passages of the river. For the Most High then shewed signs for them, and held still the flood, till they were passed over. For through that country there was a great way to go (across the ocean*), namely, of a year and a half: and the same region is called Arsareth. Then dwelt they there* (The Americas*) until the latter time* (Our time today*); and now when they shall begin to come* (after the Second Coming of Christ!*) ...But those that be left behind of thy people* (the tribes of Judah, Benjamin, and Levi*) are they that are found within my borders.]*

Also the Book of Mormons, which was written by Israelites, (the indigenous American-Indian prophets) testifies concerning the origin of the American-Indians. It documents in detail how the Israelites came to settle North, South, and Central America!

<< The Book of Mormons, First Nephi 17:8 >> [And it came to pass that the Lord spake unto me (Nephi of the tribe of Ephraim, of the nation of Israel*), saying: Thou shalt construct a ship, after the manner which I shall show thee, that I may carry thy people across these waters.]*

Clearly the ancient historical records prove beyond any doubt that the American-Indian/Hispanics are descended from the Israelites!

The Book of Mormons was not written by Caucasians. It was written way before the Europeans came to the American continent. They found the book in North America and translated it! However the version of the book commonly available today has been polluted with false doctrine by the Mormon religion, in order to teach white supremacy, among other lies!

All throughout history it has been the policy of the colonial powers to keep the African-Americans and the American-Indian/Hispanics separated. As a unit the twelve tribes would be too strong for them to control and exploit. According to prophecy it is imperative that the African-Americans and the American-Indian/Hispanics seek to unite as Hebrew Israelites! The Bible says that in the last days all the tribes will be found together:

<< Jeremiah 50:33 >> [Thus saith the Lord of hosts; The children of Israel and the children of Judah were oppressed together: and all that took them captives held them fast; they refuse to let them go.]

Christian Hebrew Israelites should stop calling themselves Black, White, Indian, Spanish, Hispanics, African, French, and by any other colonial label. Israelites are not Caucasians, and are not from Africa, Europe, India, or Spain. Black is a color and you are not black in color, you're different shades of brown and yellow. The word black is a derogatory adjective, it can't be used as a noun! The Native Americans are not Indians. Indians are from India. The African-Americans and American-Indians are Israelites! Their true custom is Hebrew and original nationality is Israelite, our only identity!

THE TRUTH

GEOGRAPHY OF THE TWELVE TRIBES

The Bible provides us with the definite geographical locations as to where the original twelve tribes of Israel were dispersed to, and will be found in the last days. The geography of the twelve tribes is one of the most significant Biblical mysteries to be revealed. This proof is found mostly in Genesis chapter 49, and Deuteronomy chapter 33! These chapters describe certain social customs, geographical and historical conditions of the Israelites in the last days. These geographical conditions, without a doubt, locate and identify the descendants of the original twelve tribes of Israel, in these last days.

> << Genesis 49:1 >> [And Jacob called unto his sons, and said, Gather yourselves together, that I may tell you that which shall befall you in the last days.]

The twelve sons of Jacob gave birth to the twelve tribes of Israel. According to this Biblical verse, Jacob is about to prophesize concerning the historical and social conditions and characteristics of the true descendants of the twelve tribes in the last days. We are no doubt living in these last days now, prior to the Second Coming of Jesus Christ! The prophecies of this chapter according to verse one, will relate to conditions that would befall the Israelites in the last days, and at the same time these prophecies convey their identity and geographical location!

Genesis forty-nine and Deuteronomy thirty-three will provide us with the geography, but not the genealogy of each individual member of the tribes. Remnants of the Israelites are actually dispersed all over the world; however, the bulk of them are located in the Western Hemisphere. The tribes are also amalgamated with remnants from each other; therefore, an Israelite cannot always be one hundred percent sure of which tribe he is from based on the prophecies alone.

If you are of Western Asiatic descent, either indigenous American-Indian or African-American on your father's side of the family, and you can also relate to all the historical and social characteristics and conditions described in Genesis chapter 49 and Deuteronomy chapter 28, then you can be completely sure that according to the prophecies you are descended from the original Israelite nation! The blessings of Genesis forty-nine and Deuteronomy thirty-three literally indicate that the descendants of the original Hebrew Israelites are residing in North, South, and Central America in the last days! The Israelites inhabiting North America are indicated by the prophetic blessings of Gad, Reuben, and Judah. The blessings of Issachar and Zebulun indicates Central America. The Caribbean are indicated by the prophetic blessings of Joseph, Benjamin, Simeon and Levi! And South America is indicated through the prophetic blessings of Napthali and Asher!

North America and Canada

The blessings of the tribe of Gad indicate North America and Canada as places where a major group of Israelites will be found!

> << Genesis 49:19 >> [Gad, a troop shall overcome him: but he shall overcome at the last.]

The troop referred to is the U.S. Cavalry. The U.S. Calvary was used to commit terrorism, slaughter, and genocide against the indigenous North American-Indians!

THE TRUTH

<< Deuteronomy 33:20 >> [And of Gad he said, Blessed be he that enlargeth Gad: he dwelleth as a lion, and he teareth the arm with the crown of the head]

The American Indians lived close to the earth as hunters and warriors, as a lion. This action of tearing the arm refers to the Blood Brother ritual of the indigenous American-Indians, where the two people make a small cut in their arms and then bring the two cuts together to become blood brothers. The crown of the head refers to the bonnet with feathers, often worn by the indigenous American-Indians!

If you wanted to describe the indigenous North American-Indians, you would have to tell how the Caucasians took their land, mention the Blood Brother ritual of the North American-Indians, and describe the bonnet with feathers that only the North American-Indians use! Now that is exactly how the Bible indicates North America as a place where Israelites will be found in the last days; acknowledging the indigenous customs of the American-Indians of North America!

The next blessing to disclose North America as a habitation of the Israelites is that of Reuben. <<_Genesis_49:3_>> leads us to Florida, and the Everglades as places in North America where Israelites would be found in the last days:

<< Genesis 49:3 >> [Reuben thou art my first born, my might, and the beginning of my strength, the excellency of dignity, and of power: unstable as water.]

Excellency of dignity relates to the proud customs of the American-Indians, and also how they had preserved many of the Israelite customs. The Seminole American-Indians maintain Biblical custom by wearing turbans, and fringes:

<< Deuteronomy 22:12 >> [Thou shalt make thee fringes upon the quarters of thy vesture, wherewith thou coverest thyself.]

The wearing of fringes has always been an important Israelite custom. In addition, the Seminole American-Indians, the Navaho, and other American-Indians have a lot of Hebrew words in their languages. In fact, when the Europeans came to America, they found the Indian languages to be dialects of the Hebrew language! The American-Indian prophets wrote the Book of Mormons, about their Israelite history and migration. This book, written on gold plates, was found in a cave in North America. It was later adopted by the Mormon religion.

<< Deuteronomy 33:6 >> [Let Reuben live, and not die; and let not his men be few.]

This blessing was included because the U.S. Cavalry was trying to take the land by exterminating the American-Indians. The colonizers say, "The only good Indian is a dead Indian." If you can find it, read *The History of the American Indians*, by James Adair.

The blessing of Judah also designates North America as a geographical region where Israelites would be living in the last days:

<< Genesis 49:8 >> [...thine hand shall be at the neck of thine enemies]

THE TRUTH

This verse has to be referring to North America, because America has been the head or leader of European and Western society and the world economically, politically, and militarily. The United Nations building is located here. North America is the neck of the enemy.

> << Genesis 49:10 >> *[The scepter shall not depart from Judah, nor a lawgiver from between his feet, until Shiloh come* (Jesus Christ)*; and unto him* (Christ) *shall the gathering of the people be.]*

Christ is returning to gather the descendants of the original Israelites into a nation again. The last Judite king to rule was Zedekiah, about two thousand six hundred years ago. Because of wickedness, rulership of the kingdom was taken away from the Judite kings and passed on to Levi during the Maccabeeian kingdom. The Romans destroyed the Maccabees kingdom, and the three tribes were scattered and taken into captivity. Christ will restore the kingdom, and set up 12,000 princes out of each tribe, to rule the kingdom of Heaven forever!

When trying to understand scriptures, it is important to remember that the word Judah is not only a tribal name, but also the name of the nation, because after the death of Solomon the kingdom was divided in two. The northern part was called Israel, and the southern was called Judah. Very often when you see the word Judah in the scriptures, it is referring to all twelve tribes, because at the time the prophets were writing those scriptures Judah was the name used for the entire nation, to include all twelve tribes! Here is an example:

> << Zechariah 12:7-9 >> *[The Lord also shall save the tents (inhabitants of the nation) of Judah first, that the glory of the house of David; and the glory of the inhabitants of Jerusalem do not magnify themselves against Judah.]*

Tents represent the entire nation, not just the tribe; for example:

> << Jeremiah 30:18 >> *[Thus saith the Lord, I will bring again the captivity of Jacob's tents, and have mercy on his dwelling places.]*

No one is to lord over the nation, all glory is to God. The Most High God does not want any person or group to glorify themselves over the twelve tribes. The glory is to the Father alone, not to man!

You can prove that the word Judah in this case means the nation and not the specific tribe because verse one says, *[..The word of the Lord to Israel.]* However, at that time the nation was being called Judah!

> << Zechariah 12:8 >> *[In that day shall the Lord defend the inhabitants of Jerusalem; and he that is feeble among them in that day shall be as David; and the house of David shall be as Gods* (referring to the government: 12,000 out of each tribe: Revelation Chapter 7)*, and as the angels of the Lord before them!]*

We see that without a doubt, there is a great future for the original descendants of the Hebrew Israelites, although we have nothing now and are constantly being disrespected while the heathens have everything. But the one thing we have as a people that the heathens don't have is a future.

In prophecy, the Bible often refers to Christ by his ancestral name, David. It was Israelite custom to call a person by their ancestor's name!

THE TRUTH

<< *Ezekiel 34:23,24* >> *[And I set up one shepherd over them, and he shall feed them, even my servant David* (referring to Christ*); he shall feed them, and he shall be their shepherd. And I the Lord will be their God, and my servant David a prince among them; I the Lord have spoken it.]*

But we know that Christ is the prince and the shepherd referred to here, not David the son of Solomon. The prophecy was referring to Christ by his ancestral name. We had kings in Israel, but this was against the will of the Lord God YAHAWAH:

<< *First Samuel Chapter 8:4-8* >> *[Then all the elders of Israel gathered themselves together and came to Samuel unto Ramah, And said unto him, Behold, thou art old, and thy sons walk not in thy ways: now make us a king to judge us like all the nations. But the thing displeased Samuel, when they said, Give us a king to judge us.*

And Samuel prayed unto the Lord. And the Lord said unto Samuel, Hearken unto the voice of the people in all that they say unto thee: for they have not rejected thee, but they have rejected me, that I should not reign over them.

According to all the works which they have done since the day that I brought them up out of Egypt even unto this day, wherewith they have forsaken me, and served other gods, so do they also unto thee.]

The Hebrew Israelite government was initially a government by counsel and judges, it was in a way the first democracy. This is exactly the same kind of government that the Europeans found among the American Indians and decided to copy it when they created the United States. Government by an elected counsel and a commander in Chief came from the American Indians; nothing started with the Greeks.

<< *Jeremiah 33:17,18* >> *[For thus saith the Lord; David shall never want a man to sit upon the throne of the house of Israel.]*

This is because Christ, as the Son of God, will be our King:

<< *Luke 1:31,32* >> *[And, Behold, thou shall call his name Jesus He shall be great, and shall be called the son of the Highest: and the Lord shall give him the throne of his father David: And he shall reign over the house of Jacob forever; and of his kingdom there shall be no end.]*

THE TRUTH

Central America

The Blessing of the tribe of Issachar, indicates Mexico as one of the locations where the Israelites would be found in the last days:

>> *<< Genesis 49:14,15 >> [Issachar is a strong ass couching down between two burdens: And he saw that rest was good, and the land that it was pleasant; and bowed his shoulder to bear, and became a servant unto tribute.]*

The Mexicans are often pictured as very hard working, and they used a donkey with two large baskets of burden on each side, to transport merchandise (an ass with two burdens)! Secondly, the Mexicans are commonly depicted resting under a large sombrero hat. They celebrate many fiestas, which are days of rest and celebration.

The savage invaders from Spain forced the indigenous Mexican Indians to work as slaves for life. For centuries, few Mexican farmers owned land. Most farmers worked on haciendas, which are large estates, owned by hacendos (hacienda owners). This system bounded the farmers to the haciendas for life; a form of slavery.

The scripture describes the Mexican Indians well, in such a way that it could pertain to no other group. The indigenous people of Central America are frequently depicted with a donkey, having two loads of merchandise on each side of it and the man is seen resting under the sombrero hat. Also he wears a poncho with fringes.

The Mexican Indian customs are handed down from the original Israelites. Recall that fringes pertain to Israelite laws and customs, which is why the American-Indians used them extensively on their garments:

>> *<< Numbers 15:38 >> [Speak unto the children of Israel, and bid them that they make them fringes in the borders of their garments throughout their generations.]*

The blessings of Zebulun also serve to define the indigenous Central American Indians as Israelites; the area ranging from Guatemala to Panama:

>> *<< Genesis 49:13 >> [Zebulun shall dwell at the haven of the sea; and he shall be for an haven of ships.]*

This haven of ships can only be the Panama Canal. To get from the Atlantic to the Pacific Ocean, the ships must go through the Panama Canal to save valuable time and fuel! This landmark, the Panama Canal, is here being called the heaven of ships. It identifies the American-Indians of Central America to be descended from the Israelites! There is no other geographical area in the Western Hemisphere matching that description.

THE TRUTH

The Caribbean

The blessings of Joseph denominate the tropical islands of the Caribbean (such as Cuba, Puerto Rico) as places where the descendants of the Israelites will be found in the last days. Joseph had two sons Ephraim and Manasseh. Ephraim is often referred to by his father's name, Joseph.

<< *Genesis 49:22* >> [*Joseph is a fruitful bough by a well; whose branches run over the wall.*]

The Puerto Ricans and the other Hispanic American-Indians are often stigmatized as having many children:, being fruitful.

<< *Genesis 49:25* >> [*...The Almighty, who shall bless thee with blessings of the deep that lieth under, blessings of the breast and of the womb.*]

The deep that lieth under refers to the ocean. Therefore, this must be pertaining to islands. The blessings of the deep refer to the good tropical weather, and other blessings of the sea. Blessings of the breast and of the womb pertain to motherhood and childbearing.

<< *Deuteronomy 33:13 to 17* >> [*And of Joseph he said, Blessed of the Lord be his land, for the precious things of heaven, for the dew, and for the deep that lieth beneath... And for the precious things of the earth and for the fullness thereof.*]

These conditions are found on the tropical islands of the West Indies. To this day, the imperialists have been destroying, stealing, and exploiting the resources of the islands. The people are denied economic self-determination and political power. Death squads are constantly murdering the leaders of the indigenous people. As a result, the indigenous people suffer poverty, discrimination, miseducation, and more. They are forced to live in harsh, crowded conditions, resulting in a high incidence of violence, incest, and child abuse.

<< *Deuteronomy 33:17* >>: [*...they are the ten thousand of Ephraim, and they are the thousands of Manasseh.*]

Joseph had two sons, Ephraim and Manasseh. Only the islanders of indigenous American Indian and African-American descent are Israelites. The ones with Caucasian fathers are not Israelites, because it is the genealogy along the lines of the father only that determines true nationality; this is according to Biblical law!

The blessings of Simeon and Levi denote the Island of Hispaniola as a geographical location of the Israelites in the last days:

<< *Genesis 49:5* >> [*Simeon and Levi are brethren; instruments of cruelty are in their habitations.*]

All the tribes are brethren, but it means that the two tribes would live closely together as two countries on the same island: the Haitian Republic and the Dominican Republic!

THE TRUTH

The Haitians were the first people to successfully revolt against colonial slavery in the Western Hemisphere. They independently and singularly defeated the Caucasians several times in battle, and set up the first free and independent nation in the Western Hemisphere.

Also it was the Haitians that masterminded the liberation of South America from European colonial forces! The Haitian President Petion was called: "L'auteur de la Liberte de L'Amerique du Sude", meaning "Author of the liberation of South America". Simon Bolivar, who was one of the ambassadors from South America who had come to Haiti seeking military help, gave him this title!

The Haitian forces helped to liberate Venezuela, Peru, Bolivia and others. However, in recent times imperialistic forces have infiltrated the South American governments with economic and political terrorists. They use covert activities, false religions, mind control, and propaganda to oppress and exploit the indigenous native American people!

The Blessing of the tribe of Benjamin also directs us to the Caribbean as a place that would be inhabited by the descendants of the original Israelites in the last days:

<< *Genesis 49:27* >> *[Benjamin shall ravin as a wolf: in the morning he shall devour the prey, and at night he shall divide the spoil.]*

Jamaicans are a people of grassroots revolution. For example they are known for the revolutionary themes in their songs.

<< *Deuteronomy 33:12* >> *[And of Benjamin he said, The beloved of the Lord shall dwell in safety by him; and the Lord shall cover him all the day long, and he shall dwell between his shoulders.]*

This scripture tells us of a tropical island location. The shoulders of God are probably referring to the seas and the sky that envelops the islands with tropical weather.

The blessings of the tribe of Dan designate the chain of islands ranging from the Virgin Islands to Trinidad and Tobago as a region where Israelites would be found living in the last days.

<< *Genesis 49:17* >> *[Dan shall be a serpent by the way, an adder in the path.]*

A string of about one hundred islands, beginning with the Virgin Islands, forms the shape of a serpent. They end with Trinidad and Tobago as the head of that geographical serpent, near two channels. One channel is called Dragon's Mouth, and the other is called Serpent's Mouth.

This is the only grouping of islands in the great way or path called the Atlantic Ocean that forms the shape of a serpent! During the European invasion of the Americas, many Asiatic people were brought there in chains and forced to work as slaves.

<< *Judges 5:17* >> *[Gilead abode beyond Jordan: and why did Dan remain in ships? Asher continued on the sea shore, and abode in his breaches.]*

The Danites have always lived their lives by the sea. And this also is the exact custom and lifestyle of the indigenous Carib American-Indians! Asher's blessing also identifies Brazil, a very extensive coastline in that region.

THE TRUTH

<< *Deuteronomy 33:22* >>: [*And of Dan he said, is a lion's whelp* (a young lion is fierce*): he shall leap from Bashan.*]

The word Caribbean means cannibals. It refers to the fierceness of the attacks that the Carib Indians would launch against the European imperialists who were invading their islands! The phrase "He shall leap" refers to the raiding and pillaging of the Caribs against the colonial settlers.

South America

The blessings of the tribe of Asher identify the region from Colombia to Uruguay, including Brazil, as one of the geographical locations where Israelites will be living in the last days.

<< *Genesis 49:20* >> [*Out of Asher his bread shall be fat, and he shall yield royal dainties.*]

South America is very rich in minerals, vegetation, and cattle. The land is very plentiful. Consider the Amazon forests of Brazil, which are rich in mineral, and timber and also the oil fields of Colombia, and Venezuela.

<< *Deuteronomy 33:24-27* >> [*And of Asher he said, Let Asher be blessed with children; let him be acceptable to his brethren, And let him dip his foot in oil. Thy shoes shall be iron and brass and as thy days, so shall thy strength be.*
    There is none like unto the God of Jeshurun, who rideth up on the heaven in thy help, and in his excellency on the sky. The eternal Lord is thy refuge, and underneath are the everlasting arms: and he shall thrust out the enemy from before thee; and shall say Destroy them.]

The Brazilian American-Indians and African-Americans will eventually prevail against their colonial oppressors!

The blessings of the tribe of Napthali discloses the area of Argentina and Chile as a geographical region inhabited by the descendants of the Israelites in the last days:

<< *Deuteronomy 33:23* >> [*And of Naphtali he said, O Napthali, satisfied with favor, and full with the blessings of the Lord: possess thou the West and the South.*]

As far South as you can get in the Western World is the tip of South America: Argentina and Chile. This gives us another important geographical location where a major portion of the original tribes of Hebrew Israelites will be found in the last days!

It has been proven in many ways that the original Israelites are of Asiatic ancestry, and that the only true descendants of the original Hebrew Israelites are the people called African-Americans, and American-Indian/Hispanics of North, South, and Central America!

Genesis forty-nine and Deuteronomy thirty-three prophetically indicate North, South, and Central America as places where the bulk of the descendants of the twelve tribes of Israel will be found in the last days! Undoubtedly, the African-Americans and American-Indians living in those regions match the prophetic, social, ethnic, and all the historical conditions that would serve to identify the Israelites according to Deuteronomy chapter twenty-eight.

Because of the Biblical and historical evidence found in Deuteronomy twenty-eight, and the geographical evidence indicated by Genesis forty-nine, we can say beyond any doubt that the African-Americans and American-Indian/Hispanics are the original descendants of the Hebrew Israel. Obviously, the Caucasians who are claiming to be Jews in Palestine today are impostors!

The ancestors of the American-Indians migrated to America by ships after the king of Babylon had expelled them from their land in Samaria (Israel). The remaining three tribes of Israel plus remnants of the other tribes, called the nation of Judah, were overthrown and expelled from Palestine by the Romans in AD 70. After which they sought to establish settlements in North West Africa and certain provinces of the Roman Empire, such as Spain and Portugal. Hebrew Israelite communities can be found in many countries today: Asia, the Pacific, Africa, remnants among the Gypsies and the Sephardim of Spain and Yemen.

The Hebrew Israelites suffered from constant political and religious persecution. Eventually the Roman Catholic Church, using a system of torture they call the inquisition, succeeded in exterminating and expelling all the Israelites out of the Roman Empire and its colonies. The Africans and Arabs eventually captured the Israelite refugees, who sold the original Jews into slavery to the Americas for guns, wine, and silver. The scriptures refer to the Israelites as the sons of God:

> << Isaiah 41:8 >> [But thou, Israel, art my servant, Jacob whom I have chosen, the seed of Abraham, my friend.]
> << Exodus 4:22 >> [And thou shalt say unto Pharaoh, Thus saith the Lord, Israel is my son, even my first born.]

An Israelite is ordained a prince and a son of the Lord God YAHAWAH only by conforming to the image of God by upholding the laws and understanding the principles and wisdom of the Bible. An Israelite honors Jesus Christ as his Lord and Savior.

The African-Americans and American-Indians are the original seed of Israel; destined to put on the incorruptible image and likeness of the Lord God YAHAWAH. The Israelites must first repent of their evil ways and learn to be respectful, loving, and obedient. They must return to their true Biblical custom and identity. Above all, they must accept the real Jesus Christ as Lord, Savior, and the only intercessor between man and God! The Israelites must also seek to teach the Biblical truth to the world.

The Original Hebrew Language

The Language is an important part of a person's culture and identity. The original Hebrew language spoken by the Israelites is very different from the so-called Modern Hebrew. The original characters were different, and the sounds were very different. The impostor Caucasians who are claiming to be Jews do not speak nor write the true original Hebrew!

When the Israelites were in captivity under the Babylonians in 440 BC Ezra the scribe adopted the so-called Assyrian (Ezra Script) characters for the Hebrew language. And the Hebrew has always been read from right to left. I will list the true Hebrew alphabet, followed by the original sounds. Israelites must learn the original Hebrew! Hebrew is our language as Israelites, and therefore it is part of our identity, heritage and laws! The Lord YAHAWAH commands that we, the twelve tribes of Israel, return to our own language.

THE TRUTH

<< Zephaniah 3:9 >> *[For then will I return to the people a pure language, that they may all call upon the name of the Lord, to serve him with one consent.]*

The above diagram illustrates the original Hebrew alphabet. The word Hebrew is derived from the name of Eber as in << Genesis 10:21 and 24 >>. The word means from the past: as in ancient. Because at the time of the confusion of tongues and the rebellion at Babel, Eber chose to keep the customs of the past, which were handed down from Adam. Adam was the first Hebrew!

THE PURE HEBREW

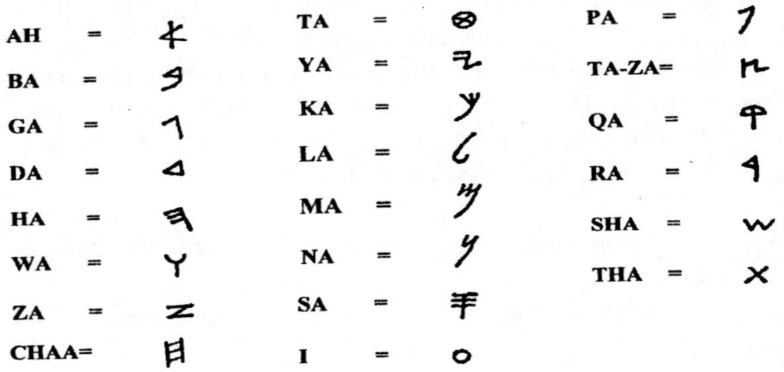

AH	=	𝄐	TA	=	⊗	PA	=	7
BA	=	𝟛	YA	=	⇃	TA-ZA	=	ᴨ
GA	=	˥	KA	=	ƴ	QA	=	ϙ
DA	=	◁	LA	=	ℓ	RA	=	˧
HA	=	�	MA	=	ᵐ	SHA	=	w
WA	=	Y	NA	=	⅄	THA	=	X
ZA	=	z	SA	=	ⅲ			
CHAA	=	⅄	I	=	o			

<< Jeremiah 10:16 >> *[The portion of Jacob is not like them: for he is the first and former of all things; and Israel is the rod of his inheritance: The Lord of host is his name.]*

<< Acts 26:14 >> *[And when we were all fallen to the earth, I heard a voice speaking unto me, and saying in the Hebrew tongue]*

The above verse proves that Jesus Christ spake in Hebrew to the people. The gospel was first taught in Hebrew, by Hebrews speaking to other Hebrews. It was not originally in Greek or Latin! Hebrew is our language, it is important and we must learn and preserve the original custom, it is a major part of our identity! Knowing the original Hebrew language allows us to know the proper way of pronouncing Hebrew words. If we want to say God's name properly we have to know the true Hebrew. We have no "Jay" or "ho" sound in the original Hebrew, therefore God's name cannot be "Jehovah". It is YAHAWAH, which means He is to be, or I AM. The name of Jesus in Hebrew cannot be "Yashouah, or anything similar because we have no "ou", "o", or similar vowel sounds in the pure Hebrew language. The true name of the Savior (Jesus) is Yahawashy, which means He saves, or savior. The name Christ means Anointed or Chosen; the name Christ in Hebrew is Mashayak. To say Jesus Christ in Hebrew we say Mashayak Yahawashy.

THE TRUTH

HISTORY AND PROPHECY

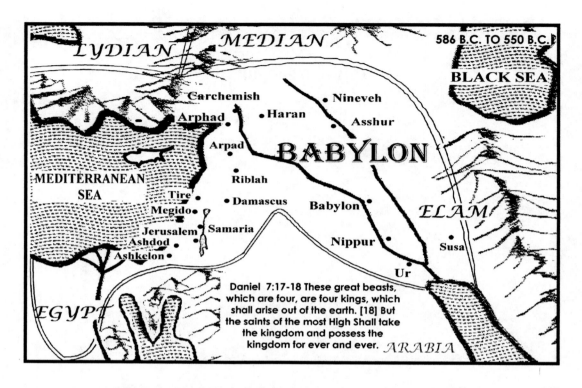

Daniel 7:17-18 These great beasts, which are four, are four kings, which shall arise out of the earth. [18] But the saints of the most High Shall take the kingdom and possess the kingdom for ever and ever.

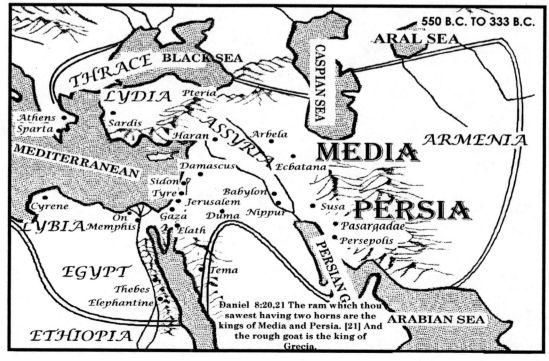

Daniel 8:20,21 The ram which thou sawest having two horns are the kings of Media and Persia. [21] And the rough goat is the king of Grecia.

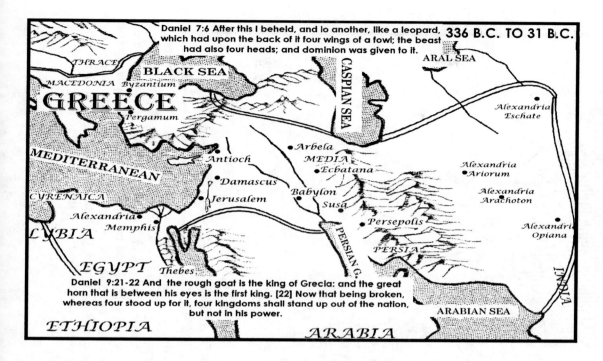

Daniel 7:6 After this I beheld, and lo another, like a leopard, which had upon the back of it four wings of a fowl; the beast had also four heads; and dominion was given to it.

336 B.C. TO 31 B.C.

Daniel 9:21-22 And the rough goat is the king of Grecia: and the great horn that is between his eyes is the first king. [22] Now that being broken, whereas four stood up for it, four kingdoms shall stand up out of the nation, but not in his power.

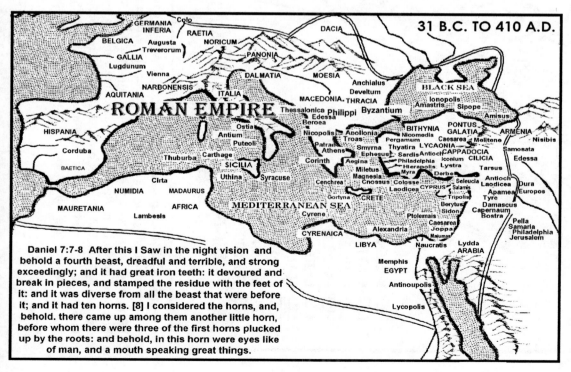

31 B.C. TO 410 A.D.

Daniel 7:7-8 After this I Saw in the night vision and behold a fourth beast, dreadful and terrible, and strong exceedingly; and it had great iron teeth: it devoured and break in pieces, and stamped the residue with the feet of it: and it was diverse from all the beast that were before it; and it had ten horns. [8] I considered the horns, and, behold. there came up among them another little horn, before whom there were three of the first horns plucked up by the roots: and behold, in this horn were eyes like of man, and a mouth speaking great things.

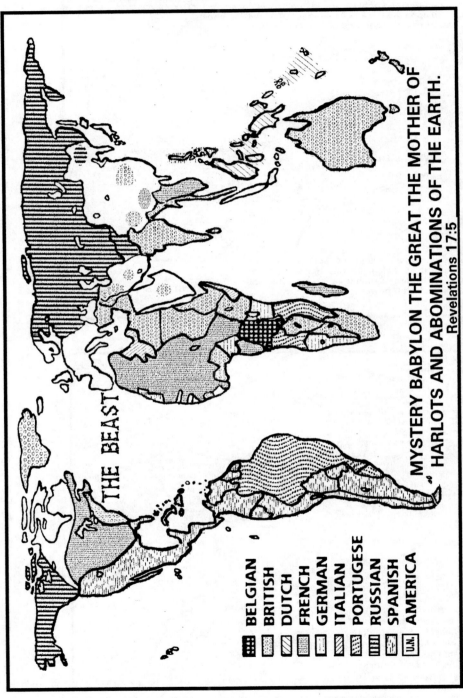

THE BEAST

MYSTERY BABYLON THE GREAT THE MOTHER OF HARLOTS AND ABOMINATIONS OF THE EARTH.
Revelations 17:5

BELGIAN
BRITISH
DUTCH
FRENCH
GERMAN
ITALIAN
PORTUGESE
RUSSIAN
SPANISH
AMERICA

Daniel 7:23-26 Thus he said, The fourth beast shall be the fourth kingdom upon the earth, which shall be diverse from all kingdoms, and shall devour the whole earth, and shall tread it down, and break it in pieces. [24] And the ten horns out of this kingdom are ten kings that shall rise: and another shall rise after them; and he shall be diverse from the first, and he shall subdue three kings. [25] And he shall speak great words against the most High, and shall wear out the saints of the most High, and think to change times and laws: and they shall be given into his hand until a time and times and the dividing of time. [26] But the judgment shall sit, and they shall take away his dominion, to consume and to destroy it unto the end.

FROM BABYLON TO AMERICA

Now that we have explored the true identity of the nations, it is a good idea to get a brief historical perspective on the different kingdoms that have dominated the world. The Biblical prophecies pertaining to this history were concisely depicted in the seventh chapter of the book of Daniel. In 555 BCE the prophet Daniel wrote these prophecies while in captivity under the Babylonian empire:

<< *Daniel 7:1-28* >> *[In the first year of Belshazzar king of Babylon* (we were under captivity in Babylon at the time Daniel wrote the prophecies) *Daniel had a dream and visions of his head upon his bed: then he wrote the dream, and told the sum of the matters.]*

Recall, Nimrod founded the Babylonian Empire about four thousand years ago. It became a world power about 2,620 years ago, under Nabupaluser and Nebuchadnezzar. Nebuchadnezzar, the son of Nabopolassar, king of Babylon, was first succeeded by Evil-Merodach, his son. Two years later his brother-in-law, Neriglissar, murdered him. Neriglissar reigned for four years, and was succeeded by his son Leborosoarchod, who reigned for only nine months. At his death Belshazzar, the son of Evil-Merodach, was ruler for seventeen years. It was at this time that Cyrus attacked by surprise and took the city on the night of the feast! Cyrus killed Belshazzar during the great feast noted in << Daniel 5:1,30,31 >>.

<2> *[Daniel spake and said, I saw in my vision by night, and, the four winds of the heaven strove upon the great sea* (meaning many nations were at war). *And four great beasts came up from the sea, diverse one from another.]*

The term beast symbolically refer to nations:

<17 > *[These great beasts, which are four, are four kings, which shall arise out of the earth.]*

There would be four world ruling empires: the Babylonian empire (606-538 BCE) the Media Persian empire (538-330 BCE), the Greek empires (330-30 BCE), and the Roman Empire (30 BCE to the present, because the Western world is ruled by the descendants of the Greeks and Romans)!

<4> *[...The First was like a lion, and had eagle's wings:]*

A lion was used to represent the Babylonian empire, (read: Isaiah 5:29, Jeremiah 4:7); as well as eagle's wing; (Ezekiel 17:3,7, Jeremiah 48:40), for they were swift in battle.

[I beheld till the wings thereof were plucked, and it was lifted up from the earth, and made stand upon the feet as a man, and a man's heart was given to it.]

Nebuchadnezzar, the proud king of Babylon, was given a man's heart. He was turned into a very humble person. This was after the Most High cursed him, by changing him into an ox and made to eat grass. This is documented in Chapter four of Daniel.

THE TRUTH

<5> *[And behold another beast, a second, like to a bear,]*

The bear stands on two feet, symbolic of the Medes and the Persians who ruled the empire together. They were also known for their cruelty, like a bear.

[And it raised up itself on one side, and it had three ribs in the mouth of it between the teeth of it.]

This Medo-Persian Empire conquered Egypt, Babylon, and Lydia; these were the three ribs that strengthened the Medo-Persian Empire.

[And they say thus unto it, Arise, and devour much flesh. <6> And after this I beheld, and lo another, like a leopard.]

A leopard because swiftness represents the Greek Empire. Within twelve years the Macedonian Empire had conquered all the territory from Illyricium and the Adriatic Sea to India and Egypt.

[Which had upon the back of it four wings of a fowl; the beast had also four heads, and dominion was given to it.]

After Alexander died, his kingdom was divided among his four generals. Cassandra ruled Macedonia and Greece, Seleucus ruled Syria, Ptolemy ruled Egypt, and Lysimachus ruled Thrace and Bythynia.

<7> *[After this I saw in the night vision, behold a fourth beast, dreadful and terrible, and strong exceedingly; and it had great iron teeth: it devoured and break in pieces, and stamped the residue with the feet of it: and it was diverse from all the beasts that were before it, and it had ten horns.]*

This beast represents the Roman Empire. We are still in the Roman Empire today. The European nations and the colonies that came out of them are the descendants of the old Roman Empire. "Iron teeth" refers to the tanks and other high-technology weapons that arm the western world. No other empire had ever used atomic weapons before, which are dreadful and terrible. "Ten" represents division. Many different European nations and colonies came out of the Roman Empire, governing independently.

<8> *[I consider the horns, and, there came up among them another little horn (America), before whom there were three of the first horns plucked up by the roots]*

This little horn represents America. Those three horns, which were plucked up represent the British, the French, and the Spanish. America had to fight those three colonial powers in order to become an independent nation.

[And, behold, in this horn were eyes like the eyes of man, and a mouth speaking great things.]

America became the leader of the western world and all the heathens. The Western world promoted itself and claims all glory to it. They idolize themselves in front of the world, making God into their image, calling

116

themselves Jews and Christians. They destroyed morality, the human rights of a man to be a man, and destroyed the family structure by elevating women over men. They openly blaspheme against God, the Bible, and persecute the true Israelites.

<11> [I beheld till the thrones were cast down, and the ancient of days did sit, whose garment was white as snow, and the hair of his head like the pure wool: his throne was like the fiery flame, and his wheels as burning fire.]

According to Bible prophecy, the judgment of God over all of the nations of the modern Roman Empire (the Western World and other heathens) will be annihilated by fire, from nuclear war, natural and supernatural disasters. The Lord God YAHAWAH is again described as having an Afroasiatic feature, woolly hair.

<10> [A fiery stream issued and came forth from before him: thousand thousands ministered unto him, and ten thousand times ten thousand stood before him: the Judgment was set, and the books were opened.

<11> I beheld then because of the great words which the horn spake: I beheld even till the beast was slain and his body destroyed, and given to the burning flame. <12> As concerning the rest of the beasts (the other nations), they had their dominion taken away: yet their lives were prolonged for a season and time.]

The destruction of America and all other nations allied to the western world is guaranteed to take place in the near future, because those nations have despised the truth, and multiplied evil and injustice. For example, the world has presented false pictures of God and Jesus as Caucasians, and maliciously claims the Khazar Caucasians to be the Jews and Israelites. Doomsday is near for the western world. There is no future for this world; only fire.

<13> [I saw in the night visions and, behold, one like the Son of Man came with the Clouds of Heaven and came to the Ancient of days, and they brought him near before him. <14> And there was given him dominion, and glory, and a kingdom, that all people, nations, and languages, should serve him: his dominion is an everlasting dominion, which shall not pass away, and his kingdom that which shall not be destroyed.]

The Son of Man is Jesus Christ. This is a description of how Jesus Christ will return the second time, to rule the earth. He will invade the world in the chariots of fire, sometimes called The Clouds of Heaven, or UFOs today. He will come to deliver the Israelites before the nuclear destruction, the natural and supernatural disasters of doomsday.

<16> [I came near unto one of them that stood by, and asked him the truth of all this. So he told me, and made me know the interpretation of the things.

<17> These great beasts, which are four, are four kings, which shall arise out of the earth. But the saints of the Most High, (the twelve tribes of Israel) shall take the kingdom, and possess the kingdom forever and ever.]

The original twelve tribes of Israel will rule the universe forever.

THE TRUTH

<< Daniel 7:19 >> [Then I would know the truth of the fourth beast, which was diverse from all the others, exceeding dreadful, whose teeth were of iron, and his nails of brass; which devoured, and brake in pieces, and stamped the residue with his feet; <20> And of the ten horns that were in his head, and of the other which came up (America), and before whom three fell; even of that horn that had eyes, and a mouth that spake great things, whose look was more stout than his fellows.]

The fourth beast symbolizes the western world, also known as the modern Roman Empire. The ten horns represent the many different groups of European nations. "The Little Horn" represents America, which won her independence against the British, the French, and the Spanish. These three heads gave birth to America. America looks more stout and is in every way more powerful than all the other European nations.

<21> [I beheld, and the same horn made war with the Saints, and prevailed against them; <22> until the Ancient of days came, and judgment was given to the saints of the Most High; and the time came that the saints possessed the kingdom]

The original twelve tribes of Israel are the Saints. The western world has raged economic, psychological, and physical war against the African-Americans and American-Indians. The Israelites have been in slavery up to now. The chains were removed from their hands and feet, then placed upon their minds and hearts. At the return of Christ the Israelites will be delivered from the afflictions, plagues, and nuclear destruction. Then they will be set up to rule forever, and to judge and punish the other nations for their evil.

<23> [Thus he said the fourth beast shall be the fourth kingdom upon the earth, which shall be diverse from all kingdoms, and shall devour the whole earth and shall tread it down and break it in pieces.]

The Western world has devoured the earth through greed, colonialism, exploitation, and perversions. They have polluted the environment: the air, the ocean, food, and water. They have caused many plants and animals to become extinct!

<24> [And the ten horns of this kingdom are ten kings that shall arise and another shall arise after them and he shall be diverse from the first, and he shall subdue three kings. <25> And he shall speak great words against the Most High, and shall wear out the saints of the Most High, and think to change times and laws, and they shall be given into his hands until a time and times and the dividing of times]

The western world has spoken words of blasphemy, setting up "white supremacy" and teaching false religion. They have worn out the saints, by putting the African-Americans and American-Indians (Israelites) into slavery. The Europeans have changed the calendar, making the year start in January when it should start in the spring; making the day start at midnight, when it should start at sundown! They have hanged laws by allowing homosexuality and abortion, and teach perverted ideas: saying that a woman is equal to a man. They have perverted the dress code and dietary laws. They have denied a man his human rights to choose how many wives he needs, and to be king over his household. The good news is, soon the Most High will send Christ to deliver the twelve tribes of Israel, and restore our kingdom!

[But the judgment shall sit, and they shall take away his dominion to consume and to destroy it onto the end. And the kingdom and the dominion and the greatness of the kingdom under the whole heaven shall be given to the people of the saints of the Most High (the Israelites)*, whose kingdom is an everlasting kingdom and all dominion shall serve and obey him. Hitherto is the end of the matter.]*

The judgment and the destruction of the Western world and all the heathen nations is guaranteed by the will, the prophecy, and the power of God. The doom of the Caucasian domination of the world was foretold and destined to occur, even from the foundation of the world:

<< Genesis 25:21 to 26 >> [And Isaac entreated the Lord for his wife, because she was barren: and the Lord was entreated of him, and Rebecca his wife conceived. <22> And the children struggled together within her; and she said, If it be so, why am I thus? <23> And the Lord said unto her, Two nations (Israel from Jacob, and the Caucasians from Esau) *are in thy womb, and two manner of people shall be separated from thy bowels; the one people shall be stronger than the other people* (The Israelites are humanly stronger)*; and the elder shall serve the younger.]*

The Edomites are destined to be dominated by the Israelites in the kingdom to come, according to this prophecy!

<24> [And when her days to be delivered were fulfilled, behold, there were twins in her womb. <25> And the first came out Red, all over like an hairy garment and they called his name Esau (The word Esau means wasted away is he)*. <26> And after that came his brother out, and his hand took hold on Esau's heel; and his name was called Jacob.]*

Jacob pulling on Esau's heels symbolizes how the Israelites will eventually recapture the leadership of the world from the Edomites, after the Second Coming of Jesus Christ.

<< The Apocrypha 2 Esdras 6:7-10 >> [Then answered I and said, What shall be the parting asunder of the times? or when shall be the end of the first, and the beginning of it that followeth? <8> And he said unto me, From Abraham unto Isaac, when Jacob and Esau were born of him, Jacob's hand held first the heel of Esau. <9> For Esau is the end of the world, and Jacob is the beginning of it that followeth.]

Jacob was the father of the Israelites, and his name was changed to Israel:

<< Genesis 32:28 >> [Thy name shall be called no more Jacob, but Israel: for a prince hast thou power with the God and with men, and hast prevailed.]

Jacob's twelve sons became the original twelve tribes of Israel; and are today being called the African-Americans and the American-Indians of North, South, Central America, as well as the Caribbean!

THE TRUTH

The original name of the Caucasian's nations is Edom. Edom is a Hebrew word meaning red, because most Caucasians are reddish in complexion.

<< Genesis 36:8 >> *[Thus dwelt Esau in mount Seir: Esau is Edom.]*

<< Genesis 36:15 >> *[These were the Dukes of the sons of Esau: the sons of Eliaphaz the firstborn son of Esau; duke Teman, duke Omar, duke zepho, duke kenaz.]*

Some Edomites still title themselves Dukes today! The Bible uses Esau and Jacob in many allegories.

<< Malachi 1:3 >> *[I have loved you, saith the Lord. Yet ye say, wherein has thou loved us? Was not Esau Jacob's brother? Saith the lord: yet I love Jacob, And I hated Esau.]*

<< Obadiah 1:10 >> *[For thy violence against thy brother Jacob shame shall cover thee, and thou shall be cut off forever.]*

<< Revelation 13:10 >> *[He that leadeth into captivity shall go into captivity: He that killeth with the sword must be killed with the sword. Here is the patience and the faith of the saints.]*

The scriptures predicted the first coming of Christ, and the destruction of Jerusalem by the Romans, as well as the destruction of the modern Roman Empire, popularly known as the Western world. The prophecies also predicted the Second Coming of Jesus Christ as judge and ruler. An angel came to Daniel to explain:

<< Daniel 9:23-27 >> *[At the beginning of thy supplications the commandment came forth, and I am come to shew thee; for thou art greatly beloved: therefore understand the matter, and consider the vision.*
<24> Seventy weeks are determined upon thy people and upon thy holy city, to finish the transgression, and to make an end of sins, and to make reconciliation for iniquity, and to bring in everlasting righteousness, and to seal up the vision and prophecy, and to anoint the most Holy...

Knowing what the angel meant by seventy weeks is the key to understanding this prophecy. The Israelites had also reckoned time by what is called sabbatic weeks and sabbatic years, a year for a day, seven days representing seven years. For example:

<< Leviticus 25:8 >> *[And thou shalt number seven Sabbaths of years unto thee, seven times seven years; and the space of seven Sabbaths of years shall be unto thee forty and nine years.]*

Therefore to get the actual time span, multiply the seven years contained in each week into the seventy weeks, which equals four hundred and ninety years!

According to the angel, Christ's first coming was to occur within four hundred and ninety years! This first coming of Christ was for the purpose of redeeming us from our sins by his sacrifice of himself! He is the Lamb of the LORD God YAHAWAH, which takes away the sins of the world! The angel went on explaining the time intervals in detail,

THE TRUTH

<< Daniel 9:25-27 >> *[Know therefore and understand, that from the going forth of the commandment to restore and to build Jerusalem unto the Messiah the Prince shall be seven weeks, and threescore and two weeks: the street shall be built again, and the wall, even in troublous times.*

The commandment to rebuild the temple and the resettlement of the Israelites in Jerusalem was commissioned by Artaxerxes, and was directed by Ezra and Nehemiah. From that point to the beginning of the ministry of Christ is four hundred and eighty-three years, or sixty-nine weeks!

<26> And after threescore and two weeks shall the Messiah be cut off, but not for himself (Christ died for the redemption of Israel*): and the people of the prince that shall come* (the Romans coming to destroy Jerusalem) *shall destroy the city and the sanctuary; and the end thereof shall be with a flood, and unto the end of the war desolations are determined.*

The prince that shall come refers to the Romans invading Palestine. It was a Roman general named Vespatian Titus who looted and destroyed Jerusalem in AD 70, burning the temple and the city, and killing and selling into slavery all of the Israelites that did not escape by running into Africa and Asia! Now referring back to Christ, the angel explains:

<27> And he shall confirm the covenant with many for one week (seven year ministry of Christ*): and he shall cause the sacrifice and the oblation to cease, and for the overspreading of abominations he shall make it desolate, even until the consummation, and that determined shall be poured upon the desolate.]*

By offering himself on the cross, Christ fulfilled all the prophecies concerning himself as our Redeemer and all other relevant scriptures. He was the beginning and the end of all things. There could be no other after him! Also, he was the last sacrifice for all times for those that would believe in his words! After his death and resurrection, he was received in heaven; crowned King of Kings, and Lord of Lords!

The later part of this prophecy predicts the judgment that was to come upon Israel for all their abominations and simpleness. Christ himself referred to this scripture:

<< Mark 13:14 >> *[But when ye shall see the abomination of desolation, spoken of by Daniel the prophet, standing* (in the holy place*) where it ought not, let him that readeth understand.]*

This sign would refer to the Romans coming to destroy and plunder Jerusalem in AD 70. Also this same sign is to be manifested in the days before the Second Coming of Christ. We see today that the Caucasians have taken over Palestine again, this time under the false religion of Judaism, maliciously pretending to be Jews. They are described by Christ and Daniel as "the Abomination of Desolation, standing where it ought not!" This sign, Caucasians invading Palestine again, should be a warning that Christ will return any minute. Jesus Christ will come to judge, avenge, deliver, and establish the everlasting kingdom of Heaven on the Earth!

THE TRUTH

<< Daniel 12:1-13 >> [And at that time shall Michael stand up, the great prince which standeth for the children of thy people: and there shall be a time of trouble, such as never was since there was a nation even to that same time: and at that time thy people shall be delivered, every one that shall be found written in the book. <2> And many of them that sleep in the dust of the earth shall awake, some to everlasting life, and some to shame and everlasting contempt. <3> And they that be wise shall shine as the brightness of the firmament; and they that turn many to righteousness as the stars forever and ever.

<4> But thou, O Daniel, shut up the words, and seal the book, even to the time of the end: many shall run to and fro, and knowledge shall be increased. <5> Then I Daniel looked, and, behold, there stood other two, the one on this side of the bank of the river, and the other on that side of the bank of the river. <6> And one said to the man clothed in linen, which was upon the waters of the river, How long shall it be to the end of these wonders? <7> And I heard the man clothed in linen, which was upon the waters of the river, when he held up his right hand and his left hand unto heaven, and swear by him that liveth forever that it shall be for a time, times, and an half; and when he shall have accomplished to scatter the power of the holy people, all these things shall be finished.

<8> And I heard, but I understood not: then said I, O my Lord, what shall be the end of these things? <9> And he said, Go thy way, Daniel: for the words are closed up and sealed till the time of the end. <10> Many shall be purified, and made white, and tried; but the wicked shall do wickedly: and none of the wicked shall understand; but the wise shall understand. <11> And from the time that the daily sacrifice shall be taken away, and the abomination that maketh desolate set up, there shall be a thousand two hundred and ninety days. <12> Blessed is he that waiteth, and cometh to the thousand three hundred and five and thirty days. <13> But go thou thy way till the end be: for thou shalt rest, and stand in thy lot at the end of the days.]

THE TRUTH

The Chronicle of Time

Chapter eleven of Daniel contains detailed prophecies, documenting from the rise to the complete destruction of the Caucasians, otherwise known as the Edomites of the Bible. Daniel's prophecy starts from the events, which lead to the Caucasians coming into power by the defeat of the Media/Persian Empire, and it ends with the destruction of the evil empires in the last day prior to the Second Coming of Jesus! The references that can be used for understanding Daniel chapter eleven are First and Second Maccabees in the book of the Apocrypha, and also the works of Josephus, an Israelite who documented the historical events of the ancient world as they pertain to the Israelites!

It was at the time of the Media Persian Empire, about two thousand five hundred years ago, that Daniel wrote down the visions that were revealed to him!

<< Daniel 11:1 >> [Also in the first year of Darius the Mede, even I, stood to confirm and to strengthen him.]

After the destruction of the Babylonian Empire, when now the Medes and the Persians ruled, Daniel the Israelite was again given a high position in the new government because of his reputation of having great wisdom and understanding. He was made chief of the three presidents who were over the whole empire. But because Daniel was a stranger many wanted to destroy him.

<< Daniel 11:2 >> [And now shall I show thee the truth. Behold, there shall stand up yet three kings in Persia; and the fourth shall be far richer than they all: and by his strength and through his riches he shall stir up all against the realm of Grecia.]

Three kings: and Cyrus (539-529 BC), ruling first; his son Cambyses (529-522 BC), ruled after; and the third was Darius Hystaspes, the husband of the daughter of Cyrus (529-522 BC). Their son Xerxes, the fourth king, was far richer. It was said that although Xerxes fought many wars, his riches never decreased. The angel mentions the first three kings in order to arrive at Xerxes. Using his great wealth, Xerxes amassed a great army. Xerxes attacked Greece to avenge his father, Darius Hystaspes, who was defeated by Greece in 490 BC This gave Alexander, who would come later, a reason to fight against the Medes and Persians.

The other kings that ruled after Xerxes were not mentioned because they did not do anything to further antagonize Greece! They were: Artaxerxes Longimanus (465-424 BC), Xerxes II (424-423 BC), Darius II Nothus (423-404 BC), Artaxerxes II Mnemon (404-359 BC), Artaxerxes III Ochus (359-338 B.C), Arses (338-336 BC), and Darius III Codomannus (336-331 BC).

<< Daniel 11:3 >> [And a mighty king shall stand up, that shall rule with great dominion, and do according to his will.]

Alexander the Great (336-323 BC), son of Philip of Macedonia, was born a hundred years after the death of Xerxes. In retaliation, he attacked nations from Asia Minor to the Indus River, and into Egypt. (Daniel 8:4-8)

THE TRUTH

<< *Verse 4* >> *[And when he shall stand up, his kingdom shall be broken, and shall be divided toward the four winds of heaven; and not to his posterity, nor according to his dominion, which he ruled: for his kingdom shall be plucked up, even for others besides those.]*

Alexander died in Babylon at the age of thirty-two. It is believed that he either died from excessive drinking or from being poisoned. For fifteen years his brother, Philip Aridaeus and his sons, Alexander Aegus and Hercules, tried to rule the Macedonian kingdom; but they were all assassinated.

The kingdom was divided among his four chief generals, toward the four winds: 1) Seleucus Nicator (304-281 BC) ruled Syria and Babylon (east wind), 2) Lysimachus ruled Asia Minor (north wind), 3) Ptolemy Soter (304-283) ruled Egypt (south wind), and 4) Cassander ruled Greece and its neighboring countries (west wind). His generals were not of his posterity. They were not blood descendants of Alexander. His generals, who were in conflict, murdered all Alexander's children over the rulership.

<< *Daniel 8:22* >> *Now that being broken, whereas four stood up for it, four kingdoms shall stand up out of the nation, but not in his power.*

<< *Daniel 11:5* >> *[And the king of the south shall be strong, and one of his princes; and he shall be strong above him. And have dominion, his dominion shall be a great dominion.]*

Please note, the Ptolemies were Greek Caucasians, they were not originally Egyptians. They had invaded and exploited the Egyptians. The Ptolemies were named after the first Macedonian General to rule the southern realm (Egypt). Ptolemy of the south was strong for he had added Cyprus, Phoenicia, Caria, and more, to Egypt. Seleucus Nicator was for a time subject to Ptolemy. He broke away, and became stronger, possessing Syria, Babylon, Media, and the neighboring countries.

<< *Daniel 11:6* >> *[And in the end of years they shall join themselves together; for the king's daughter of the south shall come to the king of the north to make an agreement: but she shall not retain the power of the arm; neither shall he stand, nor his arm but she shall be given up, and they that brought her, and he that begot her, and he that strengthen her in these times.]*

Berenice, daughter of Ptolemy Philadelphia (283-246), king of Egypt, who was the son of Ptolemy Soter, and grand-son of Seleucus Nicator, was married to Antiochus Theos (262-246), king of Syria, to end a long bloody war on condition that Antiochus put away his wife Laodice and her children. The relationship with his new wife Berenice did not last. Antiochus recalled his former wife, Laodice, and her children. But Laodice, fearing Antiochus might recall Berenice the Ptolemy, caused Antiochus to be poisoned and Berenice and her son murdered (*"neither shall he stand"*). Seleucus Calinicus (246-227 BC), the son of Laodice was set upon the throne. The Egyptian servants that brought Berenice were killed, and her father Ptolemy that had strengthened her was dead.

<< *Daniel 11:7* >> *[But out of a branch of her root shall one stand up in his estate, which shall come with an army, and shall enter into the fortress of the king of the north, and shall deal against them, and shall prevail.]*

THE TRUTH

To avenge his sister, Ptolemy Euergetes (246-221 BC), the brother of Berenice, went to make war against Seleucus Calinicus. But Calinicus did not offer any resistance against the forces of Ptolemy. Therefore Euergetes took all of Asia from Mount Taurus to India, and returned to Egypt with much wealth and spoils of war including 40,000 talents of silver, precious vessels, and 2,500 images of their gods.

<<Daniel 11:8 >> *[And shall also carry captives into Egypt their Gods, with their princes, and with their precious vessels of silver and of gold; and he shall continue more years than the king of the north.]*

While in exile Calinicus died, and Ptolemy Euergetes outlived him by a few more years.

<<Daniel 11:9 >> *[So the king of the south shall come into his kingdom, and shall return into his own land.]*

As Ptolemy Euergetes was entering into Seleucus Calinicus' kingdom, he heard of a rebellion in Egypt. This caused him to return to Egypt and suppress the rebels. Otherwise, Euergetes would have totally destroyed Seleucus of the north.

<<Daniel 11:10 >> *[But his sons shall be stirred up, and shall assemble a multitude of great forces and one shall certainly come, and overflow, and pass through: then shall he return, and be stirred up, even to his fortress.]*

The sons of Calinicus were Seleucus Ceraunus (227-223 BC) and Antiochus the Great (223-187 BC). Ceraunus gathered a great army with the purpose of taking back the land that Ptolemy had taken from Calinicus. But while on a mission in Asia, he was poisoned by one of his generals because he could not pay the soldiers of his great forces. Then Ceraunus' brother Antiochus the Great passed through to become king, fulfilling the prophecy. This Antiochus retook all of the lost fortresses in Seleucia and Syria. He destroyed the Egyptian general Nicolaus in 219 BC, and came through Raphia, in Southern Palestine, to the frontier of Egypt ready to invade.

<<Daniel 11:11 >> *[And the king of the south shall be moved with choler, and shall come forth and fight with him, even with the king of the north: and he shall set forth a great multitude; but the multitude shall be given up into his hand.]*

Ptolemy Philopater (222-204 BC), son of Ptolemy Euergetes, was now ruling Egypt. He came to Raphia in order to retaliate with great strength against Antiochus of the north, who had a multitude of 62,000-foot soldiers, 6,000 horse, and 102 elephants. The battle was fierce, but Antiochus was defeated at Raphia and fled to Antioch, here he requested to negotiate peace with Ptolemy Philopater.

<<Daniel 11:12 >> *[And when he hath taken away the multitude, his heart shall be lifted up; and he shall cast down many ten thousands: but he shall not be strengthened by it.]*

Granted, Ptolemy Philopater had great success in battle against the Syrians of the north, and also had the opportunity to completely overthrow Antiochus, but he was mainly interested in a life of excessive pleasures and vanity. As a result, instead of completing his victory he decided to cut it short and make peace with the North. So all of his previous victories did not do him credit because his subjects became very angry with him for making peace with Antiochus on dishonorable terms at that, for Egypt did not get anything out of the treaty.

<<Daniel 11:13 >> *[For the king of the north shall return, and shall set forth a great multitude greater than the former, and shall certainly come after certain years with a great army and with much riches.]*

Fourteen years later Antiochus the great returned to fight against Egypt with another strong army. At this time, Philopater was dead and his four-year-old son Ptolemy Epiphanies (203-181 BC) was king.

<<Daniel 11:14 >> *[And in those times there shall many stand up against the king of the South: also the robbers of thy people shall exalt themselves to establish the vision; but they shall fall.]*

Both Antiochus and Philip, the king of Macedonia, united against Egypt. While Antiochus was fighting elsewhere, some of the nonconforming Israelites revolted and joined with Scopas, the Egyptian general. With their help he succeeded in capturing Palestine. Those rebel Israelites had wanted to return and build a temple in Egypt, but Antiochus returned and defeated the Egyptian general twice, first in North Palestine at Paneas, and then at Sidon! So this caused Palestine, the Pleasant Land (Daniel 8:9), to fall under Syrian control!

<<Daniel 11:15 >> *[So the king of the North shall come, and cast up a mount, and take the most fenced cities: and the arms of the South shall not withstand, neither his chosen people, neither shall there be any strength to withstand.]*

Antiochus returned, recovered Judea, and defeated Scopas. Scopas ran to Sidon with 10,000 men. Antiochus kept after them and barricaded them there, and they were forced to surrender because of hunger. Even Ptolemy's chosen people, his best generals, failed to stop Antiochus.

<<Daniel 11:16 >> *[But he that cometh against him shall do according to his will, and none shall stand before him: and he shall stand in the glorious land, which by his hand shall be consumed.]*

Antiochus defeated all the armies of Egypt that was in Palestine, and liberated all Israelites that were captives under the Egyptians.

<<Daniel 11:17 >> *[He shall also set his face to enter with the strength of his whole kingdom, and upright ones with him; thus shall he do: and he shall give him the daughter of women, corrupting her* (better translated: to destroy her, meaning Egypt): *but she shall not stand on his side, neither be for him.]*

Now Antiochus was ready to invade Egypt, but instead he decided to destroy Ptolemy by devising schemes. In 197 BC Antiochus proposed peace to Ptolemy through a treaty of marriage between Ptolemy and Cleopatra, his daughter (this is not the same Cleopatra with Mark Anthony that was to come later). Antiochus' scheme was to use his daughter Cleopatra as a trap against Ptolemy to weaken him and eventually bring about the destruction of Ptolemaic Egypt. This plan backfired against Antiochus because Cleopatra failed to betray Ptolemy. Instead she alerted Ptolemy to the plans of Antiochus, which caused Egypt to be on guard against Syria!

<<Daniel 11:18 >> *[After this shall he turn his face unto the isles, and shall take many: but a prince for his own behalf shall cause the reproach offered by him to cease; without his own reproach he shall cause it to turn upon him.]*

Antiochus organized a great navy against Ptolemaic Egypt, and conquered most of the coastal places of Greece in the Aegean Sea. But the Roman navy interfered and defeated Antiochus, driving him out of the Aegean and demanding that he pay for the expenses of the war. Therefore, by defeating Antiochus, the Romans reversed the reproach that he was trying to bring upon Rome.

<<Daniel 11:19 >> *[Then he shall turn his face toward the fort of his own land: but he shall stumble and fall, and not be found.]*

After his embarrassing defeat, Antiochus was running from city to city and proposing peace treaties to Rome. As Antiochus could not raise the money demanded by the Romans, he went around trying to collect taxes from province to province. At one place called Belus in Elymais he attempted to loot a pagan temple, but the public became outraged and killed Antiochus and his men.

<<Daniel 11:20 >> *[Then shall stand up in his estate a raiser of taxes in the glory of the kingdom: but within few days shall be destroyed, neither in anger, nor in battle.]*

Seleucus Philopator (187-176 BC) ruled after the death of his father Antiochus. It was urgent for him to come up with the money to pay the annual Roman taxes, so he imposed high taxes upon his people and also looted the temple in Jerusalem for money.

<< II Maccabees 9:23 >> *Seleucious was neither killed in anger nor in battle, he was murdered by his treasurer.*

<<Daniel 11:21 >> *[And in his estate shall stand up a vile person, to whom they shall not give the honor of the kingdom: but he shall come in peaceably, and obtain the kingdom by flatteries.]*

Antiochus, surnamed Epiphanies "the illustrious" (but commonly known as the mad man), was extremely crooked. He was a liar and a hustler. Antiochus was known for accepting bribes and fraternizing with all sorts of criminals. After the death of Seleucus Philopator, there were many individuals competing and declaring themselves king; but when Antiochus Epiphanies returned from Rome he engaged himself in bribing and flattering the military generals and leaders and begging to get their support. With their assistance, Antiochus managed to obtain the throne, but he did all this through bribery, begging and flattery.

<<Daniel 11:22 >> *[And with the arm of a flood shall they be overflown from before him, and shall be broken; yea, also the prince of the covenant.]*

THE TRUTH

The leaders and generals that Antiochus had won over through begging, flattery and bribery successfully subdued and flushed out all the other guys that were claiming rights to the throne.

In addition, Antiochus even removed Onias from office, he was the high Priest of Israel at the time ("prince of the covenant"), because of a bribe that he received from Jason, an Uncle Tom whom was sympathetic to the policies of Greece. Then Antiochus did the same thing to Jason that he did to Onias. A wicked man named Menelaus offered him an even greater sum of money for the office of High Priest. In addition, that wicked Menelaus even killed the righteous Onias in 171 BC just to show Antiochus that he was a Greek sympathizer.

Through deceitful tactics Antiochus rose to power, breaking treaties as soon as he would make them.

<<Daniel 11:23 >> *[And after the league made with him he shall work deceitfully: for he shall come up, and shall become strong with a small people.]*

Antiochus increased the size of his kingdom through malice. He would propose treaties with other nations that he would later brake. In fact, that is the same exact tactic used by the Caucasians to steal the land from the Western Indians of North, South, and Central America. Also, they use the same tactic around the world for exploiting the people and the resources of their countries. This is how Antiochus became strong with a small people.

<<Daniel 11:24 >> *[He shall enter peaceably even upon the fattest places of the province; and he shall do that which his fathers have not done, nor his father's fathers; he shall scatter among them the prey, and spoil, and riches: yea, and he shall forecast his devices against the strongholds, even for a time.]*

When Antiochus invaded the different provinces, his army committed many atrocities with extreme barbarism, looting, and burning. With all the wealth he stole from other provinces, temples, and cities, Antiochus did what his fathers had not done by distributing the stolen goods among his entire Greek subjects, and funding a variety of public entertainment programs.

<<Daniel 11:25 >> *[And he shall stir up his power and his courage against the king of the South with a great army; and the king of the South shall be stirred up to battle with a very great and mighty army; but he shall not stand: for they shall forecast devices against him.]*

Eulaeus and Lenaeus, the guardians of young Ptolemy Philometor, asked Antiochus to return the territories he had taken that belonged to Egypt. He refused. Behind this, Antiochus got himself ready for war with Egypt (I Maccabees 3:30).

Ptolemy Philometor (181-145 BC), one of the two sons from the marriage of Cleopatra of Ptolemy Epiphanes by Antiochus the Great, she was also the sister of Antiochus Epiphanes; Ptolemy Epiphanes was his nephew. The Ptolemies mobilized a great and mighty army to defeat Antiochus. The battle was fierce and the Ptolemies lost. The forces of Antiochus subdued and ruled all of Egypt, but could not defeat Alexandria in Egypt.

Antiochus did not defeat Egypt because he was stronger; he defeated them by working out devices to corrupt the captains and authorities of Ptolemy with bribes:

THE TRUTH

<< I Maccabees 1:16-19 >> [Now when the kingdom was established before Antiochus, he thought to reign over Egypt, that he might have the dominion of two realms. <17> Wherefore he entered into Egypt with a great multitude, with chariots, and elephants, and horsemen, and a great navy, <18> and made war against Ptolemy king of Egypt: but Ptolemy was afraid of him, and fled; and many were wounded to death. <19> Thus they got the strong cities in the land of Egypt, and he took the spoils thereof.]

<< Daniel 11:26 >> [Yea, they that feed of the portion of his meat shall destroy him, and his army shall overflow: and many shall fall down slain.]

Because of the briberies and other temptations offered to the administrators and captains of Ptolemy, whom he had relied on and confided in, Egypt became very corrupt and chaotic. This is the actual reason for, and the method by which, Antiochus succeeded in defeating Egypt. Eventually it came to the point where the Alexandrians set up Euergetes, the younger brother of Ptolemy, to be king over Alexandria.

<<Daniel 11:27 >> [And both these kings' heart shall be to do mischief, and they shall speak lies at one table; but it shall not prosper: for the end shall be at the time appointed.]

Antiochus proceeded to take advantage of the atmosphere of political instability in Egypt that resulted from the division between the two brothers, Philometor and Euergetes (who were his nephews). Antiochus had frequent meetings at a table with Ptolemy in Memphis, pretending to want peaceful resolutions. He pretended to be sympathetic to Ptolemy's affairs, and acted as if he was a friend. But at the same time he would also meet with Euergetes and acted in the same friendly manner. His real intention was to excite each of the two brothers against the other!

However, his two nephews were playing the same game. They acted as if they were appreciative of Antiochu's so-called friendship and concern. In reality all the peace talks were superficial lies; their true intentions were to destroy each other. It is just like the peace talks between America and Russia today. They sat down at one table and pretended to want peace when in reality they are devising ways of killing each other around the world. An examination of this chapter of Daniel will prove valuable in understanding current world events!

<<Daniel 11:28 >> [Then shall he return into his land with great riches; and his heart shall be against the holy covenant; and he shall do exploits, and return to his own land.]

Antiochus left Egypt with the valuables he had stolen and looted from his wars against Egypt and Ptolemy. As he was leaving, he heard that the Israelites were celebrating and rejoicing because of a false rumor that had spread saying Antiochus had died in Egypt. Therefore Antiochus was enraged and set his heart to punishing the people. Antiochus came into Jerusalem and looted the temple, taking all the golden vessels and the curtains from the temple, and then spread swine broth all over the altar and inside the temple. Then he murdered thousands of Israelites and sold thousands more into slavery. (II Maccabees Chapter 5)

<<Daniel 11:29 >> [At the time appointed he shall return, and come toward the South; but it shall not be as the former, or as the latter.]

His treachery was detected, and the two brothers had united. Hearing of this, Antiochus prepared to march against Alexandria a second time. Antiochus would not have the same success as when he overthrew the Egyptian army at Pelusium, or when he took Memphis (I Maccabees 1:16-20).

<<Daniel 11:30 >> *[For the ships of Chittim shall come against him: therefore he shall be grieved, and return, and have indignation against the holy covenant: so shall he do; he shall even return, and have intelligence with them that forsake the holy covenant.]*

Because Antiochus learned that the two brothers that ruled Egypt had reconciled and united, he became infuriated that his plan had not worked, and he therefore decided upon a military invasion of Egypt for a second time. But this second invasion was not successful like his former invasion. Because this time the Romans (in the ancient land of Chittim) interfered; they came to meet with Antiochus in Egypt, to demand that he make peace with his nephew or else! Therefore Antiochus had to call off the attack and bitterly withdraw from Egypt. In order to let off frustrations, Antiochus became indignant against the Israelites, and against Israelite laws and customs!

<<Daniel 11:31 >> *[And arms shall stand on his part, and they shall pollute the sanctuary of strength, and shall take away the daily sacrifice, and they shall place the abomination that maketh desolate.]*

<< II Maccabees Chapters 6 and 7 >> (Some of what Antiochus did was described as follow) *[...And to pollute also the temple in Jerusalem, and to call it the Temple of Jupiter Olympius (for a false god) ...The temple was filled with riot and revelling by the Gentiles, who dallied with harlots, and had to do with women within the circuit of the holy places, and besides that brought in things which the law forbiddeth. Neither was it lawful for a man to keep Sabbath days or ancient feasts, or to profess himself at all to be a Jew.]*
[...Moreover there went out a decree to the neighbor cities of the heathen, by the suggestion of Ptolemy against the Jews, that they should observe the same fashions and be partakers of their sacrifices: and whoso ever would not conform themselves to the manners of the Gentiles should be put to death. Then might a man have seen the present misery.]

As a result of the cruelty of the Caucasians, hundreds of thousands of Israelites were murdered in the cruelest manner; they were those who tried to keep the Hebrew customs.

<<Daniel 11:32 >> *[And such as do wickedly against the covenant shall he corrupt by flatteries: but the people that do know their power shall be strong, and do exploits.]*

Menolaus and other rebel Israelites sold out to Antiochus but at the same time certain others remained loyal to the covenant. At this time Antiochus was forcing the people to forsake the Hebrew customs and to adopt Caucasian religions and ways, or else face death.

<<Daniel 11:33 >> *[And they that understand among the people shall instruct many: yet they shall fall by the sword, and by famine, by captivity, and by spoil, many days.]*

THE TRUTH

Many Israelites resolved not to adopt the Greek customs being forced upon them, and to not eat any unclean thing; they rather choose death, that they might not profane the covenant.

< I Maccabees 1:62-64 >> [Howbeit many in Israel were fully resolved and confirmed in themselves not to eat any unclean thing. <63> Wherefore they chose rather to die, that they might not be defiled with meats, and that they might not profane the holy covenant: so then they died. <64> And there was very great wrath upon Israel.]

<<Daniel 11:34 >> [Now when they shall fall, they shall be helped with a little help: but many shall cleave to them by flatteries.]

For example, Mattathias Maccabeus and his five sons, Joannan, Simmon, Judas, Eleazar, and Jonathan rebelled against Antiochus and prospered with a small group of men (I Maccabees, Chapter II). In due time their revolt became popular and some of the hypocrites among the people used flattery to gain acceptance among the Maccabees. Judas Maccabeus and his brothers ruled with great success in many battles. Antiochus Epiphanies was to die in Babylon and was later succeeded by Antiochus Eupator.

<<Daniel 11:35 >> [And some of them of understanding shall fall, to try them, and to purge, and to make them white, even to the time of the end: because it is yet for a time appointed.]

Mysterious as it may seem, it was the Most High that was allowing all these troubles to come upon the Israelites so as to test the sincerity of their faith in him! This was to be an ongoing tribulation process for Israel. In this verse, the tribulation refers to the period from the time of Antiochus up to the destruction of America, ending the Roman Empire. It also pertains to the great tribulation period before the Second Coming of Christ!

Nothing ended with Antiochus, therefore this verse does not refer to Antiochus at all. It is a projection from that time up to the completion of the time of the gentiles to the Second Coming of Jesus Christ! It relates to the leader of the Western World, the modern Roman Empire in the last days. The head of that new gentile kingdom is America. It is also the time in the last days described in Daniel.

<< Romans 11:25 >> [...Blindness in part is happened to Israel, until the fullness of the Gentiles be come in.]

<< Daniel 12:1,2 >> [And at that time shall Michael stand up, the great prince which standeth for the children of thy people: and there shall be a time of trouble, such as never was since there was a nation even to that same time: and at that time thy people shall be delivered, everyone that shall be found written in the book. And many of them that sleep in the dust of the earth shall awake, some to everlasting life, and some to shame and everlasting contempt.]

<< Daniel 11:36 >> [And the king shall do according to his will; and he shall exalt himself above every god, and shall speak marvelous things against the God of gods, and shall prosper till the indignation be accomplished: for that is determined shall be done.]

THE TRUTH

Now, this king spoken of in verses 36 to 45 is not Antiochus, but is the future leader of the Roman Empire, in this case America! Firstly, note that in this chapter Antiochus was the one being referred to as the king of the North, because His dominion was Syria, to the North of Palestine. But to the contrary, verse 40 says concerning this new king that ["*the king of the North would come against him.*"] Secondly, Verse 36 says that this new king [would exalt himself above every god].

This was not true of Antiochus, because he worshipped Zeus. In addition, verse 45 says that this new king would meet his end in Palestine, while Antiochus died in Syria! It is the dispute over the occupation of Palestine by the Edomite Khazars (so-called Jewish) that will serve to trigger the final conflict called the Battle of Armageddon! This new king refers to America, the little horn spoken of:

> << Daniel 7:24-27 >> [*And the ten horns out of this kingdom are ten kings that shall arise: and another shall rise after them; and he shall be diverse from the first, and he shall subdue three kings. And he shall speak great words against the Most High, and shall wear out the saints of the Most High, and think to change times and laws: and they shall be given into his hand until a time and times and the dividing of time. But the judgment shall sit, and they shall take away his dominion, to consume and to destroy it unto the end.*]

This little horn is referring to America, leader of this modern Roman Empire. America had to subdue three major world powers during colonial times ("*he shall subdue three kings*") in order to become a nation: the British, the Spanish, and the French. So America is the last horn of the Roman Empire, that Daniel is prophesying about.

Although we know that the Israelites are an Asiatic people, the European political and religious institutions set up their Caucasian picture as Jesus and a god all over the world. They substituted the Bible laws with their own laws, and blaspheme against every truth in the Bible. The Israelites were worn out under the system of slavery, colonization and exploitation of North, South, and Central America.

Now many people are falsely teaching that this new king refers to a certain individual known as the Antichrist. This is in complete contradiction to the scriptures. According to the Bible, anyone who is against Christ and the truth is an Antichrist. It does not refer to a particular human being.

> << 1 John 4:1-3 >> [*Beloved, believe not every spirit, but try the spirits whether they be of the Lord YAHAWAH: because many false prophets are gone out into the world. Hereby know ye the Spirit of the Lord God: Every spirit that confesseth that Jesus Christ is come in the flesh is of God: And every spirit that confesseth not that Jesus Christ is come in the flesh is not of God: and this is that spirit of antichrist, whereof ye have heard that it should come; and even now already is it in the world.*]

In this verse, which was written about two thousand years ago, the Bible says that the spirit of the antichrist is already in the world. Therefore, it does not refer to a certain future individual, but to all the people and organizations that oppose Christ.

> <<Daniel 11:37 >> [*Neither shall he regard the god of his fathers, nor the desire of women, nor regard any god: for he shall magnify himself above all.*]

THE TRUTH

<< II Thessalonians 2:3-10 >> [Let no man deceive you by any means: for that day shall not come except there come a falling away first, and that man of sin be revealed, the son of perdition; <3> who opposeth and exalteth himself above all that is called God, or that is worshipped; so that he as God sitteth in the temple of God, shewing himself that he is God.]

For example, they show themselves as gods by presenting a Caucasian picture for Jesus Christ to people all over the world. This is an act of blasphemy, because the real Jesus Christ is Asiatic! Also, in some religions, they call their so-called priests and ministers "father"; yet the Bible says, "call no man your father that is upon the face of the earth for one is your father that is in heaven!" Thirdly, the educational institutions claim that the universe was not created, but that it is the result of a spontaneous explosion. They also teach as their educational standard that the Lord did not create man, but that mankind evolved from the apes. So in the place of God these people honor their wealth, technology, and ideas; they have replaced the word of God rebelliously!

<< II Thessalonians 2:5-10 >> [Remember ye not, that, when I was yet with you, I told you these things? <6> And now ye know what withholdeth that he might be revealed in his time. <7> For the mystery of iniquity doth already work: only he who now letteth will let, until he be taken out of the way. <8> And then shall that wicked be revealed, whom the Lord shall consume with the spirit of his mouth, and shall destroy with the brightness of his coming: <9> Even him, whose coming is after the working of Satan with all power and signs and lying wonders, And all deceivableness in them that perish; because they receive not the love of the truth, that they might be saved.]

We are living in the very last days of the modern reunited Roman Empire!

<< Daniel 11:38 >> [But in his estate shall he honor the god of forces (or fortresses): and a god whom his fathers knew not shall he honor with gold, and silver, and with precious stones, and pleasant things.]

Today, the people trust in science and technology as the source of salvation and power, rather than in the ancient pagan gods, or in the true God. They honor the god of forces; more accurately translated fortresses, referring to military might. The nations spend most of their money in the arms race, building and advancing the technology of their military forces from the conventional to the nuclear and space weapon systems.

<<Daniel 11:39 >> [thus shall he do in the most strongholds with a strange god, whom he shall acknowledge and increase with glory: and he shall cause them to rule over many, and shall divide the land for gain.]

It is with advanced military technology that this modern Roman Empire controls and rules the nations, dividing the other nations among themselves as colonies and satellites!

<< Daniel 8:23-25 >> [And in the latter time of their kingdom, when the transgressors are come to the full, a king of fierce countenance, and understanding dark sentences, shall stand up. And his power shall be mighty, but not by his own power: and he shall destroy wonderfully, and shall prosper, and practice, and shall destroy the mighty and holy people

(the original Israelites, who were and are being destroyed through mental and physical slavery). *And through his policy also he shall cause craft to prosper in his hand* (technology advanced enough to produce nuclear weapons, space travel, and genetic science*); and he shall magnify himself in his heart, and by peace shall destroy many]*

When the western colonial powers wish to invade your country, first they send in the so-called nuns, priest, and missionaries to deceive you. After that they send in the political and economic terrorists to destroy your economy and political system. Then they give you loans to trap you in a debt crisis. Eventually they send in their army disguised as so-called peacekeepers. Before you know it, your government system has been replaced, your economy is under foreign control, and your people are ignorant and in slavery!

<< *Daniel 8:25* >> *[...he shall also stand up against the Prince of princes* (they will try to fight against Jesus Christ at his Second Coming*) But he shall be broken without hand.]*

Gog and Magog in Ezekiel chapter 38, 39 describes how Antiochus (Gog) and his allies (Magog) would come up against the land of Israel to destroy it. In the last days The Khazar so-called Jew and her allies are referred to in Revelation 20:7 as the modern day Gog and Magog. They will soon be destroyed the same way Antiochus and the other enemies of the original Israelite were for coming into our land. The evil empires will be destroyed by natural and super natural disasters and by nuclear, chemical and biological war.

<< *Daniel 11:40* >> *[And at the time of the end shall the king of the south push at him: and the king of the north shall come against him like a whirlwind, with chariots, and with horsemen, and with many ships; and he shall enter into the countries, and shall overflow and pass over.]*

The destruction of the modern Roman Empire and its allies was built into their system from the start. It is the divisions within their system will eventually bring about their mutual destruction. Christ Says:

<< *Matthew 12:25* >> *[...Every kingdom divided against itself is brought to desolation; and every city or house divided against itself shall not stand: And if Satan cast out Satan, he is divided against himself; how then shall his kingdom stand?]*

According to the prophecies, Russia and the European countries (king of the North) which were in league with America will turn against America: destroying each other in the nuclear war.

<< *Revelation 17:16* >> *[and the ten horns which thou sawest upon the beast, these shall hate the whore, and shall make her desolate and naked, and shall eat her flesh, and burn her with fire.]*

<< *Daniel 11:41* >> *[He shall enter also into the glorious land, and many countries shall be overthrown: but these shall escape out of his hands, even Edom, and Moab, and the chief of the children of Ammon.]*

THE TRUTH

The modern Roman Empire will encounter some resistance from the Arab and Persian world. The glorious land is Palestine. In 1945, the military infestation of Palestine by impostors claiming to be the original Jews was initiated. If there is not a separation between church and state, there can never be democracy and equality! The impostors are descendants of the Khazars, who had converted to Judaism in about 700 AD. Today these European Khazars are falsely claiming to be Jews!

> << Mark 13:14 >> *[But when ye shall see the abomination of desolation, spoken of by Daniel the prophet, stand where it ought not, let him that readeth understand* (The Khazars occupying Palestine are an abomination according to God, recall Revelation 2:9 and 3:9), *...For in those days shall be affliction, such as was not from the beginning of the creation which God created unto this time, neither shall be.]*

It was in 70 AD that the original Asiatic Jews were expelled out of Palestine into Africa, making Palestine deserted of its original Asiatic inhabitants. According to that verse, you should see only the impostors establishing themselves in Palestine in these last days! They should not be there claiming to be Jews, because they are not the original descendants of the Asiatic Jews and Israelites. Israel today is simply a device being used by the modern Roman Empire to control, divide, and eventually conquer the Middle Eastern nations!

Although the modern Roman Empire is doing all of this wickedness blatantly, many nations and people will still remain in league with them for a time (Edom, Moab, and Amon - the Mid-East)! but eventually all of those people will become her enemies!

> << Isaiah 28:15-18,21,22 >> *[Because ye have said, We have made a covenant with death, and with hell are we at agreement; when the overflowing scourge shall pass through, it shall not come unto us: for we have made lies our refuge, and under falsehood have we hid ourselves.]*

This verse also applies to many African-Americans and American-Indians who love and adopt the wicked devices of this world, trusting and following after them!

> *[Therefore thus saith the Lord YAHAWAH, Behold, I lay in Zion for a foundation a stone, a tried stone, a precious corner stone, a sure foundation* (the truth in Jesus Christ)*: he that believeth shall not make haste. Judgment also will I lay to the line, and righteousness to plummet: and the hail shall sweep the refuge of lies, and the waters shall overflow the hiding place. And your covenant with death shall be disannulled, and your agreement with hell shall not stand; when the overflowing scourge shall pass through, then ye shall be trodden down by it,*
>
> *...For the Lord shall rise up... that he may do his strange work; and bring to pass his act, his strange act. Now therefore be ye not mockers, lest your bands be made strong: for I have heard from the Lord God of Hosts a consumption, even determined upon the whole earth.]*

> << Daniel 11:42, 43 >> *[He shall stretch forth his hand also upon the* (many) *countries: and the land of Egypt shall not escape. <43> But he shall have power over the treasures of gold*

and of silver, and over all the precious things of Egypt: and the Libyans and the Ethiopians shall be at his steps.]

Using Palestine, the modern Roman Empire will seek to achieve the complete domination of the Middle East and North Africa, and at the same time create wars and acts of imperialism through covert activities! This will set the stage for the end of the Third World War. Setting up the Khazars in Palestine to act as the Jews, will be the trigger of the Third World War. Keep in mind that many of the Jewish Khazars are ignorant of their true original identity as Khazars, and are the victims of false religion and lies!

<<Daniel 11:44 >> [but tidings out of the east (Asia) and out of the north (Europe) shall trouble him: therefore he shall go forth with great fury to destroy, and utterly to make away many.] It is in the Middle East that this final conflict will begin, and will culminate into the total destruction of the Modern Roman Empire, as Russia, America, and the other Nations turn against each other to fight a nuclear war.

<< Revelation 16:12,19 >> [And the six angel poured out his vials upon the great river Euphrates; and the water thereof was dried up, that the way of the kings of the East might be prepared ...And the great city was divided into three parts, and the cities of the nations fell: and great Babylon came in remembrance before God, to give unto her the cup of the wine of the fierceness of his wrath.]

<< Revelation 9:14-16 >> [...Loose the four angels which are bound in the great river Euphrates. And the four angels were loosed, which were prepared for an hour, and a day, and a month, and a year, for to slay the third part of men (The stage is set for that great battle). And the number of the army of the horsemen were two-hundred thousand: and I heard the number of them.]

<< Revelation 16:16 >> [And he gathered them together into a place called in the Hebrew tongue Armageddon.]

Maggedo is a valley in Palestine. The Third World War will be fought as a result of Zionist imperialism! All the world powers will mobilize their military forces against the head of this modern Roman Empire, such as the Asians, the Latin Americans, the Arabs, and even some Europeans. But the heads of the evil empire shall become furious, and seek to destroy and kill many!

<< Jeremiah 30:7 >> [For thus saith the Lord; We have heard a voice of trembling, of fear, and not of peace. Ask ye now, and see whether a man doth travail with child? Wherefore do I see every man with his hands on his loins, as a woman in travail, and all faces are turned into paleness? Alas! For that day is great, so that none is like: it is even the time of Jacob's trouble; but he shall be saved out of it. For it shall come to pass in that day,(the ones among us that repent) saith the Lord of hosts, that I will break his yoke from off thy neck, and will burst thy bonds, and strangers shall no more serve themselves of him.]

THE TRUTH

<< *Joel 2:1-3* >> [*Blow the trumpet in Zion* (Go out their and teach this truth), *and sound an alarm in my holy mountain* (warn the people)*: let all the inhabitants of the land tremble: for the day of the Lord cometh, for it is nigh at hand; A day of darkness and of clouds and thick darkness, as the morning spread upon the mountains, ...A fire devoureth before them; and behind them a flame burneth, the land is as the Garden of Eden before them, and behind them a desolate wilderness; yea, and nothing shall escape them]*

Christ will come to deliver us on the day of the nuclear war. On that day, the angels and the saints returning with Christ, will also be attacking the nations with supernatural weapons. And from the air, as we are being carried away in UFOs (chariots of salvation), we will look down and see the missiles exploding!

<< *Luke 21:18,19* >> [*But there shall not a hair of your head perish. In your patience possess ye your souls.*]

<< *Daniel 11:45* >> *And he shall plant the tabernacle of his palace between the seas in the glorious holy mountain; yet he shall come to his end, and none shall help him.*]

At the return of Christ, Doomsday will come suddenly! The times of the gentiles will have expired!

<< *Matthew 24:30,31* >> [*And then shall appear the sign of the Son of man in heaven* (the chariots of salvation, what you call UFOs) *in heaven: and then shall all the tribes of the earth mourn, and they shall see the Son of man* (Jesus Christ, an Asiatic man) *coming in the clouds of heaven with power and great glory. And he shall send his angels with a great sound of a trumpet, and they shall gather together his elect from the four winds, from one end of heaven to the other.*]

JUDGEMENT AND DOOMSDAY

We are living in the time of war, and in a time where hundreds of thousands of nuclear, chemical and biological weapons are in existence and ready to destroy at an instant! According to the Bible, Christ will return on the day of the nuclear war to miraculously deliver the believers out of the tribulation and destruction of the nuclear war and the plagues of judgement day.

The nuclear war will be a result of economic and political conflict. Impostors who are falsely claiming to be Jews will trigger it as a result of issues concerning the domination of the Middle East and the occupation of Palestine:

>> *Zechariah 12:2,3* >> *[Behold, I will make Jerusalem a cup of trembling unto all the people round about, when they shall be in the siege both against Judah and against Jerusalem. And in that day will I make Jerusalem a burdensome stone for all people: all that burden themselves with it shall be cut in pieces, though all the people of the earth be gathered together against it]!*

Palestine is the bait, the trigger of the nuclear war*!*

<< *Ezekiel 36:4,5* >> *[Therefore thus saith the Lord YAHAWAH; Surely in the fire of my jealousy have I spoken against the residue of the heathen, and against all Idumea* (Idumea= Edomites, the Caucasians of today)*, which have appointed my land into their possession with the joy of all their hearts, with despiteful minds, to cast it out for a prey.*

Prophesy therefore concerning the land of Israel, and say unto the mountains, and to the hills, to the rivers, and to the valleys, Thus saith the Lord YAHAWAH; Behold, I have spoken in my jealousy and in my fury, because ye have borne the shame of the heathen: Therefore thus saith the Lord YAHAWAH; I have lifted up mine hand, Surely the heathen shall bear their shame. But ye, O mountains of Israel, ye shall shoot forth your branches, and yield your fruits to my people Israel; for they are at hand to come.]

According to the Bible the real Jews will not be established in Palestine until after the Second Coming of Jesus Christ!

<< *Revelation 17:16* >> *[And the ten horns which thou sawest upon the beast, these shall hate the whore, and shall make her desolate and naked, and shall eat her flesh, and burn her with fire.]*

The ten horns refer to the European nations which were before divided and are now standing together to face America over the issues concerning the domination of the Middle East.

<< *Matthew 12:25* >> *[Every kingdom divided against itself is brought to desolation; and every city or house divided against itself shall not stand.]*

THE TRUTH

The modern world is divided, and it has already fought two World Wars against itself; but this Third World War will be the end of the Caucasian domination of the world. Today, we see Europe moving further and further from America and Russia and Eastern Europe are moving closer together.

The institutionalized religions often talk about the day of the Lord (Day of the Lord refers to the day when Jesus returns to judge the earth), as if the western world is going to be saved from it, and that Caucasians will be ruling in the world to come. But the opposite is true! The handwriting is on the wall, their world has been weighed in the balance, and the price is required!

<< Amos 5:18,19 >> *[Woe unto you that desire the day of the Lord! to what end is it to you? The day of the Lord is darkness* (global chaos, smoke, and dust from the nuclear war)*, and not light. As if a man did flee from a lion, and a bear met him; or went into a house, and a serpent bit him.]*

So as America is fighting with the Arabs (the lion), The Russians (the bear) will meet them. Japan and China (a serpent) will turn against America too, and they will all fire nuclear missiles at each other! The Bible also describes in detail exactly how the nuclear bombs will kill on that day.

<< Zechariah 14:12 >> *[And this shall be the plague wherewith the Lord will smite all the people that have fought against Jerusalem* (those that have oppressed the original Israelites)*; Their flesh shall consume away while they stand upon their feet, and their eyes shall consume away in their holes, and their tongue shall consume away in their mouth.]*

Only nuclear radiation can vaporize the flesh off the bones while the person is still standing. The Bible provides concrete proof that there will be a nuclear war! No one can stop the nuclear war.

<< Isaiah 14:24 >> *[The Lord of host hath sworn, saying, surely as I have thought so shall it come to pass; and as I have purposed, so shall it stand!]*

<< Isaiah 63:4 >> *[For the day of vengeance is in my heart.]*

The heathen societies of this world will not escape; they are going to be judged and punished for oppressing and exploiting the original Israelites and other righteous people of the world!

<< Jeremiah 30:16 >> *[Therefore all they that devour thee shall be devoured; and all thine adversaries, everyone of them, shall go into captivity; and they that spoiled thee shall be spoil, and all that prey upon thee will I give for a prey.]*

The nations will reap what they sow; if they've shown no mercy, they will receive no mercy:

<< Revelation 18:6 >> *[Reward her even as she rewarded you, and double unto her double according to her works* (racism, slavery, colonialism)*: in the cup which she hath filled fill to her double.]*

It is their turn to bite the bullet.

<< Revelation 13:9, 10 >> [If any man have an ear, let him hear. He that leadeth into captivity: shall go into captivity: He that killeth with the sword must be killed with the sword. Here is the patience and the faith of the saints.]

<< Obadiah 1:1-21>> [The vision of Obadiah. Thus saith the Lord GOD concerning Edom (The Western World); We have heard a rumour from the LORD, and an ambassador is sent among the heathen, Arise ye, and let us rise up against her in battle. <2> Behold, I have made thee small among the heathen: thou art greatly despised. <3> The pride of thine heart hath deceived thee, thou that dwellest in the clefts of the rock, whose habitation is high; that saith in his heart, Who shall bring me down to the ground?

<4> Though thou exalt thyself as the eagle, and though thou set thy nest among the stars, thence will I bring thee down, saith the LORD. <5> If thieves came to thee, if robbers by night, (how art thou cut off!) would they not have stolen till they had enough? if the grapegatherers came to thee, would they not leave some grapes? <6> How are the things of Esau searched out! how are his hidden things sought up! <7> All the men of thy confederacy have brought thee even to the border: the men that were at peace with thee have deceived thee, and prevailed against thee; they that eat thy bread have laid a wound under thee: there is none understanding in him.

<8> Shall I not in that day, saith the LORD, even destroy the wise men out of Edom, and understanding out of the mount of Esau? <9> And thy mighty men, O Teman, shall be dismayed, to the end that every one of the mount of Esau may be cut off by slaughter. <10> For thy violence against thy brother Jacob shame shall cover thee, and thou shalt be cut off for ever.

<11> In the day that thou stoodest on the other side, in the day that the strangers carried away captive his forces, and foreigners entered into his gates, and cast lots upon Jerusalem, even thou wast as one of them. <12> But thou shouldest not have looked on the day of thy brother in the day that he became a stranger; neither shouldest thou have rejoiced over the children of Judah in the day of their destruction; neither shouldest thou have spoken proudly in the day of distress. <13> Thou shouldest not have entered into the gate of my people in the day of their calamity; yea, thou shouldest not have looked on their affliction in the day of their calamity, nor have laid hands on their substance in the day of their calamity; <14> Neither shouldest thou have stood in the crossway, to cut off those of his that did escape; neither shouldest thou have delivered up those of his that did remain in the day of distress.

<15> For the day of the LORD is near upon all the heathen: as thou hast done, it shall be done unto thee: thy reward shall return upon thine own head. <16> For as ye have drunk upon my holy mountain, so shall all the heathen drink

continually, yea, they shall drink, and they shall swallow down, and they shall be as though they had not been.

<17> But upon mount Zion shall be deliverance, and there shall be holiness; and the house of Jacob shall possess their possessions. <18> And the house of Jacob shall be a fire, and the house of Joseph a flame, and the house of Esau for stubble, and they shall kindle in them, and devour them; and there shall not be any remaining of the house of Esau; for the LORD hath spoken it.

<19> And they of the south shall possess the mount of Esau; and they of the plain the Philistines: and they shall possess the fields of Ephraim, and the fields of Samaria: and Benjamin shall possess Gilead. <20> And the captivity of this host of the children of Israel shall possess that of the Canaanites, even unto Zarephath; and the captivity of Jerusalem, which is in Sepharad, shall possess the cities of the south. <21> And saviours shall come up on mount Zion to judge the mount of Esau; and the kingdom shall be the LORD'S.]

<<Ezekiel 38:1-23>> [And the word of the LORD came unto me, saying, <2> Son of man, set thy face against Gog,(S0-called Jews and Israeli-Khazars. They are liars like Antiochus Epiphanes, Daniel 8:23,25; 11:23,27,32) *the land of Magog* (Her allies: America, Europe) *, the chief prince of Meshech and Tubal, and prophesy against him, <3> And say, Thus saith the Lord GOD; Behold, I am against thee, O Gog, the chief prince of Meshech and Tubal: <4> And I will turn thee back, and put hooks into thy jaws, and I will bring thee forth, and all thine army, horses and horsemen, all of them clothed with all sorts of armour, even a great company with bucklers and shields, all of them handling swords: <5> Persia, Ethiopia, and Libya with them; all of them with shield and helmet: <6> Gomer, and all his bands; the house of Togarmah of the north quarters, and all his bands: and many people with thee. <7> Be thou prepared, and prepare for thyself, thou, and all thy company that are assembled unto thee, and be thou a guard unto them.*

<8> After many days thou shalt be visited: in the latter years thou shalt come into the land that is brought back from the sword, and is gathered out of many people, against the mountains of Israel, which have been always waste: but it is brought forth out of the nations, and they shall dwell safely all of them. <9> Thou shalt ascend and come like a storm (Daniel 11:40), *thou shalt be like a cloud to cover the land, thou, and all thy bands, and many people with thee.*

<10> Thus saith the Lord GOD; It shall also come to pass, that at the same time shall things come into thy mind, and thou shalt think an evil thought (Daniel 11:31-32,36): *<11> And thou shalt say, I will go up to the land of unwalled villages; I will go to them that are at rest, that dwell safely, all of them dwelling without walls, and having neither bars nor gates, <12> To take a spoil, and to take a prey; to turn thine hand upon the desolate places that are now inhabited, and upon the people that are gathered out of the nations, which have gotten cattle and goods, that dwell in the midst of the land. <13> Sheba, and Dedan, and the merchants of Tarshish, with all the young lions thereof, shall say unto thee, Art thou come to take a spoil? hast thou gathered thy company to take a prey? to carry away silver and gold, to take away cattle and goods, to*

take a great spoil?

<14> Therefore, son of man, prophesy and say unto Gog, Thus saith the Lord GOD; In that day when my people of Israel dwelleth safely, shalt thou not know it? <15> And thou shalt come from thy place out of the north parts, thou, and many people with thee, all of them riding upon horses, a great company, and a mighty army: <16> And thou shalt come up against my people of Israel, as a cloud to cover the land; it shall be in the latter days, and I will bring thee against my land, that the heathen may know me, when I shall be sanctified in thee, O Gog (Antiochus was defeated, I Maccabees 3:32,33), *before their eyes.*

<17> Thus saith the Lord GOD; Art thou he (Esau) *of whom I have spoken in old time by my servants the prophets of Israel, which prophesied in those days many years that I would bring thee against them? <18> And it shall come to pass at the same time when Gog shall come against the land of Israel, saith the Lord GOD, that my fury shall come up in my face. <19> For in my jealousy and in the fire of my wrath have I spoken, Surely in that day there shall be a great shaking in the land of Israel(nuclear war); <20> So that the fishes of the sea, and the fowls of the heaven, and the beasts of the field, and all creeping things that creep upon the earth, and all the men that are upon the face of the earth, shall shake at my presence, and the mountains shall be thrown down, and the steep places shall fall, and every wall shall fall to the ground.*

<21> And I will call for a sword against him throughout all my mountains, saith the Lord GOD: every man's sword shall be against his brother. <22> And I will plead against him with pestilence and with blood; and I will rain upon him, and upon his bands, and upon the many people that are with him, an overflowing rain, and great hailstones, fire, and brimstone. <23> Thus will I magnify myself, and sanctify myself; and I will be known in the eyes of many nations, and they shall know that I am the LORD.

<<Ezekiel 39:1-8>> [Therefore, thou son of man, prophesy against Gog, and say, Thus saith the Lord GOD; Behold, I am against thee, O Gog (The Khazar so-called Jews, Israeli, the Edomites), *the chief prince of Meshech and Tubal: <2> And I will turn thee back, and leave but the sixth part of thee, and will cause thee to come up from the north parts, and will bring thee upon the mountains of Israel: <3> And I will smite thy bow out of thy left hand, and will cause thine arrows to fall out of thy right hand.*

<4> Thou shalt fall upon the mountains of Israel, thou, and all thy bands, and the people that is with thee: I will give thee unto the ravenous birds of every sort, and to the beasts of the field to be devoured. <5> Thou shalt fall upon the open field: for I have spoken it, saith the Lord GOD. <6> And I will send a fire on Magog, and among them that dwell carelessly in the isles: and they shall know that I am the LORD. <7> So will I make my holy name known in the midst of my people Israel; and I will not let them pollute my holy name any more: and the heathen shall know that I am the LORD, the Holy One in Israel. <8> Behold, it is come, and it is done, saith the Lord GOD; this is the day whereof I have spoken.

THE TRUTH

You will see all these things happen in this very generation. Please note, most importantly, the nuclear war will take place in this generation. Christ tells us when the end will be:

<< *Matthew 24:2-7* >> *[And Jesus said unto them, see ye not all these things? Verily I say unto you, there shall not be left here one stone upon another that shall not be thrown down.]*

The nations are working to amass the material wealth in vain, and all of the renovations and constructions are in vain, for all of the office buildings that they are so proud about will very soon be reduced to ashes in the nuclear war! That is why Jesus said, "What does it profit a man to gain the whole world and loose his own soul!"

<< *Matthew 24:3-7* >> *[And as he sat upon the Mount of Olives, the disciples came unto him privately, saying, Tell us, when shall these things be? And what shall be the sign of thy coming, and of the end of the world? <4> And Jesus answered and said unto them, Take heed that no man deceives you. <5> For many shall come in my name* (using the Bible falsely*), saying, "I am Christ"* (they call themselves Christians, Jews*); and shall deceive many.*
    <4> And Ye shall hear of wars and rumors of wars: see that ye be not troubled: for all these things must come to past, but the end is not yet. <7> For nations shall rise against nations and kingdom against kingdom: and there shall be famines and pestilences, and earthquakes, in diverse places.]

And you do see all of these global crises unfolding around the world today, just like the Bible said it will happen in the last days before the Second Coming of Jesus Christ!

<< *Matthew 24:21* >> *[...For then shall be great tribulation, such as was not since the beginning of the world to this time, no, nor ever shall be* (natural disasters, plagues, nuclear war*). And except those days should be shortened, there should no flesh be saved: but for the elect's sake those days shall be shortened.]*

<< *Matthew 24:13,14* >> *[But he that shall endure to the end, the same shall be saved* (no one is saved yet, shall means in the future.) *<14> And this gospel of the kingdom* (the truth concerning the identity of the real Jews and the original Israelites) *shall be preached in all the world for a witness unto all nations; and then shall the end come.]*

<< *Matthew 24: 34* >> *[Verily I say unto you, this generation shall not pass, till all these things be fulfilled.]*

All of these signs are seen in this generation: destruction of the environment, proliferation of nuclear weapons. Therefore, the doom's day and the return of Jesus Christ will take place in this generation! Although there are political talks about peace, don't be deceived. Everything is not OK - those world leaders are not truthful.

THE TRUTH

<< First Thessalonians 5:2,3 >> [For yourselves know perfectly that the day of the Lord so cometh as a thief in the night. For when they shall say, Peace and safety; then sudden destruction cometh upon them, as travail upon a woman with child; and they shall not escape.]

<< Daniel 11:27 >> [And both of these kings' hearts shall be to do mischief, and they shall speak lies at one table; but it shall not prosper: for yet the end shall be at the time appointed.]

The promise of peace is nothing but a disguise; peace and religion was the reason given for all of the imperialistic and colonial acts. They've used the word peace like a weapon according to the Bible:

<< Daniel 8:25 >> [And through his policy also he shall cause craft to prosper in his hand; and he shall magnify in his heart, and by peace shall destroy many: he shall also stand up against the Prince of princes; but he shall be broken without hand.]

They will first send religious missionaries into your land to colonize your mind and your spirit, making you to worship their image as a god, to make you peaceful and none violent. Afterwards they invade your land with their armies and greedy corporations to exploit your people and the natural resources! Three major world wars were predicted, two have already occurred.

<< Revelation 9:12 >> [One woe is past; and behold, there come two woes more hereafter.]

Woe symbolizes war, and three such world wars were prophesied to happen! And the Third World War was to begin soon after the second:

<< Revelation 11:14 >> [The second woe is past; and, behold, the third woe cometh quickly.]

This means the Second World War took place, and the Third World War will begin soon after! In fact, the stage is already being set for the Third World War, conflicts and violent confrontations are taking place all around the world. For example, soon after the Second World War, America became involved fighting in Korea, Vietnam, and the Middle East and Europe have constant violent confrontations occurring. But these wars will escalate into Armageddon and end in nuclear destruction and the return of Christ!

The scriptures prove that the Third World War will be nuclear:

<< Second Peters 3:10 >> [But the day of the Lord will come as a thief in the night; in the which the heavens shall pass away with a great noise, and the elements shall melt with fervent heat, the Earth also and the works that are therein shall be burned up.]

Now, the only process that can cause enough heat for elements to melt is nuclear fission, and nuclear fusion reactions! These are the processes involved in the explosion of nuclear weapons. It is all in the plan of the creator to allow mankind to destroy itself, because we have rebelled against the truth, and become proud against God. The Lord says that there is only one purpose for the nuclear weapons:

THE TRUTH

<< Isaiah 54:16 >> [Behold, I have created the smith that bloweth the coals in the fire, and that bringeth forth an instrument for his work; and I have created the waster to destroy.]

The waster is the nuclear missile, which will be used! The Bible gave a visualization of the nuclear explosion saying:

<< Revelation 6:14 >> [And the heavens departed as a scroll when it is rolled together: and every mountain and island was moved out of its place.]

This verse describes what we call the mushroom cloud associated with a nuclear explosion. There can not be a doubt about the fact that there is going to be a nuclear war, and that the Caucasian Roman world is doomed, that it will be destroyed. The Bible confirms this.

<< Revelation 9:15 >> [And the four angels were loosed, which were prepared for an hour, and a day, and a month, and a year, for to slay the third part of men.]

The nuclear war will last one hour. It will take less than one hour to destroy the modern Roman Empire, and all nations that are joined to the Western world!

THE TRUTH

The Four Horsemen

The four horsemen featured in Revelation chapters six are symbolic of four phases that will culminate in the destruction of the heathen society, and the deliverance of the twelve tribes of Israel. In Matthew chapter twenty-four Jesus Christ describes the events and the time o his Second Coming. These events directly parallel those described in the four horsemen of Revelations.

<<Revelation 6:1,2>> *[And I saw when the Lamb opened one of the seals, and I heard, as it were the noise of thunder, one of the four beasts saying, Come and see. <2> And I saw, and behold a white horse* (white here is a symbol of righteousness)*: and he that sat on him had a bow; and a crown was given unto him: and he went forth conquering, and to conquer.]*

The book being opened was a book of prophecies that had to be fulfilled. The Lamb opening the book was Christ. The first horsemen represent Jesus Christ, and the bow symbolizes the gospel of the kingdom that Christ brought. A bow was used to symbolizes the gospel and judgment because the arrow reaches its mark before the rider does: as the gospel of the kingdom of the twelve tribes of Israel will be preached just before the coming of Jesus Christ.
The rider of the white horse is Jesus Christ:

<< Revelation 19:11-16 >> *[And I saw heaven opened, and behold a white horse; and he that sat on him was called faithful and true. and in righteousness he doth judge and make war. His eyes were as a flame of fire, and on his head were many crowns; and he had a name written that no man knew, but himself. And he was clothed with a vesture dipped in blood: and his name is called The Word of Lord YAHAWAH]*

We know that Jesus Christ is called **The Word** in John 1:1!

<<Revelation 6:3-17>> *[And when he had opened the second seal, I heard the second beast say, Come and see. <4> And there went out another horse that was red* (This red horse symbolizes the Edomite Caucasians)*: and power was given to him that sat thereon to take peace from the earth, and that they should kill one another* (referring to the First and Second World Wars)*: and there was given him a great sword* (This great sword represents the nuclear weapons).

<5> And when he had opened the third seal, I heard the third beast say, Come and see. And I beheld and lo a black horse (symbolizing judgment, plagues, and disaster)*; and he that sat on him had a pair of balances in his hand* (The modern Greco-Roman Empire, has been weighted in the balances, now is the time for them to pay the price for their evil, as in Daniel 5:16-31).

<6> And I heard a voice in the midst of the four beasts say, A measure of wheat for a penny, and three measures of barley for a penny (symbolizing famine, and droughts)*; and see thou hurt not the oil and the wine]*

THE TRUTH

The oil was used for anointing; here it represents the anointed people, which are all those who accept Jesus. The wine represents the new covenant in the blood of Jesus. Only the people who believe in the Lord YAHAWASHY (Jesus Christ) as their Savior will not be hurt by the judgment coming upon the people of this world.

<<*Revelation 6:7,8*>> [*And when he had opened the fourth seal, I heard the voice of the fourth beast say, Come and see. <8> And I looked and beheld a pale horse* (The word that was translated for the color pale here, is more accurately translated as green in modern English*); and his name that sat on him was Death, and Hell followed with him.*]

In Revelation, green always symbolizes the believers and the Israelites that believe in the gospel of Jesus, as in the following passage:

<< *Revelation 9:4* >> [*And it was commanded them that they should not hurt the grass of the earth, neither any green thing, neither any tree; but those men which have not the seal of the Lord YAHAWAH in their foreheads. And power was given unto them over the fourth part of the earth to kill with sword, and with hunger, and with death, and with the beast of the earth.*]

The black horse represents the 144,000, mentioned in Revelation chapter 7, and 14:3. The 144,000 will have power to judge the world.

<<*John 14:12* >> [*Verily, verily, I say unto you, He that believeth on me, the works that I do shall he do also;* **and greater** *works than these shall he do; because I go unto my Father.*

<< *Revelation 6:8-11*>> [*And I looked, and behold a pale horse: and his name that sat on him was Death, and Hell followed with him. And power was given unto them over the fourth part of the earth, to kill with sword, and with hunger, and with death, and with the beasts of the earth.*
    <9> And when he had opened the fifth seal, I saw under the altar the souls of them that were slain for the word of God, and for the testimony which they held: <10> And they cried with a loud voice, saying, How long, O Lord, holy and true, dost thou not judge and avenge our blood on them that dwell on the earth? <11> And white robes were given unto every one of them; and it was said unto them, that they should rest yet for a little season, until their fellow servants also and their brethren, that should be killed as they were, should be fulfilled..]

The time will come very soon when the Most High will give the Hebrew Israelites the spiritual power to command the elements, bring plagues, and to heal sicknesses! We will have the same kind of power the Lord YAHAWAH had given to Moses to plague the Egyptians, and the same kind of power Christ had used in performing the miracles. Then suddenly, Yahawashy will return to earth to judge, to subdue, and to punish the nations for their sins.

THE TRUTH

<< Revelation 6:12-17 >> [And I beheld when he had opened the sixth seal, and, lo, there was a great earthquake; and the sun became black as sackcloth of hair, and the moon became as blood; <13> And the stars of heaven fell unto the earth, even as a fig tree casteth her untimely figs, when she is shaken of a mighty wind. <14> And the heaven departed as a scroll when it is rolled together; and every mountain and island were moved out of their places.

<15> And the kings of the earth, and the great men, and the rich men, and the chief captains, and the mighty men, and every bondman, and every free man, hid themselves in the dens and in the rocks of the mountains; <16> And said to the mountains and rocks, Fall on us, and hide us from the face of him that sitteth on the throne, and from the wrath of the Lamb: <17> For the great day of his wrath is come; and who shall be able to stand?]

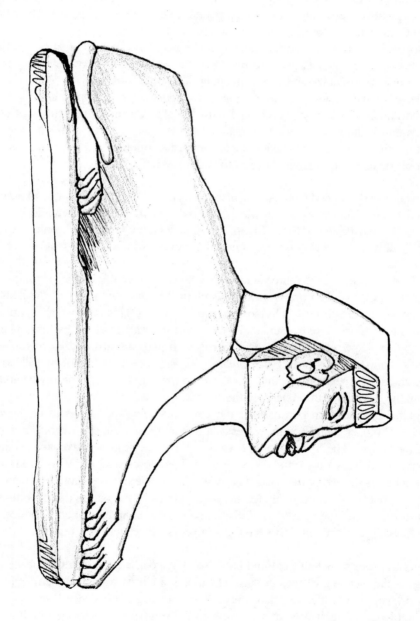

THE SPHINX

THE ZODIAC PROPHECIES AND THE SPHINX

The prophecies existed long before the Bible came to be in its present form. In fact, the prophecies concerning world events existed before man was created (to exist upon the earth). The prophecies are simply the plans, which the Creator had outlined for his creation before he formed it!

The prophecies were first revealed to mankind by way of the names of stars, and the cycles of the zodiac. In other words the very first gospel given to man was the zodiac. However, astrology is false, astrology is the pollution of the zodiac, as organized religion is the pollution of the Bible!

Knowledge of the zodiac prophecies was conveyed to Adam, approximately six thousand years ago, directly from the Almighty Creator. Teaching Adam the stellar cycles and names of stars, which names are equivalent to scriptures, did this. It was the Creator, not man, which gave each star a spiritual prophetic name! Each original star name represents an event to be accomplished upon the earth; the names are scripture! The Lord taught those prophetic names of stars and cycles to Adam, which he was to preserve and teach to his descendants after him.

Noah who was descended from Adam, also preserved and taught this sacred knowledge to his three sons: Shem, Ham, and Japhet. This spiritual knowledge from the pre-flood Adamic world was thus transferred to the people of the world after the flood. Since Shem, Ham, and Japhet are the progenitors of all people and nations upon the earth; initially, all the nations were taught the prophecies about the great Savior and Deliverer that was to come!

After the descendants of the three sons of Noah began to multiply and populate the world, some people started to pervert and misuse the pure knowledge contained in the prophecies of the zodiac, the names of stars, and the stellar cycles, to create false religions and false saviors! This confusion began at Babel. The different religions and occult practices were first created by some of the leaders of the nations. They used perverted forms of the original zodiac gospel in order to satisfy their selfish personal lust and greed for wealth and power. They used it to glorify themselves instead of the Creator. In fact, the same problem still continues to exist today. Glimpses of the zodiac Gospel can be found in various forms within the ancient myths and religions of all nations of antiquity from the Egyptians, the Asians, to the Aztecs.

The sphinx and the great pyramid are the keys to solving the mysteries of the zodiac prophecies! The word Sphinx means "binder". The Sphinx serves as a marker to indicate the true beginning and the true end of the twelve signs of the zodiac. The Sphinx consists of two parts: the head of a woman and the body of the lion. The head of the woman represents Virgo, and the body of the lion represents Leo. Virgo the head, is the true beginning of the zodiac, and Leo is the end of the zodiac! Now we know where to begin our examination of the zodiac!

Virgo is symbolic of the original Hebrew Israelite nation, the nation that would bring forth Jesus Christ, the Savior! Libra represents the price that Christ came to pay as an atonement to redeem us from sin. Scorpio represents the wounding and the fall: Jesus having to give his life. Sagittarius represents the triumph of Jesus over sin and death.

Capricorn is shown as half goat and half fish. The goat is representative of the fact that Christ died as our sin offering, as the escape goat for our sins! The blood of Christ was an atonement to redeem us to God. The lively tail of a fish represents life. Capricorn reveals that through Jesus' death, as a sin offering would comes eternal life! The blood of Christ was an atonement to redeem us back into the family of God. Aquarius shows Christ as the Water Bearer, bringing us the water of life, which is the word of truth. Pisces represents the people that are in captivity within the ocean of false philosophy and religion. Aries represents Christ as the Lamb who would come to deliver us!

The second half of the zodiac deals with the Second Coming of Jesus Christ. It starts with Taurus, depicted by a charging bull. The raging bull is a symbol of destruction, plagues, and judgment to occur in the last days, before the Second Coming of Jesus Christ. Gemini represents unity and victory for the people who accept the truth. The Scarab or a crab often represents Cancer. The hard shell of the crab protects it from the violence of the ocean around it. Similarly, the believers of truth will be protected and delivered, from the plagues and destructions of the last days. The last sign is Leo. Leo the Lion represents Christ at his Second Coming, as the conquering Lion, coming to subdue and bring judgment upon the head of the enemy!

What is called Christianity today is not new. The gospel of the zodiac is the original Christianity. We will examine details of the zodiac to see how it reveals the prophecies pertaining to the first and Second Coming of Jesus Christ, and the destiny of mankind! You can rightly say that Adam was the first Christian!

The classic myths, gods, religions, and occult practices of all the nations of antiquity are perverted forms of the original zodiac gospel, from the Egyptians and Babylonians to the Asians and the Aztecs! It is good to research all books, especially the ancient one, and read about the great teachers like: Buddha, Confucius. For example, the Egyptians preserved zodiac prophecies concerning Christ as the coming Deliverer and Redeemer in the fable of Osiris. They describe Osiris as an Asiatic man with woolly hair. Osiris, accompanied by his disciples, performed many miracles. Later he was eventually crucified on the vernal equinox, as ordered by Typhoon. He remained three days and nights to judge the dead, and he was then resurrected and ascended to heaven. As you can see, Osiris personifies the Christ that was to come!

Secondly, the Egyptians also depicted the coming Christ in the story of Horus. This story is written and illustrated on the walls of the temple of Luxor. Horus is represented in four Christian-like scenes: The Annunciation, the Immaculate Conception, the Birth, and the Adoration. Horus is a depiction of Christ, copied from the original gospel of the zodiac, which is what they call Christianity today! Consequently, all the gods of Greece and Rome were imported from Egypt, therefore, they too are polluted versions of the zodiac gospel! This knowledge was based on the gospel of the zodiac which Ham, father of the Africans, had learned from Noah.

In America, a famous myth that also conceals the original gospel of Christianity is the story of Quetzalcoatl. Quetzalcoalt was described as an Asiatic man with brown-skin and woolly hair, and possessing supernatural powers. He practiced exorcism, healing, fasting forty days, and did many miracles. When Quetzalcoatl resisted the temptations of the devil, they persecuted and crucified him on the vernal equinox. And here again is a perfect example where the original gospel was concealed in a polluted form.

All the nations had inherited the original gospel. They transformed it to create their own false gods and religions: Isis and Horus also worshipped by the Romans, Apollo and Zeus of the Greeks; Buddha, and Krishna of India, Fuhi of the Chinese, Zaha of the Japanese, Quetzalcoalt of the Mexicans, Osiris, of the Egyptians. And not only are all those false gods derived from the zodiac gospel, but upon close examinations they are found to correspond to each other. For example, the nine gods of ancient Egypt correspond to the nine Lords of the night found in the Mexican legends. The tales of Kwan-Yin, the Chinese Queen of heaven, (called Kwannon in Japan), correspond to Isis of the Egyptians.

The female goddesses are derived from the sign of Virgo. Virgo, the impregnated woman, is often used in the Bible to represent the original nation of Israel, which was to bring forth the savior Jesus Christ.

<< Revelation 12:1,2 >> [There appeared a great wonder in heaven; a woman clothed with the sun, and the moon under her feet, and upon her head a crown of twelve stars: And she being with child cried, travailing in birth, and pained to be delivered.]

THE TRUTH

If you have doubts check the Bible! The twelve stars represent the original twelve tribes of Israel, the child, of course, represents Jesus Christ!

Astrology Is False

Astrology is the perversion of the zodiac, as religion is the perversion of the Bible. The Astrologers look up to the stars like they were gods that determine events in a person's daily life; the Bible condemns this practice,

<< *Deuteronomy 17:3* >> *[...Hath gone and served other gods, and worshipped them, either the sun, the moon, or any of the hosts of heaven, which I have not commanded!]*

Clearly, the Bible condemns all occult, witchcraft practices including Astrology:

<< *Deuteronomy 18:10,11* >> *[There shall not be found among you any one that maketh his son or his daughter to pass through the fire, or that useth divination* (card readers, for example*.), or an observer of times* (the Daily Horoscopes found in magazines and news papers*), or an enchanter, or a witch, or a charmer, or a consulter with familiar spirits, or a wizard, or a necromancer. For all that do these things are an abomination unto the Lord!]*

This is because those practices are not based on truth. Astrologers are all fakes, to follow after them is to condemn yourself!

<< *Isaiah 47:13,14* >> *[Thou art wearied in the multitude of thy counsels. Let now the astrologers, the stargazers, the monthly prognosticators, stand up, and save thee from these things that shall come upon thee* (the nuclear destruction, plagues*). Behold, they shall be as stubble; the fire shall burn them; they shall not deliver themselves from the power of the flame!]*

Astrologers have no power, they will not be able to save themselves from the plagues and nuclear destruction. If the blind leads the blind, they will both fall into a pit; consulting with divinators and astrologers is Satanism, and will lead you to destruction!

Furthermore, the zodiac charts used to determine the horoscopes is an inaccurate representation of the true zodiac, the star positions on those charts are completely incorrect! For example, astrologers claim that the zodiac begins with Aries; they claim that Aries correspond to the spring equinox (the time of the year when the day and the night are of equal length, the first day of spring). This can be proven to be completely false. The zodiac and spring does not begin with Aries, because of a factor known as the precession of the equinox!

When we research Astronomy and relativistic Astrophysics, we see that because of the precession of the equinox, spring no longer occurs in Aries, it occurs now in Pisces! The precession of the equinox means that the time of year when the day and the night are equal, as the earth travels through the twelve signs of the zodiac occurs a little early every year! In other words, the earth does not completely come back to the exact same spot every year: to complete the precession cycle, such that it is 50.2" short every year; and in about 25,800 years it would return to the same spot. As a result, spring has long since left the sign of Aries and now spring occurs in

THE TRUTH

Pisces! This means that all the zodiacal cycles have shifted by one sign, making all the Astrological charts that horoscope predictions are made from, to be in error by at least one month!

But the fact is, the time that the zodiac is to start is not at all determined by the seasons! The true beginning of the zodiac is Virgo, not Aries; and it ends with Leo! Have you ever wondered why the Sphinx in Egypt was constructed? The Sphinx is a symbol marking the true beginning and the true end of the zodiac: the head of a woman, with the body of a lion! The head of a woman symbolizes Virgo, and the body of a lion symbolizes Leo! The word Sphinx means, "to bind". It binds the true beginning and the true end of the zodiac: Virgo bind with Leo! This fact serves as a key to understanding the mysteries of the zodiac! Astrology is the exploitation of the zodiac and a hoax to make money; people practicing it and other false religions will be faced with judgment!

The Tower of Babel, known in ancient times as the Seven Spheres, was a monument dedicated to the zodiac. The archeological remains of the tower have been located. At the top of this observatory was a representation of the twelve signs of the zodiac. This tower was recorded:

> << Genesis 11:4 >> [And they said one to another, Go to, let us make brick, and burn them thoroughly. And they had brick for stone, and slime for mortar. And they said, Go to, let us build a city and a tower, whose top may reach unto heaven (more accurately translated: "its top with the heaven", meaning: the ceiling was painted with a representation of the zodiac); and let us make us a name, lest we be scattered abroad upon the face of the whole earth.]

So this tower was to be a way of preserving the knowledge, if they became scattered! It was good to preserve the knowledge, but the wrong thing is that they bragged saying "Come, let us build ourselves a city, and a tower, ...and let us make a name for ourselves". Instead of giving God the glory and calling upon the name of God as in << Genesis 4:26 >> these people wanted to use the sacred knowledge to glorify themselves, and for making their own gods. This made the Lord God YAHAWAH angry, and he dispersed them!

The Sacred Zodiac

The word zodiac is from a Hebrew word ZADY meaning a way, or step, or path, referring to the path of the sun through the twelve major constellation signs. Although astrologers polluted the zodiac, astrologers did not invent the zodiac! The zodiac signs were known way before there was any Caucasian civilization in existence. Note that, the same twelve signs, and arrangements of the constellations (grouping of the stars) are common to all the classic cultures: the Aztecs, the Egyptians, and the Oriental. And as far back in history as you can trace, the signs are the same! This proves that the zodiac signs are authentic; individuals did not make them up optionally at random!

The fact is man did not invent the zodiac. According to the Bible, God made the zodiac, and set the constellations to reveal the prophecies concerning Christ! This will be proven beyond the slightest doubt! The Most High God says:

> << Job 16:19 >> [Also now, behold, my witness is in heaven, and my record is on high!]

The zodiac, like the Bible, contains the prophecies concerning Christ, as you will see shortly! The stars were not set at random in the heavens, they are accurately numbered, timed, and given prophetic names by the Creator:

THE TRUTH

<< Isaiah 40:26 >> [Lift up your eyes on high, and behold who hath created these things, that bringeth out their hosts by number (Exact numbers, and calculated motions)*: he calleth them all by names* (each star has a name corresponding to prophecy) *by the greatness of his might, for that he is strong in power; not one faileth.]*

The zodiac is the prophecies and plans of the Creator for his creation! A few of the star and constellation names are recorded in the Bible:

<< Job 26:13 >> [By his spirit he hath garnished the heavens (the Highest is the designer of the zodiac signs)*; his hand hath formed the Crooked Serpent.* (This is the name of a constellation.)*]*

<< Job 38:31-32 >> [Canst thou bind the sweet influence of Pleiades, or loose the bands of Orion? Canst thou bring forth Mazzaroth (meaning the twelve signs from Virgo to Leo) *in his season? or canst thou guide Arcturus with his sons?]*

All of those are names of various constellations. Those constellations contain prophecies:

<< Psalms 136:5 >> [To him that by wisdom made the heavens...]

<< Psalm 19:1-7 >> [The heavens declare the glory of God; and the firmament sheweth his handiwork. <2> Day unto day uttereth speech,(the zodiac contains the scriptures. It is a gospel) *and night unto night sheweth knowledge. <3> There is no speech nor language, where their voice is not heard. <4> Their line is gone out through all the earth, and their words to the end of the world. In them hath he set a tabernacle for the sun, <5> Which is as a bridegroom coming out of his chamber, and rejoiceth as a strong man to run a race. <6> His going forth is from the end of the heaven, and his circuit unto the ends of it: and there is nothing hid from the heat thereof. <7> The law of the LORD is perfect, converting the soul: the testimony of the LORD is sure, making wise the simple.]*

<< Psalm 148:3 >> [Praise ye him, sun and moon: praise him, all ye stars of light.]

The zodiac is not just a pretty picture it contains deep knowledge concerning the prophecies! The zodiac contains the history from the creation to the Second Coming of Jesus Christ! The zodiac was designated on the fourth day, of the creation.

<< Genesis 1:14 >> [And the God said, Let there be lights in the firmament of the heaven to divide the day from the night; and let them be for signs (the word translated sign here is a word referring to prophecy signs: prophecies to occur on the earth)*, and for seasons, and for days, and years.]*

154

The Hebrew word translated "seasons" in the above verse means appointed or fixed, as in events and prophecies; it does not refer to the four seasons. The zodiac was to be a pictorial representation of the prophecies concerning Christ and the nation of Israel! Recall that the zodiac is the first gospel. Now a person can not truthfully claim that the Babylonians or the Egyptians invented the zodiac. The zodiac existed before the flood, before there was a Babylonian or Egyptian empire! Adam and the people also knew the prophecies as well as the sacred Laws in the time of Noah!

<< Genesis 7:2 >> [*Of every clean beast thou shalt take to thee by seven, the male and the female: and beast that are not clean by two, the male and the female.*]

The only way Noah knew which beasts were clean and unclean was to know the Dietary Law, similar to the Biblical law. Clearly the descendants of Adam before and after the flood knew the prophecies and the Laws; way before the Babylonians, and the Egyptians existed! Originally, each of the twelve zodiac signs had three decan signs that help to explain its message. The twelve major signs and their decan signs total to forty-eight constellations! Now we will learn the truth of the individual signs of the zodiac!

The Twelve Signs Of The zodiac And Their Decans

VIRGO	**LIBRA**	**SCORPIO**	**SAGITTARIUS**
Coma	Crux	Serpens	Lyra
Bootes	Victima	Ophiuchus	Ara
Centaur	Corona	Hercules	Draco

CAPRICORN	**AQUARIUS**	**PISCES**	**ARIES**
Sagitta	Pis. Aus.	Bands	Cassiopia
Aquila	Pegasus	Androm.	Cetus
Delphinus	Cygnus	Cepheus	Perseus

TAURUS	**GEMINI**	**CANCER**	**LEO**
Orion	Lepus	Ursa Ma.	Hydra
Eridanus	Canis Ma.	Ursa Mi.	Crater
Auriga	Canis Mi.	Argo	Corvus

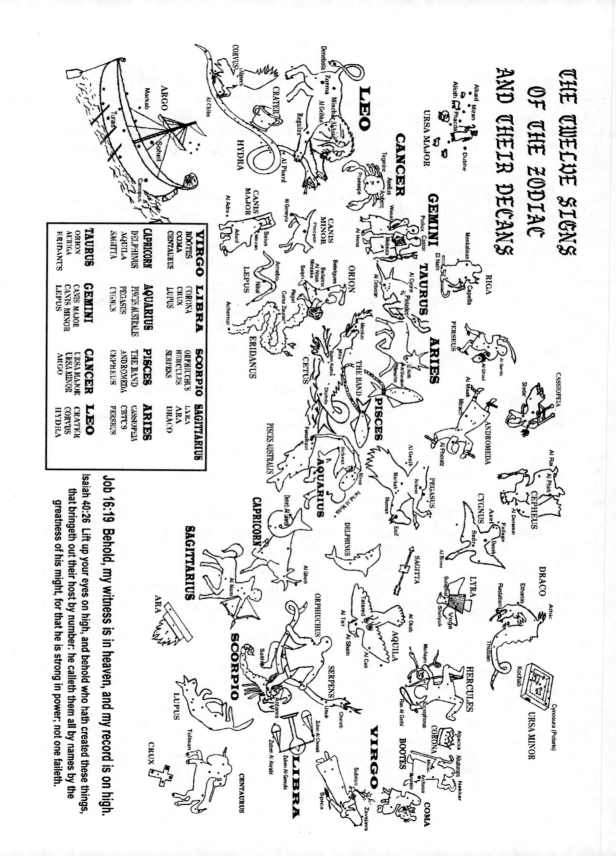

THE TWELVE SIGNS OF THE ZODIAC AND THEIR DECANS

VIRGO			LIBRA			SCORPIO			SAGITTARIUS		
BOOTES			CORONA			OPHIUCHUS			LYRA		
COMA			CRUX			HERCULES			ARA		
CENTAURUS			LUPUS			SERPENS			DRACO		

CAPRICORN			AQUARIUS			PISCES			ARIES		
DELPHINUS			PISCES AUSTRALIS			THE BAND			CASSIOPEIA		
AQUILA			PEGASUS			ANDROMEDA			CETUS		
SAGITTA			CYGNUS			CEPHEUS			PERSEUS		

TAURUS			GEMINI			CANCER			LEO		
ORION			CANIS MAJOR			URSA MAJOR			CRATER		
AURIGA			CANIS MINOR			URSA MINOR			CORVUS		
ERIDANUS			LEPUS			ARGO			HYDRA		

Job 16:19 Behold, my witness is in heaven, and my record is on high.

Isaiah 40:26 Lift up your eyes on high, and behold who hath created these things, that bringeth out their host by number: he calleth them all by the greatness of his might, for that he is strong in power; not one faileth.

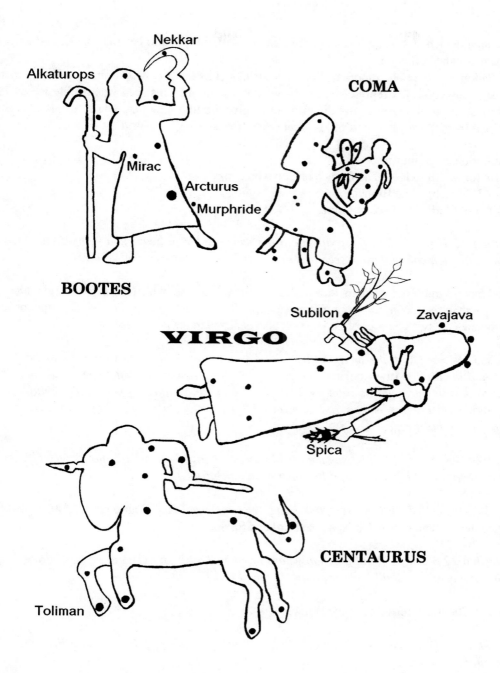

Nekkar

Alkaturops

COMA

Mirac

Arcturus

Murphride

BOOTES

Subilon

Zavajava

VIRGO

Spica

CENTAURUS

Toliman

THE TRUTH

VIRGO

This zodiac sign depicts a woman holding a child in her arm, a branch in her right hand, and an ear of corn pointing downwards in her left hand.

This constellation is a symbolic representation of Jesus Christ as the prophetic branch, and seed; a seed from the nation of Israel, symbolically represented by the woman or Virgin! This seed was manifested as Jesus Christ. As the seed must fall to the ground and die in order to give life to a new tree, Christ would also suffer death and be resurrected from the dead, as part of his great work of redeeming the world!

Stars: Zavijava - Gloriously Beautiful.
        Vindermatrix (or Al Muredin) - The Branch or Son who comes.
        Subilon (or Al Zimach) - The Branch.
        Spica - An Ear of Corn, The Seed of Corn.

<< Revelation 12:1-5 >> [And there appeared a great wonder in heaven; a woman cloth with the sun, and the moon under her feet, and upon her head a crown of twelve stars]

The sun and moon symbolize: wisdom, knowledge and understanding, which is the foundation. Note that the sun gives more light than the moon; the moon represents the Mosaic Law, and the sun is the gospel of Jesus. The twelve stars symbolize the twelve tribes of Israel, as is also depicted in the next verse.

<< Genesis 37:9 >> [And she being with child (Christ) travail in birth, and pain to be delivered... And the dragon (the Roman Empire) stood before the woman, which was ready to deliver, for to devour her child as soon as it was born. And she brought forth a man-child, who was to rule all nations with a rod of iron and her child was caught up unto Lord YAHAWAH, and to his throne.]

<< John 12:24 >> [Verily, verily, I say unto you, except a corn of wheat fall into the ground and die, it abideth alone: but if it dies, it bringeth forth much fruit.]

This Son, Christ, was to die for our sins, redeeming the Israelites and also all other Christians that have repented and accepted the truth and Jesus Christ as the Lord and Savior!

<< Zechariah 6:12 >> [...Behold the man whose name is the BRANCH; and he shall grow up out of his place, and he shall build the temple of the Lord.]

Here we see again that Christ is referred to as the Branch.

<< Isaiah 11:1 >> [And there shall come forth a rod out of the stem of Jesse, and a Branch shall grow out of his roots.]

<< Isaiah 4:2 >> [In that day shall the branch of the Lord be Beautiful and glorious...]

THE TRUTH

Zavijava: Christ the Beautiful and Glorious in His Nature and Perfect in His Character, as A Diamond.

Coma

Coma: The Desired, The Longed-For.

This constellation sign shows a woman on a chair, with her young son standing on her lap. This sign represents Christ as the desired son, and as the exalted seed!

<< Isaiah 9:6 >> *[For unto us a child is born, unto us a son is given: and the government shall be upon his shoulder: and his name shall be called Wonderful, Counsellor, the mighty Lord, The everlasting Father, The Prince of Peace.]*

<< Haggai 2:7 >> *[And I will shake all nations and the desire of all nations shall come.]*

Centaurus

Historic name: Bezeh - The despised, or Asmeath - Sin offering.

The Centaur is a half-man half-horse creature. It symbolizes the double nature of Christ: being human, and a Son of God! This double natured man would be despised and rejected by the people at his first coming.

Stars: Toliman - The Heretofore and The Here After.

<< John 1:10:11 >> *[He was in the world and the world was made by him, and the world knew him not. He came unto his own, and his own received him not.]*

<< Isaiah 53:3 >> *[He is despised and rejected of men; a man of sorrows, and acquainted with grief: and we hid as it were our faces from him; he was despised, and we esteemed him not. Surely he hath borne our grief.]*

<< Revelation 1:8 >> *[I am Alpha and Omega, the beginning and the ending.]*

THE TRUTH

Boots

Historic name: Bo - The Coming Shepherd.

This sign shows a shepherd with a staff in his right hand, and a sickle raised in his left hand. This sign symbolizes Christ as the Shepherd, coming to gather (sickle) and to lead (staff) his flock, the redeemed people!

Stars: Arcturus - He Cometh.
Nekkar – The Pierced.
Alkaturops - The Shepherd's Crook.
Mirac - The Coming Forth as an Arrow.
Murphride - Who separates (The Sheep from the goats)

<< *Zechariah 12:10* >> *[...And they shall look upon me whom they have pierced, and they shall mourn for him, as one that mourneth for his only son.]*

<< *Hebrews 13:20* >> *[Now the God of peace, that brought again from the dead our Lord Jesus, that great shepherd of the sheep, through the blood of the everlasting covenant.]*

Alpacca

CORONA

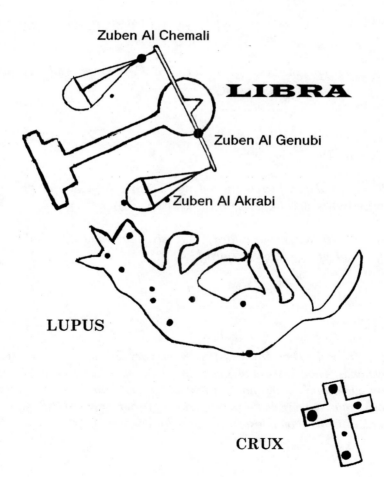

Zuben Al Chemali

LIBRA

Zuben Al Genubi

Zuben Al Akrabi

LUPUS

CRUX

THE TRUTH

LIBRA

Historic names: Al Zubena - The Purchase, Redemption Gain.
                          Mozanaim - The Pair of Scales Weighing.

This sign depicts the fact that the first coming of Christ was to pay the price for the redemption of the Israelites, by his death on the cross!

Stars: Zuben Al Genubi - The Price that is Deficient.
         Zuben Akrabi - The Price of the Conflict.
         Zuben Al Chemali - The Price that Covers.

<< Daniel 5:27 >> [TEKEL; Thou art weighed in the balances, and art found wanting.]

<< Revelation 5:9 >> [...For thou wast slain, and hast redeemed us to the Lord YAHAWAH by thy blood]

<< John 1:26 >> [...Behold the Lamb of the Lord YAHAWAH, which taketh away the sins of the world.]

Crux

Historic name: Adom - The Cutting Off.

<< Daniel 9:26 >> [And after threescore and two weeks shall the messiah be cut off, but not for himself. (Christ died as atonement for the sins of the world)]

<< John 19:30 >> [When Jesus therefore had received the vinegar, he said, it is finished: and he bowed his head, and gave up the spirit.]

Corona

Stars: Alpacca - Royal Crown.

<< Hebrews 2:7-10 >> [...Thou crownedst him with glory and honor, and didst set him over the works of thy hands: Thou hast put all things in subjection under his feet. For in that he put all in subjection under him, he left nothing that is not under him... we see Jesus, who was made a little lower than the angels for the suffering of death, crowned with glory and honor; that he by the grace of God should taste death once for every man.

THE TRUTH

Victima

Historic name: Asedah - To Be Slain.

This sign shows a dog being killed by the spear of Centaur. Symbolizing Christ was the despised sin offering, he offered to die for us! Both Victima and Centaur represent different aspects of the work of Christ. The spear of Centaur kills the dog, a humiliating animal; the fact is Christ had willingly offered his own life for us.

<< John 10:17,18 >> *[...I lay down my life, that I might take it again. No man taketh it from me, but I lay it down of my self.]*

<< Isaiah 53:3-12 >> *[He was despised and rejected of men; a man of sorrows, and acquainted with grief: and we hid as it were our faces from him; he was despised, and we esteemed him not. Surely he hath borne our griefs, and carried our sorrows: yet we esteemed him stricken, smitten of the Lord YAHAWAH, and afflicted. But he was wounded for our transgressions, he was bruised for our iniquities: the chastisement of our peace was upon him; and with his stripes we are healed. All we like sheep have gone astray; we have turned everyone to his own way; and the Lord hath laid on him the iniquity of us all.*

He was oppressed, and he was afflicted, yet he opens not his mouth: he is brought as a lamb to the slaughter, and as a sheep before her shearers is dumb, so he open not his mouth. He was taken from prison and from judgment: and who shall declare his generation? For he was cut off out of the land of the living: for the transgression of my people was he stricken. And he made his grave with the wicked, and with the rich in his death; because he had done no violence, neither was any deceit in his mouth. Yet it pleased the Lord to bruise him; he hath put him to grief: when thou shalt make his soul an offering for sin, he shall see his seed, he shall prolong his days, and the pleasure of the Lord shall prosper in his hand. He shall see of the travail of his soul, and shall be satisfied: by his knowledge shall my servant justify many; for he shall bear their iniquity. Therefore will I divide him a portion with the great, and he shall divide the spoil with the strong; because he hath poured out his soul unto death: and he was numbered with the transgressors; and he bares the sin of many and made intercession for the transgressors.]

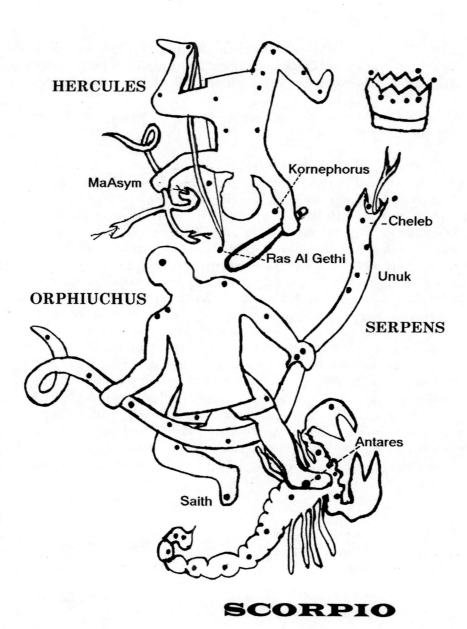

THE TRUTH

SCORPIO

Historic names: Akrab - The Conflict, or War.
                       Al Akrab - Wounding Him Who Cometh.
                       Isidis - Attack of the Enemy.

This sign depicts Christ as the mighty man, wrestling with a giant serpent. His foot is crushing the head of a scorpion, and the heel of the other foot is kicked back from the sting of the giant scorpion! This sign shows that In this spiritual battle of truth, redemption, and sacrifice, Christ would have to suffer death.

Stars: Antares (red) - The Wounding.
         Lesath - The Perverse.

Serpens

Stars: Unuk - Encompassing.
         Cheleb - The Serpent Enfolding.

<< *Genesis 3:14,15* >> *[And the Lord said unto the serpent, because thou hast done this, thou art cursed above every beast of the field; upon thy belly shalt thou go, and dust shalt thou eat all the days of thy life: And I will put enmity between thee and the woman, and between thy seed and her seed; it shall bruise thy head, and thou shall bruise his heel.]*

The scorpion symbolizes the evil elements that had caused us to fall as a nation. When Christ returns, there will be judgment, the evil empires of the world will be destroyed with Satan: to bruise a serpent's head is to kill it!

<< *Psalms 91:13* >> *[Thou shall tread upon the lion and adder: the young lion and the dragon shalt thou trample under foot.]*

Orphiuchus

Historic name: Afeichus - The Serpent Held.

Stars: Ras Al Hagus - The Head of Him Who Holds.
        Ras Al Awa - The Head of the Desired One.
        Saiph - Bruised.

<< *Psalm 22:16* >> *[Dogs have compassed me: The assembly of the wicked has enclosed me.]*

<< *Psalms 116:3* >> *[The sorrows of death compassed me, and the pains of hell got hold upon me.]*

THE TRUTH

Hercules

Historic names: Bau - The One Who Cometh.
                       Al Giscale - The Strong.

    This sign depicts a mighty man on one knee, his right heel raised slightly as if wounded, with the club in his right hand uplifted, right foot is crushing the head of Draco, his left hand is holding a triple headed snake! This sign symbolizes that when the little horn America and the other reuniting European nations comes into alliance, Christ will then return to destroy this evil society: the serpent of seven heads and ten horns!

Stars: Ras Al Gethi - The Head of Him Who Bruises; or Ras Al Awa - The Head of The Desired.
         Kornephorus - The Branch Kneeling.
         MaAsym - The Sin Offering.
         Marsic - The Wounding.
         Caiam - Punishing.

<< Psalm 118:22 >> *[The Stone (Jesus Christ) which the builders refused has become the head stone of the corner.]*

<< Revelation 20:1-3 >> *[And I saw an angel come down from heaven, having the key of the bottomless pit and a great chain in his hand. And he laid hold on the dragon, that old serpent, which is the Devil, and Satan, and bound him a thousand years, and cast him into the bottomless pit, and shut him up, and set a seal upon him, that he should deceive the nations no more, till the thousand years should be fulfilled: and after that he must be loosed a little season.]*

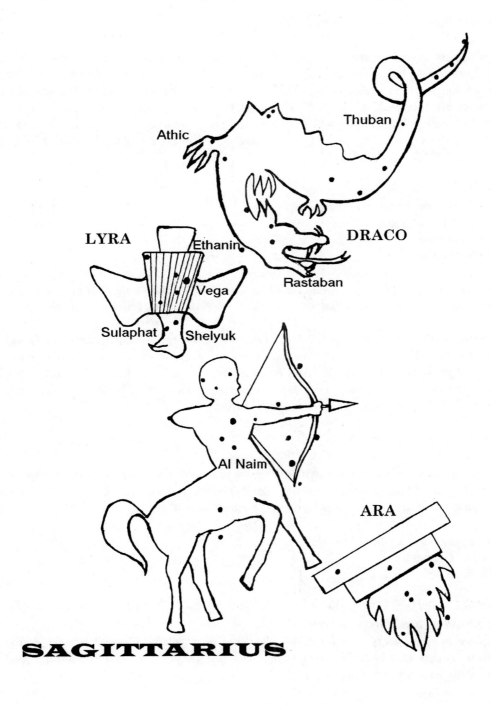

THE TRUTH

SAGITTARIUS

Historic name: Kesith - Bending of a Bow, shooting.

This sign depicts a double natured man, a centaur, aiming an arrow at the scorpion. This sign is representative of Christ's triumph over sin and evil, his victory over death, and the completion of his great work of redemption and salvation. By the sacrifice of himself, he was able to make atonement for the sins of the world, and became the intercessor between God and man. The arrow being shot forth by the Centaur is symbolic of the power of the gospel of Jesus Christ, and also of the future judgment yet to be executed upon the wicked at his Second Coming! This judgment is called The Day of The Lord. Also this is the day of the Nuclear War, in which the enemies of the gospel of truth will perish!

Stars: Al Naim - The Gracious or Delighted In.
Nushata - The Going, or Sending Forth.
Terebellum - Sent Forth Swiftly.
Al Shaula - The Dart.
Croton - The Purchaser.

<< *Revelation 6:2* >> *[And I saw, and behold a white horse: and he that sat on him had a bow; and a crown was given unto him: and he went forth conquering, and to conquer.]*

<< *II Thessalonians 2:8-10* >> *[And then shall that wicked be revealed, whom the Lord shall consume with the spirit of his mouth, and shall destroy with the brightness of his coming: Even him, whose coming is after the working of Satan with all power and signs and lying wonders, and with all deceivableness of unrighteousness in them that perish; because they receive not the love of the truth, that they might be saved.]*

Lyra

This sign shows an eagle with a harp: symbolizing the praises of Christ for his great work of redeeming mankind, the twelve tribes of Israel, and the defeating of Evil. The songs of the harp can be said to represent the gospel of truth, because the truth is a comforting song to those that listen to it.

Stars: Sulaphat - Springing Up, or Al Nest - The Eagle.
Shelyuk - The Fishing Eagle.
Vega - He Shall be Exalted.

<< *Revelation 19:1,2* >> *[...I heard a great voice of much people in heaven, saying, Alleluia; Salvation, and glory, and honor, and power, unto the Lord our Lord: For truth and righteous are his judgments: For he hath judged the great whore* (the evil empires of the world, led by America)*, which did corrupt the earth with her fornication, and hath avenged the blood of his servants at her hands.]*

THE TRUTH

Ara

Historic Names: Ara - The Alter

                         Al Mugamra - The Completion, or The Finishing, Perfecting.

This is an altar with burning fire on it. This decan symbolizes that the Judgment poured out on the enemy will be by fire (nuclear destruction)! And also that Jesus Christ had offered himself as a sheep is offered on an altar of fire, as an acceptable offering to God for atonement of our sins.

    << Revelation 20:10 >> [And the devil that deceived them was cast into the lake of fire and brimstone, where the beast and the false prophet are, and shall be tormented day and night forever and ever.]

The future is pure death and pain for this heathen world and all people that are in league with it. There can be no escape.

Draco

This red dragon represents Satan and children of Satan, which are the evil empires of the world, led by the modern Roman Empire. The Western World is the condemned serpent with seven heads and ten horns.

Stars: Rastaban - The Head of The Subtle, or The Head of The Serpent.
            Ethanin - The Long Serpent or Dragon.
            Thuban (Al Waid) - Him Who is About to be Destroyed, The Reptile.
            Grumian - The Deceiver.
            El Athik - The Fraud.
            El Asieth - The Brought Down.
            Gianser - The Punished Enemy.

    *<< Revelation 12:3,9 >> [And there appeared another wonder in heaven; and behold a great red dragon, (*Notice the color of the Devil is red.*) having seven heads and ten horns, and seven crowns upon his heads.]*

This image symbolizes completion of time: the end of the modern Roman Empire. This empire started with the Greeks and is to end with the destruction of America. Seven always represents completion, the completion of time. Ten represents division, as the ten toes divided into left and right, seen in the golden image of Daniel chapter 3.

    <12:9> [And the great dragon was cast out, that old serpent, called the devil, and Satan, which deceiveth the whole world: he was cast out into the earth and his angels with him.]

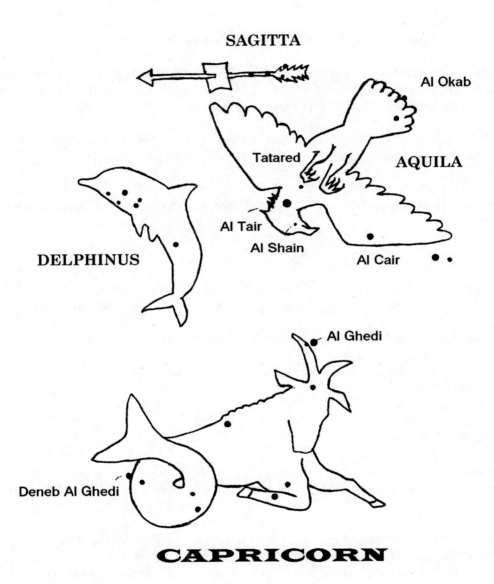

SAGITTA

Al Okab

Tatared

AQUILA

DELPHINUS

Al Tair

Al Shain

Al Cair

Al Ghedi

Deneb Al Ghedi

CAPRICORN

THE TRUTH

CAPRICORN

This sign depicts a creature, half-goat half-fish. The goat's head is bowed as if dying, the rear part of the animal is a lively tail of a fish! The goat half symbolizes the fact that Christ died as a sin offering. Capricorn represents the death and the resurrection of Christ! The Israelites had sacrificed goats as sin offerings:

<< Leviticus 9:15 >> [And he brought the people's offering, and took the goat, which was the sin offering for the people, and slew it, and offered it for sin, as the first.]

Capricorn represents the death and resurrection of Jesus Christ. The tail of the fish symbolizes liveliness and life, showing that Christ would die as an offering to make atonement for our sins, after which Christ would be resurrected back to life!

Stars: Deneb Al Gedi - The Lord, Judge, or Sacrifice Cometh.
Al Ghedi - The Kid, or Goat.

<< First Corinthians 15:3 >> [...Christ died for our sins according to the scriptures; And that he was buried, and that he rose again the third day according to the scriptures.]

Sagitta

This constellation depicts the Arrow of justice sent by the Lord YAHAWAH, as the price owed for sin. The arrow represents judgment!

<< Zechariah 12:10 >> [...And they shall look upon me whom they have pierced.]

<< Lamentation 3:12,13 >> [He hath bent his bow, and set me as a mark for the arrow. He hath caused the arrows of his quiver to enter into my reins.]

Aquila

Historic Name: Tarared - The Wounded.

The eagle flies above the earth; it symbolizes Christ, a heavenly being in the human form. The eagle is shown wounded and falling to the ground. This is symbolizing that Christ, the seed, would suffer death similar to a seed that falls to the ground and dies in order to bring forth new life!

Stars: Al Tair - The Wounding.
Tarared - The Wounding.
Al Shain - The Bright, or The Scarlet Colored.
Al Cair - The Piercing.
Al Okab - Wounded In The Heel.

THE TRUTH

<< *John 6:54-58* >>   [Christ said: *Whoso eateth my flesh, and drinketh my blood, hath eternal life; and I will raise him up at the last day. For my flesh is meat indeed* (he brought us this truth), *and my blood is drink indeed.*]

His death was for a sin offering for the Israelites and all others that believes the truth and accepts him as Lord and Savior.

Delphinus

This decan shows a fish leaping out of the water. It represents the resurrection of Christ from the dead!

<< *John 1:46* >>   [*...Thus it is written, and thus it behoved Christ to suffer, and to rise from the dead the third day*]

<< *Romans 6:3,4* >>   [*Know ye not, that so many of us as were baptized into his death? Therefore we are buried with him by baptism into death: that like Christ was raised up from the dead by the glory of the father, even so we also should walk in newness of life.*]

THE TRUTH

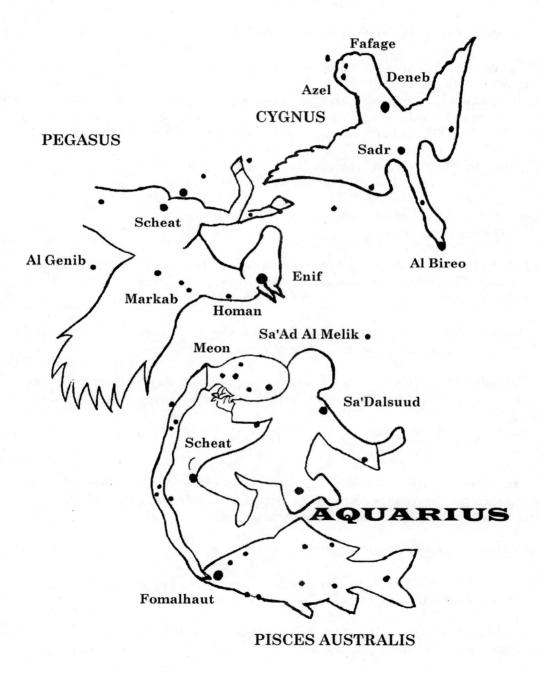

PEGASUS

CYGNUS

Fafage

Deneb

Azel

Sadr

Al Bireo

Scheat

Al Genib

Enif

Markab

Homan

Sa'Ad Al Melik

Meon

Sa'Dalsuud

Scheat

AQUARIUS

Fomalhaut

PISCES AUSTRALIS

THE TRUTH

AQUARIUS

Historic name: Hydrokoeus - The Pourer Forth of Water.

This sign depicts a man kneeling to pour out water into the mouth of a fish. His left arm is pointing towards the decans of Capricorn.

This water, according to the Bible, symbolizes the blessings being poured out: truth, wisdom, knowledge, spiritual power, and the understanding of spiritual principles. The sign represents Jesus Christ who brought us the words of the Lord YAHAWAH, and he redeemed us to receive great blessings and the kingdom!

Stars: Sa'Dalsuud - He Who Goeth and Returneth; The Pourer Out of The Stream.
Sa'Ad Al Melik (or Sa Ad Al Suud) - The Record of The Pouring Out.
Meon - Urn (Jar).
Scheat - He Who Goeth And Returneth.
Ancha - The Vessel of Pouring Out.

<< John 7:37,38 >> *[...Jesus stood and cried, saying, if any man thirst, let him come unto me and drink. He that believeth on me, as the scripture hath said, out of his belly shall flow rivers of living water.]*

<< Revelation 21:6 >> *[...It is done. I am Alpha and Omega, the beginning and the end. I will give unto him that is athirst of the fountain of the water of life freely.]*

<< Jeremiah 2:13 >> *[For my people have committed two evils; they have forsaken me the fountain of living waters, and hewed them out cisterns, broken cisterns that can hold no water.]*

Pisces Australis

This decan shows a large fish drinking the water poured out by Aquarius. This Fish represents the people whom have accepted the gospel of Jesus, and the blessings. When the time is ripe, this blessing will come to the righteous like a flood: truth, spiritual power, and everlasting life!

Stars: Fom Al Haut - The Mouth of the Fish.

<< Revelation 22:1 >> *[And he shewed me a pure river of life, clear as crystal, proceeding out of the throne of God and of the Lamb.]*

<< Revelation 22:17 >> *[...And the spirit says Come. And let him that heareth say, Come. And let him that is athirst come and whosoever will, let him take the water of life freely.]*

<< Isaiah 44:2-5 >> *[Thus saith the Lord that made thee, and formed thee from the womb, which will help thee; Fear not, O Jacob* (the Western Asiatic people, we are the original

THE TRUTH

Israelites), my servant; and thou Jerusalem whom I have chosen. For I will pour water upon him that is thirsty, and floods upon thy seed, and my blessing upon thine offspring: And they shall spring up as among the willows by the water courses. One shall say, I am the Lord's; and another shall call himself by the name of Jacob (We would wake up to our true nationality as Hebrew Israelites, when we hear this truth*); and another shall subscribe with his hand unto the Lord, and surnamed himself by the name of Israel.]*

Pegasus

Pegasus - Coming Quickly, merrily.

This decan of Aquarius shows a winged half-horse, representing Christ's speedy and swift, returning to rapture us with the flying saucers, in the Day of Judgment, from the Armageddon.

Stars: Enif - The Branch.
Homan - The Water.
Markab - Returning From Afar.
Scheat - He Who Goeth and Returneth.
Al Genib - Who Carries.
Matar - To Cause To Overflow.

<< John 14:2 >> [In my father's house there are many mansions: if it were not so, I would not have told you. I go to prepare a place for you. And if I go and prepare a place for you. I will come again, and receive you unto myself; that where I am, there you may be also.]

<< Revelation 3:11,12 >> [Behold I come quickly: hold that fast which thou hast, that no man take thy crown. Him that overcometh will I make a pillar in the temple of my Lord God YAHAWAH, and he shall go no more out: and I will write upon him the name of my Lord, and the name of the city of my Lord God YAHAWAH, which is new Jerusalem, which cometh down from my Lord God YAHAWAH.]

Cygnus

Cygnus - Who comes and goes or circles.

This decan is of a swan, as if circling overhead: like a circle Christ would go and return again!

Stars: Al Bireo - Flying Quickly.
Sadr - Who Returns As In A Circle.
Deneb - The Lord, or Judge Cometh.
Azel - Who Goes And Returns Quickly.
Fafage - The Glorious Shining Forth.

THE TRUTH

<< Acts 1:9-11 >>   [...Ye men of Galilee, why stand ye gazing up into heaven? This same Jesus, which is taken up from you into heaven, shall so come in like manner as ye have seen him go into heaven.]

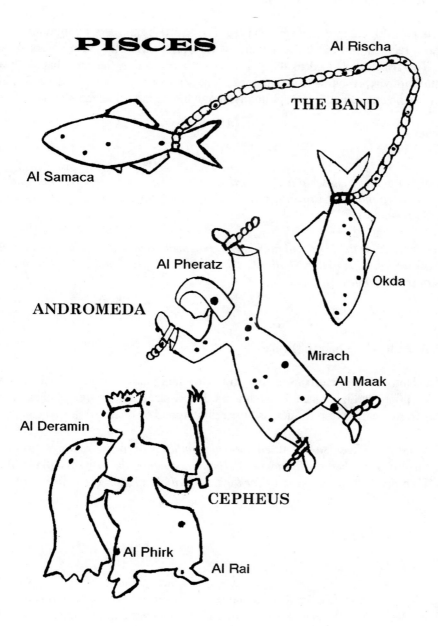

PISCES

Al Rischa

THE BAND

Al Samaca

Okda

Al Pheratz

ANDROMEDA

Mirach

Al Maak

Al Deramin

CEPHEUS

Al Phirk

Al Rai

THE TRUTH

PISCES

Historic name: Dagim - The Multitude of Fish.

This sign depicts two fish chained to a sea monster. The two fish represent the multitude of the twelve tribes of Israel, and also a remnant out of all the nations of the world, those that have accepted the truth and Yahawashy as Savior. The fish are chained to the sea monster, representing the fact that the people are in physical as well as mental captivity, resulting from ignorance. The sea monster represents the evil empires and all the forces of evil that are binding us mentally and spiritually, through deceptions and temptations!

Stars: Okda - The United.
        Al Samaca - The Upheld.

> << Jeremiah 50:33 >>   *[Thus saith the Lord of hosts: The children of Israel and the children of Judah were oppressed together: and all that took them captives held them fast; they refused to let them go.]*

> << Isaiah 141:2 >>   *[For the Lord will have mercy on Jacob, and will yet choose Israel and set them in their own land... And they shall take them captives, whose captives they were; and they shall rule over their oppressors.]*

The Band

Historic name: Al Risha - The Band or Bridle.

This decan is a chain that the sea monster uses to control and bind us, using various mind controlling tactics, including fear, deception, and ignorance. It symbolizes the physical and the mental chains that is uses to control and to mislead us from the truth, forces such as false religions and other erroneous philosophies!

> << Galatians 4:3 >>   *[Even so we, when we were children, were in bondage under the elements of this world: But when the fullness of the time was come, the Lord YAHAWAH sent forth his son... To redeem them that were under the law, that we might receive the adoption of sons.]*

Andromeda

Historic name: Siera - The Chained

This decan sign depicts a woman in chains, having her clothes torn. This decan represents Israelites and other believers in God and Jesus out of every nations of the world, who are captives under the oppression and afflictions of a carnal society, based on materialistic values, lies and injustice.

Stars: Al Pheratz - The Broken Down.
        Mirach - The Weak.

Al Maak (Al Amak) - The Struck Down.

<< *Isaiah 54:6,7* >>   [*For the Lord hath called thee as a woman forsaken and grieved in spirit, and a wife of youth, when thou wast refused, saith the Lord YAHAWAH. For a small moment have I forsaken thee; but with great mercies will I gather thee.*]

<< *Psalm 16:10* >>   [*For thou wilt not leave my soul in hell; neither wilt thou suffer thine Holy one to see corruption.*]

<< *Isaiah 52:2,3* >>   [*Shake thy self from the dust: arise, and sit down, O Jerusalem: Loose thyself from the bands of thy neck, O captive daughter of Zion. For thus saith the Lord, ye have sold your selves for nought; and ye shall be redeemed without money.*]

Cepheus

Historic name: Per-Ku-Hor; meaning - This One Comes To Rule.

This decan shows a king holding up a scepter in his left hand and a portion of his robe in the other, The heavens rotate under his right foot where the pole star is found! This decan represents Christ on his throne with all powers under his feet, because everything revolves around the Pole star, which is under his foot. The decan Cepheus communicates to us the fact that Christ is the one returning to redeem, subdue, and rule over all nations!

Stars: Al Deramin - Coming Quickly As In A Circle.
Al Phirk - The Redeemer.
Al Rai - He Who Bruises Or Breaks, The Shepherd.

<< *Isaiah 6:1* >> [*...I saw also the Lord sitting upon a throne, high and lifted up, and his train filled the temple.*]

<< *Ephesians 2:20-22* >> [*...Through Jesus Christ, when he raised him from the dead, and set him at his own right hand in the heavenly places, far above all principality, and power, and might, and dominion, and every name that is named, not only in this world, but also in that which is to come: And hath put all things under his feet, and gave him to be the head over all things.*]

<< *Colossians 1:16* >>   [*For by him were all things created, that are in heaven, and that are on earth, visible and invisible, whether they be thrones, or dominions, or principalities, or powers: all things were made by him, and for him!*]

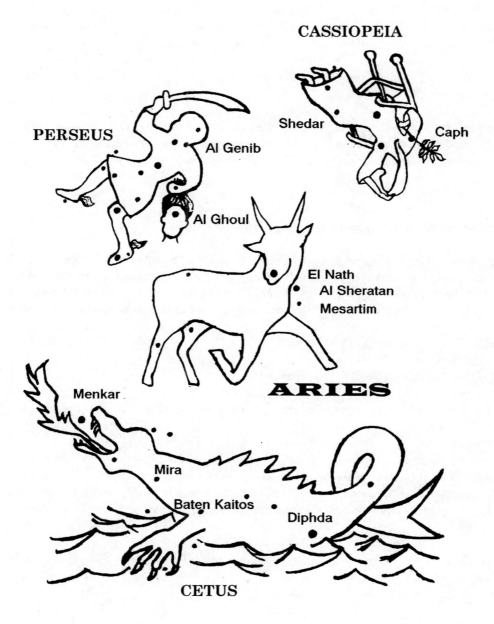

THE TRUTH

ARIES

Historic name: Talel - The Lamb Sent Forth.

This sign pictures a ram resting, with its head is turned back to look at Taurus. Its foreleg is treading the Band of Pisces. A ram is a male sheep, representing Christ who was the male sheep that died to redeem the Hebrew Israelites and other believers, as in << Genesis 22:12,13 >>, Abraham slew a ram instead of Isaac as a sacrifice to the Lord YAHAWAH! In like manner Christ was the Lamb that redeemed us with the sacrifice of himself!

Stars: Mesartim - The Bound, or The Binding.
          Al Sheratan - The Bruised, or the wounded.
          El Nath - The Wounded or The Slain.
          Salisha - The Exalted, or The Chief.
          Ras Al Thalita - Lifted Up.

<< Revelation 5:5-13 >> *[And one of the elders saith unto me, weep not: behold, the Lion of the tribe of Judah, the root of David (Christ), hath prevailed to open the book, and to loose the seven seals thereof. And I beheld, and, lo, in the midst of the throne and of the four beasts, and in the midst of the elders, stood a Lamb as it had been slain, having seven horns and seven eyes, ...the four beasts and the four and twenty elders fell down before the Lamb, ...saying, Thou art worthy to take the book, and to open the seals thereof: for thou wast slain, and hast redeemed us to the Lord YAHAWAH by thy blood]*

Cassiopeia

Cassiopeia - The Beautiful, The Enthroned, Daughter of Splendor.

This decan depicts a woman seated on a throne, holding her hair in one hand, and brushing it with a brush in the other hand. The Woman in this case is used as a symbol, representing the people of Jesus. Cassiopeia is making herself ready: symbolizing how the Israelites and the believers in Christ will strive to prepare themselves for the return of Christ by accepting the truth and learning their real identity! The western Asiatic people are the original Hebrew Israelites!

Stars: Shedar - The Freed.
          Caph - The Branch.

<< Revelation 19:7-9 >> *[Let us be glad and rejoice, and give honor to him: for the marriage of the Lamb is come, and his wife hath made her self ready. <8> And to her was granted that she should be arrayed in fine linen, clean and white: for the fine linen is the righteousness of saints. <9> And he saith unto me, Write, blessed are they which are called unto the marriage supper of the Lamb. And he saith unto me, These are the true sayings of God.]*

THE TRUTH

<< Revelation 21:2-5 >> [And I John saw the holy city, new Jerusalem, coming down from God out of heaven, prepared as a bride adorned for her husband. <3> And I heard a great voice out of heaven saying, Behold, the tabernacle of God is with men, and he will dwell with them, and they shall be his people, and God himself shall be with them, and be their God. <4> And God shall wipe away all tears from their eyes; and there shall be no more death, neither sorrow, nor crying, neither shall there be any more pain: for the former things are passed away. <5> And he that sat upon the throne said, Behold, I make all things new. And he said unto me, Write: for these words are true and faithful.]

Cetus

Historic name: Cetus - The Sea Monster.

The sea monster or dragon, is the natural enemy of the two fish. If you are a defender of truth, justice, and righteousness, you will find strong resistance and opposition from the powers that be, such as religious organizations and political institutions.

Cetus represents the powers of evil, which have placed us in physical and mental slavery. It is that same Sea Monster Leviathan (described in Job 41, Psalms 74:13,14; Isaiah 27:1; and in Revelation 12:3. In every case, it is referring to the powers of evil, working through people and institutions. Christ will destroy all evil at his Second Coming.

Stars: Diphda - The Overthrown.
Baten Kaitos - From The Belly Of The Whale.
Mira (a variable star) - The Rebel.
Menkar - The Bound, or Chained Enemy.

<< Isaiah 27:1 >> [In that day the Lord with his sore and great and strong sword shall punish Leviathan the piercing serpent, even Leviathan (the word Leviathan means crooked serpent; it is a representation of the present western world rulership) *that crooked serpent; and he shall slay the dragon that is in the sea.* (seas symbolize nations, referring to how they infiltrate and control the people)]

Perseus

Historic name: Athick - He who breaks, or The Breaker.

This decans is pictured as a man wearing a helmet and holding the head of the enemy he had just chopped off. He has wings at his ankles to represent supernatural speed. This decan represents Christ as a mighty Victor and Deliverer, who comes quickly to destroy his enemy the Western World and other heathen nations with great speed. This will be the day of the nuclear war, Armageddon, the Day of the Lord!

Stars: Rosh Satan (Caput Medusa) - The Head of The Adversary,
Al Ghoul - The Evil Spirit, and Oneh - The Subdued.

182

THE TRUTH

Al Genib - He Who Carries.
Mirfak - He Who Helps.
Athik - He Who Breaks.

<< Micah 2:12,13 >>   *[I will surely assemble, O Jacob, all of thee; I will surely gather the remnant of Israel; I will put them together as the sheep of Bozrah, as the flock in the midst of their fold: they shall make great noise by the multitude of men. The Breaker* (Christ) *is come up before them: they have broken up, and have passed through the gate, and are gone out by it: and their king shall pass before them, and the Lord on the head of men.]*

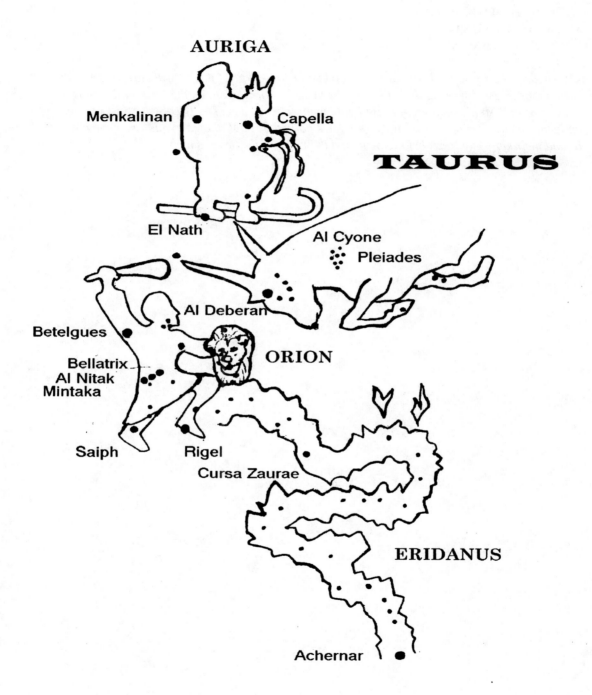

AURIGA

Menkalinan

Capella

TAURUS

El Nath

Al Cyone

Pleiades

Al Deberan

Betelgues

ORION

Bellatrix
Al Nitak
Mintaka

Saiph

Rigel

Cursa Zaurae

ERIDANUS

Achernar

THE TRUTH

TAURUS

Historic names: Rheem or Unicorn.
                       Shur - The Bull Coming, The Head or Chief Who Comes.
                       Horias - The Traveller Who Comes To Save.

This sign depicts an enraged powerful bull like creature, charging with its horns ready to push down the enemy! Taurus signifies power, strength, and fierceness. A charging bull depicts violence, symbolizing the time of judgment that we are living in: the wars, plagues, the destruction and the wrath of the Lord GOD YAHAWAH being poured out against the evil and the wicked of the world!

Stars: Pleiades (Chima) - The Accumulation, The Center.
         Al Cyone - The Center.
         Al Deberan - The Leader, or The Governor.
         El Nath - The Wounded, The Slain.
         Hyades - The Congregation.
         Palilicum - Belonging to The Judge.
         Al Thuraiya - The Abundance.
         Wasat - The Foundation.

<< Isaiah 34:2-10 >>   *[For the indignation of the Lord is upon all nations, and his fury upon all their enemies: he hath utterly destroyed them, he hath delivered them to the slaughter. <3> Their slain also shall be cast out, and their stink shall come up out of their carcass, and the mountains shall be melted with their blood. <4> And all the host of heaven shall be rolled together as a scroll: and all their host shall fall down, as the leaf falleth off from the vine, and as a falling fig from the fig tree. <5> For my sword shall be bathed in heaven: behold, it shall come down upon Edom, and upon the people of my curse, to judgment.*

<6> The sword of the Lord is filled with blood, it is made fat with fatness, and with blood of lambs and goats, with the fat of the kidneys of rams: for the Lord hath a sacrifice in Bozrah, and a great slaughter in the land of Idumea (Edomites are the Caucasians of today)*.
<7> And the unicorns shall come down with them, and the bullocks with the bulls; and their land shall be soaked with blood, and their dust made fat with fatness. <8> For it is the day of the Lord's vengeance, and the year of his recompenses for the controversy of Zion]* (for what they did to the twelve tribes of Israel, which are the western Asiatic people of today.)

<9> And the streams thereof shall be turned into pitch, and the dust thereof into brimstone, and the land thereof shall become burning pitch (natural disasters and nuclear destruction)*. <10> It shall not be quenched night nor day; the smoke thereof shall go up forever: from generation to generation it shall lie waste; none shall pass through it forever and ever.]*

The evil empires of the world are doomed. This prophecy is against the modern Babylonians, which is the so-called First World societies of today, for example America, Europe.

THE TRUTH

<< Isaiah 13:4-19 >> [The noise of a multitude in the mountains, like as of a great people; a tumultuous noise of the kingdoms of nations gathered together: the Lord of hosts mustereth the host of the battle (there are wars all over the world, This is the commencement of the LORD god YAHAWAH's Judgment; make no mistake about it, there will not be any peace until the evil empires of the world are destroyed*). <5> They come from a far country, from the end of heaven, even the Lord, and the weapons of his indignation* (nuclear missiles, chemical weapons, natural disasters), *to destroy the whole land. <6> Howl ye; for the day of the Lord is at hand; it shall come as a destruction from the Almighty.*

<7> Therefore shall all hands be faint, and every man's heart shall melt: <8> And they shall be afraid: pangs and sorrows shall take hold of them; they shall be in pain as a woman that travaileth: they shall be amazed one at another; their faces shall be as flames (you will see just how red they can get when the judgment comes). *<9> Behold, the day of the Lord cometh, cruel both with wrath and fierce anger, to lay the land desolate: and he shall destroy the sinners thereof out of it. <10> For the stars of heaven and the constellations thereof shall not give their light* (their scientists and wise men will not have any answers or solutions to save their system*): the sun shall be darkened in his going forth, and the moon shall not cause her light to shine* (his political leaders will not have the wisdom and understanding to bring about peace).

<11> And I will punished the world for their evil, and the wicked for their iniquity; and I will cause the arrogance of the proud to cease (these people will stop walking around with their heads so high up, people will know the truth and expose them.), *and I will lay low the haughtiness of the terrible. <12> I will make a man more precious than fine gold; even a man than the golden wedge of Ophir* (the African-Americans and the American-Indians will learn their Identity and stand up as real men to defend the Biblical truth, that they are the original Hebrew Israelites; it will be a miracle...)

<13> Therefore I will shake the heavens, and the earth shall remove out of her place (from the nuclear bombs), in the wrath of the Lord of hosts, and in the day of his fierce anger (there is no future in this society, it is doomed!). *<14> And it shall be as the chased roe, and as a sheep that no man taketh up: they shall every man turn to his own people, and flee every one into his own land. <15> Everyone that is found shall be thrust through; and everyone that is joined unto them shall fall by the sword. Their children also shall be dashed to pieces before their eyes; their houses shall be spoiled, and their wives ravished* (Esau, and all other nations will reap what they sow). *<16> Their children also shall be dashed to pieces before their eyes; their houses shall be spoiled, and their wives ravished.*

<17> Behold I will stir up the Medes against them (the Middle Eastern nations*), which shall not regard silver; and as for gold, they shall not delight in it. <18> Their bows also shall dash the young men in pieces; and they shall have no pity on the fruit of the womb; their eyes shall not spare children. <19> And Babylon* (America*), the glory of kingdoms, the beauty of the Chaldees Excellency, shall be as when the Lord God YAHAWAH overthrew Sodom and Gomorrah.]*

This place will be turned into a dessert, it will burn with plagues and nuclear explosions.

THE TRUTH

<< Daniel 12:1,2 >> [And at that time shall Michael stand up, the great prince which standeth for the children of thy people (Israelites)*: and their shall be a time of trouble, such as never was since there was a nation even to that same time: and at that time thy people shall be delivered, everyone that shall be found written in the book* (the twelve tribes of Israel)*. And many of them that sleep in the dust of the earth shall awake, some to everlasting life, and some to shame and everlasting contempt.]*

Orion

        Historic name: Orion - One Coming Forth As Light
                         Ur-Ana - The Light Of Heaven.

Orion, the hunter, is a famous constellation. It depicts a hunter, a mighty man, ready to strike his enemy with his uplifted club in his right hand. The sword hangs from his famous girdle of three stars. This constellation rises as Scorpio sets, symbolizing when Christ will come on the scene and the evil forces and empires will be phased out of existence! Christ is that hunter, coming with the great sword to slay and to bruise the head of that "Dragon, Serpent, or Scorpion", representing evil!

Stars: Betelguez - The Coming of The Branch.
         Bellatrix - One Hastily Coming.
         Mintaka - Dividing The Belt.
         Al Nitak - The Wounding.
         Saiph - The Bruised.
         Rigel - The Foot, One Treading Underfoot.
         Al Rai - The Bruising.

<< John 8:12 >> [Then spake Jesus again unto them, saying, I am the light of the world: he that followeth me shall not walk in darkness, but shall have the light of life.]

<< Jeremiah 16:16 >> [Behold, I will send for many fishers, saith the Lord, after will I send for many hunters, and they shall hunt them from every mountain, and from every hill, and out of the holes of the rocks.]

<< Malachi 3:1,2 >> [Behold, I will send my messenger, and he shall prepare the way before me and the Lord, whom ye seek, shall suddenly come to his temple, even the messenger of the covenant, whom ye delight in, he shall come, saith the Lord of hosts. But who may abide the day of his coming? And who shall stand when he appeareth? for he is like a refiner's fire, and like fullers' soap: And he shall sit as a refiner and purifier of silver: and he shall purify the sons of Levi and purge them as gold and silver.]

THE TRUTH

Eridanus

Eridanus - River Of The Judge.

This decan depicts a river of fire, it seems to be flowing from the foot of Orion that is lifted as if about to crush something. Eridanus is the lake of fire, representing the judgment prepared for this world. It is the nuclear furnace that awaits the wicked of this world.

Stars: Zaurae - Flowing.
             Achernar - The After Part Of The River.
             Cursa - Bent Down.

<< *Daniel 7:11* >>   *[I beheld then because of the great words which the horn spake: I beheld even till the beast* (the present Roman Empire) *was slain, and his body destroyed, and given to the burning flame.]*

<< *Revelation 20:9,10* >>   *[...and fire came down from the Lord YAHAWAH out of heaven, and devoured them. And the devil that deceived them* (the modern Roman Empire) *was cast into the lake of fire and brimstone.]*

<< *Isaiah 66:15,16* >>   *[For, behold, the Lord will come with fire, and with his Chariots like a whirlwind, to render his anger with fury, and his rebuke with flames of fire. For by fire and by his sword will the Lord plead with all flesh* (in the nuclear war): *and the slain of the Lord shall be many.]*

<< *Second Peters 3:10* >> *[But the day of the Lord will come as a thief in the night* (the nuclear war will take everyone by surprise); *in which the heavens shall pass away with a great noise* (nuclear bombs going off, destroying nations) *and the elements shall melt with fervent heat (nuclear bombs), the earth also and the works that are therein* (the buildings and the people) *shall be burned up.]*

Auriga

Historic name: Tum - One Who Subdues or Tames.

Auriga depicts a shepherd holding two little lambs in one arm, comforting and keeping them calm and protecting them from the violence going around them! This decan symbolizes how the Lord YAHAWAH will deliver and protect the twelve tribes of Israel from the tribulations of the last days and the nuclear war. Christ is that good shepherd, he will return for us; we will be lifted up into the Chariots of Salvation (the Flying Saucers), as everyone else is burning up below in the nuclear furnace!

Stars: Alioth (or Capella) - The She Goat.
             Menkalinan - The Band, or The Chain of The Goats.

THE TRUTH

<< John 10: 14 >> [(Jesus speaking) I am the good shepherd, and know my sheep, and am known of mine...And other sheep I have, which are not of this fold, them also I must bring, and they shall hear my voice; and there shall be one fold, and one shepherd.]

Christ was speaking to the original Jews, the African-Americans of today, about the rest of the twelve tribes, the American-Indians scattered throughout north, south, and central America.

<< Isaiah 40:10,11 >> [Behold, the Lord will come with strong hand, and his arm shall rule for him: behold, his reward is with him, and his work before him. He shall feed his flock like a shepherd: he shall gather the lambs with his arm, and carry them in his bosom, and shall gently lead those that are with young.]

<< Psalms 91:9-12 >> [Because thou hast made the Lord, which is my refuge, even the Most High, thy habitation (having faith in the Bible); There shall no evil befall thee, neither shall any plague come night thy dwelling. For he shall give his angels charge over thee, to keep thee in all thy ways. They shall bear thee up in their hands (we will be delivered by the UFO Chariots of Salvation.), lest thou dash thy foot against a stone.]

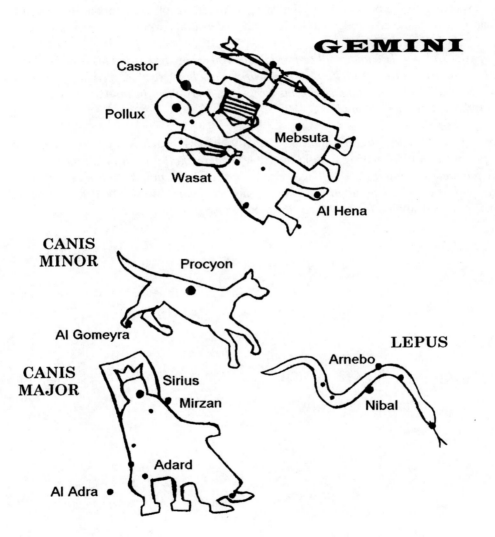

THE TRUTH

GEMINI

Historic name: Taumin - The United, The Completely Joined.

Two persons are seen: so-called Castor (Apollo), and Pollux (Hercules). Castor has an unstrung bow held up in his left hand and a harp in the other. Pollux has a club leaning in his right arm, and his left is embracing his friend about the waist. This sign represent Christ in unity with Israel. The leaning club, and the unstrung bow and arrow lifted up symbolize victory over the evil empires. The harp represents the praises of victory, and the rejoicing to come in our kingdom.

Gemini also represents the dried bones described by Ezekiel thirty-seven of the Bible. Gemini signifies the Hebrew Israelites and the other believers in Jesus, waking up and uniting, coming together after learning the truth. Gemini also characterizes the fact that When Christ appears we will be like him as if twins, and one with him; to be as sons of the Lord God YAHAWAH, ruling by his side. We are the Bride and Christ is the Bridegroom in this great reunion!

Stars: Castor - The Ruler, or Judge Coming In Haste.
Mebsuta - Treading Underfoot.
Pollux - The Ruler or Judge.
Wasat - Established, Set Up as a Foundation.
Al Hena - The Hurt or Afflicted.

<< First John 3:2 >>   *[Beloved, now are we the sons of the Lord God YAHAWAH, and it doth not yet appear what we shall be: but we know that, when he shall appear, we shall be like him; for we shall see him as he is.]*

<< Second Timothy 2:10-12 >>   *[...If we be dead with him, we shall also live with him: If we suffer, we shall also reign with him.]*

<< Revelation 19:7-16 >>   *[Let us be glad and rejoice, and give honor to him: for the marriage of the Lamb is come, and his wife hath made her self ready. And to her was granted that she should be arrayed in fine linen, clean and white: for the fine linen is the righteousness of the saints. And he saith unto me, write, blessed are they which are called unto the marriage supper of the Lamb. And he saith unto me, These sayings are true sayings of the Lord YAHAWAH. And I fell at his feet to worship him. And he said unto me, See thou do it not: I am thy fellow servant, and of thy brethren that have the testimony of Jesus: worship the Lord God YAHAWAH: for the testimony of Jesus is the spirit of prophecy.*

And I saw heaven open, and behold a white horse; and he that sat upon him was called Faithful and true, and in righteousness he doth judge and make war. His eyes were as a flame of fire, and on his head were many crowns; and he had a name written, that no man knew, but himself. And he was dressed in a vesture dipped in blood: and his name is called The Word of Lord God YAHAWAH.

And the armies, which were in heaven, followed him upon white horses, clothed in fine linen, white and clean. And out of his mouth goeth a sharp sword, that with it he should smite the nations: and he shall rule them with a rod of iron: and he treadeth the winepress of the fierceness and wrath of Almighty God YAHAWAH. And he had on his vesture and on his thigh a name written, KING OF KINGS, AND LORD OF LORDS.]

Lepus

Historic name: Lepus - Treading Underfoot.

This running animal symbolizes the enemy being chased! It is running from Sirius the prince and is located under the crushing foot of Orion. The evil empires, institutions and people with the mark of the beast, are the enemy being chased and made to flee like a shameful serpent. They are being chased out of every continent and country: Africa, South America, Asia, and The Middle East. Every nation is killing the colonizers, and terrorizing them, calling them the devil, and Satan!

Stars: Nibal - The Mad.
Arnebo - The Enemy of Him That Cometh.

<< Amos 5:18,19 >> *[Woe unto you that desire the day of the Lord! to what end is it for you? The day of the Lord is darkness, not light. As if a man did flee from a lion, and a bear met him]*

Canis Major

Historic Name: Abur - The Mighty, The Prince.

Canis Major, (some call it the Dog); originally was not a dog at all, and neither was it called the Big Dipper. Canis Major was called the Prince, named from the star Sirius. Sirius means sir or prince. It represents Christ as the mighty Prince who is to come!

Stars: Sirius - The Prince.
Ascher - The Prince Who Shall Come.
Mirzam - The Prince, The Leader, or The Chief.
Muliphen - The Leader or The Chief.
Wesen - The Bright, Shining, The Scarlet.
Al Adra - The Glorious.

Canis Minor

Historic name: Procyon - The Redeemer.

This decan is a sheep-dog. The sheep-dog guards the sheep, it redeems and protects them from the enemy. It represents Christ as our redeemer, defender, and protector, coming to defend us from our enemies!

Stars: Al Mirzam - The Ruler.
Al Shira (Procyon) - The Redeemer.

THE TRUTH

Al Gomeyra - Him Who Completes or Perfects.

<< Isaiah 49:25,26 >>   *[But thus saith the Lord, Even the captive of the mighty shall be taken away, and the prey of the terrible shall be delivered: for I will contend with him that contendeth with thee, and I will save thy children. And I will feed them that oppress thee with their own blood, as with sweet wine: and all flesh shall know that I the Lord am thy Savior and thy Redeemer, the mighty one of Jacob.]*

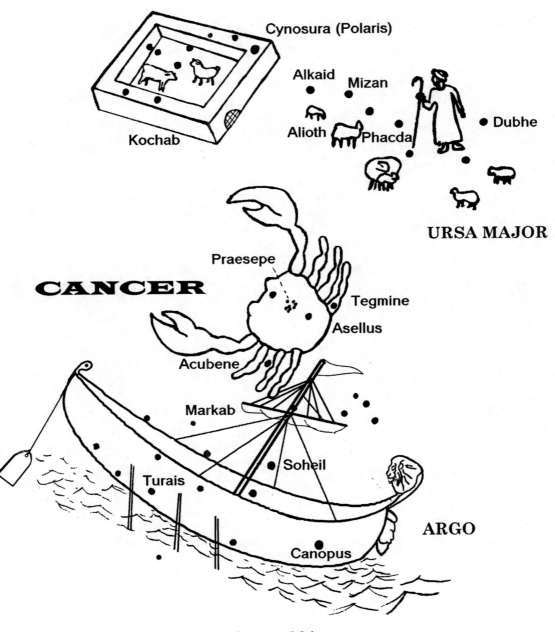

URSA MINOR

Cynosura (Polaris)

Kochab

Alkaid Mizan

Alioth Phacda Dubhe

URSA MAJOR

CANCER

Praesepe

Tegmine

Asellus

Acubene

Markab

Soheil

Turais

ARGO

Canopus

THE TRUTH

CANCER

Historic name: Al Satan - The One Who Holds, Binds, or Encircles.

This sign depicts a crab; it climbs out of the water unto the land, symbolizing our rebirth and baptism into the truth. The crab has many members or legs, symbolizing the reunited multitude of the remnant of the original Israelites and other Christians who have kept the faith of Jesus to the end.

The Redeemed will be held in safety; from the tribulations of the last days, as a crab is protected within its hard shell from the violence of the ocean around it. The returning Jesus Christ with his Chariots of Salvation will deliver the Israelites safely from the nuclear destruction!

Stars: Tegmine - Holding, Grasping.
Acubene - The Sheltering, or Hiding Place.
Al Himarein - The Kids or Lambs.
Praesepe - The Multitude, The Offspring.
Acubene - Sheltering or Hiding Place.
Ma Alaph - The Assembled Thousands.
Asellus Australis - The Southern She Ass.
Asellus Borealis - The Northern She-Ass.

<< *Revelation 21:3,4* >> [*And I heard a great voice out of heaven saying, behold, the tabernacle of God is with men, and he shall dwell with them, and they shall be his people, and God himself shall be with them, and be their God. And God shall wipe away all their tears from their eyes; and there shall be no more death, neither sorrow, nor crying, neither shall there be any more pain: for the former things are passed away.*]

Ursa Minor

Historic Name: Kochab - Waiting Him Who Cometh.

Also known as The Lesser Sheepfold. It is not a bear or a dipper. This sign depicts a flock of sheep waiting in a sheepfold. This flock symbolizes Israel and the believers in Jesus, being gathered together in the last days. It also shows that our kingdom alone will rule the world next with the good shepherd Jesus Christ as our leader! The star Polaris located in this constellation was not always the Pole Star; it was Alpha Draconis in the sign of Draco. Draco symbolizes the kingdom of Satan and his power over all of the nations of the earth. The Pole Star is now used in navigation and direction. The switch of the pole star from Draco to Ursa Minor, represents a switch in leaders: the Serpent is about to loose his leadership of the world to Christ and the Israelites, the future possessors of heaven and earth!

Stars: Kochab - Awaiting Him Who Cometh.
Cynosura (Polaris) - The Center.

When these names of stars were recorded, the Pole Star was Alpha Draconis, located in the constellation of Draco. Cynosura was prophetically named the Center. It is the precession of the equinox that caused the Pole

Star to shift to Cynosura, the new Pole Star. The Shifting of the Pole Star represents the Shifting of world Leadership, from the Serpent to Jesus Christ!

<< Jeremiah 31:10 >> *[Hear ye the word of the Lord, O ye nations, and declare it in the isles afar off, and say, He that scattered Israel will gather him, and keep him, as a shepherd doth his flock.]*

Ursa Major

Historic Name: Ash - The Assembled or Ordered Together.

Also known as The Greater Sheepfold. This sign shows a shepherd assembling a greater flock. Ursa Major and Ursa Minor represent the twelve tribes of Israel free at last in the kingdom of Heaven, reunited with Christ as their true shepherd, abiding in joy.

<< Ezekiel 37:19 >> *[Thus saith the Lord YAHAWAH; Behold, I will take the stick of Joseph, which is in the hands of Ephraim, and the tribes of Israel his fellows, and will put them with him, even with the stick of Judah, and make them one stick, and they shall be one in mine hand.]*

Stars: Dubhe - The Latter Flock.
Merach - The Purchased, The Flock.
Phacda - Visited, Guarded, Numbered.
Alioth - The She Goat.
Talita - The Little Lamb.
Al Cor - The Lamb.
Mizar - Separate or Small.
Alkaid - The Assembled.
El Kaphrah - The Protected, The Covered, The Redeemed, The Ransomed.

<< John 10:14-16 >> *[I am the good shepherd, and know my sheep, and am known of mine. As the Father knoweth me, even so know I the Father; and I lay down my life for the sheep. And other sheep I have which are not of this fold* (Christ telling the original Jews, about the rest of the twelve tribes, which are the American-Indians)*: them also I must bring, and they shall hear my voice; and there shall be one fold, and one shepherd.]*

<< Luke 12:31,32 >> *[But rather seek ye first the kingdom of the Lord God YAHAWAH; and all these things shall be added unto you. Fear not, little flock; for it is your Father's good pleasure to give you the kingdom.]*

THE TRUTH

Argo

Argo - The Company of Travelers.

This sign depicts a ship coming into homeport. A lion head on the stern decorates it; it faces the bow, and is also decorated by the head of a man at the water line, as if he is carrying the ship. This ship is the symbol of salvation, like the ark of Noah. Argo symbolizes how Christ, using the chariots, will return to deliver and carry away his possession (the twelve tribes of Israel)!

Stars: Canopus - The Possession of Him Who Cometh.
Asmidiska - The Released Who Travel.
Turais - The Possession.
Sephina - Abundance, The Multitude.
Soheil - The Desired.
Subilon - The Branch.
Markab - Returning From Afar.

<< *First Thessalonians 4:16,17* >> *[For the Lord himself shall descend from heaven with a shout, with the voice of the archangel, and the dead in Christ shall rise first: Then we which remain shall be caught up together with them in the clouds* (the clouds referred to so-called U.F.Os, the Chariots)*, to meet the Lord in the air: and so shall we ever be with the Lord.]*

<< *Matthew 24:30,31* >> *[And then shall appear the sign of the son of man in heaven: and then shall all the tribes of the earth mourn, and they shall see the son of man coming in the clouds of heaven with power and great glory. And he shall send his angels with a great sound of a trumpet, and they shall gather together his elect from the four winds, from one end of heaven to the other.]*

<< *Psalms 91:11,12* >> *[For he shall give his angels charge over thee, to keep thee in all thy ways. They shall bear thee up in their hands, lest thou dash thy foot against a stone.]*

<< *Isaiah 60:8-12* >> *[Who are these that fly as a cloud, and as doves to their windows* (Israelites being taken away in the day of the nuclear war, by Christ and the angels in the chariots)*? Surely the isles shall wait for me, and the ships of Tarshish first, to bring thy sons from far, their silver and their gold with them, unto the name of the Lord thy POWER, and to the Holy One of Israel, because he hath glorified thee.*
And the sons of strangers shall build thy walls, and their kings shall minister unto thee (The evil of the nations are going to serve under the original Hebrew Israelites, as punishment for their crimes against us.)*: for in my wrath I smote thee, but in my favor have I had mercy on thee. Therefore thy gates shall be open continually; they shall not be shut day nor night; that men may bring unto thee the forces of the Gentiles, and that their kings may be brought. For the nation and kingdom that will not serve thee shall perish; yea those nations shall be utterly wasted.]*

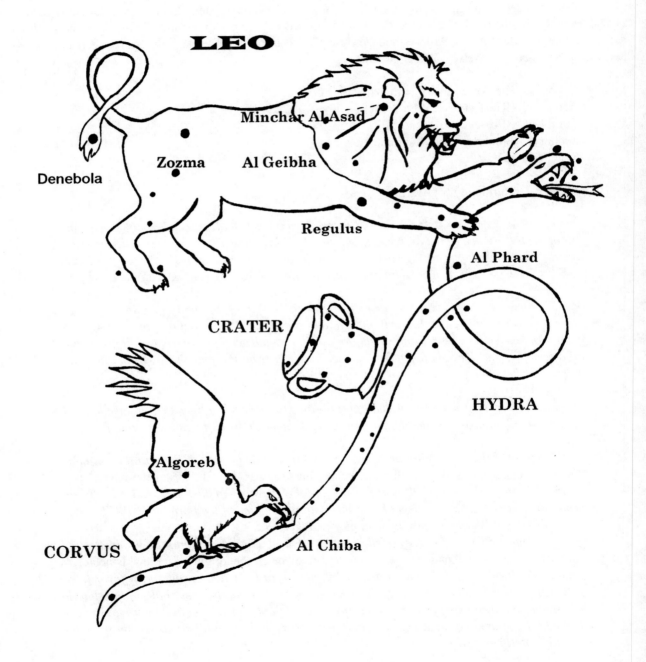

THE TRUTH

LEO

Historic name: Al Asad - The Lion Who Rends or Makes Waste.

The famous zodiac sign of Leo shows a great lion leaping forward to pounce on the head of a large serpent. The sign symbolizes the Lord MASHAYAK YAHAWASHY (Jesus Christ) coming in royalty, power, and majesty for the final conflict against the forces of evil, represented by the serpent. Christ will bring the final judgment, fierce wrath, and the violent destruction of the evil empires and institutions, on the day of the nuclear war!

Stars: Minchar Al Asad: The Lion Who Rends Or Who Makes Waste.
Al Geibha: The Exaltation.
Zozma: The Shining Forth.
Denebola: The Judge or Lord Who Comes Quickly.
Regel: The Treading Underfoot.

<< Revelation 5:5 >> *[And one of the elders saith unto me, weep not: behold, the Lion of the tribe of Judah, the Root of David, hath prevailed to open the book, and loose the seven seals thereof.]*

<< Hosea 13:7,8 >> *[Therefore I will be unto them as a Lion; as a leopard by the way will I observe them: I will meet them as a bear that is bereaved of her whelps, and will rend the caul of their heart, and there will I devour them like a Lion.]*

<< Numbers 24:8,9 >> *[The Lord brought him* (Israel) *forth out of Egypt; he hath as it were the strength of an unicorn; he shall eat up the nations his enemies, and shall break their bones, and pierce them through with his arrows. He couched, he lay down as a Lion, and as a great Lion: who shall stir him up? Blessed is he that blessed thee, and cursed is he that cursed thee.]*

Hydra

Historic name: Hidra - The Abhorred.

This decan depicts a long, winding serpent, its length covers one third of the zodiac. The paw of the Lion seems to be smashing at the head of the Serpent. A bird is pecking away at the body of this old serpent, and also a pouring bowl is placed over the body of the serpent. Finally, we observe the paw of the Leo coming down to crush the head of the serpent, to kill it.

This Serpent represents the forces of evil, along with its human allies and agents. It represents that old serpent, that dragon of seven heads and ten horns of Genesis and Revelations, being punished and destroyed. Seven represents the completion of time for the gentile kingdoms and ten represents the final stage of the divided modern Roman Empire. This destruction is soon to occur within our lifetime. The bird, Corvus represents doom for the Serpent and the bowl, Crater, represents wrath poured out upon the wicked! This wicked empire is also described in Revelations.

<< *Revelation 17:5* >> *[And upon her head was a name written, Mystery Babylon The Great, The Mother of Harlots And Abominations of the Earth.]*

Stars: Al Phard - The Separated, The Excluded, The Put Out Of the Way.

<< *Revelation 12:3,9* >> *[And there appeared another wonder in heaven; and behold a great red dragon, having seven heads and ten horns, and seven crowns upon his heads. ...And the great dragon was cast out* (colonizers and exploiters are being cast out from every nation and continent because people are starting to wake up to the truth.*), that old serpent called the Devil and Satan, which deceiveth the whole world!]*

<< *Genesis 3:14,15* >> *[And the Lord said unto the Serpent, ...I will put enmity between thee and the woman, and between thy seed* (wicked people) *and her seed* (Christians)*; it* (Christ) *shall bruise thy head* (to bruise a serpent's head is to kill it)*, and thou shall bruise his heel.]*

Bruising of the heel causes a fall: the Romans overthrew the original Jews in 70 AD.

<< *Revelation 20:10* >> *[And the Devil that deceived them was cast into the lake of fire and brimstone, where the beast and the false prophet are, and shall be tormented day and night forever and ever.]*

Crater

Historic name: Al Chas - The Cup.

This cup being poured on the serpent is a symbol of the Lord YAHAWAH's wrath coming upon the wicked empires and institutions. It is the cup of judgment!

Stars: Al Chiba - The Curse Inflicted, The Accursed.

<< *Psalms 75:8* >> *[For in the hand of the Lord there is a cup, and the wine is red; it is full of mixture; and he poureth out of the same: But the dregs thereof, all the wicked of the earth shall wring them out, and drink them.]*

<< *Revelation 14:9,10* >> *[...If any man worship the beast and his image, and received his mark in his forehead, or in his hand, The same shall drink of the wrath of the Lord God YAHAWAH, which is poured out without mixture into the cup of his indignation; and he shall be tormented with fire and brimstone in the presence of the holy angels, and in the presence of the Lamb.]*

THE TRUTH

<< Revelation 16:19 >> *[...and great Babylon* (the modern Roman Empire, *and its allies) came in remembrance before the Lord God YAHAWAH, to give unto her the cup of the wine of the fierceness of his wrath.]*

<< Revelation 18:4-6 >> *[And I heard another voice from heaven, saying, Come out of her, my people* (We must separate from evil systems and customs, and return to the original righteous customs)*, that ye be not partakers of her sins, and that ye receive not of her plagues. For her sins have reached unto heaven, and God hath remembered her iniquities. Reward her even as she rewarded you, and double unto her double according to her works: in the cup which she hath, filled to her double.]*

<< Revelation 16:1 >> *[And I heard a great voice out of the temple saying to the seven angels, Go your ways, and pour out the vials of the wrath of God upon the earth.]*

Corvus

This decan depicts a raven tearing away at the flesh of a large serpent. Ravens eat the corpses of beasts; symbolizing that this beast was slain. Corvus clearly symbolizes the complete doom and destruction that is beginning to catch up to the wicked people and the evil empires. Doomsday is at hand for the wicked at heart and for all that are practicing evil!

Stars: Algoreb: The Raven.

<< Revelation 19:17-21 >> *[And I saw an angel standing in the sun; and he cried with a loud voice, saying to all the fowls that fly in the midst of heaven, Come and gather yourselves together unto the supper of the great God Lord YAHAWAH; That ye may eat the flesh of kings, and the flesh of captains, and the flesh of mighty men, and the flesh of horses, and them that sit on them, and the flesh of all men, both free and bond, both small and great.*
And I saw the beast, and the kings of the earth, and their armies, gathered together to make war against him that sat on the horse, and against his army (Christ at his returning with the angels, will be opposed by some)*. And the beast was taken, and with him the false prophet that wrought miracles before him* (This modern Roman Empire with its political and religious leaders)*, which he deceived them that had received the mark of the beast, and them that worshipped his image* (people that had refused the truth and accepted the false teachings and customs)*. These both were cast alive into a lake of fire burning with brimstone. And the remnant were slain with the sword of him that sat upon the horse* (Christ)*, which sword proceeded out of his mouth; and all the fowls were filled with their flesh.]*

<< Jeremiah 25:30-33 >> *[Therefore prophesy thou against them all these words, and say unto them, The Lord shall roar from on high, and utter his voice from his holy habitation; he shall give a shout, as they that tread the grapes, against all the inhabitants of the earth.*
A noise shall come even to the ends of the earth; for the Lord hath a controversy with the nations, he will plead with all flesh; he will give them that are wicked to the sword, saith

the Lord. Thus saith the Lord of hosts, Behold, evil shall go forth from nation to nation, and a great whirlwind shall be raised up from coast to coast of the earth.

And the slain of the Lord shall be at that day from one end of the earth even to the other end of the earth: they shall not be lamented, neither gathered, nor buried; they shall be dung upon the ground.]

<< Matthew 6:10 >> [Thy kingdom come. Thy will be done in earth as it is in heaven.]

THE TRUTH

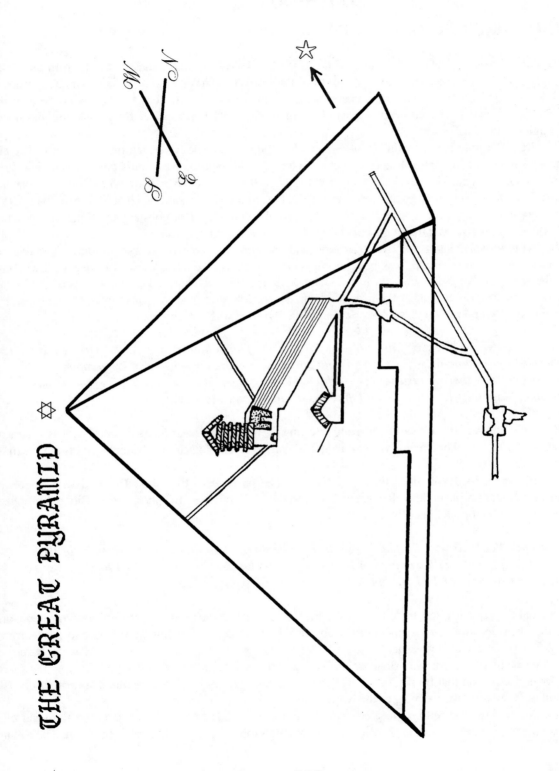

THE GREAT PYRAMID

MYSTERY OF THE GREAT PYRAMID

The entire creation declares the glory of the Lord YAHAWAH, and witnesses to his truth are found everywhere. Those who are spiritual can see the truth of the Lord YAHAWAH in all things. The design of the great pyramid was derived from the zodiac gospel handed down from Adam. It is the gospel concerning the coming of the Savior and Deliverer, Jesus Christ. The Egyptians took the gospel of the Zodiac and developed their false religions out of it.

The Great Pyramid is located in Egypt on the West Side of the Nile River, ten miles west of Cairo, and north of the ancient city of Memphis. It is constructed on top of solid rock. Its base could cover seven New York City blocks. The Great Pyramid is nearly five hundred feet high. It is made of more than 2.5 million limestone and granite blocks, two to seventy tons each. The sides of the Pyramid have a slope of 10 to 9: it rises nine feet in altitude for every ten feet up the side. The Pyramid was covered with a layer of polished limestone casing, which were jointly fitted together so well that it appears to be almost one continuous piece.

The Pyramid was constructed over four thousand one hundred and sixty years ago, during the reign of Pharaoh Cheops. At that time, Egypt was being occupied and ruled by Shemites, known as the Shepherd Kings (Hyksos). The Shepherd Kings had also abolished idol worshiping and polytheism. The Pyramid was constructed as a result of divine inspiration during the time of Noah, Shem, Job, and other prophets living at the time. The Lord referred to the Pyramid when he spoke to Job, as if the Pyramid was a microcosm of the earth:

> << Job 38:4-7 >> [Where wast thou when I laid the foundations of the earth? Declare, if thou hast understanding. <5> Or who hath stretched the line upon it? <6> Whereupon are the foundations thereof fastened? Or who laid the corner stone thereof; <7> when the Morning Stars sang together, and all the Sons of God shouted for joy?]

Obviously, this verse could not be literally referring to the earth, the earth has no corners, it is spherical. But the measurements of the Great Pyramid coincide with the astrological measurements of the earth in microcosm:

The message directly parallels that of the Bible. The purpose of the Great Pyramid was to convey spiritual, historical, and prophetic knowledge, according to the plans of the Almighty Creator. Biblical prophecy explains the true purpose of the Great Pyramid:

> << Isaiah 19:19,20 >> [In that day shall there be an altar to the Lord in the midst of the land of Egypt, and a pillar at the border thereof to the Lord. <20> And it shall be for a sign and for a witness unto the Lord of Hosts in the land of Egypt...]

Note that the verse is referring to the "Last Days". According to the prophecy, the purpose, meaning, and message of the Great Pyramid would not be revealed until the Last Days (which is now), prior to the return of Jesus Christ. The prophecy also gives us the location for the Great Pyramid. It is to be found "at the border of Egypt". In Ancient times, Egypt was divided into two kingdoms Lower Egypt and Upper Egypt; the Great Pyramid is found located on that border. It is called both an altar and a pillar. The Pyramid is a form of obelisk, which is a pillar. Peculiarly, the meaning of the word Altar in Hebrew is "Lion of God".

Now we also see the Sphinx, located near the Pyramid. It has the body of a lion and the head of a woman. It is part of the Great Pyramid complex and serves the same purpose, a witness to the truth. The Sphinx

THE TRUTH

represents the First and the Second Coming of Jesus: his First Coming as a child, born through a woman; his Second Coming as the conquering lion of the tribe of Judah! The Sphinx begins with the head of a woman and ends with the body of a lion!

According to the verse, the Pyramid was to be a sign and a witness to the gospel in the last days. The Great Pyramid was constructed to represent the gospel truth in stone, a model of the spiritual house, as confirmed by the Scriptures:

<< *Ephesians 2:20-22* >> *[And (we) are built upon the foundation of the apostles and prophets, Jesus Christ himself being the chief corner-stone;* (only a pyramid has a chief stone; the cap stone) *<21> In whom all the building fitly framed together groweth unto an Holy Temple in the Lord; <22> In whom ye also are builders together, for an habitation of God through the spirit.]*

The Capstone of the Pyramid was to represent Jesus Christ. The Capstone is five-sided and there is no place to put it until after the Pyramid is completed. It would be rejected until the last days:

<< *Psalm 118:22* >> *[The stone, which the builders refused, is become the head stone of the corner.]*

<< *I Peter 2:7,8* >> *[Unto you therefore which believe he (Jesus Christ) is precious: but unto them which be disobedient, the stone which the builders disallowed, the same is made the head of the corner, <8> And a stone of stumbling, and a rock of offense, even to them which stumble at the word, being disobedient: whereunto also they were appointed.]*

<< *Romans 9:32,33* >> *[Wherefore? Because they sought it not by faith, but as if it were by the works of the law. For they stumbled at the stumbling stone (Christ the Capstone); <33> As it is written, Behold, I lay in Sion a stumbling stone and a rock of offense: and whosoever believeth on him shall not be ashamed.]*

<< *I Corinthians 1:23* >> *[But we preach Christ crucified, unto the Jews a stumbling block, and unto the Greeks foolishness; <24> But unto them which are called, both Jews and Greeks, Christ the power of God, and the wisdom of God.]*

<< *Matthew 21:42-44* >> *[Jesus saith unto them, Did ye never read in the scriptures, The stone which the builders rejected, the same is become the head of the corner: this is the Lord's doing, and it is marvelous in our eyes? <43> Therefore say I unto you, The kingdom of God shall be taken from you, and given to a nation bringing forth the fruits thereof. <44> And whosoever shall fall on this stone shall be broken: but on whomsoever it shall fall, it will grind him to powder.]*

We are the temple of the LORD YAHAWAH, we are the spiritual building of God. Jesus Christ is our shepherd, he leads us to the Lord YAHAWAH. Christ is the Head Stone, he is the Capstone of the spiritual building.

THE TRUTH

The structural geometry, measurements, as well as the inner chambers of the Great Pyramid reveal historical and prophetic information. The date of the Pyramid construction is recorded in its structure. At the time of construction, the descending passageway was leveled in angle to the pole star, which was at the time Alpha Draconis. However, because of the precession cycle of the equinox (25,870 years), the pole star is now Polaris, no longer Alpha Draconis. And the Apex of the Pyramid was pointing at a star called Alcyone, the central star of the Pleiades, which also is the central point that the sun is circling. These factors coincided in the year 2170 B.C.E, marking the date of construction.

The entrance of the Great Pyramid is located on the north side. It is connected to a descending passage way (The path of Descent) of about four feet high and three feet wide, leading straight into a subterranean chamber (The Chamber Of Ordeal) located one hundred feet below the base of the Pyramid. The bottom of the chamber is rough, and it also has an unfinished passageway leading to nowhere.

About one thousand inches down the entrance into the descending passageway, an upward passageway (The Hall of Truth In Darkness) of about the same angle, one thousand five hundred inches long, connects to a Grand Gallery (The Hall of Truth In Light). The Grand Gallery is about thirty feet high and six feet wide. It narrows towards the top (Arch Of The Solstice) because of seven overlapping courses of stones, overhanging each other.

Three feet high vertical steps, are found at the top of the Grand Gallery which connects a low passageway (The Passage of The Vail) with an Ante-Chamber. Another passageway twice the size of the first, connects to a larger chamber constructed of polished granite (The Chamber Of Resurrection). The largest chamber contains a polished, lidless rectangular box, cut from a solid block of red granite. There are also two ventilating tubes leading to the outside. The inner chamber of the Pyramid is kept at sixty-eight degrees all year round by these ventilating tubes. There are also five hollow chambers found in the construction of the roof of this chamber. The roof is constructed of granite blocks.

Also, there is an opening leading to a well (The Well of Life) found on the floor, three feet from the entrance to the Grand Gallery (Crossing of The Pure Road of Life). This opening is very rough. The well winds down through the masonry and the rocky foundations of the Pyramid into the subterranean chamber (The Chamber of Ordeal) located directly in line with the center of the Pyramid.

There is another chamber (The Chamber of the New Birth) located twenty-five layers below the double chambers. This chamber can be reached from a horizontal passage (Path of The Coming Forth of The Regenerated Soul) adjacent to the well opening, and seventy inches from the start of the Grand Gallery. At the end of this passage, the floor drops slightly to form the base of the chamber.

The chambers and passageways of the Great Pyramid also reveal prophecies in chronological order. From the entrance of the Pyramid we encounter the descending passageway, which leads to The Chamber of Ordeal. The Chamber of Ordeal is constructed to represent hell, it is rough and unfinished. The bottom of it has a hole to represent a bottomless pit. The descending passageway represents the course of human history from the time of Adam, which has been leading the world towards hell and destruction.

An ascending passageway, called The Hall of Truth In Darkness, is encountered as we proceed down the descending passageway. It represents the chronology from the time of the giving of the law, by the Lord YAHAWAH to Moses, up to the time of the first coming of Jesus Christ. This is considered an upward trend in the spiritual course of mankind. The law was bringing us closer to the Lord YAHAWAH. When Christ came, he was able to shed light on the truth and the true meaning of the law. The law was only the shadow of the coming Jesus Christ; he was its substance!

Following the point marking the coming of Jesus, the Hall of Truth In Darkness leads into The Hall of Truth In Light. The Hall of Truth In Light represents what is known as the time of the gentiles. The seven

206

overhanging courses of stone, which makes up the walls and the roof of the chamber represents the completion of the time of the gentiles. If you recall, seven represents the completion of time. On the seventh day of creation the Lord rested and all things were completed. The end of this gallery marks the time of the tribulation and of the Second Coming of Jesus Christ.

The horizontal passageway called The Path of The Regenerated Soul, starts at the point which marks the First Coming of Jesus Christ. This passage represents the time interval from the destruction of Jerusalem by the Romans and the captivity of the Israelites to the time of the restoration of their original identity in these last days. This Path leads to the Chamber of The New Birth. This Chamber symbolizes the resurrection of the original Hebrew Israelites as a people, and the time when the world would hear the true gospel of the kingdom of the Lord YAHAWAH.

> << Romans 11:25 >> [For I would not, brethren that ye should be ignorant of this mystery, lest ye should be wise in your own conceits; that blindness in part is happened to Israel, until the fullness of the Gentiles be come in.]

The point where the three paths meet is called The Crossing Of The Pure Road Of Life. From that point there is a well that connects these passages to the Path of Descent, and the Chamber of Ordeals. This path is called the Well of Life. It represents the resurrection of Jesus Christ and all that his resurrection symbolizes.

The Hall of Truth in Light ends in a low entrance-way called The Arch of The Solstice, and it leads into a smaller chamber. It marks the end of the time of the gentile kingdoms, the last one being the present Greco-Roman Empire, composed of Europe, America, and their colonies. The smaller chamber represents the judgment when the wicked will be destroyed. This is the time of the Great Tribulation. The low passageway is directly in a vertical line with the Chamber of New Birth, representing the fact that at this same time many people will hear and awake to the Gospel of the kingdom of Heaven. A low passageway means that only the people who humble themselves to the truth of the Lord YAHAWAH will escape from the great tribulation and enter into the Kingdom of Heaven. To get through this passage the person must bow.

There is another opening at the end of the Double Hall of Truth. It is located at the end of the ceiling, to the side and leads to chambers above the Chamber of Resurrection. The remains of bats have accumulated in that passageway. Only winged creatures could have had access to this opening. This opening represents The Rapture, which will occur in the air at the Second Coming of Jesus Christ:

> << I Thessalonians 4:16,17 >> [For the Lord himself shall descend from heaven with a shout, with the voice of the archangel, and with the trump of God: and the dead in Christ shall rise first: <17> Then we which are alive and remain shall be caught up together with them in the clouds, to meet the Lord in the air: and so shall we ever be with the Lord.]

> << Matthew 24:30,31 >> [And then shall appear the sign of the Son of man in heaven (The chariots of salvation: UFOs): and then shall all the tribes of the earth mourn, and they shall see the Son of man coming in the clouds of heaven with power and great glory. <31> And he shall send his angels with a great sound of a trumpet, and they shall gather together his elect from the four winds, from one end of heaven to the other.]

The smaller chamber following the Double Hall of Truth ends in another low passageway, leading to the Chamber of Resurrection. This chamber complex represents the time in which the kingdom of heaven would be established upon the earth, a time of eternal peace and joy. In this chamber is found a lidless red granite box; it is exactly the same dimensions as the Ark of the Covenant. According to the scriptures, the Ark of the Covenant would again be seen in the kingdom:

> << *Revelation 11:19* >> *[And the temple of God was opened in heaven, and there was seen in his temple the ark of his testament: and there were lightnings, and an earthquake, and great hail.]*

THE TRUTH

FOUNDATION OF CIVILIZATION

THE PRINCIPLES OF LIFE

The first principle of life is to understand and obey the laws of God. The Lord made mankind in order to have fellowship with him; therefore, mankind must exhibit good character, in the image and likeness of the Creator! The Biblical Law teaches us how to love God and our fellow man. It is very important to return to the original Biblical customs and laws. The Biblical commandments should be the first precepts instructed to our children. You must read the books of Leviticus and Deuteronomy; they will explain many of the laws.

<< Deuteronomy 30:19 >> [I call heaven and earth to record this day against you, that I have set before you life and death, blessing and cursing: therefore choose life, that both thou and thy seed may live.]

<< Ecclesiastes 12:13 >> [Let us hear the conclusion of the whole matter: Fear God, and keep his commandments: for this is the whole duty of man.]

We, especially the original Hebrew Israelites, have to keep the Biblical customs. Realize that western culture is contrary to the laws of God. The customs and languages we have today are the result of colonization and imperialism. Concerning the Asiatic people of America, Hebrew is our custom and Israel is our nationality. The genealogy along the line of your father determines your nationality, your place of birth does not. The original Israelites have to wake up and learn the original Hebrew language and Biblical custom. We must observe all of the commandments, because it will be to our benefit!

<< Exodus 20:1-17 >> [And God spake all these words, saying, <2> I am the Lord thy God, which have brought thee out of the land of Egypt, out of the house of bondage.

<3> Thou shalt have no other gods before me.

<4> Thou shalt not make unto thee any graven image, or any likeness of any thing that is in heaven above, or that is in the earth beneath, or that is in the water under the earth: <5> thou shalt not bow down thyself to them, nor serve them: for I the Lord thy God am a jealous God, visiting the iniquity of the father upon the children unto the third and fourth generation of them that hate me; <6> and showing mercy unto thousands of them that love me, and keep my commandments.

<7> Thou shalt not take the name of the Lord thy God in vain: for the Lord will not hold him guiltless that taketh his name in vain.

<8> Remember the Sabbath day, to keep it holy. <9> Six days shalt thou labor, and do all thy work: <10> but the seventh day is the sabbath of the Lord thy God: in it thou shalt not do any work, thou, nor thy son, nor thy daughter, thy manservant, nor thy maidservant, nor thy cattle, nor thy stranger that is within thy gates: <11> for in six days the Lord made heaven and earth, the sea, and all that in them is, and rested the seventh day: wherefore the Lord blessed the sabbath day, and hallowed it.

<12> Honor thy father and thy mother: that thy days may be long upon the land which the Lord thy God giveth thee.

<13> Thou shalt not kill.

<14> Thou shalt not commit adultery.
<15> Thou shalt not steal.
<16> Thou shalt not bear false witness against thy neighbor.
<17> Thou shalt not covet thy neighbor's house, thou shalt not covet thy neighbor's wife, nor his manservant, nor his maidservant, nor his ox, nor his ass, nor any thing that is thy neighbor's.]

Idolatry is one of the biggest poisons being used to infest the minds and hearts of many so-called religious church fanatics. The Lord hates your idols and images. It is against the commandments of God to pray to any saint or person; for example, Mary. The Catholic religion is the filthiest when it comes to idolatry. God condemns it. All idolaters will be destroyed. Take all idols and images and destroy them. Throw them out of your home and save your soul.

<< Deuteronomy 7:25,26 >> [The graven images of their gods shall ye burn with fire: thou shalt not desire the silver or gold that is on them, nor take it unto thee, less thou be snared therein: for it is an abomination to the Lord thy God. <26> Neither shalt thou bring an abomination into thine house, lest thou be a cursed thing like it: but thou shalt utterly detest it, and thou shalt utterly abhor it; for it is a cursed thing.]

<< Acts 15:20 >> [But that we write unto them that they abstain from pollution of idols.]

<< Habakkuk 2:18>> [What profiteth the graven image that the maker thereof hath graven it; the molten image, and a teacher of lies, that the maker of his work trusteth therein, to make dumb idols? 19 Woe unto him that saith to the wood, Awake; to the dumb stone, Arise, it shall teach! Behold, it is laid over with gold and silver, and there is no breath at all in the midst of it. 20 But the LORD is in his holy temple: let all the earth keep silence before him.]

<<Jeremiah 2:27,28>> [Saying to a stock, Thou art my father; and to a stone, Thou hast brought me forth: for they have turned their back unto me, and not their face: but in the time of their trouble they will say, Arise, and save us. <28> But where are thy gods that thou hast made thee? let them arise, if they can save thee in the time of thy trouble: for according to the number of thy cities are thy gods, O Judah.]

<< Leviticus 26:1 >> [Ye shall make no idols nor graven image, neither rear you up a standing image, neither shall ye set up any image of stone in your land, to bow down unto it: for I am the Lord your God.]

<< Deuteronomy 7:5 >> [But thus shall ye deal with them; ye shall destroy their altars, and break down their images, and cut down their groves, and burn their images with fire.]

So-called Christianity today and many other false religions not only worship idols, they also idolize the dead and objects of death. So-called Christianity and many other religions bring dead bodies into their churches and temples. The laws of God strictly forbids all of this:

<< Numbers 19:11-16 >> [He that toucheth the dead body of any man shall be unclean seven days. <12> He shall purify himself with it on the third day, and on the seventh day he shall be clean: but if he purify not himself the third day, then the seventh day he shall not be clean. <13> Whosoever toucheth the dead body of any man that is dead, and purifieth not himself, defileth the tabernacle of the LORD; and that soul shall be cut off from Israel: because the water of separation was not sprinkled upon him, he shall be unclean; his uncleanness is yet upon him.

<14> This is the law, when a man dieth in a tent: all that come into the tent, and all that is in the tent, shall be unclean seven days. <15> And every open vessel, which hath no covering bound upon it, is unclean. <16> And whosoever toucheth one that is slain with a sword in the open fields, or a dead body, or a bone of a man, or a grave, shall be unclean seven days.]

The fact that those churches and religions bring idols and dead bodies into their congregation should prove to you that they are following Satan and there is no truth or salvation for you in there. Why do people continue to go into those false churches, temples and religions? For example, the cross is an instrument of death. Many churches idolize the cross. The Biblical laws of God forbid the idolization of any image or object specially one that is associated with death or the dead.

The true Israelites and Christians must return to the Biblical laws and Hebrew customs. The word "Hebrew" means ancient. Abraham was the ancestor of the Hebrew Israelites. We are called Hebrews because we keep the ancient customs given to Adam by God, and our ancestor, Eber, preserved it during the confusion at the tower of Babel. According to the Bible Abraham was called a Hebrew, his custom was Hebrew:

<< Genesis 14:13 >> [And there came one that had escaped, and told Abraham the Hebrew.]

Some churches are teaching that Christ did away with the Laws of the Bible. This is a big lie! Jesus Christ did not do away with the law. Jesus said:

<< Matthew 5:17-19 >> [Think not that I am come to destroy the law, or the prophets: I am come not to destroy, but to fulfill. For verily I say unto you, Till heaven and earth pass, one jot or one tittle shall in no wise pass from the Law, till all be fulfilled. Whosoever therefore shall break one of these least commandments, and shall teach men so, he shall be called the least in the kingdom of heaven: but whosoever shall do and teach them, the same shall be called great in the kingdom of heaven.]

<< Matthew 12:50 >> [For whosoever shall do the will of my father which is in heaven, the same is my brother, and sister, and mother.]

<< John 14:15 >> [If you love me, keep my commandments.]

The world religions misinterpret the meaning of the concept of grace, to provide an excuse for wickedness. According to the Bible, not everyone has grace. Only the people with true faith (knowledge) in the truth of the Bible and who do the good works commanded by it have grace.

THE TRUTH

<< Ephesians 2:7 >> [For by grace ye are saved through faith; and that not of your selves: it is the gift of the Lord YAHAWAH]

Grace only comes through upholding the truth. The truth is that the Lord YAHAWAH is the almighty God that He has only one representative, Jesus Christ; and that His words are found in the Bible. The Europeans that are claiming to be Jews in Palestine today are impostors. The original people of the Bible are the Hebrew Israelites. They are Asiatic people, the bulk of which is consisted of the African-Americans and the American-Indians, with remnants scattered all over the world!

In addition to having faith, we must also observe and promote the commandments. Everyone has to contribute to the spread of this truth!

<< James 2:17-20 >> [Even so faith, if it hath not works, is dead being alone. Yea, a man may say, Thou hast faith, and I have works: shew me thy faith without thy works, and I will shew thee my faith by my works. Thou believest that there is one God; thou doest well: the devil also believes, and trembles. But wilt thou know, O vain man, that faith without works is dead?]

We will not become perfect yet, but we of all people must observe the law. The Israelites are Lord YAHAWAH's representatives under Christ!

<< Romans 3:31 >> [Do we then make void the law through faith? God forbid: yea, we establish the law.]

<< Romans 6:1,2 >> [What shall we say then? Shall we continue in sin, that grace may abound? God forbid. How shall we, that are dead to sin live any longer therein?]

<< Matthew 7:21-23 >> [Not everyone that saith unto me, Lord, Lord, shall enter into the kingdom of heaven; but he that doeth the will of my father which is in heaven.]

<< Joshua 1:8 >> [This book of the law shall not depart out of thy mouth; but thou shall meditate therein day and night, that thou mayest observe to do according to all that is written therein: for then thou shalt make thy way prosperous, and then thou shall have good success.]

To learn the laws, you must start by reading the first five books in the Bible! Another thing to be mentioned is that we also have to obey the laws of the society we are living in, as long as they do not conflict with the laws and commandments of the Lord YAHAWAH. If you do not respect other people, and honor your elders, no one will ever respect you!

<< Romans 13:1-5 >> [Let every soul be subject unto the higher powers. For there is no power but of God: the powers that be are ordained of God. <2> Whosoever therefore resisteth the power, resisteth the ordinance of God: and they that resist shall receive to themselves damnation. <3> For rulers are not a terror to good works, but to the evil. Wilt thou then not be afraid of the power? Do that which is good, and thou shalt have praise of the same: <4> For he is the minister of God to thee for good.

THE TRUTH

But if thou do that which is evil, be afraid; for he beareth not the sword in vain: for he is the minister of God, a revenger to execute wrath upon him that doeth evil. <5> Wherefore ye must needs be subject, not only for wrath, but also for conscience sake.]

It must be made absolutely clear that the word of the Lord YAHAWAH, who is God and creator of all things, absolutely condemns homosexuality!

<< *Leviticus 20:13* >> *[If a man also lie with mankind, as he lieth with a woman, both of them have committed an abomination: they shall surely be put to death; their blood shall be upon them.]*

<< *I Corinthians 6:9* >> *[Know ye not that the unrighteous shall not inherit the kingdom of God? Be not deceived: neither fornicators, nor idolaters, nor adulterers, nor effeminates, nor abusers of themselves with mankind.]*

<< *Romans 1:26,27* >> *[For this cause God gave them up unto vile affections: for even their women did change the natural use into that which is against nature: <27> And likewise also the men, leaving the natural use of the woman, burned in their lust one toward another; men with men working that which is unseemly, and receiving in themselves that recompence of their error which was meet.]*

<< *Leviticus 18:22* >> *[Thou shalt not lie with mankind, as with womankind: it is an abomination.]*

The Dress Code

In the beginning, when God created man, he clothed him in a robe of light. Man was created to reflect the glorious image of God. The original man was the image and likeness of the heavenly even in the glorious robe of light that clothed him. And after Adam sinned and lost the glorious robe of light, God made him a garment of leather. There is a proper and an improper way to dress, there is a moral and an immoral way to appear in public. The Bible is very clear about the dress code:

<< *Deuteronomy 22:5* >> *[The woman shall not wear that which pertaineth unto a man, neither shall a man put on a woman's garment: for all that do so are an abomination unto the Lord YAHAWAH thy God.]*

A virtuous woman would only wear long dresses down to the foot! Most importantly, according to the Bible, a man should not wear feminine clothing, and a woman is not to wear any article of clothing made for men, nor cut her hair short. A woman should not take on any masculine article of fashion, nor should a man use any feminine article of fashion.

Wearing tight fitting clothes, see-through clothing, or clothing that is too short in public is a crime, for temptation is a crime. Indecent exposure is a crime! By dressing like a prostitute, a person will begin to think, feel, and act like a prostitute. Negative clothing will alter your thinking and behavior, and will also attract demons! Common sense tells you that! Those tight-fitting slut clothes are given to people in order to destroy them and the social structure by tempting people into committing adultery and fornication.

The leaders of society make it very difficult for the women, especially in the Western world, to find decent feminine clothing. Decent clothing for women is rarely found in the stores. Homosexuals, lesbians, and perverts design most of the clothing in the Western world. It is not easy for a virtuous woman in this society. A virtuous woman needs a lot of support and encouragement to overcome the pressures placed on her by society to cut her hair like a boy and dress like a pervert. You men should put your feet down and demand that your wives, sons, and daughters dress according to the Biblical law.

If women dress decently there will be less sex crimes committed against them, less temptation resulting in adultery, and more respect for women. But if they dress in a tempting way, they are asking for trouble and should not complain when they are treated as whores. We are commanded to return to the original dress code:

<< Isaiah 52:1, and in 59:9 >> [Awake, awake; put on thy strength, O Zion; put on thy beautiful garments, O Jerusalem, the jolly city, ...Awake, awake, put on strength, O arm of the Lord; as in the ancient days, in the generation of old.]

The Europeans in Palestine who falsely claim to be the Jews love to run around in all black suits, with little hats over the bald spots of their heads as a dress code. But the original Asiatic Israelites, according to the Bible, had no such customs. Originally, the Hebrew Israelites wore turbans, girdles, and warlike royal garments! We wore the royal colors: purple, royal blue, scarlet, and white. The Israelite dress code is beautiful, and royal! We wore studs of gold and silver on our garments, like true princes, and kings. For example:

<< Solomon 1:11 >> [We will make thee borders of gold with studs of silver.]

And by law, all Israelites are supposed to wear fringes on their garments, with a royal border;

<< Numbers 15:38 >> [...And the Lord spake unto Moses, saying, Speak unto the children of Israel, and bid them that they make them fringes in the borders of their garments throughout their generations, and that they put upon the fringe of the borders a ribbon of blue.]

This is a beautiful law. Israelites wore a variety of clothing articles:

<< Isaiah 3:18-23 >> [...tinkling ornaments about their feet, and their causis, and their round tires like the moon, the chains, and the bracelets, and the mufflers, the bonnets, and the ornaments of the legs, and the earrings, the rings, and nose jewels, apparel, and the mantles, and the wimples, and the crisping pins, the glasses, and the fine linen, and the hoods, and the veils.]

The men used to dress in royal, warlike, masculine garments with fringes and robes usually having two splits, one on each side.

<< 1 Maccabees 14:9 >> [The ancient men sat all in the streets, communing together of good things, and the young men put on glorious and warlike apparel]

Also a man should wear his masculine girdle. A man's girdle is usually a twenty-centimeter wide leather belt. The Lord said to Job:

<< *Job 40:7* >> *[Gird up thy loins now like a man]*

John the Baptist wore a girdle:

<< *Matthew 3:4* >> *[And the same John had his raiment of camel's hair, and a leathern girdle about his loins.]*

Jesus Christ also wears a masculine girdle:

<< *Revelation 1:13* >> *[...Girt about the paps with a golden girdle.]*

Although in this society it is not always possible, an Israelite should dress as an Israelite as often as he or she can, because it is a part of your identity! Above all, it is very important to maintain a clean appearance. Also, according to the Bible, you should not make marks, holes, cuts or tattoos on your skin: and it is good to wear your beard.

<< *Leviticus 19:27,28* >> *[Ye shall not round the corners of your heads, neither shalt thou mar the corners of thy beard. Ye shall not make any cuttings in your flesh for the dead, nor any marks upon you: I am the Lord.]*

Some Nazzarites do not cut their hair because of a religious vow. However, they never wear it in a feminine fashion. A man should not wear his hair long, like a woman. Keep it short, for we must be men.

<< *First Corinthians 11:14-16* >> *[Doth not even nature itself teach you that if a man have long hair, it is a shame unto him? But if a woman have long hair, it is a glory to her: for her hair is given her for a covering. But if any man seem to be contentious, we have no such customs.]*

However, there will be times when it will not be possible to keep your customs the way you wish to, because we are still in captivity, and we are faced with many impossible situations! In Genesis 41:14, the Egyptians made Joseph shave when he was in Egypt. People who love to follow the ways of this world are going straight to hell; and they seem to be in a hurry to get there! But you will gain the universe and eternity by learning the ways of the Lord God YAHAWAH! Christ said:

<< *Mark 8:36* >> *[For what shall it profit a man, if he shall gain the whole world, and lose his own soul?]*

THE TRUTH

Family Structure

God has established an order in the family; as in all things, there must be order:

<< *First Corinthians 11:3-9* >> *[But I would have you know, that the head of every man is Christ; and the head of the woman is the man; and the head of Christ is The Father. <7> For a man indeed, ought not to cover his head, forasmuch as he is the image and glory of the God: but the woman is the glory of the man. For the man is not of the woman; but the woman of the man. Neither was the man created for the woman; but the woman for the man.]*

There can never be any compromise about the fact that the man is to be the absolute head of his family. This is the natural and the spiritual order. A man is a man when he has learned the wisdom of God according to the Bible. The problem today is that the majority of men don't know anything about the laws of God maturity or manhood. If the men are not acting like men, how can they succeed in relationships with women? Women need real men. God's law dictates that a man is to have complete authority in all matters concerning his family. The real man is the representative of God's order and authority, not the woman. The purpose of the woman is to help the man and to nurture the family. The man's duty is to instruct, protect and defend his family. If a man has no power or authority over his wife and children he can not take proper responsibility. To remove the father from the family, or interfere with his authority is **genocide**.

<< *Ezekiel 34:31* >> *[...And ye my flock, the flock of my pasture, are men, and I am your Lord, saith the Lord Most High!]*
<< *Isaiah 13:12* >> *[I will make a man more precious than fine gold; even a man than the golden wedge of Ophir.]*

Now, believe it or not, according to the Bible, a man has the human right and the religious right to choose how many wives and concubines he needs to have. In reality, a very destructive opinion has been taught by western society: the false idea that a man can only have one wife. This is a violation of a man's human rights and religious rights on every level. This misconception has destroyed many people, relationships, and marriages unnecessarily. The Western world has been brainwashing and misleading the women into believing that there is something wrong if a man has more than one wife. According to the law of God a man is not to take another man's wife; however, he has the God given right, the human right and the religious right to choose his own wife, as well as the number of wives he needs.

But notice, in contrast, that Western civilization does not condemn homosexuality, transvestites, transsexuals, and the abortion killing of a baby. So why are they against polygamy? The fact is, throughout history, the more authentic civilizations have followed the commandments of God and allowed a man his human right to have more than one wife and/or concubines! It is a sin to take away this basic human right of mankind. Jacob, David, Solomon, and most other men of God had more than one wife!

<< *Genesis 4: 19* >> *[And Lamech took unto him two wives.]*

<< *Genesis 31:17* >> Israel had four wives. *[Then Jacob rose up, and set his sons and his wives upon camels.]*

<< Genesis 30:9 >> [When Leah saw that she had left bearing, she took Zilpah, her maid, and gave her to Jacob as a wife.]

<< Genesis 36:2 >> [Esau took his wives of the daughters of Canaan.]

<< Judges 5:30 >> [Have they not sped? ...to every man a damsel or two?]

<< Judges 8:30 >> [And Gideon had threescore and ten sons of his body begotten: for he had many wives.]

<< I Samuel 1:2 >> [And he had two wives...]

<< I Samuel 25:43 >> [David also took Ahinoam of Jezreel; and they were also both of them his wives.]

<< II Samuel 12:8 >> God said to David: [And I gave thee thy master's house, and thy master's wives (because Saul had died) into thy bosom, and gave thee the house of Israel and of Judah; and if that had been too little, I would moreover have given thee such and such things.]

<< I Chronicles 14:3 >> [And David took more wives at Jerusalem.]

<< II Chronicles 11:21 >> [And Rehoboam... For he took eighteen wives, and threescore concubines.]

<< II Chronicles 13:21 >> [But Abijah waxed mighty, and married fourteen wives.]

<< Matthew 25:1 >> Jesus Christ explained: [Then shall the kingdom of heaven be likened unto ten virgins, which took their lamps, and went forth to meet the bridegroom.]

<< Isaiah 4:1 >> [And in that day seven women shall take hold of one man, saying, we will eat our own bread, and wear our own apparel: only let us be called by thy name, to take away our reproach.]

When studying the Bible, we must take the responsibility to check out all things for our selves. An error can yield very dangerous results and confusion. A good example of this is the translation *of << I Timothy 3:2 and Titus 1:6 >>*, where we find a slight mistranslation of a single word resulting into the misinterpretation of an entire verse. This is the Greek word *mia* [Strong's #3391]. This word means first, a first, or one out of many. The Greek word that is used to represent the prime number one is *heis* [Strong's #1520]. The original scripture uses the word *mia* and not *heis* because it was not setting a count. The scripture could not at all be referring to the number of wives permitted for a bishop to have. The scripture was simply stating that a bishop should have a first wife, circumstances permitting.

THE TRUTH

<< Timothy 3:2 >> [A bishop then must be blameless, the husband of a first wife, vigilant, sober, of good behavior, given to hospitality, apt to teach]

<< Titus 1:6 >> [If any be blameless, the husband of a first wife, having faithful children not accused of riot or unruly.]

<< 1 Timothy 5:9 >> [Let not a widow be taken into the number under threescore years old, having been the wife of one man.]

In contrast, when speaking about the number of husbands a woman should have the Bible uses the word "heis", meaning one, the number one: one husband. *"Mia"* and *"heis"* are different words with separate meanings that must not be confused. In this context the word *"mia"* means first and *"heis"* means one.

In their quest for personal wealth and power, the political and religious institutions of the Western world have often mistranslated and misused the above verses making them to say "one wife" instead of "a wife". They should learn to use a dictionary. A man's human right to choose the ways of God is sacred. God and the laws of God never change. Our Lord, YAHAWAH, is the same always: a polygamist today, yesterday and forever. The scriptures of all the testaments are consistent. It is in vain to run from the Biblical truth.

Polygamy is the most beneficial and stable social structure for men, women, children and the society. Because the number of marriageable men is less than half of marriageable women, polygamy provides a solution to the lonely life of single women and fatherless children. Polygamy is good for women because they would be less susceptible to predatory men and they would not have to compete with other women for the small number of marriageable men. Over Seventy percent of homes in the western world are single parent families. Without Polygamy the large surplus of single women and fatherless children have to wait for a man to become available only when there is a divorce.

More than fifty percent of children are being raised without a father. Polygamy would reduce the burden placed on the state to provide social services for single parent homes. Polygamy would eliminate the need for social programs such as welfare and daycare, there would always be a family member around to help. There is a high rate of crime and violence in society today. Polygamy would cause a reduction in violence and juvenile crime resulting from fatherless single family homes. Polygamy would reduce the number of sexually related crime, disease and promote stability.

Polygamy cannot be a sin. The Biblical law of God allows the human right to choose Polygamy. Plural marriage has been practiced by almost every nation in the civilized world. God-loving people from around the world practice polygamy today, following the good examples set by the patriarchs of the Bible, who were diligently obeying and loving God: Moses, Abraham, Jacob, David and many more. The surplus of women cannot marry without polygamy. If polygamy was not a sin in the past it can't be a sin today because God is God and does not change. In the book of Ezekiel, since God himself claims to be a polygamist therefore polygamy cannot be a sin:

<< Ezekiel 23:1-4 >> [The word of the LORD came again unto me, saying, <2> Son of man, <u>there were two women</u>, the daughters of one mother: <3> And they committed whoredoms in Egypt; they committed whoredoms in their youth: there were their breasts pressed, and there they bruised the teats of their virginity. <4> And the names of them were Aholah the elder, and Aholibah her sister: <u>and they were mine</u>, and they bare sons

and daughters. Thus were their names; Samaria is Aholah, and Jerusalem Aholibah.]

It is a sin to tell a person that it is wrong for a man to choose how many wives he should have. It is a man's God-given personal human right. The individual alone should decide how many wives and concubines he needs to have! A man is not equal to a woman. A woman is commanded by God to have only one man as a partner. A man must never compromise when it comes to the basic principles, such as his human rights. The first rule is, a man must always treat his woman with love, respect, patience, understanding, and gentleness.

<< First Corinthians 7:3-5 >> [Let the husband render unto the wife due benevolence: and likewise also the wife unto the husband: and likewise also the wife unto the husband. <4> The wife hath not power of her own body, but the husband: and likewise also the husband hath not power of his own body, but the wife. <5> Defraud ye not one the other, except it be with consent for a time, that ye may give yourselves to fasting and prayer; and come together again, that Satan tempt you not for your incontinency.]

And a man must never divorce or put away his woman for any reason, except adultery:

<< First Corinthians 7:10 >> [...Let not the wife depart from her husband: But and if she depart, let her remain unmarried, or reconciled to her husband: and let not the husband put away his wife.]

The Virtuous Woman

The virtuous woman loves, respects, obeys, and honors her husband above all things, without any reservations. The nurturing of her family, her inner character, and intelligence are most important. A meek, humble, and modest woman is a true princess. She does not waste her time and money on whorish clothing, accessories, and makeup on her face.

<< I Timothy 2:9-15 >> [In like manner also, that women adorn themselves in modest apparel, with shamefacedness and sobriety; not with braided hair, or gold, or pearls, or costly array; But which becometh women professing godliness with good works. Let the woman learn in silence with all subjection. But I suffer not a woman to teach, nor to usurp authority over the man, but to be in silence.]

<< First Peters 3:5-7 >> [Whose adorning let it not be that outward adorning of plaiting the hair, and of wearing of gold, or of putting on of apparel; but let it be the hidden man of the heart, in that which is not corruptible, even the ornament of a meek and quiet spirit, which is in the sight of the Lord YAHAWAH of great price.

...For after this manner in old time the holy women also, trusted in the Lord YAHAWAH, adorned themselves, being in subjection unto their own husbands: Even as Sarah obeyed Abraham, calling him Lord: whose daughters ye are, as long as ye do well, and are not afraid with any amazement. Likewise, ye husbands, dwell with them according to knowledge, giving honor unto the wife, as unto the weaker vessel.]

THE TRUTH

Finding a good woman is a gift from God. You don't need to go chasing and begging. There are billions of women in the world. But only God can give you the virtuous woman.

<< *Proverbs 31:10-31* >>[*Who can find a virtuous woman? For her price is far above rubies. The heart of her husband doth safely trust in her, so that he shall have no need of spoil. She will do him good and not evil all the days of her life. <13> She seeketh wool, and flax, and worketh willingly with her hands. <14> She is like the merchants' ship; she bringeth her food from afar. <15> She riseth also while it is yet night, and giveth meat to her household, and a portion to her maidens. <16> She considereth a field, and buyeth it: with the fruit of her hands she planteth a vineyard. <17> She girdeth her loins with strength, and strengtheneth her arms. <18> She perceiveth that her merchandise is good: her candle goeth not out by night. <19> She layeth her hands to the spindle, and her hands hold the distaff.*

<20> She stretcheth out her hand to the poor; yea, she reacheth forth her hands to the needy. <21> She is not afraid of the snow for her household is clothed with scarlet. <22> She maketh herself coverings of tapestry; her clothing is silk and purple. <23> Her husband is known in the gates, when he sitteth among the elders of the land. <24> She maketh fine linen, and selleth it; and delivereth girdles unto merchants. <25> Strength and honor are her clothing; and she shall rejoice in time to come.

<26> She opens her mouth with wisdom; and in her tongue is the law of kindness. <27> She looketh well to the ways of her household, and eateth not the bread of idleness. <28> Her children arise up, and calls her blessed; her husband also, and he praiseth her <29> Many daughters have done virtuously, but thou excellest them all. <30> Favor is deceitful, and beauty is vain: but a woman that feareth the Lord, she shall be praised!]

If any of you are uncomfortable with the scriptures that are brought out, please do not judge me and accuse me falsely. Surely, there will always be some people who will be offended by the truth. Let it be known clearly, that I do not hate women! I have only love in my heart! But the following scriptures must be listed because some people will find them helpful:

<< *Isaiah 3:16* >> [*Because the daughters of Zion are haughty, and walk with stretched forth necks and wanton eyes, walking and mincing as they go and making a tinkling with their feet, ...Therefore the Lord will smite with a scab the crown of the head of the daughters of Zion, and the Lord will discover their secret parts.*]

< 24 > [*And it shall come to pass that instead of sweet smell there shall be stink; and instead of well set hair baldness, ...and burning instead of beauty.*]

<< *Jeremiah 4:30* >> [*And when thou art spoiled, what wilt thou do? Though thou clothe thyself with crimson, though thou deckest thee with ornaments of gold, though thou rentest thy face with painting, in vain shalt thou makest thyself fair; thy lovers, will despise thee, they will seek thy life.*]

<< *Proverbs 30:20* >> [*Such is the way of an adulterous woman; she eateth, and wipeth her mouth, and saith, I have done no wickedness.*]

THE TRUTH

<< Proverbs 31:3 >> [Give not thy strength unto women, nor thy ways to that which destroyeth kings.]

<< Matthew 7:6 >> [Give not that which is holy unto dogs, neither cast ye your pearls before swine, lest they trample them under their feet, and turn again and rend you.]

<< Proverbs 6:24-29 >> [To keep thee from the evil woman, from the flattery of the strange woman. Lust not after her beauty in thine heart; neither let her take thee with her eyelids. For by means of a whorish woman a man is brought to a piece of bread (She'll take the shirt off your back) ...and the adulteress will hunt for the precious life. Can a man take fire in his bosom, and his cloth not be burned? Can one go upon hot coals, and his feet not be burned! So is he that goeth in to his neighbor's wife; Whosoever toucheth her shall not be innocent!]

<< Apocrypha, Ecclesiasticus 9:8,9 >> [Turn away thine eye from a beautiful woman, and look not upon another's beauty; for many have been deceived by the beauty of a woman; herewith love is kindled as a fire. Sit not at all with another man's wife, nor sit down with her in thine arms, and spend not thy money with her at the wine; lest thine heart incline unto her, and so through thy desire thou fall into destruction.]

According to the Bible you're not even supposed to sit next to another guy's woman!

<< Proverbs 5:3-12 >> [For the lips of a strange woman drop as honeycomb, and her mouth is smoother than oil: But her end is bitter as wormwood, sharp as a two-edged sword. Her feet go down to death; her steps take hold on hell. Lest thou shouldest ponder the path of life, her ways are movable, that thou canst not know them.

Hear me now therefore, O ye children, and depart not from the words of my mouth. Remove thy way far from her, and come not nigh the door of her house: Lest thou give thine honor unto others, and thy years unto the cruel: Lest strangers be filled with thy wealth; and thy labors be in the house of a stranger; and thou mourn at the last, when thy flesh and thy body are consumed, and say, How have I hated instruction, and my heart despised reproof!]

<< Ecclesiastes 7:25-29 >> [...And I find more bitter than death the woman, whose heart is snares and nets, and her hands as bands: who so pleaseth the Lord shall escape from her; but the sinners shall be taken by her.

Behold, this have I found, saith the preacher, counting one by one, to find the account: Which yet my soul seeketh, but I find not: one man among a thousand have I found; but a woman among all those have I not found. Lo, this only have I found, that the Lord hath made man upright; but they have sought out many inventions.]

The Apocrypha - First Esdras 4:13-40 clearly shows that only with wisdom can a man overcome a wicked woman he must teach and discipline his woman if he truly loves his family!

<< Ecclesiasticus 25:13-26, Chapter 26 >> [Give me any plague, but the plague of the heart: and any wickedness, but the wickedness of a woman: and any affliction, but the

affliction from them that hate me: and any revenge, but the revenge of enemies. There is no head above the head of a serpent; and there is no wrath above the wrath of an enemy. I had rather dwell with a lion and a dragon, than to keep house with a wicked woman. The wickedness of a woman changeth her face, and darkeneth her countenance like sackcloth. Her husband shall sit among his neighbors; and when he heareth it shall sigh bitterly. All wickedness is but little to the wickedness of a woman.

Let the portion of a sinner fall upon her. As the climbing up a sandy way is to the feet of the aged, so is a wife full of words to a quiet man. Stumble not at the beauty of a woman, and desire her not for pleasure. A woman if she maintain her husband, is full of anger, impudence, and much reproach. A wicked woman abateth the courage, maketh an heavy countenance and a wounded heart: a woman who will not comfort her husband in distress maketh weak hands and feeble knees. Of the woman came the beginning of sin; through her we all die.

If she go not as thou wouldest have her, cut her off from thy flesh, and give her a bill of divorce and let her go... An evil woman is a yoke shaken to and fro: he that hath hold on her is as though he held a scorpion... The whoredom of a woman may be known in her haughty looks and eyelids, she will open her mouth, as a thirsty traveler when he hath found a fountain, and drink of every water near her: by every hedge will she sit down, and open her quiver to every arrow ...An harlot shall be counted as spittle!]

<< Micah 7:2-7 >> [The good man is perished out of the earth: and there is none upright among men: they all lie in wait for blood; they hunt every man his brother with a net. That they may do evil with both hands earnestly, the prince asketh, and the judge asketh for a reward; and the great man, he uttereth his mischievous desire: so they wrap it up. The best of them is as a brier: the most upright is sharper than a thorn hedge: the day of thy watchmen and thy visitation cometh; now shall be their perplexity.

Trust ye not in a friend, put ye not confidence in a guide: keep the doors of thy mouth from her that lieth in thy bosom (never tell your secrets). For the son dishonoureth the father, the daughter riseth up against her mother ...a man's enemies are the men of his own house. Therefore I will look unto the Lord; I will wait for my salvation: My Lord will hear me!]

The Dietary Law

The Most High also gave us a dietary law, so that we would know what food to eat and not to eat. Some foods are not made for human consumption, as you know, and they can in fact, be poisonous. You might not die right away because poisons work at different rates. Some can kill you in a minute while others can cause you to get sick and kill you in ten or twenty years. Even some of the edible food is constantly being poisoned with chemicals. Sometimes it is deliberately done for political and economical reasons. They got your body running on poison!

The reason you see so many hospitals today is because, making you sick means money! People should learn to use the herbs more often to help clean our system. Many doctors are practicing a form of witchcraft rather than medicine; they make you sick so they can charge you for the cure. The law of the Most High God teaches us which foods to eat, and not to eat:

THE TRUTH

<< Deuteronomy Chapter 14:2-20 >> *[For thou art an holy people unto the Lord thy God, and the Lord hath chosen thee to be a peculiar people unto himself, above all the nations that are upon the earth. Thou shalt not eat any abominable thing.*

These are the beasts which ye shall eat: the ox, the sheep, and the fallow deer, and the wild goat, and the pygarg, and the wild ox, and the chamois. And every beast that parteth the hoof, and cleaveth the cleft into two claws, and cheweth the cud among the beasts, that ye shall eat. Nevertheless these ye shall not eat, of them that chew the cud, or of them that divide the cloven hoof; therefore they are unclean unto you. And the swine (you're not suppose to eat pork, or any other scavenger animal; the pig is one of nature's garbage cans. It eats any filth*), because it divideth the hoof, yet cheweth not the cud, it is unclean unto you... ye shall not eat of their flesh, nor touch their dead carcass.*

These ye shall eat, of all that are in the waters: all that have fins and scales shall ye eat: and whatsoever hath not fins and scales ye may not eat (shrimps, catfish, crabs, lobsters, and all other sea scavengers are not to be eaten, they are a form of slow poison*); it is unclean unto you. Of all clean birds ye shall eat. But these are they of which ye shall not eat: the eagle, and the ossifrage, and the osprey, and the glede, and the kite, and the vulture after his kind, and every raven after his kind, and the owl, and the nighthawk, and the cuckoo, and the hawk after his kind, the little owl, and the great owl, and the swan, and the pelican, and the gier-eagle, and the cormorant, and the stork, and the heron after her kind, and the lapwing, and the bat. And every creeping thing that flyeth is unclean unto you: they shall not be eaten.]*

But of all clean fowls ye may eat. Ye shall not eat of any thing that dieth of itself: thou shalt give it unto the stranger that is in thy gates, that he may eat it; or thou mayest sell it unto an alien: for thou art a holy people unto the Lord thy Lord.

Israelites had sheep, cattle, and plenty of good meat that they were eating! Investigate the history and you'll see that the eating of meat and drinking of wine is an important part of Biblical Israelite Law. The Passover Lamb must be eaten by all Israelites! In addition to good cooking; the Israelites were also enjoying the best wines! The Passover is celebrated in the home and the drinking of wine is also a part of the celebration. When the Angels came to visit Lot in Sodom, Lot killed a cow and served the meat to them and they ate:

<< Genesis 18:8 >> *[and he took butter, and milk, and the calf which he had dressed, and set it before them; and he stood by them under the tree, and they did eat.]*

Christ himself was drinking wine and turned water into wine:

<< Genesis 49:11,12 >> *[Binding his foal unto the vine; and his ass's colt unto the choice vine; he washes his garments in wine, and his clothes in the blood of grapes <12> His eyes shall be red with wine and his teeth white with milk.]*

<< Matthew 11:19 >> *[The Son of man* (Christ) *came eating and drinking, and they say, Behold a man gluttonous, and a winebibber.]*

And remember how Noah got drunk from drinking wine?

THE TRUTH

<< Genesis 9:21 >> [And he drank of the wine, and was drunken...]

Don't let anyone tell you or any person in good health that it is wrong to drink wine, or to eat meat. Normally it is fine to do so at moderation! The Bible says:

<< Proverbs 31:6,7 >> [Give strong drink unto him that is ready to perish, and wine unto those that be of heavy hearts. Let him drink and forget his poverty, and remember his miseries no more.]

Alcoholic beverages must not be consumed in the church or the temple. If a religion allows alcohol consumption in their church or temple, it is a false religion.

<< Leviticus 10:8,9 >> [And the LORD spake unto Aaron, saying, <9> Do not drink wine nor strong drink, thou, nor thy sons with thee, when ye go into the tabernacle of the congregation, lest ye die: it shall be a statute for ever throughout your generations:

The drinking of wine is not to be done in a disorderly way, a person is not to get drunk and become uncontrollable and disrespecting others, becoming violent, and a public spectacle! Alcoholic beverages should not be consumed in the church or during the performance of any official duty. There is a time and season for all things. Know your limit and be moderate!

Circumcision:

Israelites should be circumcised according to the laws of the Bible. The Most High commanded it:

<< Genesis 17:9-27 >> [And the Lord said to Abraham, Thou shalt keep my covenant therefore, thou, and thy seed after thee in their generations (including our present generation, today). *This is my covenant, which ye shall keep, between me and you and thy seed after thee; every man-child among you shall be circumcised. And ye shall circumcise the flesh of your foreskin; and it shall be a token of the covenant betwixt me and you. And he that is eight days old shall be circumcised among you, every man child in your generations, he that is born in the house, or bought with money of any stranger, which is not of thy seed. He that is born in thy house, and he that is bought with money, must needs be circumcised: and my covenant shall be in your flesh for an everlasting covenant. And the uncircumcised man child whose flesh of his foreskin is not circumcised, that soul shall be cut off from his people; he hath broken my covenant.]*

There are two ways in which the Bible uses the word circumcision; it could also mean separation from the world:

<< First Corinthian 7:18 >> [Is any man called being circumcised? Let him not become uncircumcised. Is any called in circumcision? Let him not be circumcised.]

THE TRUTH

This can not be talking about the covenant of circumcision, where the foreskin is cut off, because there is no way you can reverse that process and replace the foreskin! You can not become physically uncircumcised after you've been circumcised! The Most High is very serious about the law of circumcision! He was going to kill Moses because Moses neglected to circumcise his child.

<< Exodus 4:24-26 >> [And it came to pass by the way in the inn, that the Lord met him, and sought to kill him. Then Zipporah took a sharp stone, and cut off the foreskin of her son, and cast it at his feet, and said, surely a bloody husband art thou to me.]

THE ISRAELITE NETWORK HOLY DAYS CALENDAR

Year	Passover	Feast of Unleavened Bread	Feast of Weeks	Feast of trumpets	Day of Atonement	Feast of Tabernacles
2000	April 20	April 21-27	June 4	Sept. 30	Oct. 9	Oct. 13-20

The Hebrew dates begin at sunset on the PREVIOUS evening and end on the dates listed above
Feast of Lights: 9th month 25th day to 10th month 3rd day. Purim: 12th month 14th, 15th day.
The Sabbath is the seventh day of the week, from friday sundown to saturday sundown.

MARCH

S	M	T	W	T	F	S*
			1	2	3	4
5	6	7	8	9	10	11
12	13	14	15	16	17	18
19	(20)	21	22	23	24	25
26	27	28	29	30	31	

APRIL

S	M	T	W	T	F	S*
						1
2	3	4	5	6	7	8
9	10	11	12	13	14	15
16	17	18	19	20	21	22
23	24	25	26	27	28	29
30						

MAY

S	M	T	W	T	F	S*
	1	2	3	4	5	6
7	8	9	10	11	12	13
14	15	16	17	18	19	20
21	22	23	24	25	26	27
28	29	30	31			

JUNE

S	M	T	W	T	F	S*
				1	2	3
4	5	6	7	8	9	10
11	12	13	14	15	16	17
18	19	20	21	22	23	24
25	26	27	28	29	30	

JULY

S	M	T	W	T	F	S*
						1
2	3	4	5	6	7	8
9	10	11	12	13	14	15
16	17	18	19	20	21	22
23	24	25	26	27	28	29
30	31					

AUGUST

S	M	T	W	T	F	S*
		1	2	3	4	5
6	7	8	9	10	11	12
13	14	15	16	17	18	19
20	21	22	23	24	25	26
27	28	29	30	31		

SEPTEMBER

S	M	T	W	T	F	S*
					1	2
3	4	5	6	7	8	9
10	11	12	13	14	15	16
17	18	19	20	21	22	23
24	25	26	27	28	29	30

OCTOBER

S	M	T	W	T	F	S*
1	2	3	4	5	6	7
8	9	10	11	12	13	14
15	16	17	18	19	20	21
22	23	24	25	26	27	28
29	30	31				

NOVEMBER

S	M	T	W	T	F	S*
		1	2	3	4	
5	6	7	8	9	10	11
12	13	14	15	16	17	18
19	20	21	22	23	24	25
26	27	28	29	30		

DECEMBER

S	M	T	W	T	F	S*
					1	2
3	4	5	6	7	8	9
10	11	12	13	14	15	16
17	18	19	20	21	22	23
24	25	26	27	28	29	30
31						

JANUARY

S	M	T	W	T	F	S*
	1	2	3	4	5	6
7	8	9	10	11	12	13
14	15	16	17	18	19	20
21	22	23	24	25	26	27
28	29	30	31			

FEBRUARY

S	M	T	W	T	F	S*
				1	2	3
4	5	6	7	8	9	10
11	12	13	14	15	16	17
18	19	20	21	22	23	
25	26	27	28			

*Sabbaths, New Moons and Holy Days ...http://israelite.net, (212) 586-5969 P.O. Box 1747 NYC 10101

Earth's Seasons Equinoxes, Solstices, Perihelion, and Aphelion

Note: D, H, M indicate day, hour, minute, respectively, of Universal Time

		d h			d h m		d h m
2000			**2000**				
Perihelion	Jan	3 05	Equinoxes	Mar	20 07 35	Sept	22 17 27
Aphelion	July	4 00	Solstices	June	21 01 48	Dec	21 13 37
2001			**2001**				
Perihelion	Jan	4 09	Equinoxes	Mar	20 13 31	Sept	22 23 05
Aphelion	July	4 14	Solstices	June	21 07 38	Dec	21 19 22
2002			**2002**				
Perihelion	Jan	2 14	Equinoxes	Mar	20 19 16	Sept	23 04 56
Aphelion	July	6 04	Solstices	June	21 13 24	Dec	22 01 15
2003			**2003**				
Perihelion	Jan	4 05	Equinoxes	Mar	21 01 00	Sept	23 10 47
Aphelion	July	4 06	Solstices	June	21 19 10	Dec	22 07 04
2004			**2004**				
Perihelion	Jan	4 18	Equinoxes	Mar	20 06 49	Sept	22 16 30
Aphelion	July	5 11	Solstices	June	21 00 57	Dec	21 12 42
2005			**2005**				
Perihelion	Jan	2 01	Equinoxes	Mar	20 12 34	Sept	22 22 23
Aphelion	July	5 05	Solstices	June	21 06 46	Dec	21 18 35

Fraction of the Moon Illuminated, 2000 at Midnight Universal Time

Day	Jan.	Feb.	Mar.	Apr.	May	June	July	Aug.	Sep.	Oct.	Nov.	Dec.
01	0.27	0.18	0.25	0.15	0.13	0.03	0.01	0.01	0.09	0.12	0.21	0.22
02	0.19	0.11	0.17	0.09	0.06	0.01	0.00	0.05	0.16	0.19	0.29	0.30
03	0.12	0.06	0.10	0.04	0.02	0.00	0.02	0.12	0.25	0.27	0.38	0.39
04	0.07	0.02	0.05	0.01	0.00	0.03	0.07	0.20	0.34	0.36	0.47	0.49
05	0.03	0.00	0.02	0.00	0.01	0.09	0.15	0.30	0.43	0.46	0.57	0.58
06	0.01	0.00	0.00	0.02	0.05	0.17	0.24	0.40	0.53	0.55	0.66	0.68
07	0.00	0.02	0.01	0.07	0.11	0.27	0.34	0.50	0.63	0.64	0.75	0.77
08	0.01	0.06	0.04	0.13	0.20	0.38	0.44	0.60	0.71	0.73	0.83	0.85
09	0.05	0.12	0.09	0.22	0.30	0.49	0.55	0.69	0.80	0.81	0.90	0.92
10	0.10	0.20	0.16	0.33	0.41	0.59	0.65	0.77	0.87	0.88	0.95	0.97
11	0.16	0.29	0.25	0.44	0.52	0.69	0.74	0.85	0.92	0.94	0.99	1.00
12	0.24	0.39	0.36	0.55	0.63	0.78	0.82	0.91	0.97	0.98	1.00	0.99
13	0.34	0.50	0.47	0.66	0.73	0.86	0.89	0.96	0.99	1.00	0.98	0.96
14	0.44	0.62	0.58	0.76	0.82	0.92	0.94	0.99	1.00	0.99	0.94	0.90
15	0.55	0.73	0.69	0.85	0.89	0.96	0.98	1.00	0.98	0.97	0.87	0.82
16	0.66	0.82	0.79	0.92	0.95	0.99	1.00	0.99	0.95	0.92	0.79	0.72
17	0.76	0.90	0.88	0.97	0.98	1.00	1.00	0.97	0.89	0.85	0.68	0.62
18	0.86	0.96	0.94	0.99	1.00	0.99	0.98	0.92	0.82	0.75	0.57	0.50
19	0.93	0.99	0.98	1.00	0.99	0.96	0.95	0.86	0.72	0.65	0.46	0.40
20	0.98	1.00	1.00	0.98	0.97	0.92	0.90	0.78	0.62	0.54	0.35	0.30
21	1.00	0.98	0.99	0.95	0.93	0.86	0.83	0.69	0.51	0.43	0.25	0.21
22	0.99	0.93	0.96	0.90	0.88	0.79	0.75	0.59	0.39	0.32	0.16	0.13
23	0.95	0.87	0.91	0.83	0.81	0.70	0.65	0.48	0.29	0.22	0.09	0.07
24	0.89	0.79	0.85	0.76	0.73	0.61	0.55	0.37	0.19	0.13	0.04	0.03
25	0.82	0.70	0.77	0.67	0.65	0.51	0.44	0.26	0.11	0.07	0.01	0.01
26	0.73	0.61	0.69	0.58	0.55	0.40	0.33	0.16	0.05	0.02	0.00	0.00
27	0.63	0.52	0.60	0.48	0.45	0.30	0.23	0.08	0.01	0.00	0.01	0.01
28	0.53	0.42	0.50	0.39	0.35	0.20	0.14	0.03	0.00	0.01	0.04	0.05
29	0.44	0.33	0.41	0.29	0.25	0.12	0.07	0.00	0.02	0.03	0.09	0.09
30	0.34		0.32	0.20	0.17	0.05	0.02	0.01	0.06	0.08	0.15	0.16
31	0.26		0.23		0.09		0.00	0.04		0.14		0.23

THE TRUTH

* The four seasons: spring, summer, fall and winter result from the fact that the tilt of the earth's axis remains constant while the earth orbits around the sun.
* The equinox occurs when the day and the nigh are equal in length and the sun rises directly above the equator.
* The spring equinox announces the arrival of spring and it is the beginning of the year.
* The summer Solstice is the longest day of the year. The sun rises towards the north during the summer solstice and towards the south during the winter solstice.

* Perihelion is the closest point that the moon approaches the earth in its orbit. At perigee the moon is moving the fastest.
* Aphelion is the farthest point in the lunar orbit, where the moon is moving the slowest. The phases of the moon result from the reflected light of the sun.
* Lunation is the time required for a complete cycle of the phases of the moon to be completed, an average of 29.51 days. From new to full, the moon is said to be waxing; from full to dark is called waining.
* The New Moon is the first observable crescent to appear after the dark moon. The first crescent is the first day of the month in the Hebrew Calendar.

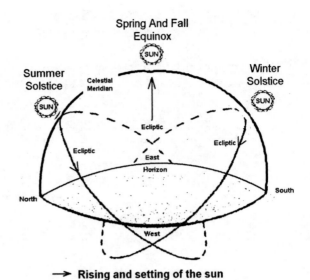

Rising and setting of the sun for the northern hemisphere

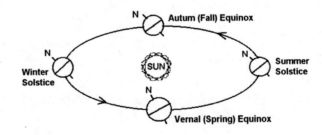

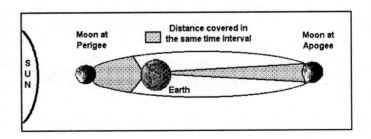

New Moon   First Quater   Full Moon   Last Quater   Last Crescent   Dark Moon

THE TRUE HOLY DAYS

To observe the true Holy Days commanded by the Lord YAHAWAH in the Bible we must first identify the original Hebrew calendar. The Hebrew calendar is calculated very different from the Western or Roman calendar of this world. The calendar consists of four independent elements of time: days, weeks, months and the year. The elements of the biblical calendar are determined only by the positions of the Sun and the moon relative to the earth.

<< Genesis 1:14-19 >> [And God said, Let there be lights in the firmament of the heaven to divide the day from the night; and let them be for signs, and for seasons, and for days, and years: 15 And let them be for lights in the firmament of the heaven to give light upon the earth: and it was so. 16 And God made two great lights; the greater light to rule the day, and the lesser light to rule the night: he made the stars also. 17 And God set them in the firmament of the heaven to give light upon the earth, 18 And to rule over the day and over the night, and to divide the light from the darkness: and God saw that it was good. 19 And the evening and the morning were the fourth day.]

The scriptures explain exactly how to determine the Hebrew calendar's days, weeks, months and year as prescribed by the laws of Lord YAHAWAH. The biblical day begins at sunset the previous evening and ends at sunset that day. The day does not start at midnight. Nothing important starts at midnight, when everyone is sleeping. A day according to the Bible is the 24-hour period from sunset to sunset.

<< Genesis 1:19 >> [And the evening and the morning were the fourth day.]

According to the Bible, the week is a seven-day cycle, starting from the first day of creation. The Israelites numbered the days but never gave names to the months or the days of the week. The names are of pagan origin. So-called Sunday is the first day of the week and so-called Saturday is the seventh day of the week. This seven-day cycle has been repeated regularly without interruption since the first day of creation.

<< Genesis 2:1-3 >> [Thus the heavens and the earth were finished, and all the host of them. 2 And on the seventh day God ended his work which he had made; and he rested on the seventh day from all his work which he had made. 3 And God blessed the seventh day, and sanctified it: because that in it he had rested from all his work which God created and made.]

According to biblical law the months are determined by the cycles of the moon. The month begins with the appearance of the first sliver of crescent light after the moon has gone dark. The first observable crescent of the moon is the first day of the month. The first day of the month is called the new moon. Some people are ignorantly using the dark moon as the new moon. This is false because the moon can remain dark for three days in a single month. You can not have two or three new moons in a single month. Secondly, the knew moon has to be observed by at least two witnesses and reported to the congregation. How can witnesses observe something invisible with their eyes? How can something be knew and it has not yet appeared? The most High is not the author of confusion. Any calculations for the new moon must be confirm by actual visual observations before the New Moon can be officially declared the first day of the month.

From the beginning, the Israelites had a system set up such that at least two witnesses would have to report the sighting of the first visible crescent of the New Moon to the counsel of the congregation. After the evidence was confirmed, the New Moon would then be proclaimed as the first day of the month throughout the nation and abroad. The average length of a month is 29.51 days, the time it takes for the moon to go through an entire cycle from new moon to half, to full, half, last crescent, and dark again. The New Moon, which appears over Jerusalem is used as the reference for Israelites around the world because that is where the temple was located. The new moon was determined from wherever the tabernacle was. We should determine all calculations such as the new moon and the equinox, using Jerusalem as the reference point.

We are commanded to observe the first day of the month, the New Moon as an important Holy Day.

>> *Psalm 81:3,4* >> *Blow up the trumpet in the new moon, in the time appointed, on our solemn feast day. <4> For this was a statute for Israel, and a law of the God of Jacob.*

<< *Numbers 10:10* >> *Also in the day of your gladness, and in your solemn days, and in the beginnings of your months, ye shall blow with the trumpets over your burnt offerings, and over the sacrifices of your peace offerings; that they may be to you for a memorial before your God: I am the LORD your God.*

<< *Numbers 28:11* >> *And in the beginnings of your months ye shall offer a burnt offering unto the LORD; two young bullocks, and one ram, seven lambs of the first year without spot.*

<< *1 Samuel 20:5* >> *And David said unto Jonathan, Behold, to morrow is the new moon, and I should not fail to sit with the king at meat: but let me go, that I may hide myself in the field unto the third day at even.*

<< *Amos 8:5* >> *Saying, When will the new moon be gone, that we may sell corn? and the sabbath, that we may set forth wheat, making the ephah small, and the shekel great, and falsifying the balances by deceit?*

<< *Isaiah 66:23* >> *And it shall come to pass, that from one new moon to*

another, and from one sabbath to another, shall all flesh come to worship before me, saith the LORD.

<< Ezekiel 45:17 >> And it shall be the prince's part to give burnt offerings, and meat offerings, and drink offerings, in the feasts, and in the new moons, and in the Sabbaths, in all solemnities of the house of Israel.

<< Ezekiel 46:3 >> Likewise the people of the land shall worship at the door of this gate before the LORD in the Sabbaths and in the new moons.

The biblical year is determined by the cycle of the sun and was independent of the lunar cycle of the months, and of the seven-day cycle of the week. The year is the period of time it takes the earth to complete one orbit about the son, a period of about 365.25 days. The cycle of the sun determines the four seasons. The year began with the spring equinox. The equinox is the time of year when the day and the night are equal and the sun is passing directly over the equator. The arrival of the spring equinox is the beginning of the year.

The first month occurs in spring and is the time of year when the Passover is to be observed. The celebration of the Passover also requires the ripening of barley, which only occurs with the arrival of spring.

<< Leviticus 23:5,10 >> In the fourteenth day of the first month at even is the LORD'S passover... 10 Speak unto the children of Israel, and say unto them, When ye be come into the land which I give unto you, and shall reap the harvest thereof, then ye shall bring a sheaf of the firstfruits of your harvest unto the priest.

The Israelite calendar is different from the Western calendar because our days, weeks, months and year is determined according to the laws of Lord YAHAWAH in the Bible by observing the cycles of the sun and the moon. Only by using the Hebrew Israelite biblical calendar can we determine the Holy days of the year. The only true Holy Days are the Festival Days commanded by the Almighty Lord YAHAWAH as found in the Bible. The true Holy Days were dictated directly to Moses and recorded in the Bible. The Holy Days of YAHAWAH are truly spiritual, significant and beneficial. The learning and keeping of the Holy Days is important because they teach us the pattern by which we must serve the Creator, and also because they reveal a deeper understanding of the First and Second Coming of Jesus Christ.

The religious and political holidays of this society are the result of confusion, greed, ignorance, and paganism. For example Halloween is derived from the worship of demons and everyone dress up like demons; Easter comes from the worship of Isis; and Christmas, from the worship of the sun god of Babylon and Egypt.

Instead of giving attention to the true Holy Days of the Creator, people spend a lot of money to celebrate colonial holidays that don't even pertain to them socially, historically, and politically. The Bible warns against following after pagan customs:

THE TRUTH

<< Jeremiah 10 >> [Hear ye the word which the Lord speaketh unto you, O house of Israel: Thus saith the Lord, learn not the way of the heathen, and be not dismayed at the signs of heaven (Astrology is false*); for the heathen are dismayed at them. For the customs of the people are vain* (their ways are wicked*): For one cutteth a tree out of the forest, the work of the hands of the workman, with the ax* (talking about how they get the Christmas tree: going into the forest and chopping it down with an ax*). They deck it with silver and with gold* (the gold and silver trimmings put on the tree*); they fasten it with hammers, that it move not. They are upright as the palm tree.]*

The Lord YAHAWAH warns us not to celebrate false heathen holidays, such as Christmas. Christmas originated from the worship of Nimrod and Satan. Christ was born in the springtime, not in December! We can not mix the worship of the true God, the Lord YAHAWAH, with a pagan festival!

The second fallacy taught about the nativity is the idea that Jesus Christ did not have a physical father on the earth. In Matthew 1:1 to 1:16 the Bible not only say that Joseph was Christ's physical father, it also gives a list of all of Christ's grandfathers!

<< Matthew 1:16 >> [And Jacob begot Joseph the husband of Mary, of whom was born Jesus, who is called Christ.]

<< Matthew 1:18 >> [...When Mary was espoused to Joseph, before they came together, she was found with child of the Holy Spirit. Then Joseph her husband, being a just man, and not willing to make her a public example, was minded to put her away privily.]

An Angel came and told Joseph not to call off his engagement because Mary was carrying a special child, and it was by a miracle of God that Joseph's sperm had impregnated her without having intercourse. Today we would have considered this pregnancy as a miraculous form of "artificial insemination".

<< Matthew 1:20 >> [...Fear not to take unto thee Mary thy wife: for that which is conceive in her (meaning she was made pregnant by the seed of Joseph by a miracle*) is of the Holy Spirit]*

It means that her child would become a great prophet! The same was said of John the Baptist:

<< Luke 1:15 >> [For he shall be great in the sight of the Lord, and shall drink neither wine nor strong drink; and he shall be filled with the Holy Spirit, even from his mother's womb.]

<< Luke 1:26,27 >> [To a virgin espoused to a man whose name was Joseph, of the house of David; and the virgin's name was Mary. And the angel came in unto her, and said...]

The angel came to Mary to deliver a message, not to have sex, which would have been adultery. The message that she was going to be impregnated in a miraculous fashion by the seed of Joseph without having intercourse.

THE TRUTH

<< Luke 1:31 >> [And behold, thou shalt conceive in thy womb, and bring forth a son, and shall call his name Jesus.]

Conception occurs only when the female egg is united with a male sperm.

<< Luke 1:34 >> [Then said Mary unto the Angel, How shall this be, seeing I know not a man?]

The Angel said in <verse 31>, that in the near future, she was going to conceive and become pregnant. God miraculously causes Mary to become pregnant with the seed of Joseph without intercourse. Joseph did not have intercourse with her until after Jesus was born, out of respect for the special child in her.

<< Matthew 1:25 >> [And knew her not till she had brought forth her firstborn son: and he called his name Jesus.]

<< Romans 1:3 >> [...Concerning his son Jesus Christ our Lord, which was made of the seed of David according to the flesh.]

The seed of life is twofold: spirit and matter. It is contained within the sperm of man. The man carries the seed, not the woman. Her egg receives and develops it. For Christ to be an original Hebrew Israelite of the tribe of Judah, he had to be from the seed of a Judite male. Joseph was that male from the line of David. The Bible says Christ descended from the seed of a man! God had miraculously caused Joseph's sperm to impregnate Mary without intercourse. Nothing is impossible for Lord YAHAWAH. The scripture says *"he knew her not"* and Mary stated *"I know not a man"*. There was no intercourse between her and Joseph according to the Bible, but he seed was that of Joseph's implanted by a miracle.

The leaders of this world have lied with regard to Christ's race, saying that he was a Caucasian. They have lied saying Christ did not have a father, and they've lied concerning Christ's birthday! Christ was not born on December 25th in the dead of winter; he was born in April during Passover. The Passover occurs on the fourteenth day after the new moon in April. People can tell lies but the elements and the seasons can never lie; they also testify as to the date of Christ's birth.

<< Luke 2:7,8 >> [And there were in the same country shepherds abiding in the field, keeping watch over their flock by night. And the Angel of the Lord came upon them ...and said For unto you is born this day in the city of David a Savior, which is Christ the Lord.]

Now how can shepherds be feeding flocks and abiding in the field in the dead of winter when the ground is frozen and there is no grass to feed the flocks? So Christ could not have been born in the wintry month of December. He was born in the spring according to the Bible.

You see it is Hebrew law that every year the Israelites have to travel to Jerusalem to keep the Feast of the Passover. According to the historical records it was also at that time that the Romans collected the taxes. It is for this reason that Mary and Joseph were traveling to Jerusalem: to pay the Roman taxes and to keep the Passover! The scriptures tell clearly the birthday of Christ:

<< Luke 2:40-42 >> [And the child grew, and waxed strong in spirit, and filled with wisdom: and the grace of the Lord was upon him (the child here is the young Christ). Now his parents

went to Jerusalem every year at the Passover (everyone should know that the Passover comes in the middle of April, the so-called Easter season*). And when he was twelve years old* (the very day Christ turned twelve years old*), they went up to Jerusalem after the custom of the feast.]*

Christ's twelfth birthday coincided with the Passover, and his parents traveled to Jerusalem to celebrate. Furthermore, when Christ was born he was not put in a dirty manger where animals feed! The word that was translated "manger" in the Bible is the same word that was used to describe the small portable cribs that was used by the Israelite women to carry their babies when they travel. And that type of crib fits on their backs! American Indian women and eastern women use the same kind of cribs today when they are traveling with their babies!

We can clearly see that, according to the Bible, Jesus Christ was not a European born on December 25th. Jesus was a Hebrew Israelite of Asiatic descent, with woolly hair, born in April, the month of Passover. Also there is no place in the Bible where it says that only three wise men came and saw the baby Jesus the Christ in a stable. The Bible said it was a group of wise men, and they found Christ in a house, not in a stable with animals:

<< *Matthew 2:11* >> *[And when they were come into the house, they saw the young child with Mary his mother, and fell down, and worshipped him: and when they had open their treasures, they presented unto him gifts; gold, frankincense, and myrrh.]*

The meaning of the Holy Days is threefold in nature: ritualistic, mystical, and prophetic. The true Holy Days, which we are called to celebrate, are given in the book of Exodus and Leviticus. The Most High desire that we observe all the Holy Days according to the manner in which He has prescribed in the Bible. Spiritually, the Holy Days teach us to attain oneness with the Lord YAHAWAH. Most importantly, the Holy Days refer prophetically to the great work that would be accomplished by Jesus Christ in leading mankind to the Lord God YAHAWAH. Each one of the Holy Days is a prophetic reference, to be accomplished in the redeeming work of Jesus Christ!

The feasts of our Lord YAHAWAH are seven in number: The Passover, Feast of Unleaven Bread, Pentecost, Memorial of Trumpets, Day of Atonement, Feast of Tabernacles and The Last Great Day. Also, in addition to the seven feasts, the Lord desires us to keep the weekly Sabbath and observe the arrival of the New Moon.

The Sabbath

<< *Genesis 2:2,3* >> *[And on the seventh day God ended his work which he had made; and he rested on the seventh day from all his work which he made. <3> And God blessed the seventh day, and sanctified it: because that in it he had rested from all his work which God created and made.]*

The Sabbath has been known as a day of rest from the very beginning of time. It is the seventh day of the week, Saturday. The true Sabbath is the rest we will find in Jesus Christ, because he is the one returning as the prince of peace. Jesus spake and said:

<< *Matthew 11:28, 29* >> *[Come unto me, all ye that labor and are heavy laden, and I will give you rest. <29> Take my yoke upon you, and learn of me; for I am meek and lowly in heart: and ye shall find rest unto your souls.]*

THE TRUTH

The Lord God *commands* that we are to keep the Sabbath because it is a prophecy to be fulfilled after the Second Coming of Jesus when we will have everlasting peace and joy.

<< *Leviticus 23:1-3* >> *[And the Lord spake unto Moses, saying, <2> Speak unto the children of Israel, and say unto them, Concerning the feasts of the Lord, which ye shall proclaim to be holy convocations, even these are my feasts. <3> Six days shall work be done: but the seventh day is the sabbath of rest, an holy convocation; ye shall do no work therein: it is the sabbath of the Lord in all your dwellings.]*

Saturday is the seventh day of the week. The Sabbath begins every Friday at sundown and lasts until Saturday at sundown the following day. A day is measured from sundown to sundown. According to Biblical law, the day does not start at midnight. The day begins at sundown the previous day. It is the day that we should rest in and reserve for spiritual activities in honor of the Lord YAHAWAH and Jesus Christ.

The seven High Holy Days are divided into three groups, thus only three separate journeys to Jerusalem were required per year. The first group is referred to as the Passover, occurring in the first month (April). It consists of the day of the Passover itself and the Feast of Unleavened bread. The second set consists of a single feast, referred to as the Feast of Pentecost (Feast of Weeks), occurring after seven weeks later, which is the sixteenth day in the third month. And the third set of high Holy Days occur in the seventh month, known as the feast of Tabernacles. It consists of the Memorial of Trumpets, on the first day; The Day of Atonement, on the tenth day; and the Feast of Tabernacles, from the fifteenth to the twenty-second day. The twenty-third day is also celebrated and is called The last Great Day.

<< *Deuteronomy 16:16* >> *[Three times in a year shall all thy males appear before the Lord thy God in the place which he shall choose; in the feast of unleavened bread, and in the feast of weeks, and in the feast of tabernacles: and they shall not appear before the Lord empty.]*

The Passover

Just as the Sabbath in a spiritual way represents an aspect of the great work of redemption by Jesus, the remaining Holy Days will serve to reveal other important aspects of the true salvation and redemption through Mashayak Yahawashy (Jesus Christ)! The Holy Days foreshadow the works that would be accomplished through the First and Second Coming of Jesus. The Holy Days are prophetic in nature, a reminder of the coming salvation.

<< *Exodus 12:1-24* >> *[And the Lord spake unto Moses and Aaron in the land of Egypt, saying, <2> This month shall be unto you the beginning of months: it shall be the first months of the year to you.]*

This verse leaves no doubt as to which month of which season is to mark the start of the year. The Passover occurs in the spring. Therefore, January, the dead of winter can not be the start of the year. Starting the calendar in January originates from pagan customs. According to the Bible the first month is to occur in the springtime. The arrival of spring occurs at the equinox and the first new moon of spring marks the first day of the first month of the year!

<< Leviticus 23:4-8>> [These are the feasts of the Lord, even holy convocations, which ye shall proclaim in their seasons. <5> In the fourteenth day of the first month at even is the Lord's Passover. <6> And on the fifteenth day of the same month is the feast of unleavened bread unto the Lord: seven days ye must eat unleavened bread. <7> In the first day ye shall have an holy convocation: ye shall do no servile work therein. <8> But ye shall offer an offering made by fire unto the Lord seven days: in the seventh day is an holy convocation: ye shall do no servile work therein.]

The Passover has its historical roots from the time that the Israelites were delivered out of captivity in Egypt:

<< Exodus 12:3-24 >> [Speak ye unto all the congregation of Israel, saying, In the tenth day of this month they shall take to them every man a lamb, according to the house of their fathers, a lamb for an house: <4> And if the household be too little for the lamb, let him and his neighbor next unto his house take it according to the number of the souls; every man according to the number of the souls; every man according to his eating shall make your count for the lamb. <5> Your lamb shall be without blemish, a male of the first year: ye shall take it out from the sheep, or from the goats: <6> And ye shall keep it up until the fourteenth day of the same month: and the whole assembly of the congregation of Israel shall kill it in the evening.

<7> And they shall take of the blood, and strike it on the upper door post of the houses, wherein they shall eat it. <8> And they shall eat the flesh in that night, roasted with fire, and unleavened bread; and with bitter herbs they shall eat it. <9> Eat not of it raw, nor sodden at all with water, but roast with fire; his head with his legs, and with the pertinence thereof. <10> And ye shall let nothing of it remain until the morning; and that which remaineth of it until the morning ye shall burn with fire.

<11> And thus shall ye eat it; with your lions girded, your shoes on your feet, and your staff in your hand; and ye shall eat it in haste: it is the Lord's Passover. <12> For I will pass through the land of Egypt this night, and will smite all the firstborn in the land of Egypt, both man and beast; and against all the gods of Egypt I will execute judgment: I am the Lord.

<13> And the blood shall be to you for a token upon the houses where ye are: and when I smite the land or Egypt. <14> And this day shall be unto you for a memorial; and ye shall keep it a feast to the Lord throughout your generations; ye shall keep it a feast by an ordinance forever. <15> Seven days shall ye eat unleavened bread; even the first day ye shall put away leaven out of your houses: for whosoever eateth leavened bread from the first day until the seventh day, that soul shall be cut off from Israel. <16> And in the first day there shall be an holy convocation, and in the seventh day there shall be an holy convocation to you; no manner of work shall be done in them, save that which every man must eat, that only may be done of you. <17> And ye shall observe the feast of unleavened bread; for in this selfsame day have I brought your armies out of the land of Egypt: therefore shall ye observe this day in your generations by an ordinance forever.

<18> In the first month, on the fourteenth day of the month at even, ye shall eat unleavened bread, until the one and twentieth day of the month at even. <19> Seven days

shall there be no leaven found in your houses: for whosoever eateth that which is leavened, even that soul shall be cut off from the congregation of Israel, whether he be a stranger, or born in the land. <20> Ye shall eat nothing leavened; in all your habitations shall ye eat unleavened bread. <21> Then Moses called for all the elders of Israel, and said unto them, Draw out and take you a lamb according to your families, and kill the Passover.

<22> And ye shall take a bunch of hyssop, and dig it in the blood that is in the basin, and strike the lintel and the two side posts with the blood that is in the basin; and none of you shall go out at the door of his house until the morning. <23> For the Lord will pass through to smite the Egyptians; and when he seeth the blood upon the lintel, and on the two side posts, the Lord will pass over the door, and will not suffer the destroyer to come in unto your houses to smite you. <24> And ye shall observe this thing for an ordinance to thee and to thy sons forever.]

The Passover marks the turning point of the Israelite captivity. After four hundred and thirty years of slavery in Egypt, The Father provided the Israelites deliverance. The Passover Lamb that the Lord had commanded the Israelites to kill and eat prior to the exodus from Egypt was also symbolic for prophetic reasons. It was the blood of the slain lamb that was used as a mark of protection against the plague of death that killed the first born of Egypt.

The Passover lamb represents Jesus. According to the scriptures Christ was without sin, the unblemished lamb (Luke 23:41, Matt. 27:4, 19, 24; Luke 15:39). It is the blood of Jesus that provides us with salvation and redeems us from the penalty of sin, which is death.

<< *John 1:29* >> *[The next day John seeth Jesus coming unto him, and saith, Behold the Lamb of God, which taketh away the sin of the world.]*

<< *Hebrews 9:22* >> *[And almost all things are by the law purged with blood; and without shedding of blood is no remission.]*

<< *I Corinthians 5:6-8* >> *[Your glorying is not good. Know ye not that a little leaven leaveneth the whole lump? <7> Purge out therefore the old leaven, that ye may be a new lump, as ye are unleavened. For Christ our Passover is sacrificed for us: <8> Therefore let us keep the feast, not with old leaven, neither with the leaven of malice and wickedness; but with the unleavened bread of sincerity and truth.]*

<< *Isaiah 53:7* >> *[He was oppressed, and he opened not his mouth: he is brought as a lamb to the slaughter, and as a sheep before her shearers is dumb, so he openeth not his mouth.]*

<< *Revelation 5:6-10* >> *[And I beheld, and lo, in the midst of the throne and of the four beasts, and in the midst of the elders, stood a Lamb as it had been slain, having seven horns and seven eyes, which are the seven Spirits of God sent forth into all the earth. <7> And he came and took the book out of the right hand of him that sat upon the throne. <8> And when he had taken the book, the four beasts and four and twenty elders fell down before the Lamb, having everyone of them harps, and golden vials full of odors, which are the prayers of saints.*

And they sung a new song, saying, Thou art worthy to take the book, and to open the seals thereof: for thou wast slain, and hast redeemed us to God by thy blood out of every kindred, and tongue, and people, and nation; <10> And hast made us unto our God kings and priests: and we shall reign on the earth.]

Christ is our Lamb of salvation, we must accept the sacrifice of his blood as our shield and the source of our redemption. Christ made this clear:

<< Luke 22:15-20 >> [And he said unto them, With desire I have desired to eat this Passover with you before I suffer: <16> For I say unto you, I will not any more eat thereof, until it be fulfilled in the kingdom of God. <17> And he took the cup, and gave thanks, and said, Take this, and divide it among yourselves: <18> For I say unto you, I will not drink of the fruit of the vine, until the kingdom of God shall come. <19> And he took bread, and gave thanks, and break it, and gave unto them, saying, This is my body which is given for you: this do in remembrance of me. <20> Likewise also the cup after supper, saying, This cup is the new testament in my blood which is shed for you.]

The Passover is the celebration of the great work of salvation accomplished by Jesus Christ by the offering of himself on the cross. Christ converted the Passover from shadow to substance. Through his blood we are liberated. When we accept Jesus we have passed from death unto life!

<< John 3:16 >> [For God so loved the world, that he gave His only begotten Son, that whosoever believeth in Him should not perish, but have everlasting life.]

<< John 11:25,26 >> [Jesus said unto her, I am the resurrection, and the life: he that believeth in me, though he were dead, yet shall he live: and whosoever liveth and believeth in me shall never die.]

The Feast of Unleavened Bread

The festival of the Passover includes the Passover Day and the Feast of Unleavened Bread. The Feast of Unleavened Bread was kept for seven days, starting with the evening of the fourteenth day. Unleavened Bread was not eaten at the Passover, but on the following evening. The fourteenth day was the day of preparation for the Feast of Unleavened Bread (John 19:14; Matthew 27:62), where all Unleavened Bread and products containing leaven had to be searched out and removed from the home. Even at the Passover day in Egypt the Israelites ate bread with leaven, but packed away the dough for the Unleavened Bread, to be used the following evening.

<< Exodus 12:34, 37 >> [And the people took their dough before it was leavened, their kneadingtroughs being bound in their clothes upon their shoulders ...And the children of Israel journeyed from Rameses to Succoth, about six hundred thousand on foot that were men, besides children.]

<< Leviticus 23:5-7 >> [In the fourteenth day of the first month at even is the Lord's Passover <6> And on the fifteenth day of the same month is the feast of unleavened bread

unto the Lord: seven days ye must eat unleavened bread. <7> In the first day ye shall have an holy convocation: ye shall do no servile work therein. <8> But ye shall offer an offering made by fire unto the Lord seven days: in the seventh day is an holy convocation: ye shall do no servile work therein.]

Because a little leaven added to the dough causes the entire lump to ferment, leaven symbolizes wickedness, worldliness, and sin, causing people to become puffed up, and self centered. The eating of unleavened bread represents separation from the wickedness of the world and from sin. The Feast of Unleavened Bread was kept for seven days. Seven is a number that is always used to represent completion, because the Lord rested on the seventh day of creation! The seven days of the Feast of Unleavened Bread represents the fact that the Lord requires us to be completely separate from sin and evil.

<< 1 Corinthians 5:6-8 >> [Your glorying is not good. Know ye not that a little leaven leaveneth the whole lump? <7> Purge out therefore the old leaven, that ye may be a new lump, as ye are unleavened. For Christ our Passover is sacrificed for us: <8> Therefore let us keep the feast, not with old leaven, neither with the leaven of malice and wickedness; but with the unleavened bread of sincerity and truth.]

Jesus Christ is the true Feast of Unleavened Bread because when we believe in him we have a new life, we are cleansed from all sins.

<< John 6:35,51 >> [And Jesus said unto them, I am the bread of life: he that cometh to me shall never hunger; and he that believeth in me shall never thirst...<51> I am the living bread which came down from heaven: if any man eat of this bread, he shall live forever: and the bread that I will give is my flesh, which I will give for the life of the world.]

We saw that the Passover symbolizes Christ sacrificing his life for us. The Feast of Unleavened Bread represents the new life of separation from that which is worldly, vain, and sinful, and turning to a new holy life in Jesus. We no longer have to offer animal sacrifices as part of these feasts because Jesus offered himself as the final offering for our sins. We must simply accept Jesus as our redeemer!

The third consecutive day of the first month was The Offering of the First Fruits. It is observed, on the sixteenth day of the first month the day following the Feast of Unleavened Bread:

<< Leviticus 23:9-14 >> [And the Lord spake unto Moses, saying, <10> Speak unto the Children of Israel, and say unto them, When ye be come into the land which I give unto you, and shall reap the harvest thereof, then ye shall bring a sheaf of the first fruits of your harvest unto the priest: <11> And he shall wave the sheaf before the Lord, to be accepted for you: on the morrow after the sabbath the priest shall wave it.

<12> And ye shall offer that day when ye wave the sheaf and he lamb without blemish of the first year for a burnt offering unto the Lord.

<13> And the meat offering thereof shall be two tenth deals of fine flour mingled with oil, an offering made by fire unto the Lord for a sweet savor: and the drink offering thereof shall be of wine, the fourth part of an hin. <14> And ye shall eat neither bread, nor parched corn,

nor green ears, until the selfsame day that ye have brought an offering unto your God: it shall be a statute forever throughout your generations in all your dwellings.]

The significant fact to keep in mind is that all of the festivals are prophetic representations of the works of Jesus Christ. The First Fruits symbolizes the resurrection of Jesus Christ and also the future resurrection of those who believe in him. The waved sheaf was to represent the entire harvests; so, too, the resurrected Jesus represents the entire body of believers to be resurrected at his Second Coming!

<< *I Corinthian 15:20-23* >> *[But Now is Christ risen from the dead, and become the first fruits of them that slept. <21> For since by man came death, by man came also the resurrection of the dead. <22> For as in Adam all die, even so in Christ shall all be made alive. <23> But every man in his own order: Christ the first fruits; afterward they that are Christ's.]*

<< *John 12:23,24* >> *[And Jesus answered them, saying, The hour is come, that the Son of man should be glorified. <24> Verily, I say unto you, Except a corn of wheat fall into the ground and die, it abideth alone: but if it die, it bringeth forth much fruit.]*

The festivals represent different aspects of the pattern we are to follow in order to receive the salvation. In The First Fruits we see that the best part of the harvest was consecrated and given to the Lord. In the same way, Christ gave the best that he could to God, he gave his life for us. We also have to offer the first fruit of ourselves to the Most High. It is not enough that we separate ourselves from evil, but we must then devote our lives to serving the Lord YAHAWAH by following the teachings of Jesus!

<< *Luke 11:23-26*>> *[He that is not with me is against me: and he that gathereth not with me scattereth. <24> When the unclean spirit is gone out of a man, he walketh through dry places, seeking rest; and finding none, he saith, I will return unto my house whence I came out. <25> And when he cometh, he findeth it swept and garnished. <26> Then goeth he, and taketh to him seven other spirits more wicked than himself; and they enter in, and dwell there: and the last state of that man is worse than the first.]*

The Feast of Pentecost

As we have seen earlier, the Holy Days are in three groups. The second of the three groups is called The Feast of Pentecost, which required a second journey to Jerusalem. Please note that the forty-nine days, (or seven Sabbaths) between the Feast of First Fruits and the Feast of Pentecost is known as The Feast of Weeks. We can read the details of these feasts:

<< *Leviticus 23:15-22* >> *[And ye shall count unto you from the morrow after the sabbath, from the day that ye brought the sheaf of the wave offering; seven Sabbaths shall be complete: <16> Even unto the morrow after the seventh sabbath shall ye number fifty days; and ye shall offer a new meat offering unto the Lord. <17> Ye shall bring out of your habitations two wave loaves of two tenth deals: they shall be baked with leaven; they are the first fruits unto the Lord. <18> And ye shall offer with the bread seven lambs without blemish of the first*

year, and one young bullock, and two rams: they shall be for a burnt offering unto the Lord, with their meat offering, and their drink offerings, even an offering made by fire, of sweet savor unto the Lord.

<19> Then ye shall sacrifice one kid of the goats for a sin offering, and two lambs of the first year for a sacrifice of peace offerings. <20> And the priest shall wave them with the bread of the first fruits for a wave offering before the Lord, with the two lambs: they shall be holy to the Lord for the priest. <21> And ye shall proclaim on the selfsame day, that it may be an holy convocation unto you: ye shall do no servile work therein: it shall be a statute forever in all your dwellings throughout your generations.

<22> And when ye reap the harvest of your land, thou shalt not make clean riddance of the corners of thy field when thou reapest, neither shalt thou gather any gleaning of thy harvest: thou shalt leave them unto the poor, and to the stranger: I am the Lord your God.]

The Feast of Pentecost is directly related to the offering of the First Fruits: The First Fruit offerings marks the beginning of the harvest, the Feast of Pentecost marks the end of the harvest! The Feast of Pentecost represents the outpouring of the Holy Spirit upon the believers and uniting them with Jesus Christ. The Creator has a day set apart to harvest the true believers into salvation. The first fruit of this harvest was Jesus Christ, and also the disciples that believed in Christ. The second part, or end of the harvest, is the last days at the Second Coming of Christ when the Hebrew Israelites and the multitude of believers will be harvested out of this world and delivered into the Kingdom of Heaven.

<< Revelation 14:14,15 >> [And I looked, and behold a white cloud, and upon the cloud one sat like unto the Son of man, having on his hand a sharp sickle. <15> And another angel came out of the temple, crying with a loud voice to him that sat on the cloud, Thrust in thy sickle, and reap; for the harvest of the earth is ripe.]

Jesus had commanded the disciples to stay in Jerusalem and wait for the Holy Spirit from the Father to come:

<< John 14:16, (14:26; 15:26) >> [But the Comforter, which the Father will send in my name, he shall teach you all things, and bring to remembrance, whatsoever I have said unto you.]

Fifty days after the resurrection of Jesus, on the day of the Feast of Pentecost, the Holy Spirit descended upon all the believers that had gathered:

<< Acts 2:1-22, 37-41 >> [And when the day of Pentecost was fully come, they were all with one accord in one place. <2> And suddenly there came a sound from heaven as of a rushing mighty wind, and it filled all the house where they were sitting. <3> And there appeared unto them cloven tongues like as of fire, and it sat upon each of them. <4> And they were all filled with the Holy Spirit, and began to speak with other tongues, as the Spirit gave them utterance.

<5> And there were dwelling at Jerusalem Jews, devout men, out of every nation under heaven. <6> Now when this was noised abroad, the multitude came together, and were confounded, because that every man heard them speak in his own language. <7> And they

were all amazed and marvelled, saying one to another. Behold, are not all these which speak Galilean? <8> And how hear we every man in our tongue, wherein we were born? <9> Parthians, and Medes, and Elamites, and the dwellers in Mesopotamia, and in Judea, and Cappadocia, in Pontus, and Asia, <10> Phrygia, and Pamphylia, in Egypt, and in the parts of Libya about Cyrene, and strangers of Rome, Jews and proselytes, <11> Cretes and Arabians, we do hear them speak in our tongues the wonderful works of God. <12> And they were all amazed, and were in doubt, saying one to another, What meaneth this? <13> Others mocking and said, These men are full of new wine.

<14> But Peter, standing up with the eleven, lifted up his voice, and said unto them, Ye men of Judea, and all ye that dwell at Jerusalem, be this known unto you, and hearken to my words: <15> For these are not drunken, as ye suppose, seeing it is but the third hour of the day. <16> But this is that which was spoken by the prophet Joel (Ch.2:28-32); <17> And it shall come to pass in the last days, saith God, I will pour out of my Spirit upon all flesh: and your sons and your daughters shall prophesy, and your old men shall dream dreams: <18> And on my servants and on my handmaidens I will pour out in those days of my Spirit; and they shall prophesy: <19> And I will shew wonders in heaven above, and sighs in the earth beneath; blood, and fire, and vapor of smoke: <20> The sun shall be turned into darkness, and the moon into blood, before that great and notable day of the Lord come: <21> And it shall come to pass, that whosoever shall call upon the name of the Lord shall be saved <22> Ye men of Israel, hear these words; Jesus of Nazareth, a man approved of God among you by miracles and wonders and signs, which God did by him in the midst of you, as ye yourselves also know....

<37> Now when they heard this, they were pricked in their hearts, and said unto Peter and to the rest of the apostles, Men and brethren, what shall we do? <38> Then Peter said unto them, Repent, and be baptized every one of you in the name of Jesus Christ for the remission of sins, and ye shall receive the gift of the Holy Spirit. <39> For the promise is unto you, and to your children, and to all that are afar off, even as many as the Lord our God shall call. <40> And with many other words did not he testify and exhort, saying, Save yourselves from this untoward generation. <41> Then they that gladly received his word were baptized: and the same day there were added unto them about three thousand souls.]

The Feast of Pentecost represents the Holy Spirit descending and uniting us as one in Christ! The Believers were given the power to speak different foreign languages so that there would be no separation between them, and so that they could spread the gospel to all nations in different languages. The Feast of Pentecost also represents the outpouring of spiritual power: giving strength where there was weakness, giving light where there was darkness. Again, in these last days, the Lord will soon give us the spiritual power to defeat all enemies of the truth!

The Feast of Pentecost includes the entire harvest, to symbolize the salvation of all the believers. Bread with leaven was offered at the Feast of Pentecost, to represent the sinful condition of the believers. However, the Feast of Pentecost also included the sin offering, the burnt offering, and the peace offering to cover the transgressions. But now, we are the loaf of bread with leaven, and Jesus Christ has become our offering to the Father for our sins. Christ is our wave offering because he showed himself many times after his resurrection. And Jesus is our wheat offering, like a seed that has fallen to the earth and is resurrected.

THE TRUTH

The Memorial of Blowing of Trumpets

The third set of the three festivals is known in a collective sense as The Feast of Tabernacles, occurring on the seventh month. The three Holy Days celebrated on the sabbatic month are The Feast of Trumpets, The Day of Atonement, The Feast of Tabernacles, plus the Last Great Day. The prophecies associated with the Passover, Unleavened Bread, and Pentecost have already been realized historically; however, the Feast of Trumpets, Day of Atonement, the Feast of Tabernacles and the Last Great Day pertain to prophecies yet to be realized in the near future.

Let us examine The Feast of Trumpets occurring on the first day of the seventh month. It involves the blowing of two silver trumpets:

<< Leviticus 23:23-25 >> [And the Lord spake unto Moses, saying, <24> Speak unto the Children of Israel, saying, In the seventh month, in the first day of the month, shall ye have a sabbath, a memorial of blowing of trumpets, an holy convocation. <25> Ye shall do no servile work therein: but shall offer an offering made by fire unto the Lord.]

The blowing of the trumpets was to be done only by the priests. It was used as a way of communicating to the people in announcing special occasions, for example the Holy Days, the Sabbath, the arrival of the New Moon, an invitation to gather, an alarm of war, and before important announcements as well.

<< Numbers 10:1-10 >> [And the Lord spake unto Moses, saying, <2> Make thee two trumpets of silver; of a whole piece shalt thou make them: that thou mayest use them for the calling of the assembly, and for the journeying of the camps. <3> And when they shall blow with them, all the assembly shall assemble themselves to thee at the door of the tabernacle of the congregation. <4> And if they blow but with one trumpet, then the princes, which are heads of the thousands of Israel shall gather themselves unto thee. <5> When ye blow an alarm, then the camps that lie on the east parts shall go forward. <6> When ye blow an alarm the second time, then the camps that lie on the south side shall take their journey: they shall blow an alarm for their journeys. <7> But when the congregation is to be gathered together, ye shall blow, but ye shall not sound an alarm.

<8> And the sons of Aaron, the priests, shall blow with the trumpets; and they shall be to you for an ordinance forever throughout your generations. <9> And if ye go to war in your land against the enemy that oppresseth you, then ye shall blow an alarm with the trumpets; and ye shall be remembered before the Lord your God, and ye shall be saved from your enemies. <10> Also in the day of your gladness, and in your solemn days, and in the beginnings of your months, ye shall blow with the trumpets over your burnt offerings, and over the sacrifices for a memorial before your God: I am the Lord your God.]

The Feast of Trumpets represents the call to resurrect the lost tribe of Israel to return to their true identity and for the world to accept the true gospel of the kingdom of Heaven. As Christ was in the grave for three days, the three months separating the Day of Pentecost and the Day of Trumpets represent the time period of the gentiles when the true Hebrew Israelites were in oppression. They were dead to the truth, and dead to their true history and identity. To blow the trumpets symbolizes the teaching of the true gospel, which would awake the world and the original Israelites to their identity and eliminate the false gospels. Historically, the announcement of the gospel is compared to a trumpet:

<< *Revelation 4:1* >> *[After this I looked, and, behold, a door was opened in heaven: and the first voice which I heard was as it were of a trumpet talking with me; which said, Come up hither, and I will shew thee things which must be hereafter.]*

The time has now arrived for the world to learn the true gospel of the kingdom of Heaven, including the identity of the people of whom the Bible is talking about: the original Asiatic Hebrew Israelites. Ezekiel describes the resurrection of the Hebrew Israelites:

<< *Ezekiel 37:1-14* >> *[The hand of the Lord was upon me, and carried me out in the spirit of the Lord, and set me down in the midst of the valley which was full of bones* (a valley of dry bones represent the low mental, spiritual, and social condition of the real Hebrews)*, <2> And caused me to pass by them round about: and, behold, there were very many in the open valley; and, lo, they were very dry. <3> And he said unto me, Son of man, can these bones live? And I answered, O Lord God, thou knowest.*

<4> Again he said unto me, Prophesy upon these bones, and say unto them, O ye dry bones, hear the word of the Lord. <5> Thus saith the Lord God unto these bones; Behold, I will cause breath (knowledge) *to enter in to you, and ye shall live: <6> And I will lay sinews upon you, and will bring up flesh upon you, and cover you with skin, and put breath in you and ye shall live* (to live means that the Israelites would wake up to the true gospel, learn their true identity and customs)*; and ye shall know that I am the Lord.*

<7> So I prophesied (to blow the trumpet of truth) *as I was commanded: and as I prophesied, there was a noise, and behold a shaking, and the bones came together, bone to his bone. <8> And when I beheld, lo, the sinews and the flesh came up upon them, and the skin covered them above: but there was no breath in them.*(No breath in them because as we begin to wake up to our identity and acquiring knowledge, that will not be enough. We will also need to develop an understanding of the work of Jesus Christ and of his love. This first stage is only a carnal revival.)

<9> Then said he unto me, Prophesy unto the wind, prophesy, son of man, and say to the wind, Thus saith the Lord God; Come from the four winds, O breath, and breathe upon these slain, that they may live. <10> So I prophesied as he commanded me, and the breath came into them, and they lived, and stood up upon their feet, and exceeding great army (After the Israelites have learned about their true nationality, they will not be able to unite until they have learned to love the Lord YAHAWAH and their brothers like Christ loved .This is the baptism in Jesus Christ. This is the spiritual "born-again".)

<11> Then he said unto me, Son of man, these bones are the whole house of Israel: behold, they say, Our bones are dried, and our hope is lost; we are cut off for our parts. <12> Therefore prophesy and say unto them, Thus saith the Lord God; Behold, O my people, I will open your graves, and cause you to come up out of your graves, and bring you into the land of Israel. <13> And ye shall know that I am the Lord, when I have opened your graves, O my people, and brought you up out of your graves, <14> And shall put my spirit in you,

and ye shall live, and I shall place you in your own land: than shall ye know that I the Lord have spoken it, and performed it, saith the Lord.]

Two trumpets were blown at The Feast of Trumpets. Similarly, Ezekiel was told twice, to prophesy unto the bones, to represent the blowing of the two trumpets. The first time that Ezekiel was told to prophesy, the dry bones became corpses. This will come to pass when the Israelites all over the world reclaim their true identity and the European Khazars are exposed as impostor Jews. The second time he prophesied, the breath entered the corpses and they came alive and were united into a great army. This second and last blowing of the trumpets will take place at the Second Coming of Jesus Christ when he returns to deliver us and establish his kingdom:

<< *I Thessalonians 4:16-18* >> *[For the Lord himself shall descend from heaven with a shout, with the voice of the archangel, and with the trump of God: and the dead in Christ shall rise first: <17> Then we which are alive and remain shall be caught up together with them in the clouds, to meet the Lords, to meet the Lord in the air: and so shall we ever be with the Lord. <18> Wherefore comfort one another with these words.]*

<< *I Corinthians 15:50-54* >> *[Now this I say, brethren, that flesh and blood cannot inherit the kingdom of God; neither doth corruption inherit incorruption. <51> Behold, I shew you a mystery; We shall not all sleep, but we shall all be changed. <52> In a moment, in the twinkling of an eye, at the last trump: for the trumpet shall sound, and the dead shall be raised incorruptible, and we shall be changed. <53> For this corruptible must put on incorruption, and this mortal must put on immortality. <54> So when this corruptible shall have put on incorruption, and this mortal shall have put on immortality, then shall be brought to pass the saying that is written. Death is swallowed up in victory. <55> O death, where is thy sting? O grave, where is thy victory?]*

<< *Matthew 24:30,31* >> *[And then shall appear the sign of the Son of man in heaven: and then shall all the tribes of the earth mourn, and they shall see the Son of man coming in the clouds of heaven with power and great glory. <31> And he shall send his angels with a great sound of a trumpet, and they shall gather together his elect from the four winds, from one end of heaven to the other.]*

The Day of Atonement

The second prophetic feast yet to be accomplished is The Day of Atonement, occurring the tenth day of the seventh month. This was the most important day of the year. On The Day of Atonement the people were to humble and humiliate themselves before the Lord and confess their sins. It was the only time in the year that the high priest was allowed access beyond the veil of the temple into the Holy of Holies, to make an annual atonement for sins. Let's read the details of the Day of Atonement:

<< *Leviticus 23:26-32* >> *[And the Lord spake unto Moses, saying, <27> Also on the tenth day of this seventh month there shall be a day of atonement: it shall be an holy convocation unto you; and ye shall afflict your souls, and offer an offering made by fire unto the Lord. <28> And ye shall do no work in that same day: for it is a day of atonement, to make an*

atonement for you before the Lord your God. <29> For whatsoever soul it be that shall not be afflicted in that same day, he shall be cut off from among his people. <30> And whatsoever soul it be that doeth any work in that same day, the same soul will I destroy from among his people. <31> Ye shall do no manner of work: it shall be a statute forever throughout your generations in all your dwellings. <32> It shall be unto you a sabbath of rest, and ye shall afflict your souls: in the ninth day of the month at even, from even unto even, shall ye celebrate your sabbath.]

The Lord provided the Day of Atonement as a temporary covering for our sins. The following verses will give further information on the occurrences of that day:

<< Leviticus 16:1-14 >> [And the Lord spake unto Moses after the death of the two sons of Aaron, when they offered before the Lord, and died; <2> And the Lord said unto Moses, Speak unto Aaron thy brother, that he come not at all times into the holy place within the veil before the mercy seat, which is upon the ark; that he die not: for I will appear in the cloud upon the mercy seat. <3>Thus shall Aaron come into the holy place: with a young bullock for a sin offering, and a ram for a burnt offering. <4> He shall put on the holy linen coat, and he shall have the linen breeches upon his flesh, and shall be girded with a linen girdle, and with the linen mitre shall he be attired: these are holy garments; therefore shall he wash his flesh in water, and so put them on.

<5> And he shall take of the congregation of the children of Israel two kids of the goats for a sin offering, and one ram for a burnt offering. <6> And Aaron shall offer his bullock of the sin offering, which is for himself and make an atonement for himself, and for his house. <7> And Aaron shall take the two goats, and present them before the Lord at the door of the tabernacle of the congregation. <8> And Aaron shall cast lots upon the two goats; one lot for the Lord, and the other lot for the scapegoat. <9> And Aaron shall bring the goat upon which the Lord's lot fell, and offer him for a sin offering. <10> But the goat, on which the lot fell to be the scapegoat, shall be presented alive before the Lord, to make an atonement with him. and to let him go for a scapegoat into the wilderness.

<11> And Aaron shall bring the bullock to the sin offering, which is for himself, and shall make an atonement for himself, and for his house, and shall kill the bullock of the sin offering which is for himself: <12> And he shall take a censer full of burning coals of fire from off the altar before the Lord, and his hands full of sweet incense beaten small, and bring it within the veil: <13> And he shall put the incense upon the fire before the Lord, that the cloud of the incense may cover the mercy seat that is upon the testimony, that he die not: <14> And he shall take of the blood of the bullock, and sprinkle it with his finger upon the mercy seat eastward; and before the mercy seat shall he sprinkle of the blood with his finger seven times.]

<< Leviticus 16:20-27 >> [And when he hath made an end of reconciling the holy place, and the tabernacle of the congregation, and the altar, he shall bring the live goat: <21> And Aaron shall lay both his hands upon the head of the live goat, and confess over him all the iniquities of the children of Israel, and all their transgressions in all their sins, putting them upon the head of the goat, and shall send him away by the hand of a fit man into the

wilderness: <22> And the goat shall bear upon him all their iniquities unto a land not inhabited: and he shall let go the goat in the wilderness.] Jesus Christ was the true scapegoat for us, he carried all of our sins:

<< *Isaiah 53:6* >> *[...and the Lord had laid on him the iniquity of us all.]*

<< *Leviticus 16:23-27* >> *[And Aaron shall come into the tabernacle of the congregation, and shall put off the linen garments, which he put on when he went into the holy place, and shall leave them there: <24> And he shall wash his flesh with water in the holy place, and put on his garments, and come forth, and offer his burnt offering, and the burnt offering of the people, and make an atonement for himself, and for the people, <25> And the fat of the sin offering shall he burn upon the altar. <26> And he that let go the goat for the scapegoat shall wash his clothes, and bathe his flesh in water, and afterward come into the camp. <27> And the bullock for the sin offering, and the goat for the sins offering, whose blood was brought in to make atonement in the holy place shall one carry forth without the camp; and they shall burn in the fire their skins, and their flesh, and their dung.]*

We also know that the Burnt Offering was symbolic of Jesus Christ; he was our absolute offering for sin:

<< *II Corinthians 5:21* >> *[For he had made him to be sin for us, who knew no sin; that we might be made the righteousness of the Lord YAHAWAH in him.]*

The prophetic significance of the Day of Atonement has been realized in the works of Christ. Jesus Christ is the true atonement. It was the great work of redemption by Jesus Christ that not only covered our sins, but has completely removed our sins and justifies us for salvation. The Bible explains this in further detail:

<< *Hebrews 9:1-16, 24-28* >> *[Then verily the first covenant had also ordinances of divine service, and a worldly sanctuary. <2> For there was a tabernacle made; the first, wherein was the candlestick, and the table, and the shewbread; which is called the sanctuary. <3> And after the second veil, the tabernacle which is called the Holiest of all; <4> Which had the golden censer, and the ark of the covenant overlaid round about with gold, wherein was the golden pot that had manna, and Aaron's rod that budded, and the tables of the covenant; <5> And over it the cherubim of glory shadowing the mercyseat; of which we cannot now speak particularly.*

<6> Now when these things were thus ordained, the priests went always into the first tabernacle, accomplishing the service of God. <7> But into the second went the high priest alone once every year not without blood (Christ went on the cross alone)*, which he offered for himself, and for the errors of the people: <8> The Holy Spirit this signifying, that the way into the holiest of all was not yet made manifest, while as the first tabernacle was yet standing: <9> Which was a figure for the time then present, in which were offered both gifts, and sacrifices, that could not make him that did the service perfect, as pertaining to the conscience; <10> Which stood only in meats and drinks, and divers washing, and carnal ordinances, imposed on them until the time of reformation.*

<11> But Christ being come an high priest of good things to come, by a greater and more perfect tabernacle, not made with hands, that is to say, not of this building; <12> Neither by the blood of goats and calves, but buy his own blood he entered in once into the holy place, having obtained eternal redemption for us. <13> For if the blood of bulls and of goats, and the ashes of an heifer sprinkling the unclean, sanctifieth to the purifying of the flesh: <14> How much more shall the blood of Christ, who through the eternal Spirit offered himself without spot to God, purge your conscience from dead works to serve the living God? <15> And for this cause he is the mediator of the new testament, that by means of death, for the redemption of the transgressions that were under the first testament, they which are called might receive the promise of eternal inheritance. <16> For where a testament is, there must also of necessity be the death of the testator...

...<24> For Christ is not entered into the holy places made with hands, which are the figures of the true; but into heaven itself, now to appear in the presence of God for us: <25> Nor yet that he should offer himself often, as the high priest enterreth into the holy place every year with blood of others; <26> For then must he often have suffered since the foundation of the world: but now once in the end of the world hath he appeared to put away sin by the sacrifice of himself. <27> And as it is appointed unto men once to die, but after this the judgment: <28> So Christ was once offered to bear the sins of many; and unto them that look for him shall he appear the second time without sin unto salvation.]

The Feast of Tabernacles

The Feast of Tabernacles was observed for seven days, starting on the seventh month fifteenth day to the twenty-first. The feast of tabernacles represents the Millenium reign of Christ at his Second Coming, in which the kingdom of heaven will be established on earth and the Israelites are established in the kingdom. We are to dwell in booths seven days to remind us of how the Lord God YAHAWAH did not forsake us in Egypt and in the wilderness. He gave us divine protection, provided for all of our needs and delivered us into a land flowing with milk and honey.

<< Leviticus 23:33-44 >> [And the LORD spake unto Moses, saying, <34> Speak unto the children of Israel, saying, The fifteenth day of this seventh month shall be the feast of tabernacles for seven days unto the LORD. <35> On the first day shall be an holy convocation: ye shall do no servile work therein. <36> Seven days ye shall offer an offering made by fire unto the LORD: on the eighth day shall be an holy convocation unto you; and ye shall offer an offering made by fire unto the LORD: it is a solemn assembly; and ye shall do no servile work therein.

<37> These are the feasts of the LORD, which ye shall proclaim to be holy convocations, to offer an offering made by fire unto the LORD, a burnt offering, and a meat offering, a sacrifice, and drink offerings, every thing upon his day: <38> Beside the Sabbaths of the LORD, and beside your gifts, and beside all your vows, and beside all your freewill offerings, which ye give unto the LORD. <39> Also in the fifteenth day of the seventh month, when ye have gathered in the fruit of the land, ye shall keep a feast unto the LORD seven days: on the first day shall be a sabbath, and on the eighth day shall be a sabbath. <40> And ye shall take you on the first day the boughs of goodly

trees, branches of palm trees, and the boughs of thick trees, and willows of the brook; and ye shall rejoice before the LORD your God seven days. <41> And ye shall keep it a feast unto the LORD seven days in the year. It shall be a statute forever in your generations: ye shall celebrate it in the seventh month. <42> Ye shall dwell in booths seven days; all that are Israelites born shall dwell in booths: <43> That your generations may know that I made the children of Israel to dwell in booths, when I brought them out of the land of Egypt: I am the LORD your God. <44> And Moses declared unto the children of Israel the feasts of the LORD.]

<< Deuteronomy 16:13 >> *[Thou shalt observe the feast of tabernacles seven days, after that thou hast gathered in thy corn and thy wine: <14> And thou shalt rejoice in thy feast, thou, and thy son, and thy daughter, and thy manservant, and thy maidservant, and the Levite, the stranger, and the fatherless, and the widow, that are within thy gates.]*

<< Nehemiah 8:13-18 >> *[And on the second day were gathered together the chief of the fathers of all the people, the priests, and the Levites, unto Ezra the scribe, even to understand the words of the law. <14> And they found written in the law which the LORD had commanded by Moses, that the children of Israel should dwell in booths in the feast of the seventh month: <15> And that they should publish and proclaim in all their cities, and in Jerusalem, saying, Go forth unto the mount, and fetch olive branches, and pine branches, and myrtle branches, and palm branches, and branches of thick trees, to make booths, as it is written. <16> So the people went forth, and brought them, and made themselves booths, every one upon the roof of his house, and in their courts, and in the courts of the house of God, and in the street of the water gate, and in the street of the gate of Ephraim. <17> And all the congregation of them that were come again out of the captivity made booths, and sat under the booths: for since the days of Joshua the son of Nun unto that day had not the children of Israel done so. And there was very great gladness. <18> Also day by day, from the first day unto the last day, he read in the book of the law of God. And they kept the feast seven days; and on the eighth day was a solemn assembly, according unto the manner.]*

Jesus and his disciples observed the Feast of Tabernacles:

<< John 7:2-14, 37,38 >> *[Now the Jews' feast of tabernacles was at hand. <3> His brethren therefore said unto him, Depart hence, and go into Judaea, that thy disciples also may see the works that thou doest. <4> For there is no man that doeth any thing in secret, and he himself seeketh to be known openly. If thou do these things, shew thyself to the world. <5> For neither did his brethren believe in him. <6> Then Jesus said unto them, My time is not yet come: but your time is alway ready. <7> The world cannot hate you; but me it hateth, because I testify of it, that the works thereof are evil. <8> Go ye up unto this feast: I go not up yet unto this feast; for my time is not yet full come. <9> When he had said these words unto them, he abode still in Galilee. <10> But when his brethren were gone up, then went he also up unto the feast, not openly, but as it were in*

secret. <11> Then the Jews sought him at the feast, and said, Where is he? <12> And there was much murmuring among the people concerning him: for some said, He is a good man: others said, Nay; but he deceiveth the people. <13> Howbeit no man spake openly of him for fear of the Jews. <14> Now about the midst of the feast Jesus went up into the temple, and taught. <37> In the last day, that great day of the feast, Jesus stood and cried, saying, If any man thirst, let him come unto me, and drink. <38> He that believeth on me, as the scripture hath said, out of his belly shall flow rivers of living water. <39> But this spake he of the Spirit, which they that believe on him should receive: for the Holy Ghost was not yet given; because that Jesus was not yet glorified.]

The Passover, Feast of Unleavened Bread, and Pentecost were historical in nature, while the last three feasts are prophetic. The Feast of Passover represents the crucifixion, the Feast of Unleavened Bread is walking the new life of sanctification in Christ, The Feast of Pentecost is the outpouring of the Holy Spirit. The Feast of Trumpets Symbolizes the declaration of the true gospel of the kingdom in these last days. The Day of Atonement represent the Second coming of Christ. The Feast of Tabernacles stands for the establishment of the kingdom of heaven on earth. The Last Great Day represents the day of the White Throne Judgement when all souls will be resurrected and judged.

<< Hebrews 4:1-8 >> [Let us therefore fear, lest, a promise being left us of entering into his rest, any of you should seem to come short of it. <2> For unto us was the gospel preached, as well as unto them: but the word preached did not profit them, not being mixed with faith in them that heard it. <3> For we which have believed do enter into rest, as he said, As I have sworn in my wrath, if they shall enter into my rest: although the works were finished from the foundation of the world. <4> For he spake in a certain place of the seventh day on this wise, And God did rest the seventh day from all his works. <5> And in this place again, If they shall enter into my rest. <6> Seeing therefore it remaineth that some must enter therein, and they to whom it was first preached entered not in because of unbelief: <7> Again, he limiteth a certain day, saying in David, To day, after so long a time; as it is said, To day if ye will hear his voice, harden not your hearts. <8> For if Jesus had given them rest, then would he not afterward have spoken of another day. <9> There remaineth therefore a rest to the people of God.]

<< Micah 4:1-5 >> [But in the last days it shall come to pass, that the mountain of the house of the LORD shall be established in the top of the mountains, and it shall be exalted above the hills; and people shall flow unto it. <2> And many nations shall come, and say, Come, and let us go up to the mountain of the LORD, and to the house of the God of Jacob; and he will teach us of his ways, and we will walk in his paths: for the law shall go forth of Zion, and the word of the LORD from Jerusalem. <3> And he shall judge among many people, and rebuke strong nations afar off; and they shall beat their swords into plowshares, and their spears into pruninghooks: nation shall not lift up a sword against nation, neither shall they learn war any more. <4> But they shall sit every man under his vine and under his fig tree; and none shall make them afraid: for the mouth of the LORD of hosts hath spoken it. <5> For all people will walk every one in

the name of his god, and we will walk in the name of the LORD our God for ever and ever.]

<< Isaiah 11:6-9 >> [The wolf also shall dwell with the lamb, and the leopard shall lie down with the kid; and the calf and the young lion and the fatling together; and a little child shall lead them. <7> And the cow and the bear shall feed; their young ones shall lie down together: and the lion shall eat straw like the ox. <8> And the sucking child shall play on the hole of the asp, and the weaned child shall put his hand on the cockatrice' den. <9> They shall not hurt nor destroy in all my holy mountain: for the earth shall be full of the knowledge of the LORD, as the waters cover the sea.]

Last Great Day

The Last great Day represents the Day of the White Throne judgement, when every soul will be resurrected and presented for judgement.

<< Numbers 29:35 >> [On the eighth day ye shall have a solemn assembly: ye shall do no servile work therein]

<< Matthew 25:32 >> [And before him shall be gathered all nations: and he shall separate them one from another, as a shepherd divideth his sheep from the goats.]

<< Revelation 21:1 >> [And I saw a new heaven and a new earth: for the first heaven and the first earth were passed away; and there was no more sea.]

<< Revelation 20:5 >> [But the rest of the dead lived not again until the thousand years were finished. This is the first resurrection. <6> Blessed and holy is he that hath part in the first resurrection: on such the second death hath no power, but they shall be priests of God and of Christ, and shall reign with him a thousand years. <11> And I saw a great white throne, and him that sat on it, from whose face the earth and the heaven fled away; and there was found no place for them.]

In addition to the major Holy Days and the festivals of Hanukkah and Purim, we also observed the new moons. The new moon marks the beginning of the month:

<< Psalm 81:3 >> [Blow up the trumpet in the new moon, in the time appointed, on our solemn feast day.]

<<< Isaiah 66:23 >> [And it shall come to pass, that from one new moon to another, and from one sabbath to another, shall all flesh come to worship before me, saith the LORD.]

The Hebrew Israelites, which are scattered all over the world, must first of all reclaim their true identity and they must repent of all their wicked ways and accept Christ as their savior. This is the only way for us to end our captivity! We can not blame anyone else except ourselves! The African-Americans and American-Indians must recover their true identities as Israelites. Then they should humble themselves before The Lord for their sins, and lay their sins upon Christ, accepting his death as atonement for their sins.

Jesus came to rend the Veil, which separated man from the Creator. Until we return to Christ as our Savior, reclaim our true identity, and repent of our ignorance and stupidity, their will always be a Veil separating us and the glory of the kingdom:

<< II Corinthians 3:15,16 >> [But even unto this day, when Moses is read, the Vail is upon their heart. <16> Nevertheless when it shall turn to the Lord, the Veil shall be taken away.]

<< Matthew 28:51 >> [And, behold, the veil of the temple was rent in twain from the top to bottom; and the earth did quake, and the rocks rent.]

The learning and observance of all the Holy Days, including the Sabbath, New Moon and even the festival days of Chanukah (9th month 25th day to 10th month 3rd day, *I Maccabees 4*) and Purim (12th month 14th to 15th day, *Esther 9:21*) are all important days. You may request a calendar of the Holy days from the Israelite Network. They teach us the design by which we must serve the Creator. Also they reveal a deeper understanding of the works concerning the First and Second Coming of Jesus Christ. Above all, keeping of the Holy Days is a commandment from God, which we must obey. Failure to obey God's commandments will result in being cursed.

Tithes and Offerings

A lamp has to be maintained by adding fuel to it so that it may continue to give us light. In the same way those who benefit from the work of the ministers of God need to support the ministry. A tithe is defined as one-tenth of all material possessions of a person. The Lord God commands the people to pay tithes and offerings to the priests that minister unto them so that they may continue to serve the community.

<< Leviticus 27:30 >> [And all the tithe of the land, whether of the seed of the land, or of the fruit of the tree, is the LORD'S: it is holy unto the LORD.]

<< Numbers 18:21 >>[And, behold, I have given the children of Levi all the tenth in Israel for an inheritance, for their service which they serve, even the service of the tabernacle of the congregation.]

<< Nehemiah 10:37 >> [And that we should bring the firstfruits of our dough, and our offerings, and the fruit of all manner of trees, of wine and of oil, unto the priests, to the chambers of the house of our God; and the tithes of our ground unto the Levites, that the same Levites might have the tithes in all the cities of our tillage].

<< Deuteronomy 14:29 >> [And the Levites, (because he hath no part nor inheritance with thee,) and the stranger, and the fatherless, and the widow, which are within thy gates, shall come, and shall eat and be satisfied; that the LORD thy God may bless thee in all the work of thine hand which thou doest.]

THE TRUTH

<< Malachi 3:7 >> [Even from the days of your fathers ye are gone away from mine ordinances, and have not kept them. Return unto me, and I will return unto you, saith the LORD of hosts. But ye said, Wherein shall we return?

<8> Will a man rob God? Yet ye have robbed me. But ye say, Wherein have we robbed thee? In tithes and offerings. <9> Ye are cursed with a curse: for ye have robbed me, even this whole nation. <10> Bring ye all the tithes into the storehouse, that there may be meat in mine house, and prove me now herewith, saith the LORD of hosts, if I will not open you the windows of heaven, and pour you out a blessing, that there shall not be room enough to receive it.]

<< Timothy 5:17, 18 >> [Let the elders that rule well be counted worthy of double honour, especially they who labour in the word and doctrine18 For the scripture saith, Thou shalt not muzzle the ox that treadeth out the corn. And, The labourer is worthy of his reward.]

It is very important not to rob God or his servants. Do not invite a curse. Give your tithes and offerings as commanded by the Lord God so that we may continue to bring out this truth and help people with needs. You are welcome to contact The Israelite Network on the World Wide at: http://israelite.net or at P.O. Box 1747, NYC, NY 10101. Also, the Israelite Network would welcome your support in other forms, not just materially. You can help us distribute this book. Help bring out the truth of the Bible to the world by any means necessary.

FALSEHOOD OF RELIGION

God gave man a law, not religions. From the beginning of history, all of the world's major problems have been caused by man-made religions. The religions have changed all of the important laws of God and have hidden the truth in order to enrich and to glorify themselves instead of God. There are several different religions in the world; however, there is only one truth. Only the truth is real, all of those various man-made religions are ignorant, selfish, and full of lies. Man-made religion is a barrier against the ultimate truth, keeping people from experiencing reality; it chains the mind, keeping it from transcending and experiencing the mysteries of existence! Being committed to a false man-made religion is the same as being racist if not worst!

The preachers of the false version of modern Christianity are often ministers of racism, teaching white supremacy. They do so by elevating a Caucasian image of Jesus Christ, although the Bible says that Christ was Hebrew Israelite of Asiatic descent. His hair texture was woolly and his complexion was like burnt brass. The religious, educational, and political institutions are also deceiving people by supporting the deceptive European Khazars living in Palestine, who are falsely claiming to be Jews. The so-called Jewish people of today are not the Jews of the Bible. They are the descendants of the Khazar Empire who have converted to Judaism! This is an act of blasphemy! The real Jews are the western Asiatic people of America, remnants of whom are also scattered all over the world!

Where did all the different religions come from? According to the Bible, the Lord gave man a LAW not a religion! The churches are responsible for the destruction of many families. The religious women spend all day in the church, gossiping, and giving away their poor husband's money to the dumb preacher who is constantly rationalizing and justifying them in their evil deeds. That is why the churches are mostly composed of women. According to the Bible, a woman should be home with her husband, helping him and caring for her family. The Lord exposes those false preachers for what they are:

<< Isaiah 56:10,11 >> [His watchmen are blind: they are all ignorant (all of them)*, they cannot bark; sleeping, lying down, and loving to slumber* (lazy)*. Yea, they are greedy dogs which can never have enough* (the false preachers are only out to make money)*. And they are shepherds that can not understand: they all look to their own way, everyone for his gain, from his quarter.]*

<< Micah 3:11 >> [The heads thereof judge for reward, and the priests thereof teach for hire, and the prophets thereof divine for money.]

<< Ezekiel 13:1>> [And the word of the LORD came unto me, saying, <2> Son of man, prophesy against the prophets of Israel that prophesy, and say thou unto them that prophesy out of their own hearts, Hear ye the word of the LORD; <3> Thus saith the Lord GOD; Woe unto the foolish prophets, that follow their own spirit, and have seen nothing! <4> O Israel, <u>thy prophets are like the foxes in the deserts.</u>

<5> Ye have not gone up into the gaps, neither made up the hedge for the house of Israel to stand in the battle in the day of the LORD. <6> They have seen vanity and lying divination, saying, The LORD saith: and the LORD hath not sent them: and they have made others to hope that they would confirm the word. <7> Have ye not seen a

vain vision, and have ye not spoken a lying divination, whereas ye say, The LORD saith it; albeit I have not spoken?

<8> Therefore thus saith the Lord GOD; Because ye have spoken vanity, and seen lies, therefore, behold, I am against you, saith the Lord GOD. <9> And mine hand shall be upon the prophets that see vanity, and that divine lies: they shall not be in the assembly of my people, neither shall they be written in the writing of the house of Israel, neither shall they enter into the land of Israel; and ye shall know that I am the Lord GOD. <10> Because, even because they have seduced my people, saying, Peace; and there was no peace; and one built up a wall, and, lo, others daubed it with untempered morter: <11> Say unto them which daub it with untempered morter, that it shall fall: there shall be an overflowing shower; and ye, O great hailstones, shall fall; and a stormy wind shall rend it.

<12> Lo, when the wall is fallen, shall it not be said unto you, Where is the daubing wherewith ye have daubed it? <13> Therefore thus saith the Lord GOD; I will even rend it with a stormy wind in my fury; and there shall be an overflowing shower in mine anger, and great hailstones in my fury to consume it. <14> So will I break down the wall that ye have daubed with untempered morter, and bring it down to the ground, so that the foundation thereof shall be discovered, and it shall fall, and ye shall be consumed in the midst thereof: and ye shall know that I am the LORD.

<15> Thus will I accomplish my wrath upon the wall, and upon them that have daubed it with untempered morter, and will say unto you, The wall is no more, neither they that daubed it; <16> To wit, the prophets of Israel which prophesy concerning Jerusalem, and which see visions of peace for her, and there is no peace, saith the Lord GOD.]

<< Deuteronomy 13:5 >> *[And that prophet, or that dreamer of dreams, shall be put to death; because he hath spoken to turn you away from the Lord.]*

The following scriptures can be a good guideline in helping the churches and preachers to adjust their attitude:

<< II Corinthians 10:12 >> *[For we dare not make ourselves of the number, or compare ourselves with some that commend themselves: but they measuring themselves by themselves, and comparing themselves among themselves, are not wise.]*

<< Luke 18:14 >> *[I tell you, this man went down to his house justified rather than the other: for every one that exalteth himself shall be abased; and he that humbleth himself shall be exalted.]*

<< I Corinthians 4:5-7 >> *[Therefore judge nothing before the time, until the Lord come, who both will bring to light the hidden things of darkness, and will make manifest the counsels of the hearts: and then shall every man have praise of God. <6> And these things, brethren, I have in a figure transferred to myself and to Apollos for your sakes; that ye might learn in us not to think of men above that which is written, that no one of* *you be puffed up for one against another. <7> For who maketh thee to differ from another? and what hast thou that thou didst not receive? now if thou didst receive it, why dost thou glory, as if thou hadst not received it?]*

<< *I Peter 5:1-3* >> *[The elders which are among you I exhort, who am also an elder, and a witness of the sufferings of Christ, and also a partaker of the glory that shall be revealed: <2> Feed the flock of God which is among you, taking the oversight thereof, not by constraint, but willingly; not for filthy lucre, but of a ready mind; <3> Neither as being lords over God's heritage, but being ensamples to the flock.]*

<< *Matthew 20:25-27* >> *[But Jesus called them unto him, and said, Ye know that the princes of the Gentiles exercise dominion over them, and they that are great exercise authority upon them. <26> But it shall not be so among you: but whosoever will be great among you, let him be your minister; <27> And whosoever will be chief among you, let him be your servant: 28 Even as the Son of man came not to be ministered unto, but to minister, and to give his life a ransom for many.]*

<< *I Corinthians 7:22* >> *[For he that is called in the Lord, being a servant, is the Lord's freeman: likewise also he that is called, being free, is Christ's servant. 23 Ye are bought with a price; be not ye the servants of men.]*

<< *Numbers 11:29* >> *[And Moses said unto him, Enviest thou for my sake? would God that all the LORD'S people were prophets, and that the LORD would put his spirit upon them!]*

<< *I Corinthians 14:30-32* >> *[If any thing be revealed to another that sitteth by, let the first hold his peace. <31> For ye may all prophesy one by one, that all may learn, and all may be comforted. <32> And the spirits of the prophets are subject to the prophets.]*

<< *Luke 9:49, 50* >> *[And John answered and said, Master, we saw one casting out devils in thy name; and we forbade him, because he followeth not with us. <50> And Jesus said unto him, Forbid him not: for he that is not against us is for us.]*

<< *Revelation 5:9, 10* >> *[And they sung a new song, saying, Thou art worthy to take the book, and to open the seals thereof: for thou wast slain, and hast redeemed us to God by thy blood out of every kindred, and tongue, and people, and nation; <10> And hast made us unto our God kings and priests: and we shall reign on the earth.]*

<< *Philippians 2:2-9* >> *[Fulfil ye my joy, that ye be like-minded, having the same love, being of one accord, of one mind. <3> Let nothing be done through strife or vainglory; but in lowliness of mind let each esteem other better than themselves. <4> Look not every man on his own things, but every man also on the things of others. <5> Let this mind be in you, which was also in Christ Jesus: <6> Who, being in the form of*

THE TRUTH

God, thought it not robbery to be equal with God: <7> But made himself of no reputation, and took upon him the form of a servant, and was made in the likeness of men: <8> And being found in fashion as a man, he humbled himself, and became obedient unto death, even the death of the cross.<9> Wherefore God also hath highly exalted him, and given him a name which is above every name:]

You don't need to go to any man-made temple or church to worship the Lord God YAHAWAH.

<< *Matthew 18:20* >> *[For where two or three are gathered together in my name, there am I in the midst of them.]*

You can study with your friends, any place where you're comfortable. Make sure you're using the King James translation; it is the most accurate English language Bible! Stay away from other Modern English translations; they were maliciously mistranslated by the modern religions to teach you their false religions, to deceive you and to create a colonial mentality in people! This blasphemy is the work of the modern religious and political organizations! The Lord's temple is the heart of his people, not some church building:

<< *Acts 17:24* >> *[The Lord that made the world and all things therein, seeing that he is Lord of heaven and earth, dwell not in temples made with hands.]*

<< *Jeremiah 7:4* >> *[Trust ye not in lying words, saying, The temple of the Lord, the temple of the Lord YAHAWAH, The temple of the Lord, are these.]*

The Lord's people are his temple, not the so-called churches and synagogues, full of idols.

<< *1 Corinthians 3:16,17* >> *[Know ye not that ye are the temple of the Lord, and that the spirit of the Lord dwelleth in you? If any man defile the temple of the Lord, him shall the Lord destroy; for the temple of the Lord is holy, which temple you are.]*

You don't need a church to pray. The best place to pray is some place private.

<< *Matthew 6:1-8* >> *[Take heed that ye do not your alms (your prayers) before men, to be seen of them: otherwise ye have no reward of your Father which is in heaven. Therefore when thou doest thine alms, do not sound a trumpet before thee, as the hypocrites do in the synagogues and in the streets, that they may have glory of men Verily I say unto you, they have their reward. But when thou doest alms, let not thy left hand know what thy right hand doeth: that thine alms may be in secret: and thy Father which seeth in secret himself shall reward thee openly.*

And when thou prayest, thou shalt not be as the hypocrites are: for they love to pray standing in the synagogues and in the corners of the streets, that they may be seen of men. Verily I say unto you, They have their reward. But thou, when thou prayest, enter into thy closet, and when thou hast shut thy door, pray to thy Father which is in secret; and thy Father which seeth in secret shall reward thee openly. But when ye pray, use not vain repetitions, as the heathens do (like that satanic false religion: the Roman Catholics)*: for they think that they* *shall be heard for their much speaking. Be not ye therefore like unto them: for your father knoweth what thing ye have need of before ye ask him.]*

And you must not praise those false religious leaders with any glorifying title like Pope or Father. Jesus Christ taught and said:

<< *Matthew 23:9,10* >> *[Call no man your father upon the Earth: for one is your father, which is in heaven! <10> Neither be ye called masters: for one is your Master, even Christ.]*

The word "pope" is Latin, it means father, "Pope John Paul" of the Catholic church is not a Pope, the Lord in heaven is our only father. That guy is not John, and he is not Paul either, those were Asiatic Hebrew Israelites. His real name is Carol Rogitler. Any preacher who calls himself FATHER or Pope is an antichrist.

And the prophets Paul and Peter were not the ones who started the Roman Catholic Church, a sun worshipper named Constantine formed that evil false religion in 329 AD. There are many books revealing the truth about the so-called Roman Catholic Church: for example read, The <u>Two Babylons</u>, by Alexander Hislop. You should read about the history of the Catholic Church and the inquisition. That religion is Satan's seat!

The Catholic religion has absolutely nothing to do with the Bible, but all lies and perversions of Biblical truth can be traced back to the Roman Catholic religion. So many good and innocent people in the Catholic church and in other false religions are being misled and exploited. False religion is the mother of colonialism and genocide. Their teachings were adopted from paganism and devil worship, not of Biblical origin at all. In reality, Catholicism is the worship of demons started by Nimrod of the Babylonian Empire! Catholic festivals such as Christmas and Easter can all be traced back to the Babylonian religion.

Nimrod killed his father and married his mother. Nimrod built Babylon and set himself as the king and his mother (wife) as his queen. He led the people to rebel against the Lord. Then Nimrod proclaimed himself a god called Moloch. He also practiced human sacrifice and developed the false religion of astrology!

It was Shem that killed Nimrod in order to stop that false religion and satanic worship. Nimrod's mother, whom he had married, declared her self-a goddess and had babies sacrificed to her! And she would have the sign of the cross cut into the baby's chest and their hearts taken out to please Nimrod! The cross or X sign was the first initial in the name of Tamuzz, the son of Semiramus; it was also used as an emblem to identify cult members. That is the true origin of the sign of the cross; it is the sign of death to symbolize Satanism! The people wept when Nimrod died and declared an annual weeping for Nimrod; this is the origin of the Catholic celebration called Lent! All of these Catholic, modern Christianity, religious traditions, and so-called holidays are purely satanic in origin!

When Semiramis became pregnant, she claimed to have been a virgin impregnated by the false god Molock. She claimed that her son, Tammuz, was Nimrod reincarnated, and that she was the spirit of god incarnated in a woman. She called herself the queen of heaven! This is the real so-called virgin that the Catholics and other false religions around the world pray to. That is the origin of the so-called trinity idea and the worship of Mary. Mary is a mask representation of Semiramis! And all the nations at Babylon, except for the Hebrews and a few others, adopted this worship of Molock! The word "Hebrew" means past, as in ancient. They called us Hebrews because we kept the customs of the past. The Hebrew customs are the same customs that the Lord YAHAWAH gave to Adam.

When the nations began to migrate to other lands, they took the false Babylonian religion with them and eventually customized it to their culture and environment. Now, this mother goddess of Babylon is known by different names in different nations: in China she is called Shing Moo, in Phoenicia she is known as Astoreth, in

THE TRUTH

Asia Minor as Diana (Acts 19:27), and in Egypt as Isis! Today it is maliciously called Mary to blaspheme the scriptures! They have the world blindly worshipping a false god! The Bible is about Christ not Mary. Salvation is through Christ not Mary:

> << Acts 4:10-12 >> *[Be it known unto you all, and to all the people of Israel, that by the name of Jesus Christ of Nazareth, whom ye crucified, whom the Lord YAHAWAH raised from the dead ...Neither is there salvation in any other: for there is none other name under heaven given among men, whereby we must be saved.]*

And Christ wants us to pray to the Lord, the Father, whose name is YAHAWAH. The so-called Catholic religion and all other religions have deceived the world into worshipping Satan through idols and other means. You can see that the image in all churches is no other then that of the devil! Only the devil would desire to replace the Creator! And exploited

Modern, culture, philosophy, law, science, and religion is being misused and exploited. It is used to trick, deceive and murder. They are being used as tools of colonialism, exploitation and capitalism. They are used to teach hatred towards the Most High, the Bible, and Asiatic people. They are used to set up and to teach white supremacy and to make you a carbon copy of the devil! The words of the religious, educational and political leaders of this world are poisonous lies! For example, the Native American Indians say, "the white man speaks with a fork tongue." This is true of most political and religious leaders around the world, regardless of race.

> << Psalms 58:3,4 >> *[The wicked are estranged from the womb: they go astray as soon as they be born, speaking lies. Their poison is like the deaf adder that stoppeth her ear.]*

Speaking In Tongues

Many of churches profess to have what they call the Holy Ghost. Now, there is no such a thing as ghost; the word properly translated is "Spirit", Holy Spirit. Now, those people claiming to have this so-called Holy Ghost also claim they can speak in tongues. One group calls itself the Pentecostals. They claim to speak in tongues because the Holy Ghost has entered their bodies. They demonstrate this by making all kinds of silly and unintelligible sounds and wild movements. But according to the Bible, speaking in tongues mean speaking in different foreign languages. It does not mean acting silly and making completely unintelligible sounds. Those ignorant hypocritical church people look as if they are demon infested!

The so-called Pentecostal try to justify their philosophy by misinterpreting the scriptures of the Bible. But if they had cared enough to examine the scriptures closely, this false religion could never have deceived them. The day of Pentecost is originally called the Feast of Weeks (Deuteronomy 16:10). It is easily seen that by "tongues" the Bible means different languages:

> << Acts 2:1-11 >> *[And when the day of Pentecost was fully come, they were all with one accord in one place <2> And suddenly there came from heaven as of a rushing mighty wind, and it filled all the house where they were sitting. <3> And there appeared unto them cloven tongues like as of fire, and it sat upon each of them. <4> And they were all filled with the Holy Ghost* (this should have been translated Holy Spirit), *and began to speak with other tongues (*in different languages*), as the spirit gave them utterance.]*

THE TRUTH

The next verse actually names what nation or regions the specific languages came from, intelligible languages regularly spoken by various people!

> *<5> [And there were dwelling at Jerusalem Jews, devout men, out of every nation (the tongues were the tongues spoken by those nations) under heaven. <6> Now when this was noised abroad, the multitude came together, and were confounded, because that every man heard them speak in his own language.]*

These were languages that other people could speak, geographical, national languages like we have Spanish, French, English, Arabic today, not some mumble-jumble sound that does not make sense.

> *<7> [And they were all amazed and marvelled, saying one to another, Behold, are not all these which speak Galilean? <8> And how hear we every man in our own tongues, wherein we were born?]*

Meaning the tongues were different national languages, and that by a miracle the congregation was gifted to speak! A list of the different countries are given here:

> *<9> [Parthians, and Medes, and Elamites, and the dwellers in Mesopotamia, and Judea, and Cappadocia, in Pontus, and Asia, <10> Phrygia, and Pamphylia, in Egypt, and in the parts of Libya about Cyrene, and strangers of Rome, Jews and proselytes, <11> Cretes and Arabians, we do hear them speak in our tongues the wonderful works of the Lord.]*

> *<< First Corinthians. 14:27 >> [If any man speak in an unknown tongue, let it be by two or at the most by three, and let one interpret.]*

If the so-called preachers and priests wish to speak in Latin or some other language, the Bible says that they should bring interpreters. But that jumping around and screaming, which they claim to be speaking in tongues, is demonic, insane and unintelligible, and can not be interpreted! The so-called Pentecostals and other church people should stop this foolishness; it is a sign that identifies unbelievers! Know for sure that when you see them jumping up and down in their churches, they are either acting or are completely demon possessed. They might have an evil spirit making them act so foolishly!

The religious and educational institutions of this world have created all kinds of new bibles in order to maliciously change and retranslate the Bible falsely, for political, economic, and psychological reasons. These changes are also designed to hide the identity of the original Hebrew Israelites and to replace the true God with their idols.

If you are reading in English, get the King James 1611 version of the Bible. It is usually more accurate than other translations. Don't waste your time with the new versions, revisions, and translations. They are inaccurate. Get a complete Bible, containing both the old and New Testament together. And get an Apocrypha too. The Apocrypha is another important set of books that the religious leaders had removed from the Bible because it was telling the truth about the atrocities of Greco-Roman history. Also read the works of Josephus.

You must get a complete Bible, not just a New Testament. You will not understand the New Testament if you don't know the Old Testament. The reason why they are trying to separate and take away the Old Testament is to hide the truth. We have a responsibility to know the complete Bible. Jesus emphasized this.

THE TRUTH

<< Matthew 5:17 >> [Think not that I am come to destroy the law or the prophets: I am not come to destroy but to fulfill.]

<< Revelation 22:18,19 >>: [If any man shall add unto these things, the lord shall add unto him the plagues that are written in this book: And if any man shall take away from the words of this prophecy, the lord shall take away his part out of the book of life, and out of the holy city, and from the things which are written in this book!]

The reason why the world is in ignorance and darkness is because the educational and religious institutions have conspired to deliberately deceive people in order to control and exploit them for selfish and materialistic purposes, such as personal, political, and economic power. Ignorance and fear are your two worst enemies. We have been taught lies deliberately! As a result, masses of people have been brought down to a very low condition spiritually, intellectually, morally, and politically.

The Israelites have become the least of all people because we abandoned the truth. For example, we are calling our selves by every kind of false name and identity, rather than Hebrew Israelites: our true original national identity. We have become as low as the dust. That is why the Lord God told Adam: *<< Genesis 3:19 >> [...for dust thou art, and unto dust shalt thou return.]*

<< Hosea 4:6 >> [My people are destroyed for lack of knowledge: because thou hast rejected knowledge, I will also reject thee, that thou shalt be no priest to me: seeing thou hast forgotten the law of thy Lord YAHAWAH, I will also forget thy children.]

The Most High spoke to the twelve tribes of Israel, saying:

<< Ezekiel 16:24-63 >> [Thou hast played the whore also with the Assyrian, (following after the pagan ways of the western world and of other heathens) *because thou wast insatiable; yea, thou hast played the harlot with them, and yet couldest not be satisfied, ...How weak is thine mind, saith the Lord, seeing thou doest all these things, the work of an imperious whorish woman, ... But as a wife that committeth adultery, which taketh strangers instead of her husband!*

They give gifts to all whores: but thou givest thy gift to all thy lovers, and hirest them, that they may come unto thee on every side for thy whoredom. And the contrary is in thee from other woman, whereas none followeth thee to commit whoredom: in that thou givest a reward, and no reward is given unto thee, therefore thou art contrary. Wherefore, O harlot, hear the word of the Lord... (The Lord is comparing their wickedness to that of a whore)

< 44> ...Behold, every one that useth proverbs shall use this proverb against thee, saying, as is the mother, so is the daughter. Thou art thy mother's daughter, that lotheth her husband and her children; and thou art the sister of thy sisters, which loathed their husbands and children: your mother was a Hittite, and your father an Amorite. And thine elder sister is Samaria, she and her daughters that dwell at thy left hand: and thy younger sister that dwelleth at thy right hand is Sodom and her daughter.

Yet hast thou not walked after their ways, nor done after their abominations: but, as if that were a very little thing, thou wast corrupt more than they in all thy ways. As I live, saith the Lord YAHAWAH, *Sodom thy sister hath not done, nor her daughters, as thou hast done, thou and thy daughters. <51> Neither hath Samaria committed half of thy sins; but thou hast multiplied thy sins more than they, and hast justified thy sisters in all the abominations that thou hast done* (that is why I had said, the wickedness of the Afro-Americans and Hispanics are making the Caucasians look good.)

<59> ...For thus saith the Lord YAHAWAH; I will even deal with thee as thou hast done, which hast despised the oath in breaking my covenant. Nevertheless I will remember my covenant with thee in the days of thy youth, and I will establish unto thee an everlasting covenant. ...And I will establish my covenant with thee; and thou shalt know that I am the Lord: That thou mayest remember, and be confounded, and never open thy mouth any more because of thy shame, when I am pacified toward thee for all that thou hast done, saith the Lord.]

As if it was not embarrassing enough that we treat each other so wickedly, the Bible says that we are more stupid than an ox or a donkey, the two dumbest animals on earth:

<< *Isaiah 1:2-9* >> [*Hear, O heavens, and give ear, O earth: for the Lord hath spoken, I have nourished and brought up children* (the twelve tribes of Israel) *and they have rebelled against me. The ox knoweth his owner and the ass his master's* crib (the donkey knows the way back to his stable): *but Israel doth not know, my people doth not consider. Ah sinful nation, a people laden with iniquity, a seed of evildoers, children that are corrupter: they have forsaken the Lord, they have provoked the Holy One of Israel unto anger, they are gone away backward. Why should ye be stricken any more?*

Ye will revolt more and more: the whole head is sick (corruption: none of the past leaders stood for our true nationality as Israelites; instead those false pastors have taught us to look up to a false colonial image for Christ), *and the whole heart faint. From the sole of the foot even unto the head there is no soundness in it* (from the least among them to the greatest); *but wounds, and bruises, and putrefying sores: they have not been closed, neither bound up, neither mollified with ointment* (No one had done anything about teaching this gospel of the kingdom and identifying the original twelve tribes of Israel).

Your country is desolate, your cities burned with fire (The Hebrew Israelites have been living in slums for the longest time): *your land, strangers devour it in your presence, and it is desolate, as overthrown by strangers. And the daughter of Zion is left as a cottage in a vineyard* (in ghettos, and huts), *as a lodge in a garden of cucumbers, as a besieged city. Except the Lord of hosts had left unto us a very small remnant, we should have been as Sodom, and we should have been like unto Gomorra.]*

All this happened to us because we are following after the ways of this wicked world instead of the precepts of the Lord YAHAWAH and the real Jesus Christ according to the true Bible. Christ told the cowards to their faces:

<< *John 8:44* >> [*Ye are of your father the devil, and the lust of your father ye will do, He was a murderer from the beginning, and abode not in the truth, because there is no truth in him]*

THE TRUTH

The people will always be suffering for as long as they have those negative attitudes. Read chapters five and six of Ezekiel.

<< *Matthew 23:23-39* >> [*Woe unto you, scribes and* Pharisees (modern day popular religious and political leaders), *hypocrites! for ye pay tithe of mint and anise and cummin, and have omitted the weightier matters of law, judgment, mercy, and faith: these ought ye to have done, and not to leave the other undone. <24> Ye blind guides, which strain at a gnat, and swallow a camel.*

<25> *Woe unto you, scribes and Pharisees, hypocrites! For ye make clean the outside of the cup and of the platter, but within they are full of extortion and excess. <26> Thou blind Pharisee, cleanse first that which is within the cup and platter, that the outside of them may be clean also. <27> Woe unto you, scribes and Pharisees, hypocrites! For ye are like unto whited sepulchers, which indeed appear beautiful outward, but are within full of dead men's bones, and of all uncleanness. <28> Even so ye also outward appear righteous unto men, but within ye are full of hypocrisy and iniquity.*

<29> *Woe unto you, scribes and Pharisees* (your modern day ministers and politicians), *hypocrites! because ye build the tombs of the prophets, and garnish the sepulchers of the righteous. <30> And say, If we had been in the days of our fathers, we would not have been partakers with them in the blood of the prophets. <31> Wherefore ye be witnesses unto yourselves, that ye are the children of them which killed the prophets... <32> Fill ye up then the measure of your fathers. <33> Ye serpents* (low life), *ye generation of vipers, how can ye escape the damnation of hell.* (That is why the Most High allowed the Israelites to come into slavery!)

<34> *Wherefore, behold, I send unto you prophets, and wise men, and scribes: and some of them ye shall kill and crucify; and some of them shall ye scourge in your Synagogues, and persecute them from city to city: <35> That upon you may come all the righteous blood shed upon the earth, from the blood of righteous Abel unto the blood of Zacharias son of Barachias, whom ye slew between the temple and the altar. <36> Verily I say unto you, All these things shall come upon this generation.*

<37> *O Jerusalem, Jerusalem, thou that killest the prophets, and stonest them which are sent unto thee, how often would I have gathered thy children, even as a hen gathereth her chickens under her wings, and ye would not! Behold, your house is desolate. <39> For I say unto you, ye shall not see me henceforth, till ye shall say, Blessed is he that cometh in the name of the Lord.*]

For as long as the people continue to be simple and ignorant, cruel and disrespectful, they will continue to suffer. And the majority of them will have to die because they will not listen to truth! However, the solution to this, if you want to see people out of slavery, is to teach them the Biblical truth and the identity of the original Israelites! This is a commandment from YAHAWAH!

<< *Ezekiel 2:3-7*>> [*And he said unto me, son of man I sent thee to the Children of Israel, to a rebellious nation that hath rebelled against me: they and their fathers have transgressed against me, even unto this very day. <4> For they are impudent children and stiffhearted*

(hammer-heads). *I do send thee unto them, Thus saith the Lord YAHAWAH. <5> And they, whether they will hear, or whether they will forbear, for they are a rebellious house; yet shall know that there hath been a prophet among them.]* Once you've told them what the Most High had said, your job is done!

<6> [And thou, son of man, be not afraid of them, neither be afraid of their words, though briers and thorns be with thee, and thou doest dwell among scorpions: be not afraid of their words, nor be dismayed at their looks, though they be a rebellious house. <7> And thou shalt speak my words unto them, whether they will hear, or whether they will forbear: for they are a most rebellious house]

<< Ezekiel 3:4-9 >> [And he said unto me, son of man, go get thee unto the house of Israel, speak with my words unto them. <5> For thou art not sent to a people of a strange speech and of a hard language, but to the house of Israel; <6> not to many people of a strange speech and of an hard language, whose words thou canst not understand. Surely, had I sent thee to them, they would have hearkened unto thee. <7> But the house of Israel will not hearken unto thee; for they will not hearken unto me: for all the house of Israel are impudent and hardhearted. <8> Behold, I have made thy face strong against their faces, and thy forehead strong against their foreheads. <9> As an adamant harder than flint have I made thy forehead: fear them not, neither be dismayed at their looks, though they be a rebellious house.]

How can you call yourself a human being and not stand to defend your own heritage and identity as the original Hebrew Israelites? You must defend and spread this truth! Another problem that is caused by ignorance, is envy! Envy is one of the greatest obstacles keeping people from uniting and working together! If one person is trying to do something positive, another goes out of his way to cause his brother to fail. Christ and his disciples were faced with the same problem:

<< Acts 13:45 >> [But when the Jews saw the multitudes, they were filled with envy, and spake against those things which were spoken by Paul, contradicting and blaspheming.]

<< Matthew 27:18 [For he (Jesus) *knew that for envy they had delivered him.* (to the Romans*)]*

Besides envy, there are other problems that we need to overcome: ignorance, fear, pride, jealousy, competition, and prejudice against others, otherwise there can be no unity and no progress! According to the Bible, politics and economics can not solve our problem. Our problem is spiritual! We have to start by learning the truth about our origin, our purpose, and our destiny! Once we know our true identity, the inferiority complex and the self-hatred will vanish instantly! And after we have discarded the negative attitudes and habits, unity will be the result, and with that comes all prosperity!

<< Isaiah 52:3 >> [For thus saith the Lord, Ye have sold your selves for nought; and ye shall be redeemed without money.]

THE TRUTH

<< John 15:12,13 >> [This is my commandment, That ye love one another, as I have loved you. Greater love hath no man than this that he lay down his life for his friends.]

<< Corinthians 13:1>> [Though I speak with the tongues of men and of angels, and have not charity, I am become as sounding brass, or a tinkling cymbal. <2> And though I have the gift of prophecy, and understand all mysteries, and all knowledge; and though I have all faith, so that I could remove mountains, and have not charity, I am nothing. <3> And though I bestow all my goods to feed the poor, and though I give my body to be burned, and have not charity, it profiteth me nothing.

<4> Charity suffereth long, and is kind; charity envieth not; charity vaunteth not itself, is not puffed up, <5> Doth not behave itself unseemly, seeketh not her own, is not easily provoked, thinketh no evil; < 6> Rejoiceth not in iniquity, but rejoiceth in the truth; < 7> Beareth all things, believeth all things, hopeth all things, endureth all things. <8> Charity never faileth: but whether there be prophecies, they shall fail; whether there be tongues, they shall cease; whether there be knowledge, it shall vanish away.

<9> For we know in part, and we prophesy in part. <10> But when that which is perfect is come, then that which is in part shall be done away. <11> When I was a child, I spake as a child, I understood as a child, I thought as a child: but when I became a man, I put away childish things. <12> For now we see through a glass, darkly; but then face to face: now I know in part; but then shall I know even as also I am known.< 13> And now abideth faith, hope, charity, these three; but the greatest of these is charity.]

THE TRUTH

SALVATION AND DESTINY

SPIRITUAL WARFARE

Spiritual warfare is the most risky of all warfare: you can lose both your life and your everlasting soul. The problems we perceive in the physical world are but a shadow of the spiritual battle, which is the true reality: the conflict between the forces of good and the forces of evil. The survival and destiny of the soul is the objective of this battle. To defeat Satan and his host of demons we must at all times have a strong love for the word of the LORD YAHAWAH and have a loving attitude towards our fellow man.

We must not go into spiritual warfare unprepared; we must arm ourselves. As in all battles we must identify the enemy, learn the nature of the warfare in terms of the weapons involved and the tactics that can be used by both sides for either offensive or defensive purposes. Our prime enemy is Satan the devil and his demons who have rebelled against God. They are deliberately hostile spiritual beings to both God and man, and they seek to destroy the sons of God, and keep the kingdom of heaven from being established on earth.

The things we can not see with our eyes are often more powerful than what we do see. Satan and his many legions of demons are very real and have the power to rule the entire earth at this time. Satan's best weapons are deception, stealth, temptation, and demonization. It is difficult to fight an enemy if you are not aware of him. Satan and his host of demons are invisible beings in constant opposition to the law and order of God and seeking to destroy mankind. Demons can be detected through their powerful activities and influences in the world and upon other beings, both animals and humans. The acts of Satan prove that he is not an abstraction, but a personal being.

Satan is envious of mankind and does not believe in disinterested love. The goal of Satan is to destroy the people of God, keep the kingdom of heaven from being established on earth, and to neutralize, eliminate, and replace the true God with his own image claiming glory for himself. Satan plans to do this by destroying the truth of the Bible and replacing it with deceitful lies, and by maliciously turning mankind from God through carnal and materialistic temptations.

Satan rebels against God because he desires to attain the power, glory, and rulership away from the true living God, the LORD YAHAWAH, and to replace the Almighty. The word "Satan" means accuser, or enemy. Satan is the adversary of mankind, the accuser of God and righteous people. The word "Devil" means deceiver or slanderer. Satan leads the forces of evil against the Almighty and against mankind. Satan uses various deceptive mechanisms to incite and tempt mankind into committing evil: separating man from God.

Satan the Devil is not an abstraction, he is a very real entity acting as his own person. Satan is also known by other names such as Beelzebub, the ruler of the demons. In addition, there are several other demons in league with Satan, which have united in rebellion against the Almighty God. These other demons are often referred to as evil spirits, unclean spirits, fallen angels, and principalities.

The Almighty God did not create Satan evil. He was an angelic being who rebelled against the Almighty God. When God made the world, man was ordained to have dominion over the creation and to inherit the physical and spiritual universe as sons of God, to dominate even the angelic world, and to have co-rulership with God. Satan became envious of mankind because of the great love between man and God, and has been the accuser of mankind, inciting mankind to do evil, using lies, cunning and deceit in order to separate man from God.

<< I Corinthians 6:3 >> [Know ye not that we shall judge angels? How much more things that pertain to this life?]

THE TRUTH

Satan desired to have dominion over the creation instead of Adam, so he became the adversary of man and God, leading the forces of evil in opposition to God, the Israelites, and the church. For this reason, Satan and other angels who joined in the rebellion were condemned and expelled from heaven.

<< II Peter 2:4 >> [For if God spared not the angels that sinned, but cast them down to hell, and delivered them into chains of darkness, to be reserved unto judgment.]

<< Jude 6,7,8 >> [And the angels which kept not their first estate, but left their own habitation, he hath reserved in everlasting chains under darkness unto the judgment of the great day. <7> Even as Sodom and Gomorrha, and the cities about them in like manner, giving themselves over to fornication, and going after strange flesh, are set forth for an example, suffering the vengeance of eternal fire. <8> Likewise also these filthy dreamers defile the flesh, despise dominion, and speak evil of dignities.]

<< Revelation 12:9 >> [And the great dragon was cast out, that old serpent called the Devil, and Satan, which deceiveth the whole world: he was cast out into the earth, and his angels were cast out with him.]

This scripture in Revelations also makes it clear that the Serpent in Genesis was Satan the Devil. And that Satan and his angels used to live in heaven at first but committed sin, and were later expelled from heaven. The Serpent knew what God had said to Adam and Eve and was able to speak. It obviously could not have been an ordinary snake. The Serpent was serving as a medium, possessed by the evil spirit of Satan. In the third chapter of Genesis, it was Satan the Devil that came to Eve through the medium of a serpent and tempted Eve.

The tree of life and the tree of the knowledge of good and evil were also symbolic, and so was the fruit just as the serpent was symbolic of Satan. It could not have been the eating of a physical fruit that brought about the mortality of Adam and Eve. Jesus explained this point:

<< Matthew 15:11 >> [Not that which goeth into the mouth defileth a man; but that which cometh out of the mouth, this defileth a man.]

<< Genesis 3:1-7 >> [Now the serpent was more subtle than any beast of the field which the Lord God had made. And he said unto the woman. Yea, hath God said, ye shall not eat of every tree of the garden? And the woman said unto the serpent, We may eat of the fruit of the trees of the garden: But of the fruits of the tree which is in the midst in the garden, God hath said, Ye shall not eat of it neither shall ye touch it, lest ye die.

For God doth know that in the day ye eat thereof, then your eyes shall be opened, and ye shall be as gods, knowing good and evil. And when the woman saw that the tree was good for food, and that it was pleasant to the eyes, and a tree to be desired to make one wise, she took of the fruit thereof, and did eat, and gave also unto her husband with her, and he did eat.

And the eyes of them both were opened, and they knew that they were naked; and they sewed fig leaves together, and made themselves aprons.]

THE TRUTH

Since the fruit was symbolic, so were the tree of life and the tree of the knowledge of good and evil. The tree of the knowledge of good and evil was said to be located in the midst of the garden. Specifically speaking, what did the tree of life and the tree of the knowledge of good and evil represent?

<< Proverb 13:12 >> [Hope deferred maketh the heart sick: but when the desire cometh, it is the tree of life.]

Basically, desire fulfilled is the tree of life, success and joy!

<< Revelation 22:14 >> [Blessed are they that do his commandments, that they may have right to the tree of life, and may enter in through the gates of the city.]

Ultimately, a person who has fulfilled the ideal of creation has the tree of life. This is a person who puts God first in their life, obeys his words, and receives the blessings of God. The tree of the knowledge of good and evil, is the tree of judgment. A person who makes himself the judge of what is good and evil, instead of looking to the Almighty LORD YAHAWAH for leadership and judgment of what is right or wrong. This is an individual who creates his own standards of truth and places himself at the center of life instead of God.

The woman desired the fruit to get wisdom for herself because she thought that knowledge would make her independent from God. People like that begins to seek knowledge as a way to gain personal power and to live independently from God and the principles established by the word of God. This person starts to depend on his or her own wisdom and knowledge as a means of salvation, instead of having faith in God. A person who has eaten the fruit of the tree of the knowledge of good and evil does not trust God's words, instead he trusts in his own carnal wisdom and knowledge as the source of his welfare and salvation.

This is a person who has decided to make himself Lord and God: he replaces God as the center of life! This person usually makes up his own false gods and religions, in his own image, to serve his own selfish purposes. Today, many people believe that science and technology are the solutions to the problems of the world. If this were true there would not be so much greed, injustice, and violence in the world today. Science and technology are very helpful, but because man has turned from God, the technology is being used to exploit people and to destroy the environment. It is vanity; man can not hope to replace God!

Eve became the embodiment of the tree of the knowledge of good and evil. Her fruits are either the children of good or of evil. Because she committed spiritual fornication with Satan in the garden, listening to her own mind and emotions instead of obeying God's law. Satan deceived her into believing she could have power and become independent from God. Mankind would inherit this evil nature from Satan through the spiritual fornication of Eve with Satan. That is why Jesus called the people a generation of vipers whose father is the Devil:

<< John 8:44 >> [Ye are of your father the Devil. and the lust of your father ye will do. He was a murderer from the beginning, and abode not in the truth, because the truth is not in him. When he speaketh a lie, he speaketh of his own: for he is a liar, and the father of it.]

<< Matthew 23:33 >> [Ye serpents, ye generation of vipers, how can ye escape the damnation of hell.]

THE TRUTH

The Almighty God LORD YAHAWAH has the ultimate control over all things visible and invisible, material and spiritual, including the devil and his demons. Satan can not do anything except God allows him, and he can go no further than what God allows.

<< John 19:11 >> *[Jesus answered, Thou couldest have no power at all against me, except it were given thee from above...]*

The Almighty God has dominion over all powers in the creation whether it is good or evil. Satan is not more powerful than God at any time.

<< Isaiah 45:6,7 >> *[That they may know from the rising of the sun, and from the west, that there is none beside me. I am the Lord, and there is none else. <7> I form the light, and create darkness: I make peace, and create evil: I the Lord do all these things.]*

<< Deuteronomy 32:39 >> *[See now that I, even I, am he, and there is no god with me: I kill, and I make alive; I wound, and I heal: neither is there any that can deliver out of my hand.]*

<< I Samuel 2:6,7 >> *[The Lord killeth, and maketh alive: he bringeth down to the grave, and bringeth up. <7> The Lord maketh poor, and maketh rich: he bringeth low, and lifteth up.]*

<< Exodus 4:24 >> *[And it came to pass by the way in the inn, that the Lord met him, and sought to kill him.]*

<< I Samuel 16:14 >> *[But the Spirit of the Lord departed from Saul, and an evil spirit from the Lord troubled him.]*

<< II Samuel 24:15,16 >> *[So the Lord sent a pestilence upon Israel from the morning even to the time appointed: and there died of the people from Dan even to Beer-Sheba seventy thousand men. <16> And when the angel stretched out his hand upon Jerusalem to destroy it, the Lord repented him of the evil, and said to the angel that destroyed the people, It is enough: stay now thine hand. And the angel of the Lord was by the threshingplace of Araunah the Jebusite.]*

<< Romans 13:1 >> *[...For there is no power but of God: the powers that be are ordained of God.]*

Satan is not an independent force. He is subordinate to God's will. But Satan is very hostile to God's servants and challenges the righteousness of God, as well as the rightfulness of God's dominion. Satan operates in a very systematic and organized way, achieving his goals using lies, trickery, and deceit. Satan has power not as Lord, but as an executioner. The Bible illustrates the nature of spiritual warfare:

<< II Corinthians 10:3-5 >> *[For though we walk in the flesh, we do not war after the flesh <4> (For the weapons of our warfare are not carnal, but mighty through God to the pulling*

down of strong holds;) <5> Casting down imaginations, and every high thing that exalteth itself against the knowledge of God, and bringing into captivity every thought to the obedience of Christ.]

Though we walk in the flesh in the usual manner as human beings, we do have powerful and subtle enemies on the spiritual level. We need to arm ourselves spiritually in the power of the Almighty LORD YAHAWAH to withstand the powerful and ruthless attacks of Satan, his host of demons, and his human agents. The spiritual attacks of Satan are manifested in our daily mental, emotional, and physical trials, perils, and tribulations. Many thoughts and emotions that we perceive are not really our own, but are broadcasted to us by Satan and his evil spirits, in order to mislead, confuse, and control our minds. Satan is constantly trying to deceive us with false religions, man-made idols, false preachers, false gods, false sciences and perverted ideas. If we know the truth and the love of the Almighty LORD YAHAWAH, we can put Satan and his agents to shame, and turn their lies against them.

The weapons of our warfare is primarily the atonement made by the Lord Jesus Christ, his death and resurrection, and the shedding of his blood for our sins in order to redeem us to the family of the LORD God YAHAWAH. Our secondary line of defense against Satan is the wisdom, knowledge, understanding from the Bible. Above all, we must be in constant prayer to the Almighty LORD YAHAWAH, seeking his wisdom and deliverance. To study and to learn the Bible is imperative: the pure word of God is mighty. It is the absolute truth and no man-made imagination nor philosophy can stand before it. Our wisdom, knowledge and understanding must come from, and will ultimately lead to, the Almighty Father in heaven, and to our everlasting life with great joy and glory.

<< Ephesians 6:11-18 >> [Put on the whole armor of God, that ye may be able to stand against the wiles of the devil. <12> For we wrestle not against flesh and blood, but against principalities, against powers, against the rulers of the darkness of this world, against spiritual wickedness in high places. <13> Wherefore take unto you the whole armor of God, that ye may be able to withstand in the evil day, and having done all, to stand.

<14> Stand therefore, having your loins girt about with truth, and having on the breastplate of righteousness; <15> And your feet shod with the preparation of the gospel of peace; <16> Above all, taking the shield of faith wherewith ye shall be able to quench all the fiery darts of the wicked. <17> And take the helmet of salvation and the sword of the Spirit, which is the word of God: <18> Praying always with all prayer and supplication in the Spirit, and watching thereunto with all perseverance and supplication for all saints.]

Make no mistake about it, we are in the midst of an all-out war, and there have already been many casualties at every level. Don't be the next casualty of Satan. Not only do you need to arm yourself with the whole armor of God, you must also attain the skills and experience to use your spiritual armor. The word of the Almighty, the law and the testimony of the Bible, and the redeeming work of Jesus Christ are your armor in this daily spiritual battle. The wiles of the Devil include all of the tricks, deceptions, and temptations, used by the devil to trap and put you into slavery and destroy you.

Satan and his forces are not human, they are not flesh and blood, they are extraordinary beings. You must be aware of the nature of this enemy. We are fighting principalities and the rulers of darkness, which implies high-ranking demons in the government of Satan's kingdom. We must therefore be wise. We are fighting spiritual wickedness in high places, which implies evil forces that are highly organized, focused and using very subtle lies, false science and religions disguised as truth. Knowing the word of God, keeping the commandments, and applying discipline, wisdom, knowledge, and understanding, is the only way to defeat Satan.

Stand ready for combat therefore with your spiritual armor. Our weapons and armor are not physical, the gospel of Jesus Christ, the commandments, and the love of LORD YAHAWAH make up our arsenal against Satan. The breastplate of righteousness represents a good conscience before the Lord. We must be pure in heart and mind. We should not seek to justify ourselves in our own eyes by following false religions and philosophies, but rather to admit that we are sinners, seeking repentance, that we may have forgiveness of our sins and salvation through the blood of Jesus Christ our redeemer.

Faith is our shield, faith is knowledge: the knowledge of the laws and the testimony of the Bible and the redeeming work of our Savior. We can be confident in battle because we are justified by the atonement made by our Lord and Savior, the MASHAYAK. Constant prayer, learning, and living our lives according to the doctrines of righteousness found in the Bible, will provide us with protection against Satan, against his demons, and against his agents of evil.

Satan the Devil now dominates all the nations of the world. Satan controls all aspects of religion, economics, and politics of every nation. The people seem to crave violence and are lusting after evil daily. The world is growing more and more perverted and corrupt every day. Homosexuals and lesbians are leading the nations. A real man is being denied the power, authority and a man's right to lead his family. The word "civilization" has no meaning anymore in the western world. Satan dominates the world with evil.

<< John 14:30 >> [Hereafter I will not talk much with you: for the prince of this world cometh, and hath nothing in me.]

<< Psalm 96:5 >> [For all the gods of the nations are idols; but the Lord made the heavens.]

<< I Corinthians 10:20 >> [But I say, that the things which the Gentiles sacrifice, they sacrifice to devils, and not to God; and I would not that ye should have fellowship with devils.]

<< John 8:44 >> [Ye are of your father the devil, and the lusts of your father ye will do. He was a murderer from the beginning and abode not in the truth, because there is no truth in him. When he speaketh a lie, he speaketh of his own: for he is a father of it.]

<< Revelation 2:9 >> [I know thy works, and tribulation and poverty, (but thou art rich) and I know the blasphemy of them which say they are Jews and are not. but are the synagogue of Satan.]

The Bible describes Satan as "The prince of this world" to make it clear that the world is under the domination of Satan the Devil. That is why there is no justice in the world for the righteous man. His rights are constantly violated, he is denied all access to prosperity. Corrupt leaders, teaching false values and objectives are leading the vast majority of the people. The synagogues and churches are under the direct domination of Satan the Devil. The people are being made to serve idols and false gods, which are all demons in disguise. Satan is described as a murderer and the father of lies, who dominates the whole world, leading it to death and destruction.

THE TRUTH

<< Daniel 11:12,13 >> [Then said he unto me, Fear not, Daniel: for from the first day that thou didst set thine heart to understand, and to chasten thyself before thy God, thy words were heard, and I am come for thy words. <13> But the prince of the kingdom of Persia withstood me one and twenty days: but lo, Michael, one of the chief princes, came to help me.]

<< Revelation 16:14 >> [For they are the spirits of devils, working miracles, which go forth unto the kings of the earth and of the whole world, to gather them to the battle of that great day of God Almighty.]

Satan the Devil is the author of the confusion and the wars occurring among the nations. He dominates all of the nations of the world, for the purpose of bringing about the total destruction of mankind. One of the demons assigned by Satan to dominate over Persia, had the power to resist and oppose even Arch-angel Michael, one of the most powerful among the angels of God. Satan organizes his kingdom in a military fashion, with princes, generals, administrators, and agents. Satan has ruling demons set up in an organized fashion to rule over: families, societies, communities, companies, neighborhoods, and states, dominating every nation to carry out his evil devices in opposition to God and the righteous.

Satan the Devil is the author of all confusion. He operates through his many legions, hosts of demons, and human agents, to resist, oppose, and defile the righteous. Satan is constantly using evil devices such as deception, lies, and demonization, to create afflictions, destructions, murder, and war among nations. We must fight back against Satan with full spiritual armor.

<< Matthew 10:16 >> [Behold, I send you forth as sheep in the midst of wolves: be ye therefore wise as serpents, and harmless as doves.]

<< I Peter 5:8 >> [Be sober, be vigilant; because your adversary the devil, as a roaring lion, walketh about, seeking who he may devour.]

Satan, his demons, and his agents are at work day and night. The Bible clearly describes Satan as our adversary, seeking to ruin us by every means necessary. To survive, we must love the LORD YAHAWAH and his commandments with all of our hearts and have love for each other. If Satan succeeds at keeping us from loving each other and away from the words of God, then we are doomed.

<< II Corinthians 4:3,4 >> [But if our gospel is hid, it is hid to them that are lost: <4> In whom the god of this world hath blinded the minds of them which believe not, lest the light of the gospel of Christ, which is the image of God, should shine unto them.]

<< Luke 22:31 >> [And the Lord said, Satan hath desired to have you, that he may sift you as wheat; <32> But I have prayed for thee, that thy faith fail not: and when thou art converted, strengthen thy brethren.]

Satan the Devil has power to demonize. Demonization is often erroneously referred to as demon possession. Satan cannot posses us because we belong to God. Satan and his demons have no legitimate right to dwell in our bodies; we are the temple of God. Satan enters and demonizes a being only by invitation. Sin is the doorway for Satan to enter our bodies and minds, and to control our actions, thoughts, and emotions.

<< *Luke 22:3* >> *[Then entered Satan into Judas surnamed Iscariot, being of the number of the twelve.]*

Demonization of a person or an animal can manifest itself in a variety of effects and behaviors, including the demonstration of supernatural strength and other abilities. Often not only one, but also several related demons indwell a person at the same time. A group of demons is called a legion. Demonization can also cause mental and physical diseases. Many of the problems that plague our society today are signs of demonization, such as the fascination with the occult, the immoral and indecent way that people dress and behave. Demonization often results in physical affliction, emotional instability, psychic and physical pain. Demonized people often have a tendency to refuse the wearing of decent clothing, seeking to go about naked. Demonized people often have a fascination with the dead and a desire to dwell among the tombs or desolate and ruinous places.

<< *Mark 5:2-9,15* >> *[And when he had come out of the ship, immediately there met him out of the tombs a man with unclean spirit, <3> who had his dwelling among the tombs; and no man could bind him, no, not with chains: <4> Because that he had been often bound with fetters and chains, and the chains had been plucked asunder by him, and the fetters broken in pieces: neither could any man tame him.*

<5> And always, night and day, he was in the mountains, and in the tombs, crying, and cutting himself with stones. <6> But when he saw Jesus afar off, he ran and worshipped him, <7> And cried with a loud voice, and said, What have I to do with thee, Jesus, thou Son of the Most High God? I adjure thee by God, that thou torment me not. <8> For he said unto him, Come out of the man, thou unclean spirit. <9> And he asked him, what is thy name? And he answered, saying, My name is Legion: for we are many. Many devils were entered into him.]

The perils of Job, for example, also illustrate significantly the powers of Satan to cause afflictions, death, plagues, and natural disasters such as storms:

<< *Job 1:6-22, 2:1-7* >> *[Now there was a day when the sons of God came to present themselves before the Lord, and Satan came also among them. <7> And the Lord said unto Satan, Whence comest thou? Then Satan answered the Lord, and said, From going to and fro in the earth, and from walking up and down in it.*

<8> And the Lord said unto Satan, Hast thou considered my servant Job, that there is none like him in the earth, a perfect and an upright man one that feareth God, and escheweth evil? <9> Then Satan answered the Lord and said, Doth Job fear God for naught? <10> Hast not thou made a hedge about him, and about his house, and about all that he hath on every side thou hast blessed the work of his hands, and his substance is increased in the land.

<11> But put forth thine hand now, and touch all that he hath, and he will curse thee to thy face. <12> And the Lord said unto Satan, Behold, all that he hath is in thy power, only upon himself put not forth thine hand. So Satan went forth from the presence of the Lord.

<13> And there was a day when his sons and his daughters were eating and drinking wine in their eldest brother's house: <14>. And there came a messenger unto Job, and said, The oxen were plowing, and the asses feeding beside them: <15> And the Sabeans fell upon them, and took them away; yea, they have slain the servants with the edge of the sword; and I only am escaped alone to tell thee.

<16> While he was yet speaking, there came also another, and said, The fire of God is fallen from heaven, and hath burned up the sheep, and the servants, and consumed them; and I only am escaped alone to tell thee.

<17> While he was yet speaking, there came also another, and said, The Chaldeans made out three bands, and fell upon the camels, and have carried them away, yea, and slain the servants with the edge of the sword; and I only am escaped alone to tell thee.

<18> While he was yet speaking, there came also another, and said, Thy sons and thy daughters were eating and drinking wine in their eldest brother's house: <19> And, behold, there came a great wind from the wilderness, and smote the four corners of the house, and it fell upon the young men, and they are dead; and I only am escaped alone to tell thee.

<20> Then Job arose, and rent his mantle, and shaved his head, and fell down upon the ground, and worshipped, <21> And said, Naked came I out of my mother's womb, and naked shall I return thither: the LORD gave, and the LORD hath taken away; blessed be the name of the LORD. <22> In all this Job sinned not, nor charged God foolishly.]

<< Job 2:1-13 >> [Again there was a day when the sons of God came to present themselves before the Lord, and Satan came also among them to present himself before the Lord. <2> And the Lord said unto Satan, From whence comest thou? And Satan answered the Lord, and said, From going to and fro in the earth, and from walking up and down in it.

<3> And the Lord said unto Satan, Hast thou considered my servant Job, that there is none like him in the earth, a perfect and an upright man, one that feareth God, and escheweth evil? and still he holdeth fast his integrity, although thou movest me against him, to destroy him without cause. <4> And Satan answered the Lord, and said, Skin for skin, yea, all that a man hath will he give for his like. <5> But put forth thine hand now, and touch his bone and his flesh, and he will curse thee to thy face.
<6> And the Lord said unto Satan, Behold, he is in thine hand; but save his life. <7> So went Satan forth from the presence of the Lord, and smote Job with sore boils from the sole of his foot unto his crown.

<8>. And he took him a potsherd to scrape himself withal; and he sat down among the ashes. <9> Then said his wife unto him, Dost thou still retain thine integrity? Curse God, and die. <10> But he said unto her, Thou speakest as one of the foolish women speaketh. What? Shall we receive good at the hand of God, and shall we not receive evil? In all this did not Job sin with his lips.

<11> Now when Job's three friends heard of all this evil that was come upon him, they came every one from his own place; Eliphaz the Temanite, and Bildad the Shuhite, and Zophar the Naamathite: for they had made an appointment together to come to mourn with him and to comfort him. <12> And when they lifted up their eyes afar off, and knew him not, they lifted up their voice, and wept; and they rent every one his mantle, and sprinkled dust upon their heads toward heaven. <13> So they sat down with him upon the ground seven

days and seven nights and none spake a word unto him: for they saw that his grief was very great.]

<< Job 42:10-17 >> [And the LORD turned the captivity of Job, when he prayed for his friends: also the LORD gave Job twice as much as he had before. <11> Then came there unto him all his brethren, and all his sisters, and all they that had been of his acquaintance before, and did eat bread with him in his house: and they bemoaned him, and comforted him over all the evil that the LORD had brought upon him: every man also gave him a piece of money, and every one an earring of gold.

<12> So the LORD blessed the latter end of Job more than his beginning: for he had fourteen thousand sheep, and six thousand camels, and a thousand yoke of oxen, and a thousand she asses. <13> He had also seven sons and three daughters. <14> And he called the name of the first, Jemima; and the name of the second, Kezia; and the name of the third, Keren-happuch. <15> And in all the land were no women found so fair as the daughters of Job: and their father gave them inheritance among their brethren. <16> After this lived Job an hundred and forty years, and saw his sons, and his sons', even four generations. <17> So Job died, being old and full of days. So the Lord blessed the latter end of Job more than his beginning: for he had fourteen thousand sheep, and six thousand camels, and a thousand yoke of oxen, and a thousand she asses.]

In addition to being able to demonize people, afflicting them psychologically, and physically, Satan has great supernatural powers to bring about natural disasters and plagues, to accomplish his murderous and evil purposes. The plagues and afflictions of Satan upon Job reveal Satan's vicious and murderous intentions.

Basically, Satan in his constant effort to accuse God and man, was charging that the only reason Job served God was because God gave him a lot of material wealth and protection. And If God were to take these things away from Job, or any other servant of God, that servant would abandon the LORD God YAHAWAH Ultimately, God removed his protection from Job and Satan was allowed to test Job to reveal what was in Job's heart.

Satan was proven a liar again. God's servants do not serve him only for selfish considerations, but because of their love for God. Whenever our love for the Almighty LORD YAHAWAH is strong and unconditional, and whenever we apply wisdom, knowledge, and understanding, Satan will always be defeated.

The Lord has the ultimate control of all forces good and evil. For example, Satan was ordered not to take Job's life by the LORD YAHAWAH; Satan did not dare to challenge God's order and authority. Satan is often depicted as a rival against God, constantly accusing man and God:

<< Zechariah 3:1, 2 >> [And he showed me Joshua the high priest standing before the angel of the Lord, and Satan standing at his right hand to resist him. <2> And the Lord said unto Satan, The Lord rebuke thee, O Satan; even the Lord that hath chosen Jerusalem rebuke thee: is not this a brand plucked out of the fire?]

The scriptures of the Bible reveal clearly the nature of the kingdom of Satan, and how he has operated to destroy mankind throughout history. The actions of Satan throughout history has been a constant effort to prevent the reconciliation of mankind to God by trying to prevent and hinder Jesus Christ, the chosen seed of promise, from coming and restoring the kingdom of heaven on earth.

THE TRUTH

Satan has been trying to cause to stumble and to bring about the destruction of the patriarchs and the Israelites, so that he could block the lineage of the chosen seed, Jesus Christ, to keep Christ from coming to earth and fulfilling the prophecies. In his constant effort to destroy the lineage of the promised Savior and Deliverer, Satan tempted the patriarchs and the Israelites, deceived, and perverted them with evil and falsehood, in an attempt to block the Seed of Promise:

<< *Deuteronomy 32:16-21* >> *[They provoked him to jealousy with strange gods, with abominations provoked they him to anger. <17> They sacrificed unto devils, not to God; to gods whom they knew not, to new gods that came newly up, whom your fathers feared not. <18> Of the Rock that begot thee thou art unmindful, and hast forgotten God that formed thee.*

<19> And when the LORD saw it, he abhorred them, because of the provoking of his sons, and of his daughters. <20> And he said, I will hide my face from them, I will see what their end shall be: for they are a very froward generation, children in whom is no faith. <21> They have moved me to jealousy with that which is not God; they have provoked me to anger with their vanities: and I will move them to jealousy with those which are not a people; I will provoke them to anger with a foolish nation.]

The scriptures give many examples of how Satan constantly attacks and provokes the Servants of God, and the kings of Israel into doing evil, and often using the gentile kingdoms to pervert and destroy the Israelites:

<< *I Chronicles 21:1* >> *[And Satan stood up against Israel, and provoked David to number Israel.]*

<< *I Kings 11:11* >> *[Wherefore the Lord said unto Solomon, forasmuch as this is done of thee, and thou hast not kept my covenant and my statutes, which I have commanded thee, I will surely rend the kingdom from thee, and will give it to thy servant.]*

<< *Ezekiel 21:25-27* >> *[And thou, profane wicked prince of Israel, whose day is come, when iniquity shall have an end, <26> Thus saith the Lord God; Remove the diadem, and take off the crown: this shall not be the same: exalt him that is low, and abase him that is high. <27> I will overturn it: and it shall be no more, until he come whose right it is; and I will give it him.]*

<< *II Chronicles 36:15-21* >> *[And the Lord God of their fathers sent to them by his messengers, rising up quickly, and sending; because he had compassion on his people and on his dwelling place: 16> But they mocked the messengers of God, and despised his words, and misused his prophets, until the wrath of the LORD arose against his people, till there was no remedy. <17> Therefore he brought upon them the king of the Chaldees, who slew their young men with the sword in the house of their sanctuary, and had no compassion upon young man or maiden, old man, or him that stooped for age: he gave them all into his hand.*

<18> And all the vessels of the house of God, great and small, and the treasures of the house of the LORD, and the treasures of the king, and of his princes; all these he brought to Babylon. <19> And they burnt the house of God, and brake down the wall of Jerusalem,

and burnt all the palaces thereof with fire, and destroyed all the goodly vessels thereof. <20> And them that had escaped from the sword carried he away to Babylon; where they were servants to him and his sons until the reign of the kingdom of Persia: <21> To fulfill the word of the LORD by the mouth of Jeremiah, until the land had enjoyed her Sabbaths: for as long as she lay desolate she kept sabbath, to fulfill threescore and ten years.]

Because of the great love and mercy of the Lord YAHAWAH, he sent many prophets and teachers, and has always been willing to forgive us and bless us whenever we repented from our evil and return to the Lord YAHAWAH. The Most High protected the Israelites until Yahawashy, our Lord and Savior, the seed of promise would come.

<< Ezra 1:1-6 >> Now in the first year of Cyrus king of Persia, that the word of the Lord by the mouth of Jeremiah might be fulfilled, the Lord stirred up the spirit of Cyrus king of Persia, that he made a proclamation throughout all his kingdom, and put it also in writing, saying, <2> Thus saith Cyrus king of Persia, The Lord God of heaven hath given me all the kingdoms of the earth; and he hath charged me to build him a house at Jerusalem, which is in Judah. <3> Who is there among you of all his people? His God be with him, and let him go up to Jerusalem, which is in Judah, and build the house of the Lord God of Israel, (he is the God,) which is in Jerusalem.

<4> And whosoever remaineth in any place where he sojourneth, let the men of his place help him with silver, and with gold, and with goods, and with beasts, beside the freewill offering for the house of God that is in Jerusalem. <5> Then rose up the chief of the fathers of Judah and Benjamin, and the priests, and the Levites, with all them whose spirit God had raised, to go up to build the house of the Lord which is in Jerusalem. <6> And all they that were about them strengthened their hands with vessels of silver, with gold, with goods, and with beasts, and with precious things, beside all that was willingly offered.]

When the Chosen Savior, Jesus Christ the Mashayak came to earth, Satan was attempting to destroy him from the first day. The entire life of Jesus Christ had been a struggle against Satan. Satan tried everything he could to destroy and to kill Jesus.

<< Matthew 2:13 >> [And when they were departed, behold the angel of the Lord appeareth to Joseph in a dream, saying, Arise, and take the young child and his mother, and flee into Egypt, and be thou there until I bring thee word: for Herod will seek the young child to destroy him.]

As in the Garden of Eden, Satan tempted Jesus with his famous three prong temptation: he challenged Jesus' devotion to God, he tested Jesus to see whether Jesus would use spiritual power selfishly, and he tested Jesus on dominionship, to see whether Jesus would accept any shortcuts to kingship.

<< Matthew 4:1-11 >> [Then was Jesus led up of the spirit into the wilderness to be tempted of the devil. <2> And when he had fasted forty days and forty nights, he was afterward hungry. <3> And when the tempter came to him, he said, If thou be the Son of God, command

that these stones be made bread. <4> But he answered and said, It is written, Man shall not live by bread alone, but by every word that proceedeth out of the mouth of God.

<5> Then the devil taketh him up into the holy city, and setteth him on a pinnacle of the temple. <6> And saith unto him, If thou be the Son of God, cast thyself down: for it is written, He shall give his angels charge concerning thee: and in their hands they shall bear thee up, less at any time thou dash thy foot against a stone.
<7> Jesus said unto him, It is written again, Thou shalt not tempt the Lord thy God.

<8> Again, the devil taketh him up into an exceedingly high mountain, and showeth him all the kingdoms of the world, and the glory of them; <9> And saith unto him, All these things will I give thee, if thou wilt fall down and worship me. <10> Then saith Jesus unto him, Get thee hence, Satan: for it is written, Thou shalt worship the Lord thy God, and him only shalt thou serve. <11> Then the devil leaveth him, and behold, angels came and ministered unto him.]

<< Luke 4:13 >> [And when the devil had ended all the temptation, he departed from him for a season.]

Satan had often tempted Christ and the disciples to follow strange thoughts and ideas that contradict the will of the Almighty God YAHAWAH.

<< Matthew 16:21-23 >> [From that time forth began Jesus to shew unto his disciples, how that he must go unto Jerusalem, and suffer many things of the elders and chief priests and scribes, and be killed, and raised again the third day. <22> Then Peter took him, and began to rebuke him, saying, Be it far from thee, Lord: this shall not be unto thee.

<23> But he turned, and said unto Peter, Get thee behind me, Satan: for thou art an offense unto me: for thou savourest not the things of God, but those that be of men.]

Satan tried to use human agents, the government, religious leaders, and even the disciples, in his attempt to trap and destroy Jesus Christ.

<< Matthew 22:15 >> [Then went the Pharisees, and took counsel how they might entangle him in his talk.]

<< Luke 22:3 >> [Then entered Satan into Judas surnamed Iscariot, being of the number of the twelve.]

<< John 13:26,27 >> [Jesus answered, He it is, to whom I shall give a sop, when I have dipped it. And when he had dipped the sop, he gave it to Judas Iscariot, the son of Simon. <27> And after the sop Satan entered into him. Then said Jesus unto him, That thou doest, do quickly.]

<< Luke 22:52,53 >> [Then Jesus said unto the chief priests, and captains of the temple and the elders, which were come to him, Be ye come out, as against a thief, with swords and

staves? <53> When I was daily with you in the temple, ye stretched forth no hands against me: but this is your hour, and the power of darkness.]

Following the death and resurrection of Jesus Christ, Satan continued to wage constant war against the disciples and the church in an attempt to destroy the plans of God. To this date, Satan dominates all of the world's churches and synagogues. Satan wages an incessant fight to destroy the believers, and he never stops his accusations against the righteous.

Satan and his agents have transformed themselves into preachers and religious leaders, disguising their true nature in order to mislead the people away from the worship of the true God, the Almighty, the LORD YAHAWAH:

<< II Corinthians 11:13-15 >> [For such are false apostles, deceitful workers, transforming themselves into apostles of Christ. <14> And no marvel; for Satan himself is transformed into an angel of light. <15> Therefore it is no great thing if his ministers also be transformed as the ministers of righteousness; whose end shall be according to their works.]

<< I Timothy 4:1,2 >> [Now the Spirit speaketh expressly, that in the latter times some shall depart from the faith, giving heed to seducing spirits, and doctrines of devils: <2> Speaking lies in hypocrisy; having their conscience sealed with a hot iron.]

<< Colossians 2:18 >> [Let no man beguile you of your reward in a voluntary humility and worshipping of angels, intruding into those things which he hath not seen, vainly puffed up by his fleshly mind.]

<< Acts 19:27 >> [So that not only this our craft is in danger to be set at nought; but also that the temple of the great goddess Diana should be despised, and her magnificence should be destroyed, whom all Asia and the world worshippeth.]

<< Revelation 2:9 >> [I know thy works, and tribulation and poverty, but thou art rich, and I know the blasphemy of them which say they are Jews, and are not, but are the synagogue of Satan.]

<< Luke 8:12 >> [Those by the way side are they that hear; then cometh the devil, and taketh away the word out of their hearts, lest they should believe and be saved.]

<< II Corinthians 12:7 >> [And lest I should be exalted above measure through the abundance of the revelations, there was given to me a thorn in the flesh, the messenger of Satan to buffet me, lest I should be exalted above measure.]

The door way for demonization is sin. When a person sin Satan sees it as an open invitation. The sin could be either one of commission or omission. The goal of the demons is to resist, defile, accuse, condemn, and destroy human beings through pressure, deceptions, temptations, afflictions, and to control a person through demonization. Sin is the doorway through which demons enter and control a person.

THE TRUTH

<< II peter 2:14 >> [Having eyes full of adultery, and that cannot cease from sin, beguiling unstable souls: a heart they have exercised with covetous practices; cursed children.]

<< Ephesians 2:2,3 >> [Wherein in time past ye walked according to the course of this world, according to the prince of the power of the air, the spirit that now worketh in the children of disobedience: <3> Among whom also we all had our conversation in times past in the lust of our flesh, fulfilling the desires of the flesh and of the mind; and were by nature the children of wrath, even as others.]

<< James 1:13-15 >> [Let no man say when he is tempted, I am tempted of God: for God cannot be tempted with evil, neither tempteth he any man: <14> But every man is tempted, when he is drawn away of his own lust, and enticed. <15> Then when lust hath conceived, it bringeth forth sin: and sin, when it is finished, bringeth forth death.]

<< James 4:4 >> [Ye adulterers and adulteresses, know ye not that the friendship of the world is enmity with God? whosoever therefore will be a friend of the world is the enemy of God.]

<< II Corinthians 11:3 >> [But I Fear, lest by any means, as the serpent beguiled Eve through his subtlety, so your minds should be corrupted from the simplicity that is in Christ.]

<< I John 3:8 >> [He that committeth sin is of the devil; for the devil sinneth from the beginning. For this purpose the Son of God was manifested, that he might destroy the works of the devil.

Jesus Christ redeemed us to God and defeated Satan by the sacrifice of his life for us. He is the Lamb of God, which takes away the sins of the world. Christ's victory over Satan is twofold: a present reality of the atonement before God, and a future promise of his Second Coming to establish the kingdom of heaven on the earth. Although Satan has been defeated and his power dissolved, the total abolishment of Satan and his ultimate doom is reserved for the Day of Judgment at the Second Coming of Jesus Christ. Christ has successfully redeemed those who have accepted him as their Savior to God.

<< Romans 5:12 >> [Wherefore, as by one man sin entered into the world, and death by sin; and so death passed upon all men, for that all have sinned.]

<< Revelation 12:10,11 >> [And I heard a loud voice saying in heaven, Now is come salvation and strength, and the kingdom of our God, and the power of his Christ: for the accuser of our brethren is cast down, which accused them before our God day and night. <11> And they overcame him by the blood of the Lamb, and by the word of their testimony; and they loved not their lives unto death.]

<< Acts 4:10-12 >> [Be it known unto you all, and to all the people of Israel, that by the name of Jesus Christ of Nazareth, whom ye crucified, whom the LORD YAHAWAH raised

from the dead ...Neither is there salvation in any other: for there is none other name under heaven given among men, whereby we must be saved.]

The resurrection of Jesus represents the defeat of Satan: the Second Coming of Jesus marks the complete doom and destruction of Satan, known as the Day of the Lord. Satan has no power over those who keep their faith in Jesus Christ, and keep the commandments of the Bible.

<< *I Corinthians 15:20-28* >> *[But now is Christ risen from the dead, and become the Firstfruits of them that slept. <21> For since by man came death, by man came also the resurrection of the dead. <22> For as in Adam all die, even so in Christ shall all be made alive. <23> But every man in his own order: Christ the Firstfruits; afterward they that are Christ's at his coming. <24> Then cometh the end, when he shall have delivered up the kingdom to god, even the Father, when he shall have put down all rule and all authority and power. <25> For he must reign, till he hath put all enemies under his feet.*

<26> The last enemy that shall be destroyed is death. <27> For he hath put all things under his feet. But when he saith all things are put under him, it is manifest that he is accepted, which did put all things under him. <28> And when all things shall be subdued unto him, then shall the Son also himself be subject unto him that put all things under him that God may be all in all.]

<< *Matthew 28:18* >> *[And Jesus came and spake unto them, saying, All power is given to me in heaven and in earth.]*

The power of Jesus over Satan was clearly manifested in his numerous acts of casting out demons. Not only was this a sign of the authority of Jesus over Satan, but also a representation of the kingdom of heaven on earth. Christ is mightier than Satan and is able to bind Satan at will.

<< *Matthew 12:22-27* >> *[Then was brought unto him one possessed with a devil, blind, and dumb: and he healed him, insomuch that the blind and dumb both spoke and saw. <23> And all the people were amazed, and said, Is not this the son of David? <24> But when the Pharisees heard it, they said, This fellow doth not cast out devils, but by Beelzebub the prince of the devils.*

<25> And Jesus knew their thoughts, and said unto them, Every kingdom divided against itself is brought to desolation; and every city or house divided against itself shall not stand: <26> And if Satan cast out Satan, he is divided against himself; how shall then his kingdom stand? <27> And if I by Beelzebub cast out devils, by whom do your children cast them out? therefore they shall be your judges.]

<< *Luke 11:17-22* >> *[But he, knowing their thoughts, said unto them, Every kingdom divided against itself is brought to desolation; and a house divided against a house falleth. <18> If Satan also be divided against himself, how shall his kingdom stand? Because ye say that I cast out devils through Beelzebub. <19> And if I by Beelzebub cast out devils, by whom do your sons cast them out? Therefore shall they be your judges. <20> But if I with the finger of God cast out devils, no doubt the kingdom of God is come upon you. <21> When a strong*

man armed keepeth his palace, his goods are in peace: <22> But when a stronger than he shall come upon him, he taketh from him all his armor wherein he trusted, and divideth his spoils.]

Satan recognizes Jesus as the Son of God:

<< *Luke 4:33-35* >> *[And in the synagogue there was a man, which had a spirit of an unclean devil, and cried out with a loud voice, <34> Saying, Let us alone; What have we to do with thee, thou Jesus of Nazareth? art thou come to destroy us? I know thee who thou art; the Holy One of God. <35> And Jesus rebuked him, saying, Hold thy peace, and come out of him. And when the devil had thrown him in the midst, he came out of him and hurt him not.]*

The scriptures clearly illustrate that demons can speak in their own person. A demonized person has an alien personality, his own personality is suppressed. His thoughts, his emotions, and actions are dictated by the demons. Keep in mind, too, that there is a difference between temptation and demonization. However, a person who has been tempted into doing an evil act still retains his own personality and the control of his own actions. The Bible also distinguishes between sickness and demonization. Not all sicknesses are caused by demons. A doctor can often cure a sick person. Jesus was casting out demons from people that were demonized, healing people that were sick, and rebuking people that had been deceived by false religion and philosophy.

<< *Matthew 4:24* >> *[And his fame went throughout all Syria: and they brought unto him all sick people that were taken with diverse diseases and torments, and those which were possessed with devils, and those that had the palsy; and he healed them.]*

<< *Matthew 9:12* >> *[But when Jesus heard that, he said unto them, They that be whole need not a physician, but they that are sick.]*

<< *Matthew 9:32,33* >> *[As they went out, behold they brought to him a dumb man possessed with a devil. <33> And when the devil was cast out, the dumb spake: and the multitudes marvelled, saying, It was never so seen in Israel.]*

<< *Matthew 17:15-18* >> *[...Lord, have mercy on my son: for he is lunatic and sore vexed: for ofttimes he falleth into the fire, and oft into the water. <16> And I brought him to thy disciples, and they could not cure him. <17> Then Jesus answered and said, O faithless and perverse generation, how long shall I suffer you? Bring him hither to me. <18> And Jesus rebuked the devil; and he departed out of the child: and the child was cured from that hour.]*

<< *Luke 11:14* >> *[And he was casting out devils, and it was dumb. And it came to pass, when the devil was gone out, the dumb spake; and the people wondered.]*

<< *Luke 7:21* >> *[And in that same hour he cured many of their infirmities and plagues, and of evil spirits; and unto many that were blind he gave sight.]*

THE TRUTH

<< Luke 8:2 >> [And certain women, which had been healed of evil spirits and infirmities, Mary called Magdalene, out of whom went seven devils.]

<< Colossians 2:15 >> [And having spoiled principalities and powers, he made a show of them openly, triumphing over them in it.]

Those who believe in Jesus Christ as the Chosen Savior have been given the absolute power to confront, cast out, and defeat Satan and all evil spirits. Jesus Christ has already defeated Satan and abolished the powers of Satan. Christ suffered and died in order to make the atonement for our sins and has conquered death through his resurrection. By so doing, Christ has fulfilled the prophecies, defeated Satan, and has given his believers power over evil spirits and demons to resist and defeat Satan and his agents. Our faith, the power of the atonement made by the blood of Christ, as well as knowledge of the scriptures, constitute an invincible armor against Satan in the spiritual warfare.

<< I Corinthians 15:55-57 >> [O death, where is thy sting? O grave, where is thy victory? <56> The sting of death is sin; and the strength of sin is the law. <57> But thanks be to God, which giveth us the victory through our Lord Jesus Christ.]

<< Hebrews 2:14,15 >> [Forasmuch then as the children are partakers of flesh and blood, he also himself likewise took part of the same; that through death he might destroy him that had the power of death, that is, the devil <15> And deliver them who through fear of death were all their lifetime subject to bondage.]

Deliverance is the process by which demons are expelled from a demonized person or other mediums. We have this Power now. If our faith is strong in the Lord, and if we apply the principles of love, wisdom, knowledge, understanding and faith, we will defeat Satan, and cast out any demon. We have been granted this power over Satan.

<< Matthew 16:18,19 >> [And I said unto thee, That thou art Peter, and upon this rock I will build my church; and the gates of hell shall not prevail against it <19> And I will give unto thee the keys of the kingdom of heaven: and whatsoever thou shalt bind on earth shall be bound in heaven: and whatsoever thou shalt loose on earth shall be loosed in heaven.]

<< Mark 11:23 >> [For verily I say unto you, That whosoever shall say unto this mountain, Be thou removed, and be thou cast into the sea; and shall not doubt in his heart, but shall believe that those things which he saith shall come to pass; he shall have whatsoever he saith.]

Spiritual warfare is different from prayer. We don't have to pray to God, asking for Satan to be cast out of a person. If our faith is strong, we have the power to command Satan or any evil spirit, in the name of the Chosen Savior, and the evil spirit will flee. God has already given us the power to cast out Satan and all demons. We simply need to exercise that power by commanding Satan to be cast out in the name of Jesus, i.e. by the power of the blood of Jesus that was shed on the cross; which has redeemed us to the Lord YAHAWAH.

THE TRUTH

We are responsible to use this spiritual power to protect ourselves from Satan, and help to free others as well. The tactics of casting out demons (deliverance) can also be done on the part of another in order to free the will of that person from the domination of the demons, so that the person can choose to repent and seek the righteousness of the Lord YAHAWAH. We have the power to command and to cast out demons from others- our families, communities, institutions and ourselves; to prevent Satan from dominating our lives and leading us to destruction.

<< *Luke 9:1* >> *[Then he called his twelve disciples together, and gave them power and authority over all devils, and to cure diseases.]*

<< *Acts 1:8* >> *[But ye shall receive power, after that the Holy Spirit is come upon you: and ye shall be witnesses unto me both in Jerusalem, and in all Judea, and in Samaria, and unto the utmost part of the earth.]*

<< *Mark 16:17,18* >> *[And these signs shall follow them that believe; In my name shall they cast out devils; they shall speak with new tongues; <18> They shall take up serpents; and if they drink any deadly thing, it shall not hurt them; they shall lay hands on the sick, and they shall recover.]*

<< *Acts 2:4* >> *[And they were all filled with the Holy Spirit and began to speak with other tongues, as the Spirit gave utterance.]*

<< *Luke 10:17-20* >> *[And the seventy returned again with Joy, saying, Lord, even the devils are subject unto us through thy name. <18> And he said unto them, I beheld Satan as lightning falls from heaven. <19> Behold, I give unto you power to tread on serpents and scorpions, and over all the power of the enemy: and nothing shall by any means hurt you. <20> Notwithstanding in this rejoice not, that the spirits are subject to you; but rather rejoice, because your names are written in heaven.]*

<< *Mark 6:13* >> *[And they cast out many devils, and anointed with oil many that were sick, and healed them]*

<< *I Corinthians 12:7-14* >> *[But the manifestation of the Spirit is given to every man to profit withal. <8> For to one is given by the Spirit the word of wisdom; to another the word of knowledge by the same Spirit; <9> To another faith by the same Spirit; to another the gifts of healing by the same Spirit; <10> To another the working of miracles; to another prophecy; to another discerning of spirits; to another diverse kinds of tongues; to another the interpretation of tongues: <11> But all these worketh that one and the selfsame Spirit, dividing to every man severally as he will. <12> For as the body is one, and hath many members, and all the members of that one body, being many, are one body: so also is Christ. <13> For by one Spirit are we all baptized into one body, whether we be Jews or Gentiles, whether we be bond or free; and have been all made to drink into one Spirit. <14> For the body is not one member, but many.]*

THE TRUTH

If we want deliverance from Satan and evil spirits, we must keep our faith strong in the word of the Lord YAHAWAH. The truth of the Bible is the key to freedom.

<< *Joel 2:32* >> *[And it shall come to pass, that whosoever shall call on the name of the Lord shall be delivered: for in Zion and in Jerusalem shall be deliverance, as the Lord hath said, and in the remnant whom the Lord shall call.]*

<< *Psalm 18:2* >> *[The Lord is my rock, and my fortress, and my deliverer; my God, my strength, in whom I will trust; my buckler, and the horn of my salvation, and my high tower.]*

To defeat Satan and his afflictions, and to prevent demonization, we must become knowledgeable of the laws and the scriptures of the Bible and follow them. All wisdom comes from God. The truth is our armor.

<< *John 8:32* >> *[And ye shall know the truth, and the truth shall make you free.]*

<< *Psalms 119:105* >> *[Thy word is a lamp unto my feet, and a light unto my path.]*

<< *Hebrews 4:12* >> *[For the word of God is quick, and powerful, and sharper than any two-edged sword, piercing even to the dividing asunder of soul and spirit, and of the joints and marrow, and is a discerner of the thoughts and intents of the heart.]*

<< *I Peter 2:2* >> *[As newborn babes, desire the sincere milk of the word, that ye may grow thereby.]*

<< *Matthew 4:4* >> *[But he answered and said, It is written, Man shall not live by bread alone, but by every word that proceedeth out of the mouth of God.]*

To identify the presence of evil spirits we must first be able to detect them by observing the effects they are having. We can analyze the kinds of symptoms and problems a person may display in order to identify the kind of evil spirit that is afflicting that person (or entity). We can detect demons by the kind of physical, mental, and spiritual afflictions they cause to a person. Demons can cause addictions to drugs, alcohol, or sex, for example. Demons also cause irrational thoughts, emotions, behavioral and psychological patterns. In addition to detecting demons by their effect on a person, the presence of evil spirits can also be revealed supernaturally. A person may be given the supernatural gift of discernment, to be able to perceive the presence and the nature of evil spirits. All demons are not the same. We must learn the different ways to detect and expel each type.

When Satan attacks we must be able to recognize the workings of Satan. Anything that contradicts the words and the laws of God is from Satan. We must guard our thoughts and emotions also, because some of the thoughts and feelings we perceive are not our own, they originated with Satan. Once we have become aware of the demons that have attacked, tempted, or deceived us to sin, we must honestly repent of our evil. We must discard bad habits and addictions. We must seek moderation. Lusts and greed are the doorways of demonization through which demons tempt and enter a person. We must resist Satan and repent from sin. We must present ourselves in all humility before the Lord YAHAWAH, and truthfully confess our sins to him.

THE TRUTH

<< *Ephesians 2:12* >> *[That at that time ye were without Christ, being aliens from the commonwealth of Israel, and strangers from the covenants of promise, having no hope, and without God in the world.]*

<< *Galatians 5:19-21,24* >> *[Now the works of the flesh are manifest, which are these; adultery, fornication, uncleanness, lasciviousness, <20> Idolatry, witchcraft, hatred, variance, emulations, wrath, strife, sedition, heresies, <21> Envying, murders, drunkenness, revellings, and such like: of the which I tell you before, as I have also told you in time past, that they which do such things shall not inherit the kingdom of God. <24> And they that are Christ's have crucified the flesh with the affections and lusts.]*

<< *I John 5:18,19* >> *[We know that whosoever is born of God sinneth not; but he that is begotten of God keepeth himself, and that wicked one toucheth him not. And we know that we are of God, and the whole world lieth in wickedness.]*

<< *Psalms 32:5* >> *[I acknowledged my sin unto thee, and mine iniquity have I not hid. I said, I will confess my transgressions unto the Lord; and thou forgavest the iniquity of my sin. Selah.*

<< *Psalm 139:23, 24* >> *[Search me, O God, and know my thoughts: <24> And see if there be any wicked way in me, and lead me in the way everlasting.]*

<< *James 5:16* >> *[Confess your faults one to another, and pray one for another, that ye may be healed. The effectual fervent prayer of a righteous man availeth much.]*

<< *James 4:6,7* >> *[But he giveth more grace. Wherefore he saith, God resisteth the proud, but giveth grace unto the humble. <7> Submit yourselves therefore to God. Resist the devil, and he will flee from you.]*

<< *Ezekiel 20:43* >> *[And there shall ye remember your ways, and all your doings, wherein ye have been defiled; and ye shall loathe yourselves in your own sight for all your evils that ye have committed.]*

<< *Matthew 3:7,8* >> *[But when he saw many of the Pharisees and Sadducees come to his baptism, he said unto them, O generation of vipers, who hath warned you to flee from the wrath to come? <8> Bring forth therefore fruits meet for repentance.]*

<< *Acts 19:18,19* >> *[And many that believed came, and confessed, and showed their deeds. <19> Many of them also which used curious arts brought their books together, and burned them before all men: and they counted the price of them, and found it fifty thousand pieces of silver.]*

<< *I John 1:9* >> *[If we confess our sins, he is faithful and just to forgive us our sins, and to cleanse us from all unrighteousness.]*

THE TRUTH

To deliver ourselves from demonization and retain deliverance so that Satan does not demonize us again, we must arm ourselves with the spiritual armor of God and meditate on the scriptures day and night. Always be on the lookout for signs of negativism and evil; demons are very subtle. We must also learn to differentiate the origin of our thoughts and emotions, evil thoughts and emotions from Satan must not be tolerated. Eliminate your bad habits. Once a sin is discovered it must be confessed to God immediately, because sins are the doorway for demons and evil spirits to enter and dwell within a person, eventually dominating that person.

Rebuke Satan by quoting the scriptures accurately, and he will flee from you. Give thanks and praise to the Lord YAHAWAH always, and keep a strong faith in the scriptures.

<< *Psalms 1:1-3* >> [*Blessed is the man that walketh not in the counsel of the ungodly, nor standeth in the way of sinners, nor sitteth in the seat of the scornful. <2> But his delight is in the law of the Lord; and in his law doth he meditate day and night. <3> And he shall be like a tree planted by the rivers of water, that bringeth forth his fruit in his season; and whatsoever he doeth shall prosper.*]

We must not neglect to pray regularly, to keep your faith strong, and ask for the blessings of Lord YAHAWAH. We must pray regularly, both in private and with others. We should also pray for each other. Pray to express also your thankfulness to God.

<< *I Thessalonians 5:17* >> [*Pray without ceasing.*]

Once we have successfully cast out the evil spirits from ourselves or from some other medium, we must take steps to prevent that evil spirit from returning. We must then fill our life with spiritual activities. We must commit ourselves to the ministry with all of our hearts, or else the evil spirit will seek to demonize us again.

<< *Matthew 12:43-45* >> [*When the unclean spirit is gone out of a man, he walketh through dry places, seeking rest, finding none. <44> Then he saith, I will return into my house from whence I came out; and when he is come, he findeth it empty, swept, and garnished. <45> Then goeth he, and taketh with himself seven other spirits more wicked than himself, and they enter in and dwell there: and the last state of the man is worst than the first. Even so shall it be also unto this wicked generation.*]

<< *Galatians 5:22,23* >> [*But the fruit of the spirit is love, peace, long suffering, gentleness, goodness, faith, Meekness, temperance: against such there is no law.*]

Once we have committed ourselves to serving God, and filling our lives with spiritual activities, prayer, fellowship, and faith, we will be completely protected from demonization. Living a life means to love God and to love our fellow man. If we do not love each other, we cannot retain deliverance from evil. We must keep our minds and hearts free of evil thoughts and desires, keeping our faith strong in the Lord.

To expel demons that are tempting us into doing evil, we must always have a compassionate and loving heart, and we must be patient with each other. Remove all hate from your heart and replace it with forgiveness, wisdom, and understanding. Seek knowledge at all times.

THE TRUTH

<< *Matthew 6:14,15* >> [*For if ye forgive men their trespasses, your heavenly Father will also forgive you. <15> But if ye forgive not men their trespasses, neither will your Father forgive your trespasses.*]

<< *Amos 3:3* >> [*Can two walk together, except they be agreed?*]

<< *Matthew 18:21-35* >> [*Then came Peter to him, and said, Lord, how often shall my brother sin against me, and I forgive him? Till seven times? <22> Jesus saith unto him, I say not unto thee, Until seven times but until seventy times seven.*

<23> Therefore is the kingdom of heaven likened unto a certain king, which would take account of his servants. <24> And when he had begun to reckon, one was brought unto him, which owed him ten thousand talents. <25> But forasmuch as he had not to pay, his lord commanded him to be sold, and his wife, and children, and all that he had, and payment to be made. <26> The servant therefore fell down, and worshipped him, saying, Lord, have patience with me, and I will pay thee all. <27> Then the lord of that servant was moved with compassion, and loosed him, and forgave him the debt.

<28> But the same servant went out, and found one of his fellow servants, which owed him a hundred pence: and he laid hands on him, and took him by the throat, saying, Pay me that thou owest. <29> And his fellow servant fell down at his feet, and besought him, saying, Have patience with me, and I will pay thee all. <30> And he would not: but went and cast him into prison, till he should pay the debt.

<31> So when his fellow servants saw what was done, they were very sorry, and came and told unto their lord all that was done. <32> Then his lord, after that he had called him, said unto him, O thou wicked servant, I forgave thee all that debt, because thou desiredst me: <33> Shouldest not thou also have had compassion on thy fellow servant, even as I had pity on thee? <34> And his lord was wroth, and delivered him to the tormentors, till he should pay all that was due unto him. <35> So likewise shall my heavenly Father do also unto you, if ye from your hearts forgive not every one his brother their trespasses.]

<< *Ephesians 5:25,26* >> [*Husbands, love your wives, even as Christ also loved the church, and gave himself for it; <26> That he might sanctify and cleansed it with the washing of water by the word.*]

<< *I John 1:9-11* >> [*He that saith he is in the light and hateth his brother, is in darkness even until now. <10> He that loveth his brother abideth in the light, and there is none occasion of stumbling in him. <11> But he that hateth his brother is in darkness, and walketh in the darkness, and knoweth not whither he goeth, because that darkness hath blinded him.*]

<< *John 15:10* >> [*If ye keep my commandments, ye shall abide in my love; even as I have kept my Father's commandments, abide in his love.*]

<< *Matthew 6:21-23* >> [*For where your treasure is, there will your heart be also.*]

THE TRUTH

<< *James 1:22-25* >> [*But be ye doers of the word, and not hearers only, deceiving your own selves. <23> For if any be a hearer of the word, and not a doer, he is like unto a man beholding his natural face in a glass; <24> For he beholdeth himself, and goeth his way, and straightway forgetteth what manner of men he was. <25> But whoso looketh into the perfect law of liberty, and continueth therein, he being not a forgetful hearer, but a doer of the work, this man shall be blessed in his deed.*]

Our battle against Satan will not be in vain. The victory will be ours, and the rewards will be great:

<< *Revelation 2:7, 11, 26* >> [*He that hath an ear, let him hear what the Spirit saith unto the churches; To him that overcometh will I give to eat of the tree of life, which is in the midst of the paradise of God.*
<11>... He that hath an ear, let him hear what the Spirit saith unto the churches; He that overcometh shall not be hurt of the second death.
<26>... And he that overcometh, and keepeth my works unto the end, to him will I give power over the nations]

<< *Revelation 3:21* >> [*To him that overcometh will I grant to sit with me in my throne, even as I also overcame, and am set down with my Father in his throne.*]

<< *Revelation 21:7* >> [*He that overcometh shall inherit all things; and I will be his God, and he shall be my son.*]

Satan's World Is Doomed

Satan has dominated this world for nearly six thousand years. The end of Satan's kingdom is near. It will be within this generation. This period of time that we are now living in is known as the times of the gentiles, when heathenism has replaced the truth, and material lust has replaced love. It is a time when evil rules the earth. However, This era is quickly coming to an end. According to prophecy, the eternal kingdom of the Lord YAHAWAH is soon to be established! And the LORD YAHAWAH will restore the identity and kingdom of the original Israelites. The kingdoms of this world today belong to Satan and they will all soon be destroyed at the Second Coming of Lord YAHAWASHY, who is known as Jesus Christ!

The other nations had their rulership and kingdom; Satan gave them power and wealth in exchange for their rebellion. The gentiles wanted glory for themselves and to satisfy their own evil lusts, therefore they have conspired in league with Satan:

A) To replace the truth with false religions in order to have control over the minds of the people, making their own laws contradictory to the laws of God so as to exploit the public.
B) To replace the true God with their own images and concepts in order to have power and glory for themselves. (When people are given a false idea for God, it can easily turn them into atheists.)
C) To destroy the identity of the original Israelites because the original Israelites represent the kingdom of heaven and the glory of the true God.

There were three major gentile kingdoms prior to the present (modern) form of the Edomite Greco-Roman Empire. Nimrod started the Babylonian kingdom. Then the Media Persian Empire took over the

THE TRUTH

Babylonian Empire and ruled for about 200 years. The Greek Empire defeated the Persians. It lasted for about 300 years. And now the Roman Empire (Edomites: Europeans, Americans and all other European colony nations, etc.) has emerged from the Greeks. They have been ruling as divided groups of nations through many falls and revivals.

The Edomite and heathen rulership will end with civil war, moral, and economic collapse, coupled with chemical, biological and nuclear war. The resurrection of the truth of God, the exposing of Satan, the revelation of the identity of the original Israelites, and the Second Coming of Jesus will guarantee the absolute destruction of the gentile rulership, and the end of Edomite domination. The destiny of world history is presented here in a nutshell:

<< *Daniel 9:17,18* >> *[These great beasts which are four, are four kings, which shall arise out of the earth. But the saints of the Most High shall take the kingdom, and possess the kingdom forever and ever!]*

<< *Psalms 50:5* >> *[Gather my saints together unto me; those that have made a covenant with me by sacrifice.]*

This verse tells us whom the true saints are, the people who have made a covenant with the LORD YAHAWAH, the original Israelites. The Holy Covenants were made with Abraham, Isaac, and Jacob. Christ will reestablish the kingdom of the Hebrew Israelites after the destruction of this modern world.

The satanic realm has dominated the gentile kingdoms that have been established on this earth. The Gentiles have always rejected the true God and followed the satanic path. That is why the demons said to Jesus:

<< *Matthew 8:29* >> *[What have we to do with thee, Jesus, thou Son of God? art thou come hither to torment us before the time?]*

Clearly, this means that Satan knows that his time is limited and will soon end! The word "devil" is derived from the word diabolos, meaning deceiver. And the word "Satan" means adversary or enemy. These words could also be used to describe anyone, regardless of nationality; anyone who is either a deceiver or an enemy of the LORD YAHAWAH! Of course, there are spiritual demons too; however, when the Bible speaks in historical or prophetic terms, the word devil is often used in describing a system or power structure, like a nation under the domination of Satan. The present Greco-Roman Empire is identified as the kingdom of the Devil and Satan!

This is not to say that all of the people of that empire are devils, but that the system is controlled by the devil: educationally, socially, politically, and in all aspects. Secondly, the vast majority of the people of that system have adopted the evil ways of Satan, selling their soul. The Bible proves beyond a doubt that the Western world is the head of the present demonic kingdom:

<< *Revelation 12:3* >> *[And there appeared another wonder in heaven; and behold a great red dragon, having seven heads and ten horns, and seven crowns upon his heads.]*

This dragon beast or serpent symbolizes the gentile dominion. "Beasts" symbolize nations. In the book of Daniel, the number seven identifies the completion of the time of the gentiles. Seven always represents completion in time, as in the Creation. Therefore, this empire will exit at the end, at the completion of the time of the gentiles.

THE TRUTH

This is to occur at the end of the sixth millennium since the beginning of the creation. We are living in that time now. This beast with seven heads and ten horns represents the entire world, headed by America, under Satan. It is referring to this modern form of the Greco-Roman Empire. It began with the Greeks and will soon end in the present with the destruction of America and the other nations.

And of course we know that Biblically, ten is a symbol of division: as the ten fingers are divided between the two hands, and ten toes are divided among the two feet. In the last days, the kingdom of Satan would be strong but divided into many powerful nations, Eastern and Western. The Greco-Roman Empire consists of the entire western world, including the Europe, America, and also the colonies that come from them, as well as the nations in league with them: Asian, Eastern and Western nations. It is all really one system, one economy, and one philosophy based on greed, lies, lust, injustice, and exploitation.

No other group fits the description of the beast with seven heads and ten horns except this present divided world, led by the Euro-Caucasians, and headed by the impostor Khazars (so-called Jewish). They are originally known as the Edomites in the Bible. They are the dominant rulers of this present world, in full league with the philosophy of Satan!

The beast with seven heads and ten horns symbolizes this present form of the Greco-Roman Empire. It has no future except doom, because of the evil way in which it has been dominating the world, polluting the truth, blaspheming the name of LORD YAHAWAH, and destroying the identity of the original Israelites. It is blasphemy for them to claim themselves to be Jews, Christians, or call the Roman Empire "Holy". The Greco-Roman Empire is the source of all the filth in the world. Civilization ended with the Greco-Roman Empire!

<< Revelation 12:9 >> [And the great dragon was cast out, that old serpent, called the Devil, and Satan, which deceiveth the whole world]

The nations are beginning to wake up to the deceptions and illusions of western philosophy and religion, and are trying to cast off the yoke of colonialism and mental slavery. As the knowledge begins to increase and the light of truth is seen, the colonialist vultures and bloodsuckers are being chased out from every continent on the earth by war, terrorism, and other methods. The song of many nations today is "Yankee go Home" and every oppressed nation around the world is calling the imperialist nations "Devil" and "Satan". No other people can fit that description of the devil's children at this present time and history confirms it!

The man made religions of the world are the greatest enemy of the truth. They have been teaching lies: saying that Jesus was born December twenty-fifth for example, when the Bible confirms that Christ was born in April, and teaching that Sunday is the Sabbath when the Bible says that the Sabbath is Saturday. The Bible law says that the man is head of the woman, but this western world has given the woman the power over the man. The Bible condemns homosexuality and supports polygamy, but this society denies a man's human right to choose the number of his wives and they support homosexuality and abortion instead. The list where this society is constantly crucifying Christ and the laws of God goes on and on!

This society is the agent of Satan on this earth. This society is the Devil Lucifer. The Bible makes it clear that the name Lucifer refers to a society and people, not only a spirit being! The scriptures reveal the understanding and the proper context of the term Lucifer. The prophecies indicate that the leaders (political, religious, economic, and social) of this world are the true enemies of the LORD YAHAWAH:

<< Job 9:24 >> [The earth is given into the hands of the wicked: he covereth the faces of the judges thereof; (The modern Roman Empire is manipulating every country and leader around the world.) *if not, where, and who is he?]*

THE TRUTH

To know who the wicked are you just have to look and see who or what nation the people of the world are following... It is modern western society. Perverts lead the Western society. God says, if they are not the devil, then you tell him who the devil is! According to the Bible, they are born wicked.

>   << Psalms 58:3,4 >> [The wicked are estranged from the womb: they go astray as soon as they be born, speaking lies. Their poison is like the deaf adder that stoppeth her ear.]

The Antichrist

Every living person walking around must have flesh and skin on that flesh, and that skin has to be a certain complexion. It is wrong to picture Jesus as a European. An antichrist is simply anyone that denies the Asiatic identity of Jesus Christ and of the original Hebrew Israelites!

>   << First John 4:2,3 >> [Hereby know ye the spirit of God: Every spirit that confesses that Jesus Christ is come in the flesh is of God: And every spirit that confesseth not that Jesus Christ is come in the flesh is not of God: and this is that spirit of Antichrist, whereof ye have heard that it should come; and even now already is it in the world!]

>   << II Thessalonians 2:3,4 >> [Let no man deceive you by any means: for that day shall not come except there come a falling away first, and that man of sin be revealed, the son of perdition; who opposeth and exalteth himself above all that is called God, or that is worshipped; so that he as God sitteth in the temple of God, shewing himself that he is God.]

Even if what Jesus Christ looks like is not important, the truth is always important. To produce a false image for Christ is to tell a lie. Jesus Christ had features of the Asiatic type. Caucasian pictures are presented for God and for Jesus Christ to people all over the world. God Jesus Christ, the angels, the prophets, and the Israelites are presented in Caucasian pictures (illustrations, paintings, etc.) to people all over the world. This fact would serve to identify exactly, with a picture, who is the leading man of sin on this earth. The whole world is following the western image and philosophy. This is an act of blasphemy, because the real Jesus Christ is Asiatic! He was not a Caucasian.

>   << II Thessalonians 2:5-10 >> [Remember ye not, that, when I was yet with you, I told you these things? <6> And now ye know what withholdeth that he might be revealed in his time. <7> For the mystery of iniquity doth already work: only he who now letteth will let, until he be taken out of the way. <8> And then shall that wicked be revealed, whom the Lord shall consume with the spirit of his mouth, and shall destroy with the brightness of his coming: <9> Even him, whose coming is after the working of Satan with all power and signs and lying wonders, <10> And deceivableness of unrighteousness in them that perish; because they receive not the love of the truth, that they might be saved.]

In their religions (for example the Catholic), they call their priests "father"; the Bible says, "call no man your father that is upon the face of the earth for one is your Father that is in heaven!" Thirdly, the leaders of the world have also deceived people in their educational institutions, claiming that the universe was not created but that it is the result of a spontaneous explosion. They also deceitfully teach as their educational standard that the Lord did not create man, but that man evolved from apes. So in the place of God, these people honor their wealth, technology, and ideas; they have rebelliously replaced the word of God!

The kingdom of Satan is identified with the mark of the beast, SIX-SIX-SIX. Beast represents kingdom in the Bible. The mark of the beast, marks or identifies the philosophy of a kingdom. The mark does not refer to any specific individual, but to the entire philosophy of the western society in general.

> << *Revelation 13:14-18* >> *[...And deceiveth them that dwell on the earth by the means of those miracles which he had power to do in the sight of the beast; saying to them that dwell on the earth, that they should make an image to the beast, which had the wound by a sword, and did live. <15> And he had power to give life unto the image of the beast, that the image of the beast should both speak, and cause that as many as would not worship the image of the beast should be killed.*
>
> <16> *And he causeth all both small and great, rich and poor, free and bond, to receive a mark in their right hand, or in their foreheads: <17> Here is Wisdom, Let him that hath understanding count the number of the beast: for it is the number of a man; and his number is Six hundred threescore and six.]*

The number is the number of a man, not a spirit. A score is twenty, and three scores is sixty (666). Six is a number that represents man because on the sixth day God made man (Genesis 1:26). Three is a number that identifies God and Jesus. Because Christ was resurrected after three days in the tomb, as a sign of his divinity, (Matthew 12:40). So therefore, three sixes is a man who is claiming himself to be the god of the Bible. The mark was received on the forehead, which is where the brain is. To receive the mark of the beast in your forehead means to accept their philosophy into your mind and believing in it. Receiving the mark in your right hand means to live, work, and support that philosophy. This means rejecting the Bible, practicing a philosophy of being self centered, and motivated by lust and greed; instead of a life centered around the Almighty God Lord YAHAWAH.

They "made and image to the Beast". For centuries, all over the world, Caucasians have been claiming to be Jews and Christians. But, the original Jews and Christians are people of Asiatic descent. Some Caucasians have also gone around the world, making and displaying their own European images and statues as Jesus and God. It is clear that according to the Bible and history, that not one of the ancestors of Jesus was European. The Caucasians have claimed to be the Jews, Christ, the angels and have even set up their picture as God all over the world. Therefore, the Western world and its allies have to be the red dragon with seven heads and ten horns, having the mark Six, six, six. The Western world under Satan is the leader of this symbolic Beast, according to the Bible!

> << *Revelation 3:9* >> *[Behold, I will make them of the synagogue of Satan, which say they are Jews, and are not but do lie; behold, I will make them to come and worship before thy feet, and to know that I have loved thee.]*

The Most High was prophesying concerning this modern day Greco-Roman Empire; also known prophetically as Babylon, Egypt, Sodom and Gomorra, Lucifer. The word Lucifer means brightness, it occurs as such once in the Bible; to symbolize a nation only, a nation that is damned and doomed.

THE TRUTH

<< Isaiah 14:1-24 >> [*For the Lord will have mercy on Jacob, and will yet choose Israel, and set them in their own land: and the strangers shall be joined with them, and they shall cleave to the house of Jacob. <2> And the people shall take them and bring them to their place: and the house of Israel shall possess them in the land of the Lord for servants and handmaids: and they shall take them captives, whose captives they were: and they shall rule over their oppressors.* (Everyone who had us as slaves will become our slaves in the Kingdom of Heaven: an eye for an eye.)

<3> And it shall come to past in the day that the Lord shall give thee rest from thy sorrow, (speaking to the Israelites about the last days, when Christ would restore the kingdom of heaven; see verse one.) *and from thy fear, and from the hard bondage wherein thou was made to serve,* (the slavery of the Asiatic people in the colonial world) *<4> That thou shalt take up this proverb against the king of Babylon,* (The Euro-American world is the modern Babylon, Egypt, Sodom and Gomorra according to Revelation and other prophecies. The subject here is clearly a nation and people, not the spiritual demon, Satan) *and say, how hath the oppressor ceased! The golden city ceased!*

<5> The Lord hath broken the staff of the wicked, and the scepter of the rulers (The Western European nations and other colonial powers that are in league with them have been loosing control of their empire around the world.) *<6> He who smote the people in wrath with a continual stroke, he that ruled the nations in anger* (the hate, terror, slavery, racism, injustice, and exploitation) *is persecuted and none hindereth. <7> The whole earth is at rest, and is quiet: they break forth into singing. <8> Yea, the fir trees* (the trees again symbolize nations) *rejoice at thee, and the cedars of Lebanon, saying, since thou art laid down, no feller is come up against us.*

<9> Hell from beneath is moved for thee to meet thee at thy coming: (now it is their time to start catching hell; hell in this case is clearly a condition on the earth) *it stirreth up the dead for thee, even all the chief ones of the earth; it hath raised up from their thrones all the kings of the nations. <10> All they shall speak and say unto thee, Art thou also become weak as we? Art thou become like unto us? <11> Thy pump is brought down to the grave and the noise of thy viols: the worm is spread under thee, and the worms cover thee.*

Corruption is everywhere in the political, economic, religious and educational system of the Euro-American world today. Homosexuality and abortion is exploding, morality is nonexistent in western society. The environment is in a catastrophic state. The economic system is a time bomb ready to collapse.

<12> How art thou fallen from heaven O Lucifer, son of the morning! (The Greco-Roman Empire is falling from their "heaven" or rulership position. They have been the stars of the earth.) *How art thou cut to the ground, which didst weaken the nations!*

On a global scale, the Euro-Americans are the primary people to have lead in the evil to colonized and perverted the civilizations, destroyed the environment, and blasphemed against God, Christ, the angels, the Israelites, and the Bible.

<13> For Thou hast said in thine heart, I will ascend into heaven, I will exalt my throne above the stars of God: (with their space program) *<14> I will sit also upon the mount of the congregation, in the sides of the north; I will be like the Most High.* (They Colonized the Americas and Palestine, and are maliciously promoting the Khazar converts to be Jews. They have deceived the world into accepting a Caucasian image for God, and Caucasians as the Jews.) *<15> Yet thou shalt be brought down to hell, to the sides of the pit.*

<16> They that see thee shall narrowly look upon thee (If Lucifer was referring to a spirit you could not look and see him with your eyes, this is a nation on this earth), *and consider thee, saying, Is this the man that made the earth to tremble, that did shake kingdoms;* (He is called a man, because Lucifer refers to people), *<17> That made the world as a wilderness* (Because of greed, they have polluted the air, the ocean, and caused extinction of many plants and animals, promoted homosexuality and abortion of babies, mass genocide), *and destroyed the cities thereof; that open not the house of his prisoner?]*

The Israelites are still in physical as well as mental slavery, prisoners in fear, with no education, no justice and no respect. The system has stolen and destroyed the Hebrew culture, the minds, the history, the identity and nationality of the original Hebrew Israelites who are derogatorily being called minorities, Negroes, Hispanics, Blacks and Indians today.

[<18> All the kings of the nations, even all of them, lie in glory, every one in his own house. <19> But thou art cast out of the grave like an abominable branch, and as the raiment of those that are slain, thrust through with the sword, that go down to the stones of the pit; as a carcass trodden under feet. <20> Thou shalt not be joined to them in burial, because thou hast destroyed thy land, and slain thy people. The seed of evildoers shall never be renowned.

<21> Prepare a slaughter for his children for the iniquity of their fathers; (Do you know what that means??) *that they do not rise, nor possess the land, nor fill the face of the world with cities. <22> For I will rise up against them, saith the Lord of hosts, and cut off from Babylon: the name, and remnant, and son, and nephew, saith the Lord.]*

The Bible reveals clearly that the word Lucifer was used only as a title referring to an empire symbolically called Babylon. Prophetically this is the modern Greco-Roman Empire of Euro-America and its allies. A spirit does not have sons and nephews, or land; therefore, Lucifer has to be referring to people. As you read further it becomes clear that Lucifer refers to the modern Euro-American Roman Empire, which is destined for destruction.

<< Isaiah 14:23,24 >> [I will also make it a possession for the bittern, and pools of water: and I will sweep it with the bosom of destruction, saith the Lord of hosts. (There is no future for this perverted society, the stage is being set up for the doom of judgement day) *<24> The Lord of hosts hath sworn, saying, Surely as I have thought, so shall it come to pass; and as I have purposed, so shall it stand!]*

Other scriptures also prove that it is nations and people who are the agents of Satan the Devil and who are deceiving the world and who are claiming the glory of God for themselves. For example, the Prince of Tyrus is another prophetic representation of the modern Edomite kingdom, consisting of Europe, her colonies, America, and other nations in league with them.

<< Ezekiel 28:2,6-10 >> [Son of man, say unto the prince of Tyrus, Thus saith the Lord God Because thine heart is lifted up, and thou hast said, I am a god, I sit in the seat of God, in the midst of the seas; yet thou art a man, and not god, though thou set thine heart as the heart of a god.]

As a nation, only the Edomites (Caucasians) have set up their own image as the God of the Bible, Jesus Christ, the prophets, and the angels of the Bible. Nobody else is doing this, therefore, we see clearly that this prophecy has to be referring to the present Euro-American, Greco-Roman Empire. Their mentality is explained in the following verses:

<6> [Therefore thus saith the LORD YAHAWAH; Because thou hast set thine heart as the heart of god (thinking they are superior to other people*); <7> Behold, therefore I will bring strangers upon thee, the terrible of the nations* (terrorists*): and they shall draw their swords against the beauty of thy wisdom, and they shall defile thy brightness. <8> They shall bring thee down to the pit, and thou shalt die the deaths of them that are slain in the midst of the seas.*

<9> Wilt thou yet say before him that slayeth thee, I am god? But thou shalt be a man, and no god in the hand of him that slayeth thee! I have spoken it, saith the LORD YAHAWAH <10> Thou shalt die the deaths of the uncircumcised by the hand of strangers: for I have spoken it saith the Lord God.

<11> Moreover the word of the Lord came unto me, saying, <12> Son of man, take up a lamentation upon the king of Tyrus, and say unto him, Thus saith the Lord God; Thou sealest up the sum, full of wisdom, and perfect in beauty. <13> Thou hast been in Eden the garden of God; every precious stone was thy covering, the sardius, topaz, and the diamond, the beryl, the onyx, and the jasper, the sapphire, the emerald, and the carbuncle, and gold: the workmanship of thy tabrets and of thy pipes was prepared in thee in the day that thou wast created.

<14> Thou art the anointed cherub that covereth; and I have set thee so: thou wast upon the holy mountain of God; thou hast walked up and down in the midst of the stones of fire. <15> Thou wast perfect in thy ways from the day that thou wast created till iniquity was found in thee. <16> By the multitude of thy merchandise they have filled the midst of thee with violence, and thou hast sinned: therefore I will destroy thee. O covering cherub, from the midst of the stones of fire.

<17> Thine heart was lifted up (proud minded) *because of thy beauty, thou hast corrupted thy wisdom by reason of thy brightness: I will cast thee to the ground, I will lay thee before kings, that they may behold thee. <18> Thou hast defiled thy sanctuaries by the multitude of thine iniquities, by the iniquities of thy traffic; therefore will I bring forth a fire from the midst of thee, it shall devour thee, and I will bring thee to ashes upon the earth in the sight of all them that behold thee. <19> All they that know thee among the people shall be astonished at thee, thou shall be a terror, and never shalt thou be any more.]*

THE TRUTH

The time has now arrived for the wicked rulers of this society to begin paying in the flesh for blaspheming and teaching lies against the Bible. Because these social and historical events have been unfolding exactly as predicted, we are able to identify who the terms Lucifer, the Devil, and Satan refer to on this earth! And that is how we know that the Bible is true, because all of these things are happening exactly the way that the Bible said they would. Judgment Day is coming for this world and there will be no escape:

> << John 12:31 >> [Now is the judgment of this world: now shall the prince of this world be cast out.]

> << Revelation 12:9 >> [And the great dragon was cast out, that old serpent, called the Devil, and Satan, which deceiveth the whole world: he was cast out into the earth and his angels with him.]

> << Revelation 20:10 >> [And the devil that deceived them was cast into the lake of fire and brimstone, where the beast and the false prophet are, and shall be tormented day and night forever and ever.]

We have discovered what "Antichrist" is referring to: all people that make up lies about the existence of, or misrepresent the physical features of the living Jesus Christ, and anyone who rebels against the doctrines of the Bible. Only an antichrist would tell you that Christ had no color, and/or create a non-Asiatic image of Christ. If the appearance of Christ did not matter, then why is it that they have been fanatically displaying European images of Christ all over the world?

It has been made clear that Satan the Devil is not an abstraction. Satan is a real entity, acting as his own person. Also, the following terms refer to people upon the earth who are acting as agents of Satan, and they are not always referring to spiritual beings: Devil, Satan, Lucifer, Six-Six-Six, The Beast, and Antichrist. The Devil is anyone who deceives people from following the Lord God YAHAWAH. The word Satan can also be used to describe any person who is an enemy of the Lord God YAHAWAH. The word Lucifer can also refer to anyone who tries to exalt himself or herself above the Lord God YAHAWAH. "666" is any person who seeks to replace God or God's laws, or believes that he is the god. And the Antichrist is anyone who denies that Christ came in the flesh as an Asiatic man!

The scriptures reveal Satan the Devil as a defeated foe whose days are numbered. The scriptures also teach us how to identify and defeat Satan in spiritual warfare. The Lord God YAHAWAH promises us salvation, joy, eternal life, and the kingdom of heaven as our reward for resisting Satan. Those that follow the ways of Satan will face the judgment and eternal hell and damnation!

THE TRUTH

SALVATION

The Lord YAHAWAH created mankind to share his love with. True love is the reason why the Lord YAHAWAH desires to save mankind from judgement, doomsday and eternal suffering. Mankind has rejected the laws of God and abandoned the true God. As a result of this decision, people are suffering under all sorts of captivity, fear, ignorance, oppression and pain. The world is in a state of physical, moral, and spiritual decay and chaos. From His great love, the Lord YAHAWAH has provided us a way to be redeemed, a way for mankind to be readopted into the family of God. He offered us a Savior, The Lord Mashayak Yahawashy (Jesus Christ), the intercessor whose life was given as atonement for our sins.

<< John 3:16 >> [For God so love the world, that he gave his only begotten son, that whosoever believeth in him should not perish, but have everlasting life.]

The Salvation offered by the Lord God YAHAWAH is twofold: the first promise is redemption through the atonement made for us by Jesus Christ at his First Coming, through his death and resurrection. The Second promise of the Lord YAHAWAH is the restoration of the original twelve tribes of Israel as the Kingdom of Heaven on the earth at the Second Coming of Jesus Christ. The kingdom of heaven will be ruled by Christ and the twelve tribes of Israel. The Israelites will rule all nations and people according to the laws and judgements of YAHAWAH. Christ will come as the Judge, the Avenger, the Deliverer, the King of kings and Lord of lords.

All nations are commanded to return to God through faith in Jesus Christ according to the Bible. The people that do will have mercy, the ones that rebel will face judgement and hell. There is no other way to escape the coming destruction, the day of judgement, and the everlasting torment of hell. God offers the chance for salvation to all nations and people that would obey and serve him.

The following scriptures reveal that God is not partial; he loves and blesses all people and nations that keep his commandments.

<< Genesis 12:3 >> [And I will bless them that bless thee (the Israelites)*, and curse him that curseth thee: and in thee shall all families of the earth be blessed.]*

<< Exodus 12:48,49 >> [And when a stranger shall sojourn with thee, and will keep the passover to the LORD, let all his males be circumcised, and then let him come near and keep it; and he shall be as one that is born in the land: for no uncircumcised person shall eat thereof. <49> One law shall be to him that is homeborn, and unto the stranger that sojourneth among you.]

<< Ezekiel 47:22>> [And it shall come to pass, that ye shall divide it by lot for an inheritance unto you, and to the strangers that sojourn among you, which shall beget children among you: and they shall be unto you as born in the country among the children of Israel; they shall have inheritance with you among the tribes of Israel.]

<< 1 Kings 8:41-43 >> [Moreover concerning a stranger, that is not of thy people Israel, but cometh out of a far country for thy name's sake; 42 (For they shall hear of thy

great name, and of thy strong hand, and of thy stretched out arm;) when he shall come and pray toward this house; 43 Hear thou in heaven thy dwelling place, and do according to all that the stranger calleth to thee for: that all people of the earth may know thy name, to fear thee, as do thy people Israel; and that they may know that this house, which I have builded, is called by thy name.]

<< *Jeremiah 39:16* >> *[Go and speak to Ebedmelech the Ethiopian, saying, Thus saith the LORD of hosts, the God of Israel; Behold, I will bring my words upon this city for evil, and not for good; and they shall be accomplished in that day before thee. 17 But I will deliver thee in that day, saith the LORD: and thou shalt not be given into the hand of the men of whom thou art afraid. 18 For I will surely deliver thee, and thou shalt not fall by the sword, but thy life shall be for a prey unto thee: because thou hast put thy trust in me, saith the LORD.]*

<< *Ruth 1:4* >> *And they took them wives of the women of Moab; the name of the one was Orpah, and the name of the other Ruth: and they dwelled there about ten years.*

<< *Ruth 1:16* >> *And Ruth* (The Moabitest woman) *said, Intreat me not to leave thee, or to return from following after thee: for whither thou goest, I will go; and where thou lodgest, I will lodge: thy people shall be my people, and thy God my God*

<< *Ruth 2:12* >> *The LORD recompense thy work, and a full reward be given thee of the LORD God of Israel, under whose wings thou*(The Moabitest woman) *art come to trust.*

<< *Ruth 3:11* >> *And now, my daughter* (The Moabitest woman), *fear not; I will do to thee all that thou requirest: for all the city of my people doth know that thou art a virtuous woman.*

<< *Ruth 4:11*>> *And all the people that were in the gate, and the elders, said, We are witnesses. The LORD make the woman* (The Moabitest woman) *that is come into thine house like Rachel and like Leah, which two did build the house of Israel: and do thou worthily in Ephratah, and be famous in Bethlehem.*

<< *Numbers 12:1-11* >> *[And Miriam and Aaron spake against Moses because of the Ethiopian woman whom he had married: for he had married an Ethiopian woman. 2 And they said, Hath the LORD indeed spoken only by Moses? hath he not spoken also by us? And the LORD heard it. 3 (Now the man Moses was very meek, above all the men which were upon the face of the earth.) 4 And the LORD spake suddenly unto Moses, and unto Aaron, and unto Miriam, Come out ye three unto the tabernacle of the congregation. And they three came out.*
5 And the LORD came down in the pillar of the cloud, and stood in the door of the tabernacle, and called Aaron and Miriam: and they both came forth. 6 And he said, Hear now my words: If there be a prophet among you, I the LORD will make myself

known unto him in a vision, and will speak unto him in a dream. 7 My servant Moses is not so, who is faithful in all mine house. 8 With him will I speak mouth to mouth, even apparently, and not in dark speeches; and the similitude of the LORD shall he behold: wherefore then were ye not afraid to speak against my servant Moses?

9 And the anger of the LORD was kindled against them; and he departed. 10 And the cloud departed from off the tabernacle; and, behold, Miriam became leprous, white as snow: and Aaron looked upon Miriam, and, behold, she was leprous. 11 And Aaron said unto Moses, Alas, my lord, I beseech thee, lay not the sin upon us, wherein we have done foolishly, and wherein we have sinned.]

<< Matthew 28:19,20 >> *[Go ye therefore, and teach all nations, baptizing them in the name of the Father, and of the Son, and of the Holy Ghost: <20> Teaching them to observe all things whatsoever I have commanded you: and, lo, I am with you alway, even unto the end of the world. Amen.]*

<< Ephesians 3:6 >> *[That the Gentiles should be fellowheirs, and of the same body, and partakers of his promise in Christ by the gospel]*

<< 1 John 2:2 >> *[And he is the propitiation for our sins: and not for ours only, but also for the sins of the whole world.]*

<< John 1:11,12 >> *[He came unto his own, and his own received him not. <12> But as many as received him, to them gave he power to become the sons of God, even to them that believe on his name.]*

<< Matthew 3:9 >> *[And think not to say within yourselves, We have Abraham to our father: for I say unto you, that God is able of these stones to raise up children unto Abraham.]*

<< Matthew 8:10-12 >> *[When Jesus heard it, he marvelled, and said to them that followed, Verily I say unto you, I have not found so great faith, no, not in Israel. <11> And I say unto you, That many shall come from the east and west, and shall sit down with Abraham, and Isaac, and Jacob, in the kingdom of heaven. <12> But the children of the kingdom shall be cast out into outer darkness: there shall be weeping and gnashing of teeth.]*

<< Luke 10:29-37 >> *[But he, willing to justify himself, said unto Jesus, And who is my neighbour? 30 And Jesus answering said, A certain man went down from Jerusalem to Jericho, and fell among thieves, which stripped him of his raiment, and wounded him, and departed, leaving him half dead. 31 And by chance there came down a certain priest that way: and when he saw him, he passed by on the other side. 32 And likewise a Levite, when he was at the place, came and looked on him, and passed by on the other side.*

33 But a certain Samaritan, as he journeyed, came where he was: and when he saw him, he had compassion on him, 34 And went to him, and bound up his wounds, pouring in oil and wine, and set him on his own beast, and brought him to an inn, and took care of him. 35 And on the morrow when he departed, he took out two pence, and gave them to the host, and said unto him, Take care of him; and whatsoever thou spendest more, when I come again, I will repay thee.

36 Which now of these three, thinkest thou, was neighbour unto him that fell among the thieves? 37 And he said, He that shewed mercy on him. Then said Jesus unto him, Go, and do thou likewise.]

<< *Galatians 3:28,29* >> *[There is neither Jew nor Greek, there is neither bond nor free, there is neither male nor female: for ye are all one in Christ Jesus. <29> And if ye be Christ's, then are ye Abraham's seed, and heirs according to the promise.]*

<< *Revelation 7:9,10* >> *[After this I beheld, and, lo, a great multitude, which no man could number, of all nations, and kindreds, and people, and tongues, stood before the throne, and before the Lamb, clothed with white robes, and palms in their hands; <10> And cried with a loud voice, saying, Salvation to our God which sitteth upon the throne, and unto the Lamb.]*

<< *Deuteronomy 23:7* >> *[Thou shalt not abhor an Edomite; for he is thy brother: thou shalt not abhor an Egyptian; because thou wast a stranger in his land.]*

<< *Romans 9:24-26* >> *[Even us, whom he hath called, not of the Jews only, but also of the Gentiles? <25> As he saith also in Osee, I will call them my people, which were not my people; and her beloved, which was not beloved. <26> And it shall come to pass, that in the place where it was said unto them, Ye are not my people; there shall they be called the children of the living God.]*

To receive the salvation that is promised by God we have to first realize that God created us because he wants to share his love and goodness with us. Our wickedness and sins have separated us from God. We must realize and confess with our mouth that we are all sinners who have forsaken the commandments of God, and pray to God for forgiveness. If we can be humble enough to accept this truth, only then are we able to begin our journey to salvation. To receive the salvation of God we must confess to God in prayer and repent of our sins. We must also accept Mashayak Yahawashy (Jesus Christ) as our Lord and Savior, are baptized, and follow the commandments of the Bible. Before we can receive salvation and communion with the Lord God YAHAWAH, our sins need to be atoned for and forgiven.

We must confess to the fact that we are sinners.

<< *Romans 6:23*>> *[For the wages of sin is death; but the gift of God is eternal life through Jesus Christ our Lord.]*

<< *Romans 5:8* >> *[But God commendeth his love toward us, in that, while we were yet sinners, Christ died for us.]*

THE TRUTH

<< Romans 3:22,23 >> *[Even the righteousness of God which is by faith of Jesus Christ unto all and upon all them that believe: for there is no difference: <23> For all have sinned, and come short of the glory of God.]*

<< Romans 3:10 >> *[As it is written, There is none righteous, no, not one.]*

<< 1 John 5:19 >> *[And we know that we are of God, and the whole world lieth in wickedness.]*

We cannot save ourselves, a price must be paid for our sins.

<< Isaiah 53:6 >> *[All we like sheep have gone astray; we have turned every one to his own way; and the LORD hath laid on him the iniquity of us all.]*

<< 1 Timothy 1:15 >> *[This is a faithful saying, and worthy of all acceptation, that Christ Jesus came into the world to save sinners; of whom I am chief.]*

<< Matthew 26:28 >> *[For this is my blood of the New Testament, which is shed for many for the remission of sin.]*

<< Hebrews 9:19-28 >> *[For when Moses had spoken every precept to all the people according to the law, he took the blood of calves and of goats, with water, and scarlet wool, and hyssop, and sprinkled both the book, and all the people, <20> Saying, This is the blood of the testament which God hath enjoined unto you. <21> Moreover he sprinkled with blood both the tabernacle, and all the vessels of the ministry. 22 And almost all things are by the law purged with blood; and without shedding of blood is no remission. <23> It was therefore necessary that the patterns of things in the heavens should be purified with these; but the heavenly things themselves with better sacrifices than these. <24> For Christ is not entered into the holy places made with hands, which are the figures of the true; but into heaven itself, now to appear in the presence of God for us: <25> Nor yet that he should offer himself often, as the high priest entereth into the holy place every year with blood of others; <26> For then must he often have suffered since the foundation of the world: but now once in the end of the world hath he appeared to put away sin by the sacrifice of himself. <27> And as it is appointed unto men once to die, but after this the judgment: <28> So Christ was once offered to bear the sins of many; and unto them that look for him shall he appear the second time without sin unto salvation.]*

<< 1 Peter 2:24 >> *[Whom his own self bears our sins in his own body on the tree, that we, being dead to sins, should live unto righteousness: by whose stripes ye were healed.]*

<< John 19:30 >> *[When Jesus therefore had received the vinegar, he said, It is finished: and he bowed his head, and gave up the ghost.]*

<< *Mark 15:38*>> [*And the veil of the temple was rent in twain from the top to the bottom.*]

<< *2 Corinthians 5:19-21* >> [*To wit, that God was in Christ, reconciling the world unto himself, not imputing their trespasses unto them; and hath committed unto us the word of reconciliation. <20> Now then we are ambassadors for Christ, as though God did beseech you by us: we pray you in Christ's stead, be ye reconciled to God. <21> For he hath made him to be sin for us, who knew no sin; that we might be made the righteousness of God in him.*]

We must accept the sacrifice of Yahawashy (Jesus Christ) as the atonement for our sins.

<< *Romans 5:7-21* >> [*For scarcely for a righteous man will one die: yet peradventure for a good man some would even dare to die. <8> But God commendeth his love toward us, in that, while we were yet sinners, Christ died for us. <9> Much more then, being now justified by his blood, we shall be saved from wrath through him. <10> For if, when we were enemies, we were reconciled to God by the death of his Son, much more, being reconciled, we shall be saved by his life. <11> And not only so, but we also joy in God through our Lord Jesus Christ, by whom we have now received the atonement.*

<12> Wherefore, as by one man sin entered into the world, and death by sin; and so death passed upon all men, for that all have sinned: <13> For until the law sin was in the world: but sin is not imputed when there is no law. <14> Nevertheless death reigned from Adam to Moses, even over them that had not sinned after the similitude of Adam's transgression, who is the figure of him that was to come. <15> But not as the offence, so also is the free gift. For if through the offence of one many be dead, much more the grace of God, and the gift by grace, which is by one man, Jesus Christ, hath abounded unto many. <16> And not as it was by one that sinned, so is the gift: for the judgment was by one to condemnation, but the free gift is of many offences unto justification. <17> For if by one man's offence death reigned by one; much more they which receive abundance of grace and of the gift of righteousness shall reign in life by one, Jesus Christ.

<18> Therefore as by the offence of one judgment came upon all men to condemnation; even so by the righteousness of one the free gift came upon all men unto justification of life. <19> For as by one man's disobedience many were made sinners, so by the obedience of one shall many be made righteous. <20> Moreover the law entered, that the offence might abound. But where sin abounded, grace did much more abound: <21> That as sin hath reigned unto death, even so might grace reign through righteousness unto eternal life by Jesus Christ our Lord.]

<< *Romans 2:13* >> [*For not the hearers of the law are just before God, but the doers of the law shall be justified.*]

<< *James 2:17* >> [*Even so faith, if it hath not works, is dead, being alone.*]

THE TRUTH

<< Romans 5:9>> [Much more then, being now justified by his blood, we shall be saved from wrath through him.]

<< 1 Corinthians 15:3,4 >> [For I delivered unto you first of all that which I also received, how that Christ died for our sins according to the scriptures; <4> And that he was buried, and that he rose again the third day according to the scriptures.]

<< Acts 4:10-12 >> [Be it known unto you all, and to all the people of Israel, that by the name of Jesus Christ of Nazareth, whom ye crucified, whom God raised from the dead, even by him doth this man stand here before you whole. <11> This is the stone which was set at nought of you builders, which is become the head of the corner. <12> Neither is there salvation in any other: for there is none other name under heaven given among men, whereby we must be saved.]

<< John 14:6 >> [Jesus saith unto him, I am the way, the truth, and the life: no man cometh unto the Father, but by me.]

<< John 11:25-27 >> [Jesus said unto her, I am the resurrection, and the life: he that believeth in me, though he were dead, yet shall he live: <26> And whosoever liveth and believeth in me shall never die. Believest thou this? <27> She saith unto him, Yea, Lord: I believe that thou art the Christ, the Son of God, which should come into the world.]

<< Revelation 3:20 >> [Behold, I stand at the door, and knock: if any man hear my voice, and open the door, I will come in to him, and will sup with him, and he with me.]

<< John 1:12 >> [But as many as received him, to them gave he power to become the sons of God, even to them that believe on his name.]

<< Galatians 2:20 >> [I am crucified with Christ: nevertheless I live; yet not I, but Christ liveth in me: and the life which I now live in the flesh I live by the faith of the Son of God, who loved me, and gave himself for me.]

<< 1 Peter 3:18 >> [For Christ also hath once suffered for sins, the just for the unjust, that he might bring us to God, being put to death in the flesh, but quickened by the Spirit.]

Baptism is required

<< Romans 6:1-8>> [What shall we say then? Shall we continue in sin, that grace may abound? <2> God forbid. How shall we, that are dead to sin, live any longer therein? <3> Know ye not, that so many of us as were baptized into Jesus Christ were baptized into his death? <4> Therefore we are buried with him by baptism into death: that like as Christ was raised up from the dead by the glory of the Father, even so we also should walk in newness of life. <5> For if we have been planted together in the likeness of his

death, we shall be also in the likeness of his resurrection: <6> Knowing this, that our old man is crucified with him, that the body of sin might be destroyed, that henceforth we should not serve sin. <7> For he that is dead is freed from sin. <8> Now if we be dead with Christ, we believe that we shall also live with him.]

<< John 3:3-6 >> *[Jesus answered and said unto him, Verily, verily, I say unto thee, Except a man be born again, he cannot see the kingdom of God. <4> Nicodemus saith unto him, How can a man be born when he is old? Can he enter the second time into his mother's womb, and be born? <5> Jesus answered, Verily, verily, I say unto thee, Except a man be born of water and of the Spirit, he cannot enter into the kingdom of God. <6> That which is born of the flesh is flesh; and that which is born of the Spirit is spirit.]*

<< Romans 10:9-13 >> *[That if thou shalt confess with thy mouth the Lord Jesus, and shalt believe in thine heart that God hath raised him from the dead, thou shalt be saved. <10> For with the heart man believeth unto righteousness; and with the mouth confession is made unto salvation. <11> For the scripture saith, Whosoever believeth on him shall not be ashamed. <12> For there is no difference between the Jew and the Greek: for the same Lord over all is rich unto all that call upon him. <13> For whosoever shall call upon the name of the Lord shall be saved.]*

<< Mark 11:30 >> *[The baptism of John, was it from heaven, or of men? Answer me. <31> And they reasoned with themselves, saying, If we shall say, From heaven; he will say, Why then did ye not believe him?]*

<< Mark 1:4 >> *[John did baptize in the wilderness, and preach the baptism of repentance for the remission of sins.]*

<< Luke 7:29 >> *[And all the people that heard him, and the publicans, justified God, being baptized with the baptism of John.]*

<< Luke 3:7 >> *[Then said he to the multitude that came forth to be baptized of him, O generation of vipers, who hath warned you to flee from the wrath to come?]*

<< Luke 7:29,30 >> *[And all the people that heard him, and the publicans, justified God, being baptized with the baptism of John. <30> But the Pharisees and lawyers rejected the counsel of God against themselves, being not baptized of him.]*

<< Acts 19:4,5 >> *[Then said Paul, John verily baptized with the baptism of repentance, saying unto the people, that they should believe on him which should come after him, that is, on Christ Jesus. <5> When they heard this, they were baptized in the name of the Lord Jesus.]*

THE TRUTH

<< Luke 3:16 >> [John answered, saying unto them all, I indeed baptize you with water; but one mightier than I cometh, the latchet of whose shoes I am not worthy to unloose: he shall baptize you with the Holy Ghost and with fire.]

<< Mark 10:38-39 >> [But Jesus said unto them, Ye know not what ye ask: can ye drink of the cup that I drink of? and be baptized with the baptism that I am baptized with? <39> And they said unto him, We can. And Jesus said unto them, Ye shall indeed drink of the cup that I drink of; and with the baptism that I am baptized withal shall ye be baptized.]

<< Colossians 2:11-17 >> [In whom also ye are circumcised with the circumcision made without hands, in putting off the body of the sins of the flesh by the circumcision of Christ: <12> Buried with him in baptism, wherein also ye are risen with him through the faith of the operation of God, who hath raised him from the dead. <13> And you, being dead in your sins and the uncircumcision of your flesh, hath he quickened together with him, having forgiven you all trespasses; <14> Blotting out the handwriting of ordinances that was against us, which was contrary to us, and took it out of the way, nailing it to his cross; <15> And having spoiled principalities and powers, he made a shew of them openly, triumphing over them in it. <16> Let no man therefore judge you in meat, or in drink, or in respect of an holy day, or of the new moon, or of the sabbath days: <17> Which are a shadow of things to come; but the body is of Christ.]

<< Mark 16:15-18 >> [And he said unto them, Go ye into all the world, and preach the gospel to every creature. <16> He that believeth and is baptized shall be saved; but he that believeth not shall be damned. <17> And these signs shall follow them that believe; In my name shall they cast out devils; they shall speak with new tongues; <18> They shall take up serpents; and if they drink any deadly thing, it shall not hurt them; they shall lay hands on the sick, and they shall recover.]

<< Acts 8:12-17 >> [But when they believed Philip preaching the things concerning the kingdom of God, and the name of Jesus Christ, they were baptized, both men and women. <13> Then Simon himself believed also: and when he was baptized, he continued with Philip, and wondered, beholding the miracles and signs which were done. <14> Now when the apostles which were at Jerusalem heard that Samaria had received the word of God, they sent unto them Peter and John: <15> Who, when they were come down, prayed for them, that they might receive the Holy Ghost: <16> For as yet he was fallen upon none of them: only they were baptized in the name of the Lord Jesus. <17> Then laid they their hands on them, and they received the Holy Ghost.]

<< Acts 8:36-38 >> [And as they went on their way, they came unto a certain water: and the eunuch said, See, here is water; what doth hinder me to be baptized? <37> And Philip said, If thou believest with all thine heart, thou mayest. And he answered and said, I believe that Jesus Christ is the Son of God. <38> And he commanded the chariot to

stand still: and they went down both into the water, both Philip and the eunuch; and he baptized him.]

<< 1 Corinthians 12:13 >> *[For by one Spirit are we all baptized into one body, whether we be Jews or Gentiles, whether we be bond or free; and have been all made to drink into one Spirit.]*

<< Acts 3:19 >> *[Repent ye therefore, and be converted, that your sins may be blotted out, when the times of refreshing shall come from the presence of the Lord.]*

<< Acts 2:37-39 >> *[Now when they heard this, they were pricked in their hearts, and said unto Peter and to the rest of the apostles, Men and brethren, what shall we do? <38> Then Peter said unto them, Repent, and be baptized every one of you in the name of Jesus Christ for the remission of sins, and ye shall receive the gift of the Holy Ghost. <39> For the promise is unto you, and to your children, and to all that are afar off, even as many as the Lord our God shall call.]*

Repent and surrender to the Lord YAHAWAH through Christ.

<< Ephesians 2:8,9 >> *[For by grace are ye saved through faith; and that not of yourselves: it is the gift of God: <9> Not of works, lest any man should boast.]*

<< Ephesians 4:1-6 >> *[therefore, the prisoner of the Lord, beseech you that ye walk worthy of the vocation wherewith ye are called, <2> With all lowliness and meekness, with long suffering, forbearing one another in love; <3> Endeavouring to keep the unity of the Spirit in the bond of peace. <4> There is one body, and one Spirit, even as ye are called in one hope of your calling; <5> One Lord, one faith, one baptism, <6> One God and Father of all, who is above all, and through all, and in you all.]*

<< 1 John 5:18 >> *[We know that whosoever is born of God sinneth not; but he that is begotten of God keepeth himself, and that wicked one toucheth him not.]*

<< Philippians 2:12 >> *[Wherefore, my beloved, as ye have always obeyed, not as in my presence only, but now much more in my absence, work out your own salvation with fear and trembling.]*

<< Galatians 5:22-25 >> *[But the fruit of the Spirit is love, joy, peace, long suffering, gentleness, goodness, faith, <23> Meekness, temperance: against such there is no law. <24> And they that are Christ's have crucified the flesh with the affections and lusts. <25> If we live in the Spirit, let us also walk in the Spirit.]*

<< Matthew 28:19 >> *[Go ye therefore, and teach all nations, baptizing them in the name of the Father, and of the Son, and of the Holy Ghost.]*

THE TRUTH

Restoration of the Hebrew Israelites

All nations have been enjoying life in their own country, having their own land and rulership, except for the original Hebrew Israelites. The Israelites have been scattered all over the earth for over two thousand years. One of the main mission objectives of Jesus Christ is the reestablishment of the Israelite nation and the identity of its people. When the Israelites were delivered out of Egypt the Lord had accepted the blood of the Passover Lamb as the price of their redemption. But the blood of Jesus is the actual atonement that guarantees the reestablishment of the Israelites as a kingdom!

<< *Exodus 12:43* >> [*And the Lord said unto Moses and Aaron, this is the ordinance of the Passover: there shall no stranger eat thereof!*]

Misusing the Bible, this society's religion teaches that Christ died for the whole world, without mentioning the fact that part of his mission was to lay the foundation for the reestablishment of the original Hebrew Israelites. Christ died for the world, but what does the scripture mean by the word "world"? The word "world" here was translated from a term that means society. There are many worlds (or societies), for example, the Chinese world, the Western world, the music world, and the boxing world. In light of the scriptures, Christ couldn't have meant the entire earth because he says in (I John 2:15) "love not the world". The world or society that Christ was referring to in John 3:16, the one he loved and died for, is the society of the Hebrew Israelites and the true Christians. The true Israelites will be the foundation of the kingdom of heaven on earth.

<< *First John 2:15* >> [*Love not the world, neither the things that are in the world. If any man love the world, the love of the father is not in him.*]

<< *St. John 17:9,14* >> Jesus spake and said: [*I pray for them: I pray not for the world, but for them which thou has given me; for they are thine... <14> I have given them thy word; and the world hath hated them, because they are not of the world, even as I am not of the world.*]

A true Christian is a person who has accepted the truth from the bible and confesses the afro-asiatic identity of the Israelites, observes the laws of YAHAWAH and has the Mashayak Yahawashy (Jesus Christ) as their Lord and Savior. The original Israelites as well as the true Christians who believe in the real God, are constantly the victims of discrimination and oppression in today's society. The nation of the original Hebrew Israelites is referred to in the Bible as the kingdom of Heaven.

<< *Matthew 11:12* >> [*And from the days of John the Baptist until now the kingdom of heaven suffereth violence, and violence take it by force.*]

Now, if the kingdom of heaven was in space it could not suffer violence. The original Israelites (African-Americans, Native Americans, and Hispanics) are the kingdom of heaven on earth, suffering violence from the Greco-Roman (Western) world and from other heathens! That is why Christ says:

<< *Luke 17:20,21* >> [*...behold, the kingdom of the Lord is within you.*]

Concerning the mission of Jesus, the Bible says:

THE TRUTH

<< Matthew 1:21 >> [And she shall bring forth a son, and thou shalt call his name Jesus: for he shall save his people from their sins.]

The word "his" is a possessive pronoun, like mine and theirs. The people of Christ in this case are the twelve tribes of Israel, those who will accept his teachings and keep his commandments!

<< Matthew 10:5 and 6 >> [These twelve Jesus sent forth and commanded them, saying, Go not into the way of the Gentiles, and into any city of the Samaritans enter ye not: (Samaritans were Ethiopian impostors claiming to be Jews) *But go rather to the lost sheep of the house of Israel.]*

Christ commanded the disciples specifically to go only to the Israelites, because one of the main mission objectives of Jesus is to lay the foundations for the reestablishment of the true Israelites as a nation! The other nations are in their worlds and are ruling their own lands. Their rulership is part of their salvation. But the Israelites have been scattered. There is a world to come and a salvation to come belonging to the Israelites! We are the only people wandering around in oppression, without an identity and without a land - for nearly two thousand years.

<< John 14:30 >> [Hereafter I will not talk much with you: for the prince of this world cometh and hath nothing in me.]

Christ is referring to the Greco-Roman Empire and the nations derived from it. They will not stand for this truth. Christ's kingdom is the one to come, and he makes it clear that those nations now ruling the world have no part in the rulership of the kingdom of heaven:

<< Matthew 12:31 >> [Now is the judgment of this world: now shall the prince of this world be cast out.]

It is true that the heathens may have the world and all of its wealth and power, but they do not have a future in terms of rulership. Judgement Day is at hand. Christ tried to explain this to a Greek woman:

<< Matthew 15:22-26 >> [And, behold, a woman of Canaan came out of the same coast, and cried unto him, saying, have mercy on me, O Lord, thou son of David; my daughter is grievously vexed with a devil. But he answered her not a word.]

This woman was an immigrant living in Canaan. We learn of this woman's nationality:

<< Mark 7:26 >> [The woman was a Greek ...And his disciples came and besought him, saying, Send her away; for she crieth after us (because at the time, the disciples wanted to concentrate on the restoration of the Israelites. She was not an Israelite). *But he* (Jesus) *answered and said, I am not sent but unto the lost sheep of the house of Israel.*

Then came she and worshipped him, and saying, Lord, help me. But he answered and said, it is not meet to take the children's bread, and cast it to dogs.]

THE TRUTH

Jesus Christ made it clear that the main goal of his mission was the redemption and restoration of the Israelite kingdom on earth. In another example Christ had to straighten out this Ethiopian woman who was thinking that the Ethiopians were Jews:

<< St. John 4:7- 21 >> *[There cometh a woman of Samaria to draw water: Jesus saith unto her, give me to drink... Then saith the woman of Samaria unto him, How is it that thou, being a Jew, askest drink of me, a woman of Samaria? For the Jews have no dealing with the Samaritans.]*

Again, you can see that the people knew that there was a difference between Israel and those other nations practicing their own man-made Jewish religion! That Ethiopian woman went on saying*:*

<< John 4:20, 21 >> *[Our fathers worshipped in this mountain; and ye say, that in Jerusalem is the place where men are to worship. Jesus saith unto her, Woman, believe me, the hour cometh, when ye shall neither in this mountain, nor yet at Jerusalem, worship the father. Ye worship ye know not what: we know what we worship: for salvation is of the Jews]*

Salvation as far as rulership pertains to the reestablishment of the original twelve tribes of Israelite. The land belongs to the real Israelites, not to the Ethiopians or the Caucasian Khazars, nor any other nation.

<< Verse 23 >> *[But the hour cometh and now is, when the true worshippers (*the original twelve tribes of Israel*) shall worship the Father in spirit and in truth: for the Father seeketh such to worship him.]*

The majority of the westerns Asiatic people of North, South and Central America are not Africans. Africans are descended from Ham, we are Israelites from Shem! The Africans had the Israelites as captives before the Caucasian Edomites did. The Arab merchants were the middlemen who sold the Israelites to the Caucasians. When the Israelites fled into Africa, after being run out of Palestine by the Romans, the Africans captured the Israelites as slaves and used to take them and offer them as human sacrifices to their pagan gods.

The Lord is only looking for Israelites when it comes to the reestablishment of the nation in Palestine. We are not Africans or Arabs and should not be called by the identity of other nations. The Ethiopians, the Arabs, the Caucasians and the Africans were selling us as slaves, and they had us as slaves! And now, some of them are falsely claiming our identity, calling themselves Israelis, Jews and Jewish. The Most High God will judge all nations that have afflicted us:

<< Zephaniah 2:12 >> *[Ye Ethiopians also, ye shall be slain by my sword (*with war and famine*).]*

According to the Bible, the twelve tribes of Israel are chosen by the Lord YAHAWAH to receive the salvation and be reestablished as the rulers in the kingdom of heaven on earth with Jesus Christ as King!

THE TRUTH

<< Isaiah 41:8 >> *[But thou Israel, art my servant, Jacob whom I have chosen, the seed of Abraham my friend.]*

God will save a remnant of people from every nation. Just knowing the truth and knowing ones identity as Israelite is not enough to guarantee salvation. We have to keep the commandments: know Christ and practice His love. Not all Israelites will be saved because the majority of them have chosen gentile customs and ways, and no longer serving the Lord YAHAWAH. The word "gentile" refers to custom not nation. Israelites are sometimes called gentiles when they are following non-Hebrew customs and are not keeping the Biblical law. There are many Israelites that have gone into gentile customs and are calling themselves by gentile names. The apostle Paul had Roman citizenship and was calling himself by a Roman name at one time. But Paul was an Israelite, from the tribe of Benjamin:

<< Romans 11:1 >> *[I say then, Hath God cast away his people? God forbid. For I also am an Israelite, of the seed of Abraham, of the tribe of Benjamin.]*

Israelites that have gone into gentile customs have be referred to as gentiles, but they are not natural gentiles; they are only calling themselves by gentile names like we call ourselves "Americans", "West Indians", "Hispanics", and "Africans"; but we are actually the original twelve tribes of Israel!

<< First Corinthians 1:1, 2 >> *[Now concerning spiritual gifts, brethren (He is talking to fellow Israelites), I would not have you ignorant. Ye know that ye were Gentiles, carried away unto these dumb idols, even as ye were led.]*

<< Acts 15:17 >> *[That the residue of men might seek after the Lord, and all the Gentiles, upon whom my name is called, saith the Lord.]*

The only people that have the Lord's name are the twelve tribes of Israel. The word "Israel" means "He Is The Prince Of God".

<< John 7:35 >> *[Then said the Jews among themselves, whither will he go, that we shall not find him? Will he go unto the dispersed among the Gentiles?]*

Israelites are scattered among all the nations. We must reestablish our original identity. Israelites can be classified into two groups: the ones that know their identity and are keeping the customs are called the Hebrew Israelites or Jews; the other groups don't know that they are Israelites and are keeping gentile customs, they are referred to as Gentiles! But there is really no difference between any two Israelites, whether one calls himself Jamaican, American, or Indian, or Hispanics. We are all from the same seed.

<< Galatians 3:26-29 >> *[For ye are all children of the Father by faith in Christ Jesus. For as many of you as have been baptized into Christ have put on Christ. There is neither Jew nor Greek, there is neither bond nor free, there is neither male nor female: for ye are one in Christ Jesus. And If ye be Christ's, then are ye Abraham's seed, and heirs according to the promise.]*

THE TRUTH

Notice the word "seed" here is referring to genealogy. The progenitors of the Hebrew Israelites were Abraham, Isaac, and Jacob, from whom the twelve tribes of Israel were born. Jacob's name was changed to Israel (meaning: the Prince of God) after the Lord blessed him. The LORD GOD YAHAWAH made the promise to the twelve tribes through Abraham, Isaac, and Jacob. The bulk of the descendants of the twelve tribes of Israel are the African-Americans and Native American-Indians. Remnants are also scattered all over the world. Here is a list of scriptures containing some of the promises that the Lord YAHAWAH made specifically to the Hebrew Israelites:

<< Genesis 12:1-3 >> [Now the Lord had said unto Abraham, Get thee out of thy country, and from thy kindred, and from thy father's house, unto a land that I will shew thee: <2> And I will make of thee a great nation, and I will bless thee, and make thy name great; and thou shalt be a blessing: <3> And I will bless them that bless thee, and curse him that curseth thee: and in thee shall all the nations of the earth be blessed.]

<< Genesis 17:1-8 >> [And when Abram was ninety years old and nine, the LORD appeared to Abram, and said unto him, I am the Almighty God; walk before me, and be thou perfect. <2> And I will make my covenant between me and thee, and will multiply thee exceedingly. <3> And Abram fell on his face: and God talked with him, saying, <4> As for me, behold, my covenant is with thee, and thou shalt be a father of many nations. <5> Neither shall thy name any more be called Abram, but thy name shall be Abraham; for a father of many nations have I made thee. <6> And I will make thee exceeding fruitful, and I will make nations of thee, and kings shall come out of thee.
<7> And I will establish my covenant between me and thee and thy seed after thee in their generations for an everlasting covenant, to be a God unto thee, and to thy seed after thee. <8> And I will give unto thee, and to thy seed after thee, the land wherein thou art a stranger, all the land of Canaan, for an everlasting possession; and I will be their God.]

<< Genesis 15:18 >> [In the same day the Lord made a covenant with Abraham, saying, Unto thy seed have I given this land, from the river of Egypt unto the great river, the river Euphrates.]

<< Genesis 14:19 >> [And he blessed him and said, Blessed be **Abraham** of the Most High God, **possessor of heaven and earth**]

<< Genesis 17:19 >> [And God said, Sarah thy wife shall bear thee a son indeed; and thou shalt call his name Isaac: and I will establish my covenant with him for an everlasting covenant, and with his seed after him.]

<< Genesis 26:2-5 >> [And the Lord appeared unto (Isaac) him, and said, Go not down into Egypt; dwell in the land which I shall tell thee of: <3> Sojourn in this land, and I will bless thee; for unto thee, and unto thy seed, I will give all these countries, and I will perform the oath which I swore unto Abraham thy father; <4> And I will make thy seed to multiply as the stars of heaven, and will give unto thy seed all these countries; and in thy seed shall all the

nations of the earth be blessed; <5> Because that Abraham obeyed my voice and kept my commandments, my statutes, and my laws.]

<< *Genesis 28:13-15* >> *[And, behold, the Lord stood above it, and said, I am the Lord God of Abraham thy father, and the God of Isaac: the land whereon thou (Jacob) liest, to thee will I give it, and to thy seed (the Israelites); <14> And thy seed shall be as the dust of the earth, and thou shalt spread abroad to the west, and to the east, and to the north and to the south: and in thee shall all the families of the earth be blessed.]*

<< *Deuteronomy 30:1-10* >> *[And it shall come to pass, when all these things are come upon thee (speaking to the twelve tribes of Israel), the blessing and the curse, which I have set before thee, and thou shalt call them to mind among all the nations, whither the Lord thy God hath driven thee, <2> And shalt return unto the Lord thy God, and shalt obey his voice according to all that I have commanded thee this day, thou and thy children, with all thine heart, and with all thy soul; <3> That then the Lord thy God will turn thy captivity, and have compassion upon thee, and will return and gather thee from all the nations, whither the Lord thy God hath scattered thee.*

<4> If any of thine be driven out unto the utmost parts of heaven, from thence will the Lord thy God gather thee, and from thence will he fetch thee; <5> And the Lord thy God will bring thee into the land which thy fathers possessed; and thou shalt possess it; and he will do thee good, and multiply thee above thy fathers. <6> And the Lord thy God will circumcise thine heart, and the heart of thy seed, to love the Lord thy God with all thine heart, and with all thy soul, that thou mayest live. <7> And the Lord thy God will put all these curses upon thine enemies, and on them that hate thee, which persecuted thee.

<8> And thou shalt return and obey the voice of the Lord, and do all his commandments, which I commanded this day. <9> And the Lord thy God will make thee plenteous in every work of thine hand, in the fruit of thy cattle, and in the fruit of thy land, for good: for the Lord will again rejoice over thy fathers: <10> If thou shalt hearken unto the voice of the Lord thy God, to keep his commandments and his statutes which are written in this book of the law, and if thou turn unto the LORD thy God with all thine heart, and with all thy soul.]

<< *I Peters 2:9* >> *[But ye are a chosen generation, a royal priesthood, an holy nation, a peculiar people; that ye should shew forth the praises of him who hath called you out of darkness into his marvelous light.]*

<< *Deuteronomy 14:2* >> *[For thou art an holy people unto the LORD thy God, and the LORD hath chosen thee to be a peculiar people unto himself, above all the nations that are upon the earth.]*

From his great love, the Lord YAHAWAH has offered salvation to all nations who have accepted the teachings and the atonement in the true Jesus Christ. And the Lord promises to restore the original Hebrew Israelites. The original Israelites are expected to wake up and assume their original identity as Hebrew Israelites. It is time to reject those colonial names and derogatory labels, as well as the false customs and religions.

THE TRUTH

The Bible explains in detail how the Lord YAHAWAH plans to restore the identity, nationality, and the rulership to the Hebrew Israelites:

<< *Hosea 2:23* >> *[And I will sow her unto me in the earth; and I will have mercy upon her that had not mercy; and I will say to them which were not my people* (Israelites that had been cursed and rejected), *Thou art my people; and they shall say, thou art my God.]*

<< *Isaiah 44:5,6* >> *[One shall say, I am the Lord's; and another shall call himself by the name of Jacob; and another shall subscribe with his hands unto the Lord, and surname himself Israel.]*

This wicked world is about to loose its current state of salvation. Salvation can mean rulership. There is soon to be a change of rulership in the world! The modern Greco-Roman World, The Western society, is about to loose their present salvation of rulership. This is due to the crimes and injustices that have been committed against the nations, the Israelites, against the planet, for teaching lies on the Bible, and for blaspheming the name of the Lord YAHAWAH, and Jesus Christ!

<< *Amos 9:8 to 10* >> *[Behold, the eyes of the Lord are upon the sinful kingdom, and I will destroy it from of the face of the earth* (by civil war, chaos, nuclear destruction); *saving that I will not utterly destroy the house of Jacob, saith the Lord. <9> For, lo, I will command, and I will sift the house of Israel among all nations like corn is sifted in a sieve, yet shall not the least grain fall upon the earth.*

<10> All the sinners of my people shall die by the sword, which say, The evil shall not overtake nor prevent us.]

The people who are practicing false religions often talk about being saved; in fact they are not saved. No one is saved yet, but we can have the hope and the knowledge of the salvation, and the forgiveness of sins. Salvation is something that we will receive at the Second Coming of Jesus! You could be hurt or brutally killed any minute, so how are you saved? People are still lying, cheating, and being wicked so no one can say that they are saved from sins! But the blood of Jesus can take away our sins, so that those who believe in him can repent their sins and be baptized. In this way, they can be forgiven then be adopted into the kingdom of heaven when it is established on earth. Jesus himself said:

<< *Matthew 24:13* >> *[But he that shall endure to the end, the same shall be saved.]*

"Shall be saved" is in future tense, meaning that in a future time you will be saved, but not now! You can receive forgiveness and the promise of salvation after repentance and baptism, but you are not saved yet. That is why Christ has to come: to save you. He comes to save you from doomsday and from eternal hell. He will destroy this wicked world, and cast into everlasting hell all of the people that did not repent and accept his salvation. The Bible documents and explains how the Israelites had lost their salvation and how it will be restored. By the same token, it also explains the fate of this world.

THE TRUTH

<< Romans 11:11 to 27 >> [I say then, Have they stumble that they should fall? God forbid: but rather through their fall salvation is come unto the Gentiles, for to provoke them to jealousy.]

The other nations are in their kingdom, having their own land; but the Israelites are in a fallen state, as lost captives in oppression. All of this occurs because we have broken the commandments of God and have not repented and because we have gone into false religions and false gods. The people have been following the way of greed and hate, rather than love and compassion.

<< Romans 11:15 >> [For if the casting away of them be the reconciling of the world, what shall be the receiving of them be, but life from the dead?]

The Israelites are prophesied to make a great return to the true God and to the commandments of the Bible!

<< Romans 11:20 >> [And if some of the branches be broken off (Israel), and thou, being a wild olive tree, (this modern world led by the now ruling Edomites) wert grafted in among them... Boast not against the branches. But if thou boast, thou bearest not the root, but the root thee (Meaning that the Israelites are the natural rulers and the Edomite domination of the world is only temporary), Thou will say then, The branches were broken off, that I might be grafted in.
Well; because of unbelief they were broken off, Be not high minded, but fear; For if the Lord spare not the natural branches (the Israelites), take heed lest he also spare not thee.]

God took away the rulership from the Israelites because we did not obey the laws of the Bible. Paul was talking to the Roman world, warning them. However, this society has not obeyed the commandments of the Bible since Paul gave them this direct warning. Therefore, they will soon face judgement and doom. The rulership of all the heathen nations on earth will soon be terminated permanently as prophesied!

<< Romans 11:22 to 27 >> [Behold therefore the goodness and severity of the Lord: on them (Israelites) which fell, severity; but toward thee (the Western world), goodness, if thou continue in his goodness: otherwise thou also shalt be cut off (This modern Roman Empire is destined to fall).
<23> And they also, if they abide not still in unbelief (if the Israelites repent), shall be grafted in: for the Lord is able to graft them in again (The Israelites were destined to regain the rulership). For if thou were cut out of the olive tree which is wild by nature, and wert grafted contrary to nature into a good olive tree: how much more shall these, which be the natural branches, be grafted into their own olive tree?]

The scriptures describe this Edomite-dominated world as wild and unnatural. The Western world is the wild olive tree. God has put it in writing: there is a day of salvation and restoration coming for the original twelve tribes of Israel, a day when our shame, captivity and oppression will come to an end.

THE TRUTH

<< Romans 11:25-27 >> [For I would not, brethren, that ye be ignorant of this mystery, lest ye should be wise in your own conceits; that blindness in part is happened to Israel, until the fullness of the Gentiles be come.]

The nations were given a set time limit to rule, called "time of the Gentiles". This set time period has just about reached its completion when the gentiles will cease to dominate and begin to face judgement. The Israelites should now prepare for their time of salvation and rulership by repenting, uniting and propagating the true gospel.

<< Romans 11:26-27 >> [... And so all Israel shall be saved: as it is written, There shall come out of Zion the Deliverer, and shall turn away ungodliness from Jacob. <27> For this is my covenant unto them, when I shall take away their sins.]

It is as if God set a time bomb, an alarm clock and it will certainly go off on time. As surely as the heathens got to rule, the Israelites are going to rule forever! In the next world, there will be only one government on earth: the Kingdom of Heaven. In the Apocrypha, the prophet Esdras was given a clear picture by God as to when the European Edomite domination will end, and when the Israelite rulership shall begin:

<< Second Esdras 6:7-9 >> [Then answered I and said, what shall be the parting asunder of the times? or when shall be the end of the first, and the beginning of it that followeth? And he (the Angel) *said unto me, From Abraham unto Isaac, when Jacob and Esau were born of him, Jacob's hand held first the heel of Esau. For Esau* (the Caucasians) *is the end of the world, and* Jacob (the original Asiatic Israelites) *is the beginning of it that followeth.]*

Soon this evil society will disappear like smoke in the wind. The kingdom of heaven will be established and the scripture says specifically that the Israelites will be its leaders, along with Jesus Christ.

<< Romans 9:1-4 >> [I say the truth in Christ, I lie not, my conscience also bearing me witness in the Holy Ghost, <2> That I have great heaviness and continual sorrow in my heart. <3> For I could wish that myself were accursed from Christ for my brethren, my kinsmen according to the flesh: <4> Who are Israelites; to whom pertaineth the adoption, and the glory, and the covenants, and the giving of the law, and the services of the Lord, and the Promises (to rule next).]

<< Jeremiah 30:11 >> [For I am with thee to save thee: though I make a full end of all nations.]

The Israelites are found in captivity in the western world, the heathens are giving us hell every day! What do you think will happen to the nations that were and are still being cruel to the Israelites? This world is doomed and is heading for pure hell. According to the Bible, Jesus Christ came to save the Israelites as a nation and establish them as the everlasting kingdom of heaven on earth! In fact, the lord plans to destroy this society in the day of judgement, and to punish the nations for their crimes against the truth, their blasphemy against the Father, Christ, And the original Israelites!

THE TRUTH

<< *Isaiah 14:1,2* >> *[For the LORD will have mercy on Jacob, and will yet choose Israel, and set them in their own land: and the strangers shall be joined with them, and they shall cleave to the house of Jacob. 2 And the people shall take them, and bring them to their place: and the house of Israel shall possess them in the land of the LORD for servants and handmaids: and they shall take them captives, whose captives they were; and they shall rule over their oppressors.]*

<< *Isaiah 60:8-16* >> *Who are these that fly as a cloud, and as the doves to their windows? 9 Surely the isles shall wait for me, and the ships of Tarshish first, to bring thy sons from far, their silver and their gold with them, unto the name of the LORD thy God, and to the Holy One of Israel, because he hath glorified thee. 10 And the sons of strangers shall build up thy walls, and their kings shall minister unto thee: for in my wrath I smote thee, but in my favour have I had mercy on thee.*

11 Therefore thy gates shall be open continually; they shall not be shut day nor night; that men may bring unto thee the forces of the Gentiles, and that their kings may be brought. 12 For the nation and kingdom that will not serve thee shall perish; yea, those nations shall be utterly wasted. 13 The glory of Lebanon shall come unto thee, the fir tree, the pine tree, and the box together, to beautify the place of my sanctuary; and I will make the place of my feet glorious.

14 The sons also of them that afflicted thee shall come bending unto thee; and all they that despised thee shall bow themselves down at the soles of thy feet; and they shall call thee, The city of the LORD, The Zion of the Holy One of Israel. 15 Whereas thou hast been forsaken and hated, so that no man went through thee, I will make thee an eternal excellency, a joy of many generations. 16 Thou shalt also suck the milk of the Gentiles, and shalt suck the breast of kings: and thou shalt know that I the LORD am thy Saviour and thy Redeemer, the mighty One of Jacob.]

<< *Micah 4:1-4* *[But in the last days it shall come to pass, that the mountain of the house of the LORD shall be established in the top of the mountains, and it shall be exalted above the hills; and people shall flow unto it. <2> And many nations shall come, and say, Come, and let us go up to the mountain of the LORD, and to the house of the God of Jacob; and he will teach us of his ways, and we will walk in his paths: for the law shall go forth of Zion, and the word of the LORD from Jerusalem.*

<3> And he shall judge among many people, and rebuke strong nations afar off; and they shall beat their swords into plowshares, and their spears into pruninghooks: nation shall not lift up a sword against nation, neither shall they learn war any more. <4> But they shall sit every man under his vine and under his fig tree; and none shall make them afraid: for the mouth of the LORD of hosts hath spoken it.]

<< *Jeremiah 16:19* >> *[O LORD, my strength, and my fortress, and my refuge in the day of affliction, the Gentiles shall come unto thee from the ends of the earth, and shall say, Surely our fathers have inherited lies, vanity, and things wherein there is no profit.]*

THE TRUTH

Concerning the other nations, their salvation comes through their faith in Jesus, accepting the truth of the Bible, keeping the commandments and acting mercifully towards the original Israelites while the twelve tribes are in this captivity.

<< Galatians 3:6-14 >> [Even as Abraham believed God, and it was accounted to him for righteousness. <7> Know ye therefore that they which are of faith, the same are the children of Abraham. <8> And the scripture, foreseeing that God would justify the heathen through faith, preached before the gospel unto Abraham, saying, In thee shall all nations of the earth be blessed. <9> So then they which be of faith are blessed with faithful Abraham. <10> For as many as are of the works of the law are under the curse: for it is written, Cursed is every one that continueth not in all things which are written in the book of the law to do them.
<11> But that no man is justified by the law in the sight of God, it is evident: for, The just shall live by faith. <12> And the law is not of faith: but, The man that doeth them shall live in them. <13> Christ hath redeemed us from the curse of the law, being made a curse for us: for it is written, cursed is every one that hangeth on a tree: <14> That the blessing of Abraham might come on the Gentiles (the other nations) through Jesus Christ; that we might receive the promise of the Spirit through faith.]

<< Revelation 7:9 >> [And after this I beheld, and, lo, a great multitude, which no man could number, of all nations, and kindred, and tongues, and people, and tongues, stood before the Lamb, clothed with white robes, and palms in their hands; <10> And cried with a loud voice, Salvation to our God which sitteth upon the throne, and unto the Lamb.]

RESURRECTION AND REINCARNATION

Everyone would like to live forever, and it is God's pleasure to give us everlasting life. Jesus Christ came to show us the way to everlasting life. The Bible does not teach reincarnation in the same way that most other religions do. The Bible does not teach that we can be reincarnated as other kinds of animal life forms. The Lord has power over all things and has the power to bring back the spirit of a person into another body if he so chooses. In addition, the bible reveals that there will be a one-time resurrection of all people, scheduled to take place at the Second Coming of Jesus Christ. Jesus himself explains:

<< John 5:28, 29 >> [Marvel not at this: for the hour is coming, in the which all that are in the graves shall hear my voice, <29> And shall come forth; they that have done good, unto the resurrection of life; and they that have done evil, unto the resurrection of damnation.]

A few people have claimed to be capable of recollecting past life experiences, usually when under hypnosis. Some say it is proof of reincarnation. We have to be very careful. Hypnosis is like a dream state, where the person can experience their fantasies. Hypnosis is also a condition of high suggestibility when the person can be made to believe that those dreams and fantasies are real. Demons can certainly posses the mind of an individual to deceive them into believing that those hypnotic suggestions and dreams are real. The demons can also give them visions of things from the past, so that they believe that they've lived before. However, when we examine the Holy Scriptures of the Bible, the truth is brought to light. The spirit of a person does not automatically reincarnate at will. The Lord YAHAWAH has to send it.

<< Luke 16:26 >> [And beside all this, between us and you there is a great gulf fixed: so that they which would pass from hence to you cannot; neither can they pass to us, that would come from thence.]

A clear example of reincarnation in the bible is the return of Elija in the person of John the Baptist.

<< Matthew 17:10-13 >> [And his disciples asked him, saying, why then say the scribes that Elias must first come? And Jesus answered and said unto them, Elias truly shall first come, and restore all things. But I say unto you that Elias is come already, and they knew him not, but have done unto him whatsoever they listed. Likewise shall also the son of man suffer of them. Then the disciples understood that he spake to them of John the Baptist.]

<< Luke 1:13-17 >> But the angel said unto him, Fear not, Zacharias: for thy prayer is heard; and thy wife Elisabeth shall bear thee a son, and thou shalt call his name John. <14> And thou shalt have joy and gladness; and many shall rejoice at his birth. <15> For he shall be great in the sight of the Lord, and shall drink neither wine nor strong drink; and he shall be filled with the Holy Ghost, even from his mother's womb.
<16> And many of the children of Israel shall he turn to the Lord their God. <17> And he shall go before him in the spirit and power of Elija, to turn the hearts of the

fathers to the children, and the disobedient to the wisdom of the just; to make ready a people prepared for the Lord.]

<< *John 1:19-23* >> *[And this is the record of John, when the Jews sent priests and Levites from Jerusalem to ask him, who art thou? <20> And he confessed, and denied not; I am not Christ. <21> And they asked him, What then? Art thou Elias (Elija)? And he saith, I am not. Art thou that prophet? And he answered, No. <22> Then said they unto him, Who art thou? that we may give an answer to them that sent us. What sayest thou of thyself? <23> He said, I am the voice of one crying in the wilderness, Make straight the way of the Lord, as said the prophet Esaias.]*

But John the Baptist did not know that he was Elija, just like you don't remember whom you were in the previous lives. The fact is many of the disciples, and prophets of the Bible are back here today, reincarnated, teaching the truth of the Bible, just like before. But no one will know who was who and the Bible warns us not to indulge this kind of vain pursuit of genealogy because it is not yet revealed to man who he existed as in his past lives!

<< *Titus 3:9* >> *[Avoid foolish questions and genealogies.]*

We see that Reincarnation is very real according to the Bible; but all the major religions of this world are either denying the reality of reincarnation, or teaching lies concerning it! The truth is found in the Bible. All living things have a spirit in them, and that spirit never dies; it leaves the body at the time of death.

<< *Ecclesiastes 8:8* >> *[There is no man that hath power over the spirit to retain the spirit; neither hath he power in the day of death.]*

And that spirit return into a different body, of the same nationality in a future generation! A person does not come back as an animal, like a cow or an insect and you can not be reincarnated into a different nation. God is not the Author of confusion. We have all existed before, that is why Solomon says

<< *Ecclesiastes 1:9-11* >> *[The thing that hath been, it is that which shall be; and that which is done is that which shall be done: and there is no new thing under the sun (you're under the sun, so you can not be new; our spirits existed before in different bodies). Is there any thing whereof it may be said, see, this is new? it hath been already of old time which was before us. There is no remembrance of former things; neither shall there be any remembrance of things that are to come after.]*

Because you will not remember who you were in previous lives, does no mean you did not exist! Many wicked men and women, doing all kinds of evil deeds might never appear to suffer a day in their entire life, but when they be born in a future generation you can be sure they will be made to reap what they had sown! The Lord YAHAWAH promises. When the day of judgement comes, the wicked will be resurrected and punished accordingly and reincarnated as slaves.. They will reap what they have sowed!

One thing that is inherited from one generation to the other is sin. Very often the children enjoy the fruits from the sins of their ancestors, therefore, they have also inherited the punishments and curses associated with those sins.

> << *Exodus 34:7* >> *The Lord.. By no means clear the guilty; visiting the iniquity of the fathers upon the children and upon the children's children, unto the third and to the fourth generation.*

> << *John 9:1,2* >> *And as Jesus passed by, he saw a man which was blind from his birth. 2 And his disciples asked him, saying, Master, who did sin, this man, or his parents, that he was born blind?*

In other words, the descendents of the colonists and slave masters whom you're looking at today were the same individuals that were whipping your backs, killing, lynching and raping people around the world back there during the period of colonization and slavery! No one is getting away with any thing! Surely the nations will pay! They can run, but they can not hide; even if they commit suicide, they will be reincarnated to face judgement in the kingdom where there will be no mercy and no pity!

> << *Isaiah 14:21* >> *[Prepare slaughter for his children for the iniquity of their fathers; that they do not rise, nor possess the land, nor fill the face of the world with cities.]*

Christ was telling the twelve disciples that they would be reincarnated or resurrected in the last days:

> << *Matthew 19:28,29* >> *[And Jesus said unto them, Verily I say unto you, that ye which have followed me in the regeneration (or reincarnation) when the son of man shall sit in the throne of his glory, ye also shall sit upon twelve thrones, judging the twelve tribes of Israel.]*

Even Daniel was told that he would be reincarnated or resurrected in the last days!

> << *Daniel 12:13* >> *["But go thou thy way till the end be: for thou shalt rest (die), an stand in thy lot* (become reincarnated or resurrected) *at the end of the days."]*

THE TRUTH

Death is like sleep, and those who died will remain dead until the day of resurrection. The Lord told Adam clearly in Genesis:

>> *<< Genesis 3:19 >> [...Till thou return unto the ground; for out of it wast thou taken: for dust thou art, and unto dust shalt thou return.]*

>> *<< Ecclesiastic 9:5 >> [For the living know that they shall die: but the dead knows not anything.]*

>> *<< Psalms 146:4 >> [His breath goeth forth, he returneth to his earth; in that very day his thoughts perish.]*

We do not have an immortal soul. Your body is your soul. Man was made from matter and then the spirit of God brought him to life. The spirit in man survives after death and waits for the day of judgement. We are cleansed by the atonement made by the sacrificial death of Christ, not through reincarnation. If your souls were immortal, and then you would not need to look for eternal life, you would already have it. Everlasting life is a blessed gift from the Lord YAHAWAH:

>> *<< Romans 6:23 >> [For the wages of sin is death; but the gift of God is eternal life through Jesus Christ.]*

The Bible speaks of two kinds of death: the spiritual death and the physical death. The first death suffered by mankind was when Adam sinned:

>> *<< Hebrews 9:27 >> [And as it is appointed unto men once to die, after this the judgement.]*

>> *<< I Corinthians. 15:21,22 >> [For since by man came death, by man came also the resurrection of the dead. <22> For as in Adam all die, even so in Christ shall all be made alive.]*

>> *<< I Corinthians 15:50-57 >> [Now this I say, brethren, that flesh and blood cannot inherit the kingdom of God; neither doth corruption inherit incorruption. <51> Behold, I shew you a mystery; we shall not all sleep, but we shall all be changed, <52> In a moment, in the twinkling of an eye, at the last trump: for the trumpet shall sound, and the dead shall be raised incorruptible, and we shall be changed. <53> For this corruptible must put on incorruption, and this mortal must put on immortality.*
>
> *<54> So when this corruptible shall have put on incorruption, and this mortal shall have put on immortality, then shall be brought to pass the saying that is written, Death is swallowed up in victory. <55> O death, where is thy sting? O grave, where is thy victory? <56> The sting of death is sin; and the strength of sin is the law. <57> But thanks be to God, which giveth us the victory through our Lord Jesus Christ.]*

THE TRUTH

The resurrection will take place in two phases. The first resurrection will be for people who have learned and accepted the gospel while living. In the second resurrection, all the people who lived, but never had a chance to know the Lord YAHAWAH will then be resurrected and given an opportunity to accept Jesus Christ as Lord and Savior, in order to receive everlasting life. The ones that do not repent will be destroyed.

> << *Revelation 20:5,6* >> *[But the rest of the dead lived not again until the thousand years were finished. This is the first resurrection. <6> Blessed and holy is he that hath part in the first resurrection: on such the second death hath no power, But they shall be priests of God and Christ, and shall reign with him a thousand years.]*

We have a spirit in us which gives us life, and that spirit is from God. It leaves the body at the time of death. And that spirit returns to God after the body dies.

> << *Ecclesiastes. 8:8* >> *[There is no man that hath power over the spirit to retain the spirit; neither hath he power in the day of death.]*

We have prophets in the world today, as always; when the time comes, according to Revelation 11:6. The Most High will give the Israelites spiritual power like Moses and Christ had in order for us to help lead the righteous out of the great tribulation period and to plague the nations.

> << *First Corinthian 14:32* >> *[The spirits of the prophets are subject unto the prophets.]*

The same prophets that were back there are here now in these last days again to teach the truth. You can be sure that the world is treating them in the same evil ways as in the past.

> << *Revelation 11:6* >> *[These have power to shut heaven that it rains not in the day of their prophecy: and have power over waters to turn them to blood, and to smite the earth with plagues, as often as they will.]*

Jesus Christ was telling the twelve disciples that they would be resurrected at his Second Coming:

> << *Matthew 19:28,29* >> *[And Jesus said unto them, Verily I say unto you, that ye which have followed me in the regeneration when the son of man shall sit in the throne of his glory, ye also shall sit upon twelve thrones, judging the twelve tribes of Israel.]*

> << *Revelation 10:11* >> *[And he said unto me, Thou must prophesy again before many peoples, and nations, and tongues, and kings.]*

Christ will shortly return! Even Daniel was told that he would be resurrected in the last days:

THE TRUTH

<< Daniel 12:13 >> [But go thou thy way till the end be: for thou shalt rest (die)*, and stand in thy lot* (become resurrected) *at the end of the days.]*

Moses and Elija returned to earth to visit with Christ after they had been physically dead for many years. Moses had been dead for centuries.

<< St. Mark 9:4,5 >> [And there appeared unto them Elias (Elija) *with Moses: and they were talking with Jesus <5> And Peter answered and said to Jesus; Master, it is good for us to be here: and let us make three tabernacles; one for thee, and one for Moses, and one for Elias.]*

At the Second Coming of Christ, everyone that had died will be resurrected, some to face the judgement and condemnation in hell, others will be rewarded with eternal life in the kingdom of heaven.

THE DELIVERANCE AND THE UFO

The people, who wake up to the Biblical truth and obey the words of the Lord YAHAWAH, will not be destroyed in the tribulations of these last days. Christ is coming to deliver them! The Bible describes how Christ is coming:

>> *Isaiah 66:15* >> *[For behold, the Lord will come with fire* (the day of doom and judgement), *and with his chariots* (what they call U.F.Os or flying saucers), *like a whirlwind, to render his anger with fury* (to judge and to punish the wicked), *and his rebuke with flames of fire. For by fire and by his sword will the Lord plead with all flesh: and the slain of the Lord shall be many.]*

The scripture says that Christ will soon invade the nations, and that he will come with his chariots of salvation. What the Bible calls the chariots of Christ are not the kind you drag behind a horse, made of wood and metal. The chariots of salvation are the flying saucers, spiritual devices from heaven! Thousands of people per year report sightings of U.F.O's around the world, they can not all be making up a story. The truth is the U.F.Os exist and are identified in the Bible! Ezekiel saw the U.F.Os and called them clouds of fire, and a whirlwind:

<< *Ezekiel 1:4* >> *[And I looked, and, behold, a whirlwind came out of the north, a cloud, and a fire infolding itself, and a brightness was about it, and out of the midst thereof as the color of amber* (glowing, like charcoal), *out of the midst of the fire.]*

People describe the flying saucers as looking like a spinning bright light, and glowing. That is just what Ezekiel saw. More details are given:

<< *Verse 16 and 17* >> *[The appearance of the wheels and their work was like unto the color of beryl* (like a crystal): *and they four had one likeness: and their appearance and their work was as it were a wheel in the middle of a wheel.]*

That is exactly how the flying saucers are described today by the people who have seen them! They appear to be spinning like wheels. The Bible identifies the flying Chariots or U.F.Os in many other verses:

<< *Zechariah 5:1-4* >> *[Then I lifted up mine eyes, and looked, and behold a flying roll. <2> And he saith unto me, What seest thou? And I answered, I see a flying roll* (today you call it a flying saucer); *the length thereof is twenty cubits, and the breadth thereof ten cubits. <3> Then said he unto me, this is the curse that goeth forth over the face of the whole earth: for everyone that stealeth shall be cut off as on this side according to it; and everyone that sweareth shall be cut off as on that side according to it.*
<4> I will bring it forth, saith the Lord of host, and it shall enter into the house of the thief, and into the house of him that sweareth falsely by my name (the nations, institutionalized religions, evil colonial empires, etc.); *and it shall remain in the midst of his house, and shall consume it with the timber thereof and the stones thereof.]*

THE TRUTH

The angels travel in the U.F.Os, orchestrating the will of the Lord YAHAWAH on earth. Recall that the angels in the flying chariots are anthropomorphized as men of the Asiatic type! And Christ will invade the world with thousands of those flying chariots on the Day of Doom in order to save the true Israelites and Christians from the destruction!

<< *Habakkuk 3:8* >> [*Was the Lord so displeased against the rivers? was thine wrath against the sea* (rivers and seas symbolize the big and small nations), *that thou didst ride upon thine horses and thy chariots of salvation?* (Salvation from the nuclear war and doomsday)]

<< *Verse 16* >> [*...When he cometh up unto the people, he will invade them with his troops.*]

Christ's troops are the angels and the resurrected saints (Israelites and Christians) in flying saucers. The angels are the armies of Christ and of the original Hebrew Israelites. We already have an army! The angels will be at our command. No nation can ever defeat us. The angels are innumerable. Jesus Christ said:

<< *Matthew 26:53* >> [*...Thinkest thou that I cannot now pray to my father, and he shall presently give me more than twelve legions of angels?*]
<< *Psalm 68:17* >> [*The chariots of the Lord are twenty thousand, even thousands of angels.*]

The world will be invaded by thousands of angels, coming in those U.F.Os with Christ on the day of judgement, to rescue the Israelites! The Lord YAHAWAH says:

<< *Habakkuk 1:5* >> [*...Behold ye among the heathens, and regard, and wonder marvelously: for I will work a work in your days, which ye will not believe, though it be told you.*]

Whether you believe it or not make no difference; the flying saucers are real. The Israelites and the Christian believers will be saved out of the tribulations, nuclear war, and doomsday, by being carried away in the U.F.Os! The "clouds of heaven" is another name for the flying chariots, or U.F.Os. The Israelites came to America on slave ships, but will leave here first class on the flying saucers!

<< *First Thessalonians 4:16-18* >> [*For the Lord himself shall descend from heaven with a shout, with the voice of the archangel, and with the trump of God: and the dead in Christ shall rise first: then we which are alive and remain shall be caught up together with them in the clouds, to meet the Lord in the air: and so shall we ever be with the Lord.*]

<< *Matthew 24:30,31* >> [*And then shall appear the sign of the son of man in heaven* (the flying saucers): *and then shall all the tribes of the earth mourn, and they shall see the Son of man* (the MASHAYAK YAHAWASHY, meaning Jesus Christ) *coming in the clouds of heaven* (the flying saucers, the U.F.Os) *with power and great glory. And he shall send his*

angels with a great sound of a trumpet, and they shall gather together his elect from the four winds, from one end of heaven to the other.]

Only the people who accept Jesus Christ and the Biblical truth and who are doing the work commanded by the lord God YAHAWAH will be saved! The scriptures describe the sequence of events that will take place in the final hour:

<< *Revelation 11:12,13* >> *[And they heard a great voice from heaven saying unto them* (to the Israelites and Christians that are waiting for Christ), *Come up hither. And they ascended up to heaven in a cloud* (the flying saucers); *and their enemies beheld them. And the same hour was there a great earthquake* (nuclear bombs exploding, earthquakes), *and the tenth part of the city fell* (ten symbolizes a completion, meaning the destruction was total), *and in the earthquake were slain of men seven thousand* (seven symbolizes completion, everyone left in America was burned up): *and the remnant* (the Israelites and Christians that were saved by the U.F.Os) *were affrighted and gave glory to the Lord of heaven.]*

<< *Psalm 91:5-12*>> *[Thou shalt not be afraid for the terror by night* (the plagues); *nor for the arrow that flieth by day* (nuclear missiles); *Nor for the pestilence that walketh in darkness; nor for the destruction that wasteth at noonday* (the U.F.Os will attack on doomsday). *A thousand shall fall at thy side, and ten thousand at thy right hand; but it shall not come nigh thee* (because we will be above it all in the flying saucers looking down). *Only with thine eyes shalt thou behold and see the reward of the wicked. Because thou hast made the Lord, which is my refuge, even the Most High, thy habitation; There shall no evil befall thee neither shall any plague come night thy dwelling. For he shall give his angels charge over thee, to keep thee in all thy ways. They shall bear thee up in their hands, lest thou dash thy foot against a stone.]*

The original Hebrew Israelites and all of those who accepts the truth, will be in first class seats looking down at the nations getting burned up for what they did against God, the Bible, and the true Israelites! There will be no escape!

THE KINGDOM OF HEAVEN

After the tribulation, the earth will be renewed by a miracle. Then the Israelites will be ruling in their kingdom forever! As the scripture says:

<< *Revelation 21:1* >> [*And I saw a new heaven and a new earth: for the first heaven and the first earth were passed away!*]

<< *Daniel 7:27* >> [*And the kingdom and the dominion, and the greatness of the kingdom under the whole heaven, shall be given to the people of the saints of the Most High* (the original Asiatic Israelites), *whose kingdom is an everlasting kingdom, and all dominion shall serve and obey him.*]

<< *Isaiah 49:22-26* >> [*Thus saith the Lord, Behold, I will lift up mine hand to the Gentiles, and set up my standard to the people: and they shall bring thy sons in their arms, and thy daughters shall be carried upon their shoulders. <23> And kings shall be thy nursing fathers, and their queens thy nursing mothers: they shall bow down to thee with their face toward the earth, and lick up the dust of thy feet; and thou shall know that I am the Lord: for they shall not be ashamed that wait for me.*
     <25> But thus saith the LORD, Even the captives of the mighty shall be taken away, and the prey of the terrible shall be delivered: for I will contend with him (the nations) *that contendeth with thee* (the Israelites), *<26> and I will save thy children. And I will feed them that oppress thee with their own flesh; and they shall be drunken with their own blood, as with sweet wine: and all flesh shall know that I the Lord am thy Savior and thy redeemer, the mighty One of Jacob.*]

Christ is Savior and Redeemer to the Israelites as a nation, coming to reestablish their kingdom on the earth! And in that kingdom, Our rulership will be absolute and we will have the spiritual power from God as Moses had and as Christ had! Christ said:

<< *John 14:12* >> [*Verily, I say unto you, He that believeth in me, the works that I do shall he do also; and greater works than these shall he do; because I go to my father.*]

<< *Revelation 11:3-6* >> [*And I will give power unto my two witnesses.*]

Judah (the two tribes) and Israel (the ten tribes) are the two true witnesses of the Bible. The scriptures also explain how we will be given immortality:

<< *First Corinthians 15:51-55* >> [*Now this I say, brethren, that flesh and blood cannot inherit the kingdom of God; neither doth corruption inherit incorruption. <51> Behold, I shew you a mystery; we shall not all sleep, but we shall be changed, <52> In a moment, in the twinkling of an eye, at the last trump: <53> for the trumpet shall sound, and the dead shall be*

raised incorruptible, and we shall be changed. <54> For this corruptible must put on incorruption, and this mortal must put on immortality, then shall be brought to pass the saying that is written, death is swallowed up in victory.]

The making of man will be completed. We were created to be in the image and likeness of God.

<< Psalms 82:6 >> [I have said, ye are gods; and all of you are children of the Most High.]

We have a great future that we cannot even begin to imagine. According to the Bible:

<< I Corinthians 2:9 >> [...Eyes hath not seen, nor ears heard, neither have entered into the heart of man, the things which the Lord hath prepared for them that love him!]

<< Isaiah 51:16 >> [...And I have put my words in thy mouth, and I have covered thee in the shadow of my hand, that I may plant the heavens (Plant the heavens means that we will be going out to the stars and colonizing the planets and galaxies, using our flying saucers)*, and lay the foundations of the earth, and say unto Zion, Thou art my people.]*

<< Isaiah. 60:10-12 >> [And the sons of strangers shall build up thy walls and their kings shall minister unto thee: for in my wrath I smote thee, in my favor have I had mercy on thee. <11> Therefore thy gates shall be open continually; they shall not be shut day nor night; that men may bring unto thee the forces of the Gentiles, and that their kings may be brought. For the nation and king that will not serve thee shall perish; yea, those nations shall be utterly wasted.]

The new city of Jerusalem, our capital, will come straight from heaven and it will be made of all kinds of precious stone and metals:

<< Revelation 21:10-22 >> [And he carried me away in the spirit to a great and high mountain, and shewed me that great city, the holy Jerusalem, descending out of heaven from God, <11> Having the glory of God: and her light was like unto a stone most precious, even like a jasper stone, clear as crystal; <12> And had a wall great and high, and had twelve gates, and at the gates twelve angels, and names written thereon, which are the names of the twelve tribes of the children of Israel: <13> On the east three gates; on the north three gates; on the south three gates; and on the west three gates. <14> And the wall of the city had twelve foundations, and in them the names of the twelve apostles of the Lamb.
<15> And he that talked with me had a golden reed to measure the city, and the gates thereof, and the wall thereof. <16> And the city lieth foursquare, and the length is as large as the breadth: and he measured the city with the reed, twelve thousand furlongs. The length and the breadth and the height of it are equal. <17> And he measured the wall thereof, an hundred and forty and four cubits, according to the measure of a man, that is, of the angel.
<18> And the building of the wall of it was of jasper: and the city was pure gold, like unto clear glass. <19> And the foundations of the wall of the city were garnished with all manner of precious stones. The first foundation was jasper; the second, sapphire; the third, a

chalcedony; the fourth, an emerald; <20> The fifth, sardonyx; the sixth, sardius; the seventh, chrysolite; the eighth, beryl; the ninth, a topaz; the tenth, a chrysoprasus; the eleventh, a jacinth; the twelfth, an amethyst. <21> And the twelve gates were twelve pearls; every several gate was of one pearl: and the street of the city was pure gold, as it were transparent glass. <22> And I saw no temple therein: for the Lord God Almighty and the Lamb are the temple of it.]

<< Isaiah 42:9 >> *[Behold, former things are come to pass, and new things do I declare: before they spring forth I tell you of them.]*

So there will be no excuses accepted, because the Bible is available in every major language. If a person wishes to learn the truth, he has to be willing to make the sacrifices, to study and to pray!

<< Revelation 22:12-14 >> *[And behold, I come quickly; my reward is with me, to give every man according as his work shall be. <13> I am Alpha and Omega, the beginning and the end, the first and the last. <14> Blessed are they that do his commandments, that they may have right to the tree of life, and may enter in through the gates into the city. For without are dogs, and sorcerers, and whoremongers, and idolaters, and whosoever loveth and maketh a lie!]*

Don't believe any man, only believe the word of the Lord God YAHAWAH according to our Savior Mashayak Yahawashy, as written in the Bible.

<< John 7:38 >> *[He that believeth on me (Jesus) as the scripture hath said!]*

The Bible should be your guide. The truth should not be as your churches say or as he says or she says, or as you feel, but as the BIBLE says.

<< Romans 3:3,4 >> *[For what if some did not believe? shall their unbelief make the faith of God without effect <4> God forbid: yea, let God be true, but every man a liar; as it is written, That thou mightest be justified in thy sayings, and mightest overcome when thou art judged.]*

Get together with your friends and share the knowledge, grow stronger and receive freedom and joy in the truth.

<< Hebrews 10:23-25 >> *[Let us hold fast the professing of our faith without wavering; (for he is faithful that promised;) And let us consider one another to provoke unto love and to good works: not forsaking the assembling of ourselves together, as the manner of some is; but exhorting one another: and so much more, as ye see the day approaching.]*

THE PATH OF ENLIGHTENMENT

What is mankind, and why was he created? The purpose of mankind is to love God. Mankind is like a seed sown into the earth. But a seed has to go through a process of initiation, where it dies in the ground and waits for the right season. There it has to receive the water and food of life before it can develop into the great plant it was destined to become. Likewise, in the appointed season, Israelites will actualize their defining potential and become like the Father who had planted this special seed!

>*<< Psalms 82:6 >> [I have said, ye are gods; and all of you are the children of the Most High God.]*

This microcosmic seed that the Lord YAHAWAH has sown into the earth is the original twelve tribes of Israel! The earth is like an egg containing children to be delivered when the time is right. Like all seeds, Israelites and Christians have to endure and wait in due time to become what we were created to be! Our appointed time is at hand! We are Adam. We had to die because we had eaten of the fruit of disobedience. We required redemption through Jesus Christ; Christ paid the price for us as the Lamb without blemish.

An initiation process is set before this seed before it can become a mighty tree. First, it has to be buried under the earth in a dark, cold, hostile environment, where the little seed has to die as a seed. In addition, it must remain there until the appointed season (and no sooner), then it blossoms into a giant tree! Only through this rough initiation process can the seed be transformed into a gigantic tree.

Likewise, the Israelites had to go through and endure the initiation process that will transform them from simply carnal material beings into spiritual everlasting ones as sons of the Lord God YAHAWAH. To understand the initiation of Israel we must understand Jesus Christ. Christ is the guide; his life is the only path leading to that which we were created to become!

>*<< John 14:6 >> [Jesus said unto him, I am the way, the truth, and the life: no man cometh unto the Father, but by me.]*

>*<< John 1:12, 13 >> [But as many as received him, to them gave he power to become the sons of the Lord God YAHAWAH, even to them that believe on his name: Which were born, not of the flesh, nor of the will of man, but of the Almighty God YAHAWAH.]*

The initiation through Jesus starts with repentance and baptism. However, the true understanding of baptism has to be realized.

>*<< Luke 3:16 >> [John answered, saying unto them all, I indeed baptize you with water; but one mightier than I cometh, the latches of whose shoes I am not worthy to unloose: he shall baptize you with the Holy Spirit and with fire.]*

In other words, this water baptism was only symbolic of the true cleansing, the true initiation process, which was Christ. We are baptized in Christ not by being submerged in water only, but by obeying, knowing, and

THE TRUTH

understanding the words of the Lord God YAHAWAH! It is the truth that sanctifies us. Jesus Christ is that word! Christ prayed and said:

<< John 17:17 >> [Sanctify them through thy truth: thy word is truth.]

To understand that path, lets examine the events of the life of Christ in order to recognize the patterns and see the obstacles and the temptations that we have to overcome as initiates! This is important to know in advance, that way you will be able to understand the emotional, mental, and spiritual forces that you'll encounter daily as you walk in the path of truth! The first event encountered concerning Christ was the angel's announcement to the shepherds:

<< Luke 2:8-11 >> [And there were in the same country shepherds abiding in the field, keeping watch over their flock by night. And, lo, the angel of the Lord came upon them, and the glory of the Lord shone round about them: and they were sore afraid. And the angel said unto them, Fear not: for, behold, I bring you good tidings of great joy, which shall be to all people. For unto you is born this day in the city of David a Savior, which is Christ the Lord.]

The angel's coming to the shepherds was symbolic of mankind being invited as an initiate to become part of the Holy Family of the Lord YAHAWAH! Hearing this truth was your invitation to return as Hebrew Israelites and Christians, accepting the truth according to Jesus Christ. In the next event we see Herod (an Edomite) seeking to kill the newborn baby Jesus:

<< Matthew 2:13-16 >> [And when they were departed, behold, the angel of the Lord appeareth to Joseph in a dream, saying, Arise, and take the young child and his mother, and flee thou into Egypt, and be thou there until I bring thee word: for Herod will seek the young child to destroy him. When he arose, he took the young child and his mother by night, and departed into Egypt.]

Herod represents the evil world, the negative, and the past that is trying to prevent the spiritual, the new, and the righteous from manifesting! As the parable of the sower explains, once that young seed is planted many external elements will try to destroy it. Evil spirits, mental conflicts, fear, jealous people, and material lust and all things in the world will try to take you from the righteous path in Christ!

The family of Jesus fled into Egypt on a mule. The mule is a stubborn animal, it symbolizes our resistance and stubbornness to accepting the truth and doing the job we were chosen to do as defenders of this truth! You must overcome these elements!

[<15> And was there until the death of Herod: that it might be fulfilled which was spoken of the Lord by the prophet, saying, Out of Egypt have I called my son. <16> Then Herod (an Edomite), when he saw that he was mocked of the wise men, was exceeding wroth, and sent forth to slew all the children that were in Bethlehem, and in all the coasts thereof, from two years old and under, according to the time which he had diligently inquired of the wise men.]

Then we see Christ being symbolically baptized in the river:

THE TRUTH

<< *Matthew 3:13-15* >> [*Then cometh Jesus from Galilee to Jordan unto John, to be baptized of him. But John forbade him, saying I have needed to be baptized of thee, and comest thou to me? And Jesus said unto him, Suffer it so to be for now: for thus it cometh us to fulfill all righteousness. Then he suffered him.*]

The water Christ was submerged in symbolizes the torments, pains, and the sorrows of the world that the believers would go through in daily living. As Christ emerged with divine power and spiritual attributes, similarly the Israelites will emerge out of the waters of affliction and fear as new beings, with spiritual power and attributes! You must endure to the end.

Then Christ was taken into the wilderness to be tempted. He was alone: symbolizing our personal inner battles as we wrestle in the truth. Among other things we have to overcome old habits and carnal desires: ego trips, selfishness, pride, lust for materialism, envy.

<< *Matthew 4:3-11* >> [*And when the tempter came to him, he said, If thou be the Son of God, command that these stones be made bread. But he said, It is written, Man shall not live by bread alone, but by every word that proceeded out of the mouth of God.*]

Like your friend might say to you, If you love me: do this or that; think twice, that is how Satan comes. You, too, will be tempted to use your new energy, knowledge, and wisdom to fulfill materialistic desires and personal gains. Be alert against that temptation. Christ has said:

<< *Mark 8:34-38* >> [*And when he had called the people unto him with his disciples also, he said unto them, Whosoever will come after me, let him deny himself, and take up his cross, and follow me. <35> For whosoever will save his life shall lose it; but whosoever shall lose his life for my sake and the gospel's, the same shall save it. <36> For what shall it profit a man, if he shall gain the whole world, and lose his own soul? <37> Or what shall a man give in exchange for his soul? <38> Whosoever therefore shall be ashamed of me and of my words in this adulterous and sinful generation; of him also shall the Son of man be ashamed, when he cometh in the glory of his Father with the holy angels.*]

A rich man can't enter into the next kingdom; he must serve the poor and needy. Jesus explained this to the rich man:

<< *Luke 18:22-25* >> [*...Yet lackest thou one thing: sell all that thou hast, and distribute unto the poor, and thou shalt have treasures in heaven: and come follow me. And when he heard this, he was very sorrowful: for he was very rich. And when Jesus saw that he was very sorrowful, he said, How hardly shall they that have riches enter into the kingdom of God! For it is easier for a camel to go through a needle's eye, than for a rich man to enter into the kingdom of God.*]

The kingdom belongs to the poor and the meek:

THE TRUTH

<< *Matthew 5:3-5* >> *[Blessed are the poor in spirit: for theirs is the kingdom of heaven. Blessed are they that mourn: for they shall be comforted. Blessed are the meek: for they shall inherit the earth.]*

<< *Luke 16:25* >> *[But Abraham said, Son, remember that thou in thy lifetime receivedst thy good things, and likewise Lazarus evil things: But now he is comforted, and thou art tormented.]*

<< *James 2:5-7* >> *[Hearken, my beloved brethren, Hath not God chosen the poor of this world rich in faith, and heirs of the kingdom which he hath promised to them that love him? But ye have despised the poor. Do not rich men oppress you, and draw you before the judgment seats? Do not they blaspheme that worthy name by the which ye are called?]*

<< *Matthew 4:5-11* >> *[Then the devil taketh him up into the holy city, and setteth him on a pinnacle of the temple, <6> and said unto him, If thou be the Son of Lord YAHAWAH, cast thyself down: for it is written, He shall give his angels charge concerning thee: and in their hands they shall bear thee up, lest at any time thou dash thy foot against a stone. <7> Jesus said unto him, It is written again, Thou shalt not tempt the Lord thy God. <8> Again, the devil taketh him up into an exceeding high mountain, and sheweth him all the kingdoms of the world, and the glory of them; <9> And saith unto him; All these things will I give thee, If thou wilt fall down and worship me. Then saith Jesus unto him, Get thee hence, Satan: for it is written, Thou shall worship the Lord thy God, and him only shalt thou serve.]*

Many great and strong leaders have fallen and sold out when they were tempted with positions of power! private wealth, and positions of power are among the carnal, and materialistic things of this world. People seeking those things are seeking their own glory and not the glory of the Lord God YAHAWAH or of his kingdom.

<< *Matthew 6:19-34* >> *[Lay not up for yourselves treasures upon earth, where moth and rust doth corrupt, and where thieves break through and steal: <20> But lay up for yourselves treasures in heaven, where neither moth nor rust doth corrupt, and where thieves do not break through nor steal: <21> For where your treasure is, there will your heart be also.*

<22> The light of the body is the eye: if therefore thine eye be single, thy whole body shall be full of light. <23> But if thine eye be evil, thy whole body shall be full of darkness. If therefore the light that is in thee be darkness, how great is that darkness! <24> No man can serve two masters: for either he will hate the one, and love the other; or else he will hold to the one, and despise the other. Ye cannot serve God and mammon. <25> Therefore I say unto you, Take no thought for your life, what ye shall eat, or what ye shall drink; nor yet for your body, what ye shall put on. Is not the life more than meat, and the body than raiment? <26> Behold the fowls of the air: for they sow not, neither do they reap, nor gather into barns; yet your heavenly Father feedeth them. Are ye not much better than they?

<27> Which of you by taking thought can add one cubit unto his stature? <28> And why take ye thought for raiment? Consider the lilies of the field, how they grow;

they toil not, neither do they spin: <29> And yet I say unto you, That even Solomon in all his glory was not arrayed like one of these. <30> Wherefore, if God so clothe the grass of the field, which today is, and tomorrow is cast into the oven, shall he not much more clothe you, O ye of little faith? <31> Therefore take no thought, saying, What shall we eat? or, What shall we drink? or, Wherewithal shall we be clothed? <32> For after all these things do the Gentiles seek: for your heavenly Father knoweth that ye have need of all these things. <33> But seek ye first the kingdom of God, and his righteousness; and all these things shall be added unto you. <34> Take therefore no thought for the morrow: for the morrow shall take thought for the things of itself. Sufficient unto the day is the evil thereof.]

<< Matthew 11:25-28 >>: [But Jesus called them unto him, and said, Ye know that the princes of the Gentiles exercise dominion over them, and they that are great exercise authority upon them. But it shall not be so among you, but whosoever will be chief among you, let him be your servant: Even as the son of man came not to be ministered unto, but to minister and to give his life a ransom for many.]

Also, it is not good to boast about your self, nor to keep company with those that have such attitudes:

<< First Corinthians 4:6,7 >> [...that ye might learn in us not to think of men above that which is written, that no one of you may be puffed up for one against another. For who maketh thee to differ from one another? and what has thou that thou didst not receive? now if thou didst receive it why doest thou glory, as if thou hadst not received it?]

<< Second Corinthians 10:12 >> [For we dare not make ourselves of the number, or compare ourselves with some that commend themselves: but they measuring themselves by themselves, and comparing themselves among themselves, are not wise.]

And although the priority is to be united, do not be a part of any fanatical group, if according to your integrity you feel they are not teaching the truth, and with the right motives. Christ wants us to be committed to the Lord God YAHAWAH, not to groups or religions. Make sure you are teaching the truth from the Bible!

<< Luke 9:49, 50 >> [And John answered and said, Master, we saw one casting out devils in thy name; and we forbade him, because he followeth not with us. And Jesus said unto him, Forbid him not: for he that is not against us is for us.]

<< John 13:34 >> [A new commandment I give unto you, That ye love one another; as I have loved you, that ye also love one another. <35> By this shall all men know that ye are my disciples, if ye have love one to another.]

Your salvation is a personal thing between you and God; it is your unique responsibility, in which no excuses will be accepted when the judgement day arrives! Another event in this path that we should examine, is the betrayal and the crucifixion of Christ. Christ was betrayed and denied by his people, the government, his best and closest friends, and his disciples. Often times you, too, will suffer betrayal and denial by your closest allies when you are on the path of true baptism in Christ. It is very hard to teach a rebellious, fearful, ignorant and evil people. At his hour of need, Christ was looking for comfort from his disciples and he found none. There will be many times when you, too, will seek comfort from the ones you expected it from, and you will find none.

Those distressful feelings that were experienced by Christ, we, too, will suffer them in our own way: solitude, isolation, pain, embarrassment, and betrayal. Prepare yourself to deal with it, the times will come to you on your path as well. You must become accustomed to relying totally on your own inner strength, as determined by your faith in the Lord YAHAWAH. This is what Christ did, and he was resurrected to glory! A warrior must have endurance. Do not quit.

<< Matthew 23:37-39 >> [O Jerusalem, Jerusalem, thou that killest the prophets, and stonest them which are sent unto thee, how often would I have gathered thy children together, even as a hen gathereth her chickens under her wings, and ye would not! Behold, your house is left unto you desolate. For I say unto you, Ye shall not see me henceforth, until ye shall say, Blessed is he that cometh in the name of the Lord.]

<< Matthew 24:13 >> [He that shall endure unto the end, the same shall be saved.]

<< Isaiah 48:10 >> [Behold, I have refined thee, but not with silver; I have chosen thee in the furnace of affliction.]

Who was more afflicted, for the past four thousand years, than the twelve tribes of Israel? But this affliction is part of the process of making man. What Christ went through is a model or pattern: the same path we will experience in our life. Christ was crucified and they gave him vinegar to drink. The Israelites taste that bitterness and the stripes daily. As a people, the Israelites live in poverty. We feel forsaken by the Lord YAHAWAH, as Christ did when he was on that cross. This is because of our torments.

The Romans forced a crown of thorns upon the head of Christ. The pain from the thorns in his head symbolizes all the mental pains that we will have to endure in the world, those resulting from social, personal, psychological, and mental affliction, as well as from spiritual warfare.

Of the two thieves crucified with Christ, one doubted him while the other had faith. This event symbolizes our inner anguish and mental war just before the perfection! Similarly, Israelites and true Christians are being baptized with the same baptism as Christ! There will be many times when you will question your faith and even rebel temporarily. This will serve to test the truth against other beliefs. But, in the long run, all of the testing and exploring will only serve to strengthen your faith, confirm the truth, and make you wiser and more experienced! When you find yourself in mental and spiritual confrontation and warfare understand that the Bible did say it would happen that way. But you must remain strong and defend the truth! You can do this only by knowing exactly what the scriptures say.

Yes, it has to happen this way, we have to suffer because we have broken the law and the covenant that we made with the Lord YAHAWAH. We have to learn the consequences of disobedience. That is why! Christ had to suffer and die so we could have redemption. He suffered and gave himself as our sacrificial lamb:

<< Acts 17:3 >> [Opening and alleging, that Christ must needs have suffered, and risen again from the dead; and that this Jesus, whom I preached unto you, is Christ.]

THE TRUTH

If Christ did not offer himself as a ransom for humanity, we would never become reconciled to the Lord YAHAWAH. It is all part of the master plan! We suffer because of the curses associated with our sins and the sins of our ancestors. Don't be confused because you suffer, it is part of the plan. And don't think in your mind that just because you're an Israelite or a Christian and you're doing your best to keep the law, therefore you should not be suffering. Satan will always target the people who love God, to afflict and to destroy. In addition, the fact that we suffer the way we do also confirms that we are the original Israelites! You have to pay your dues and meet the requirements for the kingdom. You have to accept the suffering:

<< *Philippians 1:29* >> [*For unto you it is given in the behalf of Christ, not only to believe on him, but also to suffer for his sake*]

In reality, your endurance and suffering will be rewarded. We will all be tempted, and unfortunately at times yield to those temptations. This will result into more pain. But to make it to the kingdom, you must resist, overcome the temptations, and pray for forgiveness and strength. It is a part of growth and development. For those who choose to suffer and not yield to the temptations of the world, they will be rewarded many times over!

<< *Second Timothy 2:12* >> [*If we suffer, we shall also reign with him: if we deny him, he also will deny us*]:

<< *Matthew 10:22* >> Christ also said: [*And ye shall be hated of all men for my name's sake: but he that shall endure to the end shall be saved!*]

Don't give up! God gave us his word in writing; the Lord YAHAWAH will not forget you. He will deliver you according to his promise.

<< *First Corinthians 10:13* >> [*There hath no temptation taken you but such as is common to man: but God is faithful, who will not suffer you to be tempted above that ye are able; but will with the temptation also make a way to escape, that ye may be able to bear it.*]

<< *Second peter 2:9* >> [*The Lord knoweth how to deliver the godly out of temptations, and to reserve the unjust unto the Day of Judgment to be punished.*]

As Christ died and was resurrected, the original Israelites had to die; but they will be resurrected as a nation with all power! The resurrection of the dead to life has been the theme throughout the Bible! We can find this theme in the story of Joseph- when his own brothers tried to kill him and placed Joseph in a hole. After that, he ended up in Egypt as a righteous man with fame and fortune. There are many other people around the world who are persecuted for their righteousness and faith in Christ. They also will be redeemed by God and given salvation.

We are like Joseph placed in a hole, but we will be taken out of that hole. We are the people in the valley of dry bones in Ezekiel 37 that was resurrected! We are Job that was afflicted. We are Jonah in the belly of the whale. And we are Daniel in the Lion's den. The original Israelites will emerge alive from the lion's den. And as Daniel was placed in the furnace, so are we placed into this furnace of affliction in this world, but we will emerge and be resurrected, untouched by the fire!

THE TRUTH

<< *John 16:33* >> *[These things I have spoken unto you, that in me ye might have peace. In the world ye shall have tribulation: but be of good cheer; I have overcome the world.]*

We are the prodigal sons who have abandoned our father, the Lord YAHAWAH:

<< *Luke 15:11-24* >> *[And he said, A certain man had two sons: <12> And the younger of them said to his father, Father, give me my portion of goods that falleth to me. And he divided unto them his living. <13> And not many days after the younger son gathered all together, and took his journey into a far country, and there wasted his substance with riotous living.*
<14>And when he had spent all, there arose a mighty famine in that land; and he began to be in want. <15> And he went and joined himself to a citizen of that country; <16> and he sent him into his fields to feed swine. And he would faint have filled his belly with the husks that the swine did eat: and no man gave unto him.]

We have journeyed into materialism, a form of spiritual death and entombment; just like the prodigal son had to sink to the lowest level and eat the husks that only the swine ate. Only after this did he come to himself and was resurrected into the truth and in wisdom. The Israelites had to be brought down to that same low condition for us to understand God, repent and accept the spiritual values! Only then could we start taking the return journey to our identity and our God YAHAWAH!

<< *Luke 15:17-28*> *[And when he came to himself, he said, How many hired servants of my father's have bread enough to spare, and I perish with hunger! <18> I will arise and go to my father, and will say unto him, Father, I have sinned against heaven, and before thee, <19> And am no more worthy to be called thy son: make me as one of thy hired servants* (repentance)*. <20> And he arose, and came to his father. But when he was a great way off, his father saw him, and had compassion, and ran, and fell on his neck, and kissed him* (The Most High loves to see an Israelite wake up)*. <21> And the son said unto him, Father, I have sinned against heaven in thy sight, and am no more worthy to be called thy son. <22> But the father said to his servants, Bring forth the best robe, and put it on him; and put a ring in his hand, and shoes on his feet: <23> and bring hither the fatted calf, and kill it; and let us eat it and be merry: <24> For this my son was dead, and is alive again; he was lost and is found. And they began to be merry.]*

Can you imagine the Joy to come at the return of Jesus Christ for the original twelve tribes of Israel and the Christians?

<25> Now his elder son was in the field: and as he came and drew near to the house, he heard music and dancing. <26> And he called one of the servants, and asked what these things meant. <27> And he saith unto him, thy brother is come; and thy father hath killed the fatted calf, because he hath received him safe and sound. <28> And he was angry, and would not go in: therefore came his father out, and entreated him.]

The older son represents the forces opposing the coming of the new and the spiritually reborn. Just as Herod and the Pharisees conspired to kill Christ, similarly, be on guard so that no one causes you to leave this path of eternal life. Your own people and the ones nearest to you, will be the first ones attempting to kill the new spiritual knowledge that the Lord planted within you!

> *<29> [And he answering said to his father, Lo, these many years do I serve thee, neither transgressed I at any time thy commandment: and yet thou never gavest me a kid, that I might make merry with my friends: But as soon as this thy son was come, which hath devoured thy living with harlots, thou hast killed for him the fatted calf.]*

The older brother was jealous and envious of the younger because he came back with the spiritual gifts of wisdom and understanding as a new man. Remember, Caine killed Able because Able was righteous, and Cain was jealous and envious of his brother.

> *<< Luke 15:31,32 >> [And he said unto him, Son, thou art ever with me, and all that I have is thine. <32> It was meet that we should make merry, and be glad: for this thy brother was dead, and now is alive again; and was lost, and is found.]*

The original twelve tribes of Israel are the prodigal son and will be restored as the kingdom of heaven on earth. All nations must repent of evil, proclaim the truth, and return to our Father, the Lord YAHAWAH, through our Savior the MASHAYAK YAHAWASHY.

THE TRUTH

The Israelite Movement

Who are the Israelites? An Israelite is a blood descendent of Abraham, Isaac and Jacob, belonging to one of the twelve tribes of Israel. The bulk of the twelve tribes of Israel consist of the Asiatic people of the Western Hemisphere. A person cannot be converted into an Israelite because Israel is a nation determined by paternal genealogy (genealogy along the line of their fathers only) and not religion. The Europeans Ashkenazis who are calling themselves Jews and Israelis are impostors. Their ancestors are the Khazars who had converted to Judaism during the Dark Ages.

What do Israelites believe? We believe that there is only one true God, whose name in the Hebrew language is YAHAWAH. It is a great sin to worship, idolize, or pray to Maria or any other idol. We believe that Jesus Christ, whose name in Hebrew is Mashayak Yahawashy, is the one and only Savior and Mediator between God and man. Yahawashy will soon return as king of kings to deliver us. We believe that the Bible contains the word of God and is the final authority over all other sources of knowledge.

What makes the Israelite Network different? There are many separate organizations and denominations among the Israelites and Christians. This is because of ignorance and ego. The truth is infinite and man is finite. Let us be humble and learn together, because no one knows it all. We are all one body in Christ, learning and growing. Our little differences should not be a reason for division. Divided we fall, but united we stand.

The Israelite Network is different from most other organizations in that we do not teach hate and prejudice, or seek after personal power and glory. Part of our mission is to collaborate and work with other organizations for the purpose of spreading the true gospel of the kingdom of heaven. Some organizations do not accept the complete bible as the word of God. Some reject the New Testament and the Apocrypha. We accept the entire set of scriptures, from Genesis to Revelation, including the Apocrypha. We do not perform animal sacrifices because Yahawashy is the last and perfect sacrifice who takes away all of our sins. We believe that the acceptance of the sacrifice of Yahawashy's life on the cross for us is the only way to salvation.

The Israelites are the original Christians. But we are different from many Christian churches in this world. We believe that the religions of the world are deceived and that it is racist to portray God, Jesus, and the Israelites of the Bible with European features. The historical facts confirms that Israelites are Afro-asiatic people. Israelites despise all images and idols of worship, including the cross. The cross is an instrument of death used by the Romans to execute people. All things pertaining to the dead are unclean. It is against the laws of God in the Bible to bring any dead body or things pertaining to the dead into the church. Many churches are located in cemeteries. They bring in dead bodies into their churches and idolize images, statues and the cross of death. The Israelites believe in keeping all the laws and Holy Days of God. It is against God's laws to take part in colonial, pagan and Babylonian holiday rituals; for example, Christmas and Halloween. Regardless of our little differences, all true Christians and Israelites is one body in Christ and should treat all people lovingly.

THE TRUTH

Our mission is to multiply and replenish the earth with the goodness, understanding and love of God, by the keeping of his commandments and proclaiming the true gospel of the kingdom of YAHAWAH.

We plan to accomplish our mission in three stages:

1. To restore the true identity of the original twelve tribes of Israel.
2. To reveal the true gospel of the kingdom of Heaven, and eliminate the lies taught against God, the Bible, the Israelites, and the history.
3. To unite all true Israelites and Christians as one body in Mashayak Yahawashy (Christ). The Israelite Network was conceived as an umbrella organization to accomplish this mission.

> << Jeremiah 1:10 >> [See, I have this day set thee over the nations and over the kingdoms, to root out, and to pull down, and to destroy, and to throw down, to build, and to plant.]

> << Matthew 10:5-7 >> [These twelve Jesus sent forth, and commanded them, saying, Go not into the way of the Gentiles, and into any city of the Samaritans enter ye not: <6> But go rather to the lost sheep of the house of Israel. <7> And as ye go, preach, saying, The kingdom of heaven is at hand.]

> << Matthew 28:19, 20 >> [Go ye therefore, and teach all nations, baptizing them in the name of the Father, and of the Son, and of the Holy Ghost: <20> Teaching them to observe all things whatsoever I have commanded you: and, lo, I am with you alway, even unto the end of the world. Amen.]

What you can do: The aim of this book is to present the facts as accurately as we could so that you can derive your own conclusion. If you believe what God is saying in the Bible is true, then we recommend you do three things:

1. Pray to the Most High and ask him to keep you in the path of salvation and bless you with the wisdom, understanding and strength to meet your destiny.
2. You will need to create or join a Christian Israelite Bible study group, where you can be nurtured and grow in the knowledge of the Bible. That organization should focus on love and not hate.
3. In unity there is strength. We invite you to join forces with the Israelite Network. Start spreading the gospel of freedom today by becoming a distributor of this book: THE TRUTH. It is your responsibility. The testimony of the Bible, the original gospel of the kingdom of Heaven, must be sent around the world for a witness unto all nations so we may be redeemed and that the people may repent and learn to praise and Glorify the Lord YAHAWAH!

ANCIENT HEBREW

THE HOLY TONGUE

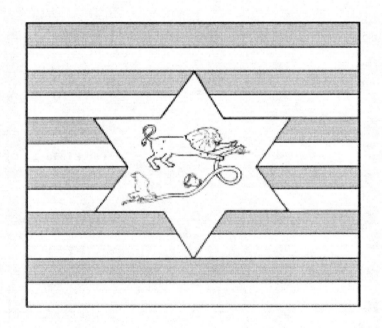

THE TRUTH

Pure Hebrew Letters			Numerical Value	Assyrian		Sample Words	
AH	=	𐤊	1	𐤀		Cattle (Ah-Lap)	𐤊𐤋𐤉
BA	=	𐤁	2	𐤁		House (Ba-Yath)	𐤁𐤉𐤕
GA	=	𐤂	3	𐤂		Camel (Ga-Mal)	𐤂𐤌𐤋
DA	=	𐤃	4	𐤃		Door (Da-lath)	𐤃𐤋𐤕
HA	=	𐤄	5	𐤅		Magnify (Ha-Dar)	𐤄𐤃𐤓
WA	=	𐤅	6	𐤅		Hook (Wa-Wa)	𐤅𐤅
ZA	=	𐤆	7	𐤆		Weapon (Za-Yan)	𐤆𐤉𐤍
CHAA	=	𐤇	8	𐤇		Destroy (Chaa-Bal)	𐤇𐤁𐤋
TA	=	𐤈	9	𐤈		Rejoice (Ta-Ab)	𐤈𐤊𐤁
YA	=	𐤉	10	𐤉		Hand (Yad)	𐤉𐤃
KA	=	𐤊	20	𐤊	𐤊	Palm of Hand (Kap)	𐤊𐤐
LA	=	𐤋	30	𐤋		The Heart (Lab)	𐤋𐤁
MA	=	𐤌	40	𐤌	𐤌	Water (Ma-Yam)	𐤌𐤉𐤌
NA	=	𐤍	50	𐤍	𐤍	Nazarite (Na-Za-Yar)	𐤍𐤆𐤉𐤓
SA	=	𐤎	60	𐤎		Support (Sa-Mak)	𐤎𐤌𐤊
I	=	𐤏	70	𐤏		Eye (I-Yan)	𐤏𐤉𐤍
PA	=	𐤐	80	𐤐	𐤐	Mouth (Pah)	𐤐𐤄
TA-ZA	=	𐤑	90	𐤑	𐤑	Sheep (Ta-Za-An)	𐤑𐤊𐤍
QA	=	𐤒	100	𐤒		Measure (Qa-Bab)	𐤒𐤁𐤁
RA	=	𐤓	200	𐤓		Head (Ra-Ash)	𐤓𐤊w
SHA	=	w	300	𐤔		Tooth (Shan)	𐤔𐤍
THA	=	𐤕	400	𐤕		Sign, End (Tha-Wa)	𐤅𐤕

The lines (__) under the Hebrew letters are used to connect two sounds together.

Hebrew – Practice

$\mathcal{K}$	$\mathcal{K}$
9	9
7	7
$\triangleleft$	$\triangleleft$
$\exists$	$\exists$
Y	Y
z	z
$\boxplus$	$\boxplus$
$\otimes$	$\otimes$
z	z
y	y
ℓ	ℓ
y	y
y	y
$\mp$	$\mp$
$\circ$	$\circ$
7	7
Λ	Λ
φ	φ
4	4
w	w
$\times$	$\times$

Assyrian – Practice	
א	א
ב	ב
ג	ג
ד	ד
ה	ה
ו	ו
ק	ק
ח	ח
ט	ט
ר	ר
כ	כ
ל	ל
מ	מ
נ	נ
ס	ס
ע	ע
פ	פ
צ	צ
ק	ק
ר	ר
ש	ש
ת	ת

ן   ם   ך   ף   ץ

THE TRUTH

Pronouns:

I (m+f) An-Ya			You (m+pl)	(Ah-Tham)	
You (m+f) Ah-Tha			You (f+Pl)	(Ah-Than)	
He (Ha-Wa-Ah)			They (m)	(Ham)	
She (Ha-Ya-Ah)			They (f)	(Han)	
We (m + f) (Ah-Nach-Na-Wa)					

To Form Feminine Adjectives Add (Ha) example:

Ta-Wab + Ha = Ta-Wa-Bah

To Form the Plural (m) Add (Yam)   Plural (f) Add (Wath)

Adjectives must agree in Number as well as in gender with the nouns Which they modify

Present Tense:

I am learning (m)	An-Ya La-Wa-Mad
I am learning (f)	An-Ya La-Wa-Mad-Hah
You're learning (m)	Ah-Thah La-Wa-Mad
You're learning (F)	Ah-Thah La-Wa-Mad-Hah
He's learning	Ha-Wa-Ah La-Wa-Mad
She's learning	Ha-Ya-Ah La-Wa-Mad-Hah
We're learning	Ah-Nach-Na-Wa La-Wa-Mad-Yam
You're learning (m+pl)	Ah-Tham La-Wa-Mad-Yam
You're learning (f+pl)	Ah-Than La-Wa-Mad-Wath
They're learning (m)	Ham La-Wa-Mad-Yam
They're learning (f)	Han La-Wa-Mad-Wath

Past Tense:

I learned (m+f)	**An-Ya La-Mad-Tha-Ya**	𐤀𐤍𐤉 𐤋𐤌𐤃𐤕𐤉
You learned (m+f)	**Ah-Tha La-Mad-Tha**	𐤀𐤕𐤄 𐤋𐤌𐤃𐤕
He learned	**Ha-Wa-Ah La-Mad**	𐤄𐤅𐤀 𐤋𐤌𐤃
She learned	**Ha-Ya-Ah La-Ma-Dah**	𐤄𐤉𐤀 𐤋𐤌𐤃𐤄
We learned	**Ah-Nach-Na-Wa La-Mad-Na-Wa**	𐤀𐤍𐤇𐤍𐤅 𐤋𐤌𐤃𐤍𐤅
You learned (m+p1)	**Ah-Tham La-Mad-Tham**	𐤀𐤕𐤌 𐤋𐤌𐤃𐤕𐤌
You learned (f+p1)	**Ah-Than La-Mad-Than**	𐤀𐤕𐤍 𐤋𐤌𐤃𐤕𐤍
They learned (m)	**Ham La-Mad-Wa**	𐤄𐤌 𐤋𐤌𐤃𐤅
They learned (f)	**Han La-Mad-Wa**	𐤄𐤍 𐤋𐤌𐤃𐤅

Future Tense:

I will learn (m +f)	**An-Ya Ah-La-Mad**	𐤀𐤍𐤉 𐤀𐤋𐤌𐤃
You will learn (m)	**Ah-Thah Tha-La-Mad**	𐤀𐤕𐤄 𐤕𐤋𐤌𐤃
You will learn (f)	**Ah-Thah Tha-La-Mad-Ya**	𐤀𐤕𐤄 𐤕𐤋𐤌𐤃𐤉
He will learn	**Ha-Wa-Ah Ya-La-Mad**	𐤄𐤅𐤀 𐤉𐤋𐤌𐤃
She will learn	**Ha-Ya-Ah Tha-La-Mad**	𐤄𐤉𐤀 𐤕𐤋𐤌𐤃
We will learn	**Ah-Nach-Na-Wa Na-La-Mad**	𐤀𐤍𐤇𐤍𐤅 𐤍𐤋𐤌𐤃
You will learn (m+pl)	**Ah-Tham Tha-La-Mad-Wa**	𐤀𐤕𐤌 𐤕𐤋𐤌𐤃𐤅
You will learn (f+p1)	**Ah-Than Tha-La-Mad-Nah**	𐤀𐤕𐤍 𐤕𐤋𐤌𐤃𐤍𐤄
They will learn (m+p1)	**Ham Ya-La-Mad-Wa**	𐤄𐤌 𐤉𐤋𐤌𐤃𐤅
They will learn (f+p1)	**Han Tha-La-Mad-Nah**	𐤄𐤍 𐤕𐤋𐤌𐤃𐤍𐤄

Possessive Adjectives:

(Sword) Chaa-Rab 𐤇𐤓𐤁 beomes (My sword) Chaa-rab-Ya 𐤇𐤓𐤁𐤉

My	**(m+f) Ya**	𐤉	**Our**	**Na-Wa**	𐤍𐤅
Your	**(m+f) Ka**	𐤊	**Your**	**(m+pl)**	𐤊𐤌
His	**Wa**	𐤅	**Your**	**(f+p1) Kan**	𐤊𐤍
Hers	**Ha**	𐤄	**Their**	**(m) Ma**	𐤌
Their (f)	**Na**	𐤍			

THE TRUTH

Conversation:

Hello / Good-bye / Peace	Sha-lam	ッ6w
Good Morning brother	Ba-Wa-Qar Ta-wab Ahch	刊长 ケY⊗ 刊PY9
What is your name	Mah Sham-ka	ッッw ∃ッ
My name is (name) son of (tribe) son of (nation).	Sham-ya__Ban_ Ban__ .	__ッ9__ッ9__2ッw
How are you/ How is your peace?	Mah Sha-lam-ka	ッッ6w ∃ッ
My peace is good thanks	Sha-lam-ya Ta-wab Tha-wa-dah	∃⊲Yx ケY⊗ 2ッ6w
Good evening sister.	I-Rab Ta-wab Ahch-wath	xY 卄长 ケY⊗ ケ⅄o
What's new?	Mah Chaa-dash	w⊲目 ∃ッ
Nothing new.	Ah-yan Chaa-Dash	w⊲目 ッ2长
Excuse me/Forgive me please.	Sa-lach-ya Ba-Ba-Qa-Sha	wP99 2目6手
Welcome	Ba-Ra-Wak	ッY99
fine/ok/Alright	Ba-Sa-Dar	4⊲手9
Ha Sha-I-Ha Tha-Shi		owx ∃ow9
The time is nine.		
Ha Sha-I-Ha Sha-Ma-Wa-Nah Wa-Ra-Bi		o⅄4Y ∃ッYッw ∃ow9
The time is eight and quarter.		
Ha Sha-I-Ha Tha-Shi Wa-Chaa-Taza-Ya		2rＢY owx ∃ow9
The time is nine and half.		
Ha Sha-I-Ha Ra-Bi La Sha-Lash		w6w6 o⅄4 ∃ow9
The time is quarter to three.		
Ha Sha-I-Ha Shath-Yam I-Sha-Rah		∃4wo ッ2xw ∃ow9
The time is twelve.		
Ha Sha-I-Ha Ah-Chaath Wa-I-Sha-Ra		4woY x 卄长 ∃ow9
The time is one and ten.		

THE TRUTH

One
(Ah-Chaad) ⟨symbol⟩

Two
(Shan-Ya) ⟨symbol⟩

Three
(Sha-Lash) ⟨symbol⟩

Four
(Ah-Ra-Bi ⟨symbol⟩

Five
(Chaa-Mash) ⟨symbol⟩

Six
(Sha-Sha) ⟨symbol⟩

Seven
(Sha-BI) ⟨symbol⟩

Eigth
(Sha-Ma-Wa-Nah) ⟨symbol⟩

Nine
(Tha-Shi) ⟨symbol⟩

Ten
(I-Sha-Ra) ⟨symbol⟩

Eleven
(Ah-Chaad-I-Sha-Ra) ⟨symbol⟩

Twelve
(Shan-Ya-I-Sha-Ra) ⟨symbol⟩

Thirteen
(Sha-Lash-I-Sha-Ra) ⟨symbol⟩

Fourteen
(Ah-Ra-Bi-I-Sha-Ra) ⟨symbol⟩

Fifteen
(Chaa-Mash-I-Sha-Ra) ⟨symbol⟩

Sixteen (Sha-Sha-I-Sha-Ra) ⟨symbol⟩

Seventeen (Sha-Bi-I-Sha-Ra) ⟨symbol⟩

Eighteen
(Sha-Ma-Wa-Nah-I-Sha-Ra) ⟨symbol⟩

Nineteen
(Tha-Shi-I-Sha-Ra) ⟨symbol⟩

Twenty
(I-Sha-Ra-Yam) ⟨symbol⟩

Thirty
(Sha-Lash-Yam) ⟨symbol⟩

Forty
(Ah-Ra-BI-Yam) ⟨symbol⟩

Fifty
(Chaa-Mash-Yam) ⟨symbol⟩

Sixty
(Sha-Sha-Yam) ⟨symbol⟩

Seventy
(Sha-BI-Yam) ⟨symbol⟩

Hundred
(Ma-Ah) ⟨symbol⟩

Two-Hundred
(Shan-Ya-Ma-Ah-Yam) ⟨symbol⟩

Three-Hundred
(Sha-Lash-Ma-Ah-Yam) ⟨symbol⟩

Thousand (Ah-Lap) ⟨symbol⟩

Two-Thousand
(Shan-Ya-Ah-Lap-Yam) ⟨symbol⟩

Three-Thousand
(Sha-Lash-Ah-Lap-Yam) ⟨symbol⟩

THE TRUTH

The Days of the Week	Ha Ya-Wam-Yam Ha Sha-Ba-Wi	
Sunday	Ya-Wam Ra-Ash-Wam	
Monday	Ya-Wam Shan-Ya	
Tuesday	Ya-Wam Sha-Lash	
Wednesday	Ya-Wam Ah-Ra-Bi	
Thursday	Ya-Wam Chaa-Mash	
Friday	Ya-Wam Sha-Sha	
Saturday	Sha-Bath	

The Months of the Year	Ha Chaa-Dash-Yam Ha Sha-Nah	
Month 1	Chaa-Dash Ra-Ash-Wan	
Month 2	Chaa-Dash ShanYa	
Month 3	Chaa-Dash Sha-Lash	
Month 4	Chaa-Dash Ah-Ra-Bi	
Month 5	Chaa-Dash Chaa -Mash	
Month 6	Chaa-Dash Sha-Sha	
Month 7	Chaa-Dash Sha-Bi	
Month 8	Chaa-Dash Sha-Ma-Wa-Nah	
Month 9	Chaa-Dash Tha-Shi	
Month 10	Chaa-Dash I-Sha-Ra	
Month 11	Chaa-Dash Ah-Chaad I-Sha-Ra	
Month 12	Chaa-Dash Shan-Ya I-Sha-Ra	

THE TRUTH

Modern Names	Biblical Names	Pronunciations & Meaning	Table of Identity
Israel	Israel	Ya-Shar-Ala Prince of God	ヨムチイwエ
Arabs	Ishmael	Ya-Sha-Mi-Ah-La God will hear	ヨムチロywエ
Asians	Japhet	Ya-path Expansion	xフエ
North Africa	Phut	Pa -Wat 	⊖Yフ
Egyptians	Mizraim, Egypt	Ma-Tazar-Yam	yエ刊しy
Sub-Saharan Africa	Canaan	Ka-Na-In	yoyy
Ethiopians	Cush, Ethiopians	Ka-Wash	wYy
India	Elam	I-Ya-Lam	yしエo
Caucasian/ Europeans	Edom, Esau	Ah-Da-Wam	yY△チ

*** The Levites and The 12 Tribes Of Israel ***

Haitians	Levi	Law-Ya Joined to me	エYし
Seminole Indians	Reuben	Ra-Aw-Ban See, it's a son	yタYチ9
Dominicans	Simeon	Sha-Mi-Wan Affliction heard	yYoyw
Afro-Americans	Judah	Ya-Ha-Wa-Dah Yahawah Thanks	ヨ△9Yヨエ
Mexicans	Issachar	Yash-Sha-Kar He is hired	9ywwエ
Guatemala to Panama	Zebulon	Za-Ba-La-Wan Dwelling	yYし9エ
Puerto Rico	Ephraim	Ah-Pa-Ra-Yam I am fruitfill	yエ刊9チ
Cubans	Manasseh	Ma-Na-Shah Made to forget	ヨwyy
Jamaicans	Benjamin	Ban-Yam-Yan Son of the Right	yエyエy9
Carib Indians	Dan	Dan Judge	y△
Columbia to Uruguay	Asher	Ah-Shar Happy	9wチ
Nor. American Indians	Gad	Gad Troop	△7
Argentina and Chile	Napthali	Na-Pa-Thal-Ya My wrestling	エしxyy

354

The Ten Commandments Ha I-Sha-Ra Ma-Taza-Wath*		×Y𝑟ᴍ𝑦 𝑓wo𝑓
1.Thou shalt have no other gods before me.	La-Ah Ya-Ha-Ya La-Ka Ah-La-Ha-Yam Ah-Chaar-Yam IL-Pan-Ya.	𝑦𝑟𝑎𝑙𝑘 𝑦𝑙 𝑧𝑎𝑧𝑘𝑙 𝑧𝑦𝑓𝑙0𝑦𝑧 𝑓𝐻𝑘𝑦𝑧
2.Thou shalt not make unto thee any graven image, nor serve them.	La-Ah Tha-I-Shah La-Ka Pa-Sal Wa-La-Ah Tha-I-Ba-Dam.	𝑙𝐹𝑓 𝑦𝑙 𝑓wo× 𝑘𝑙 𝑦𝑓𝑔o× 𝑘𝑙Y
3. Thou shalt not take the name of the Lord in vain.	La-Ah Tha-La-Qach-Ath Sham Ya-Ha-Wah Ba Sha-Wah.	𝑦w ×𝑘𝐻𝑃𝑙× 𝑘𝑙 𝑓Yw𝑔 𝑓Y𝑧𝑧
4. Remember the Sabbath day, to keep it holy.	Zakar Ha Ya-Wam Ha Sha-Bath La Qa-Dash-Wa.	×𝑔w𝑓 𝑦Y𝑧𝑓 𝑓𝑦𝑧 Yw𝑓𝑃𝑙
5. Honor thy Father and thy mother.	Ka-Bad Ah-Ba-Ka Wa Ah-Ma-Ka.	𝑦𝑦𝑘Y 𝑦𝑔𝑘 𝑔𝑔𝑦
6. Thou shalt not kill (murder).	La-Ah Tha-Ra-Tazach.	𝐻𝑟𝑓×𝑘𝑙
7. Thou shalt not commit adultery.	La-Ah Tha-Na-Ap.	𝑓𝑘𝑦×𝑘𝑙
8. Thou shalt not steal.	La-Ah Tha-Ga-Nab.	𝑔𝑦𝑟×𝑘𝑙
9. Thou shalt not bear false witness against thy neighbor.	La-Ah Tha-I-Nah Sha-Qar.	𝑓𝑦o×𝑘𝑙
10. Thou shalt not covet any thing which is thy neighbor's	La-Ah Tha-Chaa-Mad Kal Ah-Sha-Ra La Ra-I-Ka.	𝑓w𝑘 𝑙𝑦𝑔𝑦𝐻×𝑘𝑙 𝑦o𝑓𝑙

THE TRUTH

Prayer For The Anointing Of The Israelites (Numbers 6:24-26)

𐤉𐤅𐤔𐤌𐤓𐤅	𐤄𐤅𐤄𐤉	𐤉𐤋𐤓𐤊𐤅
:KA MAR SHA YA WA	WAH HA YA	KA RAK BA YA
YOU WATCHES/KEEPETH AND	THE MOST HIGH	BLESSES YOU HE

𐤊𐤋𐤓	𐤅𐤉𐤋	𐤄𐤅𐤄𐤉	𐤓𐤋𐤓
KA YA AL	WA YA PAN	WAH AH YA	AR YA
YOU UNTO	HIS FACE	THE MOST HIGH	SHINE

𐤅𐤉𐤋	𐤄𐤅𐤄𐤉	𐤓𐤔𐤉	𐤊𐤄𐤉𐤅
WA YA PAN	WAH HA YA	AH SHA YA	:KA CHAAN YA WA
HIS FACE	THE MOST HIGH	LIFT HE	TO YOU GRACIOUS AND

𐤔𐤋	𐤋𐤊	𐤅𐤉𐤔𐤌	𐤊𐤋𐤓
:LAM SHA	KA LA	SHAM YA WA	KA YA AL
PEACE	YOU TO	PLACES HE AND	YOU UNTO

𐤄𐤓𐤅	𐤊𐤓𐤁	𐤏𐤔𐤅𐤄𐤉	𐤔𐤁𐤄	𐤄𐤅𐤄𐤉
___PAH RA WA	RAK BA	SHY WA HA YA	SHAM HA BA	WAH HA YA
HEAL AND	BLESS	SAVIOR / JESUS	NAME THE IN	THE MOST HIGH

Deuteronomy 6:4

𐤄𐤅𐤄𐤉	𐤋𐤓𐤔𐤉	𐤏𐤌𐤔
WAH HA YA	LA AH SHAR YA	MI SHA
THE MOST HIGH	ISRAEL OH	HEAR

𐤃𐤓𐤊	𐤄𐤅𐤄𐤉	𐤅𐤍𐤉𐤄𐤋𐤓
CHAAD AH	WAH HA YA	WA NA YA HA LA.AH
IS ONE	YAHAWAH	OUR ALMIGHTY GOD

Greetings

𐤄𐤕𐤓	𐤊𐤓𐤁	𐤏𐤔𐤅𐤄𐤉	𐤔𐤁𐤄	𐤄𐤅𐤄𐤉
THA AH	RAK BA	SHY WA HA YA	SHAM HA BA	WAH HA YA
(BROTHER)YOU	BLESS	JESUS	NAME IN	YA-HA-WAH

𐤔𐤌𐤓𐤕𐤓	𐤏𐤔𐤅𐤄𐤉	𐤔𐤁𐤄	𐤄𐤅𐤄𐤉
THA MAR SHA	SHY WA HA YA	SHAM HA BA	WA HA YA
(SISTER)YOU WATCH	JESUS	NAME IN	YA-HA-WAH

THE TRUTH

PSALMS 121 IN HEBREW

YAN AH MA	YAM HAR HA	AL	YA YAM YAN I	SHA NA AH
WHERE FROM	THE HILLS	UNTO	MY EYES	WILL LIFT UP

AH BA MA	YA ZAR I	:YA ZAR I	AH WA BA YA
COMES FROM	MY HELP	MY HELP	SHALL COME

:TAZA RA AH WA	YAM MA SHA	SHA I	WAH HA YAH
EARTH THE AND	OF HEAVEN	MAKER	YAHAWAH

AH LA	YA GAL RA	WAT MA LA	THAN NA YA	AH LA
NOT	MY FOOT	SLIP TO	GIVES HE	NOT

WAM NA YA	AH LA	NAH HA	:YA MAR SHA	WAM NA YA
SLUMBER HE	NOT	BEHOLD	HE WATCHES	SLUMBER HE

ALA SHAR YA	MAR WA SHA	SHAN YA YA	AH LA WA
ISRAEL	HE WHO KEEPS	SLEEP	NOT AND

IL	YAH ZAL TA	WAH HA YA	YA MAR SHA	WAH HA YA
UPON	MY SHADE	YAHAWAH	MY KEEPER	YAHAWAH

AH LA YA	MASH SHA HA	MA WAM YA	:YA YAN YAM	YAD
NOT ME	SUN THE	BY DAY	MY RIGHT	HAND

:LAH YAH LA BA	RACH YA HA	AH LA WA	KAH NA YA
NIGHT IN	MOON THE	NOT AND	STRIKE

MAR SHA YA	RAI	KAL MA	YA MAR SHA YA	WAH HA YA
SHALL KEEP HE	EVIL	ALL FROM	ME SHALL KEEP HE	YAHAWAH

YA THA TAZA	MAR SHA YA	WAH HA YA	:YA PASH NA
MY GOING OUT	SHALL KEEP HE	YAHAWAH	MY SOUL

AH-MAN	:LAM WA I	ID WA	THAH I MA	YA AH WA BA WA
	FOREVER	UNTIL AND	NOW FROM	MY COMING IN AND

THE LORD'S PRAYER IN HEBREW

וקדש	שבשמים	אבנו
DASH QA	YAM MA SHA BA SHA	WA NA BA AH
HOLY	HEAVEN IN THAT	OUR FATHER

מלכותך	שמך	היה
KA WATH LAK MA	KA SHAM	YAH HA
YOUR KINGDOM	YOUR NAME	THERE BE

עשה	היה	רצונך	תבא :
SHAH I	YAH HA	KA TAZAH RA	AH BA THA
DONE	THERE BE	YOUR WANT	COME

: בשמים	היה	כו	בארץ
YAM MA SHA BA	YAH HA	WA KA	TAZA RA AH BA
HEAVEN IN	THERE BE	AS	EARTH IN

: יום	זה	לחם	נתן לנו
WAM YA	ZAH	CHAAM LA	WA NA LA THAN NA
DAY	THIS	BREAD	OUR TO GIVE

חובתנו	וסלח לנו
WA NA WATH WAB CHAA	WA NA LA LACH SA WA
OUR DEBT	OUR TO FORGIVE

: חובתינו	וסלחנו
WA NA YA WATH WAB CHAA	WA NA LACH SA KA
OUR DEBTORS	OUR FORGIVE AS

בנסיון	תביאנו	ולא
WAN YA SA NA BA	WA NA AH YA BA THA	AH LA WA
TEMPTER IN	US LEAD (OR BRING)	NOT AND

: רע	מן	הצילנו	אבל
RI	YAN MA	WA NA SHY WA HA	BAL AH
EVIL	FROM	US DELIVER	BUT

והאל	הממלכת	לך	כי
LA AH HA WA	WATH LAK MA HA	KA LA	YA KA
POWER THE AND	KINGDOM THE	YOU TO	FOR

אמן	: לעולמים	ותפארת
MAN AH	YAM LAM WA I LA	RATH AH PA THA HA WA
SO BE IT	FOR EVER	GLORY THE AND

358

THE TRUTH

Word List: English - Hebrew

All (Kal)	לכ	Beard (Za-Qa-Na)	זקן
Alone (La-Bad)	לבד	Beast-(Bah-Mah)	בהמה
Also, Too (Gam)	גם	Beautiful (Ya-Pah)	יפה
Altar (Ma-Za-Bach)	מזבח	Because (Ka-Ya)	כי
Always (Tham-Yad)	תמיד	Bed (Ma-Ma-Tah)	מטמה
Ancient, Ancestral (Za-Qan)	זקן	Before (La-Pan-Ya)	לפני
Ancient (I-Tha.Yaq)	עתיק	Beginning (Ra-Ash-Yath)	ראשית
And (Wa)	ו	Behind, Alter (Ah-Chaar-Ya)	אחרי
Angry (Qa-Tazap)	קצף	Believe (Ha-Ah-Ma-Yan)	האמין
Anoint (Ma-Shach)	משח	Behold (Ha-Nah)	הנה
Anointed (Ma-Sha-Yach)	משיח	Between (Ba-Yan)	בין
Appear (Ra-Ah)	ראה	Birds (Ta-Za-Par)	צפר
Appoint (Wa-Id)	ועד	Black (Sha-Chaa-War)	שחור
Arise (Qam)	קם	Blaze (La-Hab)	להב
As, Like (Ka)	כ	Bless (Ba-Rak)	ברך
Ascend (I-Lah)	עלה	Blood (Dam)	דם
Ask (Sha-Al)	שאל	Blue (Tha-Ka-Lath)	תכלת
Bad or Evil (Ri)	רע	Bore fruits (Ra-Ta-za-Ah)	רצא
Bag (Ya-La-Qa-Wat)	ילקוט	Book (Sa-Par)	ספר
Be (Ha-Yah)	היה	Box (Tha-Bah)	תבה
Bear (animal) (Dab)	דב	Boy (Ya-Lad)	ילד

360

THE TRUTH

Branch (I-Nap)	𐤐𐤍𐤉	Close (Sa-Gar)	𐤓𐤂𐤎
Brass (Na-Chaa-Shath)	𐤕𐤔𐤄𐤍	Cloud (I-Nan)	𐤍𐤍𐤉
Bread (La-Chaam)	𐤌𐤄𐤋	Cluster (Ash-Ka-Wal)	𐤋𐤊𐤅𐤔𐤀
Break (Sha-Bar)	𐤓𐤁𐤔	Coffee (Qa-Pah)	𐤄𐤐𐤒
Bring, Lead (Ba-Ya-Ah)	𐤀𐤆𐤁	Cold (Qar)	𐤓𐤒
Bronze (Ah-Rad)	𐤃𐤓𐤀	Collection (Ma-Qa-Wah)	𐤄𐤅𐤒𐤌
Brother (Ahch)	𐤄𐤀	Come (Ba-Ah)	𐤀𐤁
Brown (Sha-Chaam)	𐤌𐤄𐤔	Command (Taza-Wah)	𐤄𐤅𐤑
Build (Ba-Nah)	𐤄𐤍𐤁	Companion (Chaa-Bar)	𐤓𐤁𐤄
But (Ah-Bal)	𐤋𐤁𐤀	Conquer (Ma-Na-Tazach)	𐤄𐤑𐤍𐤌
Butter (Chaa-Ma-Ah)	𐤀𐤌𐤄	Counselor (Ya-Wi-Taza)	𐤑𐤅𐤉
Call (Qa-Ra)	𐤀𐤓𐤒	Cow (Pa-Rah)	𐤄𐤓𐤐
Camel (Ga-Mal)	𐤋𐤌𐤂	Create (Ba-Ra)	𐤀𐤓𐤁
Car, Chariot (Ma-Ra-Kab)	𐤁𐤊𐤓𐤌	Creep (Ra-Mash)	𐤔𐤌𐤓
Carry (Na-Sha)	𐤀𐤔𐤍	Curse (Ah-Rar)	𐤓𐤓𐤀
Cattle (Ah-Lap)	𐤐𐤋𐤀	Cut (Ka-Rath)	𐤕𐤓𐤊
Celebrate (Chaa-Gag)	𐤂𐤂𐤄	Darkness (Chaa-Shak)	𐤊𐤔𐤄
Chair (Ka-Sa)	𐤀𐤎𐤊	Daughter (Ba-Nath)	𐤕𐤍𐤁
Cheese (Ga-Ba-Ya-Nah)	𐤄𐤍𐤆𐤁𐤂	Day (Ya-Wam)	𐤌𐤅𐤉
Choose (Ba-Chaar)	𐤓𐤄𐤁	Debts (Chaa-Wab-Wath)	𐤕𐤅𐤁𐤄
Circumcise (Mal)	𐤋𐤌	Deep (Tha-Ha-Wam)	𐤌𐤅𐤄𐤕
City (I-Yar)	𐤓𐤉𐤏	Definitive (Ath)	𐤕𐤀
Cleave (Da-Baq)	𐤒𐤁𐤃	Deliver (Ha-Taza-Yal)	𐤋𐤑𐤄

THE TRUTH

English	Script	English	Script
Destroy (A-Bad)		Faith (Ah-Ma-Wan)	
Diligent (Chaa-Raw-Taza)		Father (Ah-Ba)	
Divide (Pa-Lag)		Fear (Ya-Ra)	
Do (Da)		Female (Na-Qa-Bah)	
Doing (Da-Wa)		Field (Sha-Dah)	
Door (Da-Lath)		Fight (La-Chaa-Ma)	
Down (Ma-Tah)		Fill (Ma-La)	
Dream (chaa-Lam)		Finish (Ga-Mar)	
Drink (Sha-Thah)		Fire (Ash)	
Drunk (Sha-Kar)		First (Ra-Ash-Wan)	
Dry (Ya-Ba-Shah)		Fish (Dag)	
Ear (Ah-Zan)		Flesh (Ba-Shar)	
Earth (Ah-Ra-Taza)		Fly (Ip)	
East (Qa-Dam)		Foot (Ra-Gal)	
Eat (Ah-Kal)		Forever (I-Wa-Lam-Yam)	
Eden (I-Dan)		Forget (Na-Shah)	
Empty (Ba-Haw)		Forgive, Excuse (Sa-Lach)	
End (Qa-Tazah)		Fork (Ma-Za-Lag)	
Enemy (Ah-Yab-Ya)		Form (Tha-Haw)	
Evening (I-Rab)		Friend (m) (Ra-i)	
Expense (Ra-Qa-Yai)		Fringe (Taza-Ya-Zah)	
Eye (I-Yan)		From (Ma-Yan)	
Face (Pan-Ya)		Fruit (Par-Ya)	

THE TRUTH

Garden (Gan)	𐤉𐤍	Head (Ra-Ash)	𐤅𐤊𐤀	
Garment (Ba-Gad)	𐤃𐤂𐤁	Heal (Rah-Pah)	𐤀𐤅𐤉	
Gather (Qa-Wah)	𐤀𐤉𐤒	Hear, Listen (Sha-Mi)	𐤏𐤌𐤅	
Get (Lak)	𐤉𐤋	Heart (Lab)	𐤂𐤋	
Girdle (Ah-Ba-Nat)	𐤈𐤍𐤁𐤊	Heaven (Sha-Ma-Yam)	𐤌𐤆𐤌𐤅	
Girl (Ya-La-Dah)	𐤀𐤃𐤋𐤆	Heavy (Ka-Bad)	𐤃𐤂𐤉	
Give to me (Na-Than-La-Ya)	𐤆𐤋𐤉𐤍𐤉	Hebrew language) (I-Bar-Yath)	𐤗𐤆𐤅𐤁𐤏	
Give (Na-Than)	𐤉𐤗𐤍	Help (I-Zar)	𐤀𐤆𐤏	
Glass, Cup (Ka-Was)	𐤎𐤅𐤉	Hebrite (I-Bar-Ya)	𐤆𐤅𐤁𐤏	
Glory (Tha-Pa-Ah-Rath)	𐤗𐤀𐤊𐤐𐤗	Herbs (I-Shab)	𐤁𐤅𐤏	
Gods, Powers (Ah-La-Yam)	𐤌𐤆𐤋𐤊	Here (Ka-An)	𐤉𐤊𐤉	
Good (Ta-Wab)	𐤁𐤉𐤈	High, Exalted (Ram)	𐤌𐤅	
Gracious (Ya-Chaan)	𐤉𐤇𐤆	Hills (Har-Yam)	𐤌𐤆𐤅𐤁	
Grape (I-Nab)	𐤁𐤉𐤏	Home (Ba-Yath)	𐤗𐤆𐤁	
Grass (I-Shab)	𐤁𐤅𐤏	Honey (Da-Bash)	𐤅𐤁𐤃	
Great (Ga-Dal)	𐤋𐤃𐤂	Hook (Wa-Wa)	𐤉𐤉	
Green (Ya-Ra-Qa)	𐤒𐤅𐤆	Hot (Chaam)	𐤌𐤇	
Ground (Ah-Da-Ma)	𐤀𐤌𐤃𐤊	Hour (Sha-I-Ha)	𐤀𐤅𐤅	
Grow (Taza-Mach)	𐤅𐤌𐤇	House (Ba-Yath)	𐤗𐤆𐤁	
Hair (Sha-Ir)	𐤒𐤏𐤅	Hover (Ma-Ra-Chaa-Path)	𐤗𐤐𐤇𐤅𐤌	
Hand (Yad)	𐤃𐤆	How (Ah-Yak)	𐤉𐤆𐤊	
Happy (Ah-Shar)	𐤅𐤅𐤊	If, Whether (Am)	𐤌𐤊	
Harvest (Qa-Taza-Yar)	𐤒𐤅𐤅𐤒	Hungry (Ra-Ib)	𐤂𐤅𐤅	

Image, Idol (Taza-Lam)	𐤔𐤋𐤌		Leave (I-Zab)	𐤏𐤆𐤁
In (Ba)	𐤁		Leg (Ka-Ri)	𐤊𐤓𐤏
Iron (Ba-Ra-Zal)	𐤁𐤆𐤓𐤋		Leprosy (Taza-Ra-ith)	𐤔𐤓𐤏𐤕
Irrigate (Sha-Qah)	𐤔𐤒𐤄		Letter (Mak-Thab)	𐤌𐤊𐤕𐤁
It (Ha-Wa-Ah)	𐤄𐤅𐤀		Lie, False (Ka-Zab)	𐤊𐤆𐤁
Jerusalem (Ya-Raw-Sha-Lam)	𐤉𐤓𐤅𐤔𐤋𐤌		Lie down, relcine (Sha-Kab)	𐤔𐤊𐤁
Judge (Sha-Pat)	𐤔𐤐𐤈		Light (Ah-War)	𐤀𐤅𐤓
Judgement (Ma-Sha-Pat)	𐤌𐤔𐤐𐤈		Lightning (Ba-Raq)	𐤁𐤓𐤒
Key (Ma-Pa-Thach)	𐤌𐤐𐤕𐤇		Likeness (Da-Ma-Wath)	𐤃𐤌𐤅𐤕
Kill (Ha-Rag)	𐤄𐤓𐤂		Loin, Penis (Ma-Ma-Than)	𐤌𐤌𐤕𐤍
Kind (Ma-Ya-Nah)	𐤌𐤉𐤍𐤄		Lip (Sha-Pah)	𐤔𐤐𐤄
King (Ma-Lak)	𐤌𐤋𐤊		Little (Ma-It)	𐤌𐤏𐤈
Kingdom (Ma-Lak-Wath)	𐤌𐤋𐤊𐤅𐤕		Living (Chaa-Ya)	𐤇𐤉
Kiss (Na-Shaq)	𐤍𐤔𐤒		Lion (Ah-Ra-Ya)	𐤀𐤓𐤉
Knife (Sa-Ka-Yan)	𐤎𐤊𐤉𐤍		Lock of Hair (Pa-Ri)	𐤐𐤓
Know (Ya-Di)	𐤉𐤃𐤏		Look (Ma-Ra-Ah)	𐤌𐤓𐤀
Lamb (Shah)	𐤔𐤄		Lord, Sir (Ah-Da-Wan)	𐤀𐤃𐤅𐤍
Lamp (Ma-Na-Wa-Rah)	𐤌𐤍𐤅𐤓𐤄		Love (Ah-Hab)	𐤀𐤄𐤁
Language, Tongue (La-Sha-Wan)	𐤋𐤔𐤅𐤍		Make (I-Shah)	𐤏𐤔𐤄
Last (Ah-Chaar-Wan)	𐤀𐤇𐤓𐤅𐤍		Male (Za-Ka-War)	𐤆𐤊𐤅𐤓
Law (Tha-Wa-Rah)	𐤕𐤅𐤓𐤄		Man (Ah-Yash)	𐤀𐤉𐤔
Lead (I-Wa-Pa-Rath)	𐤏𐤅𐤐𐤓𐤕		Me (Ah-Wath-Ya)	𐤀𐤅𐤕𐤉
Learn (La-Mad)	𐤋𐤌𐤃		Measure (Ma-Dad)	𐤌𐤃𐤃

English	Script	English	Script
Meet (Pa-Gash)		North (Taza-Pa-Wan)	
Mercy (Chaa-Sad)		Now (I-Thah)	
Midst, Middle (Tha-Wak)		Of (Shal)	
Milk (Chaa-Lab)		Oil (Sha-Man)	
Minute (Da-Qah)		Old (Za-Qan)	
Money (Sha-Qal)		Olive (Za-Yath)	
Moon (Ya-Rach)		On, Upon, Above (IL)	
More and Still (I-Wad)		Only (Raq)	
Morning (Ba-Wa-Qar)		Open (Pa-Thach)	
Mother (Ah-Ma)		Or (Aw)	
Mt. Sinai (Har-Sa-Yan-Ya)		Order (I-Rak)	
Multiply (Ya-Rab)		Original (Ma-Qa-War)	
Moving (Ma-Ra-Chaa-Path)		Page (Dap)	
Murder (Ra-Tazach)		Pain (Ka-Ab / Ma-Chaa-Wash)	
Music (Na-Ga-Ya-Nah)		Palm of the Hand (Kap)	
Musical (Na-Ga-Ya-Nath-Ya)		Paper (Na-Yar)	
Musician (Ma-Na-Gan)		Passover (Pa-Sach)	
Naked (I-Ram)		Past, Pass (l-Bar)	
Need (Taza-Rak)		Pay (Tha-Sha-La-Warn)	
New, month (Chaa-Dash)		Pen, Pencil (It)	
Next (Ah-Chaar)		People (Im)	
Night (La-Ya-Lah)		Phone (Da-Bar-Tha-Bah)	
No, Not (La-Ah)		Pig, Swine (Chaa-Za-Yar)	

THE TRUTH

English (Pronunciation)	Symbol	English (Pronunciation)	Symbol
Place (Ma-Ga-Wam)		River (Na-Har)	
Plate (Qa-I-Rah)		Room (Chaa-Dar)	
Please (Ba-Ba-Qa-Shah)		Rule (Ma-Ma-Sha-Lah)	
Poor (In-Ya)		Sacrifice (Za-Bach)	
Powers (Ah-La-Ha-Yam)		Say (Ah-Mar)	
Pray (Pa-Lal)		Scarlet (Sha-Nay)	
Priest (Ka-Han)		Sea (Yam)	
Punish (I-Nash)		Sea Monster (Tha-Na-Ya-Nam)	
Pupil (m) (Thal-Ma-Yad)		Season (Ma-Wa-Id)	
Purple (Ah-Ra-Ga-Man)		Seed (Za-Ri)	
Put (Sha-Path)		Sell (Ma-Kar)	
Quarter (Ra-Bi)		Semen (Sha-Ka-Bath-Za-Ri)	
Queen (Ma-La-Kah)		Send (Sha-Lach)	
Radio (Sha-Mi-Tha-Bah)		Separate (Ba-Dal)	
Rain (Ma-Tar)		Set (Na-Tha-Na)	
Read (Qa-Ra)		Sheaf (I-Mar)	
Real (Ah-Math-Ya)		Sheep (Ka-Bash)	
Red (Ah-Da-Wam)		Shield (Ma-Gan)	
Remember (Za-Kar)		Shoe (Na-IL)	
Rest (Sha-Bath)		Sign, cross (Tha-Wa)	
Rich (I-Sha-Yar)		Signs, prophetic (Ath-Wath)	
Ride (Ra-Kab)		Silver (Ka-Sap)	
Right (Yam-Yan)		Sin (Chaa-Ta)	

366

Sister (Ahch-Wath)	XYEK	Studs (Na-Qad-Yam)	ッマ◁ዋッ
Sit (Ya-Shab)	ЭWマ	Smite (Na-Kah)	ЭYッ
Sky, Firmament (Ra-Qa-YI)	oマዋ◀	Summer (Qa-Ya-Taza)	Һマዋ
Sleep (Ya-Shan)	ッWマ	Sun (Sha-Mash)	WッW
Slip (Ma-Wat)	⊗Yッ	Support (Sa-Mak)	Yッ手
Slumber (Na-Ran)	Yዋッ	Surround (Sa-Bab)	ЭЭ手
Small (Qa-Tan)	Y⊗ዋ	Swarm (Sha-Ra-Ta-Za)	Һ◀W
Smite (Ha-Kah)	ЭYЭ	Sweet (Ra-Yach)	日マ◀
Son (Ban)	Yэ	Sword (Chaa-Rab)	Э◀日
Soul (Na-Pash)	WフY	TV (Ra-Ah-Tha-Bah)	ЭэxK◀
South (Na-Gab)	эフY	Table (Shal-Chaan)	ッ日W
Speak, Word (Da-Bar)	◀э△	Take (La-Qach)	日ዋ/
Spirit (Raw-Chaa)	日◀	Taste (Ta-Im)	ッo⊗
Spoon (Ma-Kap)	フッッ	Tea (Tha-Ya-Ya)	ママx
Spring (Ah-Ba-Yab)	ЭマэK	Teacher (m) (Ma-Ah-War)	◀YKッ
Sprout (Da-Sha)	KW◁	Temptation (Na-Sa-Ya-Wan)	ッYマ手ッ
Staff (Ma-Qal)	/ዋッ	Thank You (Tha-Wa-Dah)	Э◁YX
Stand (I-Mad)	◁ッo	That (F) (Ha-Ha-Ya-Ah)	KマЭЭ
Star (Ka-Wa-Kab)	эYYッ	That (M) (Ha-Ha-Wa-Ah)	KYЭЭ
Statute (Chaaq)	ዋ日	The (Ha)	Э
Stone (A-Ban)	YэK	Then (Az)	zK
Stop (Chaa-Dal)	/◀日	There be (Ya-Ha-Ya)	マЭマ
Straight, Upright (Ya-Shar)	◀Wマ	There is are not (Ah-Yan)	ッマK

THE TRUTH

There is, are (Yash)	𐤉𐤔
There, Name (Sham)	𐤔𐤌
Therefore (La-Kan)	𐤋𐤊𐤍
These (Al-Ha)	𐤀𐤋𐤄
Think (Chaa-Shab)	𐤇𐤔𐤁
Thirst (Taza-Ma)	𐤑𐤌
This (m) (Zah)	𐤆𐤄
This (f) (Za-Ath)	𐤆𐤀𐤕
Those (m) (Ha-Ham)	𐤄𐤄𐤌
Those (f) (Ha-Han)	𐤄𐤄𐤍
Thunder (Ra-Im)	𐤓𐤏𐤌
Time (Pa-Im)	𐤐𐤏𐤌
Tin (Bad-Yal)	𐤁𐤃𐤉𐤋
To (La)	𐤋
Tomorrow (Ma-Chaar)	𐤌𐤇𐤓
Tooth (Shan)	𐤔𐤍
Touch (Na-Gi)	𐤍𐤂𐤏
Train (Ba-Ra-Zal Sa-Was)	𐤁𐤓𐤆𐤋𐤎𐤅𐤎
Tree (I-Taza)	𐤏𐤑
Tribe (Sha-Ba-Ta)	𐤔𐤁𐤈
Trumpet (Sha-Par)	𐤔𐤐𐤓
Truth (Ah-Math)	𐤀𐤌𐤕
Turban (Ma-Tazan-Path)	𐤌𐤑𐤍𐤐𐤕
Turn (Sar)	𐤎𐤓
Under (Tha-Chaath)	𐤕𐤇𐤕
Unto (Al)	𐤀𐤋
Up (La-Ma-Il)	𐤋𐤌𐤏𐤋
Vagina (Qa-Bah)	𐤒𐤁𐤄
Very (Ma-Ad)	𐤌𐤀𐤃
Voice (Qa-Wal)	𐤒𐤅𐤋
Void (Ba-Haw)	𐤁𐤄𐤅
Wait (Chaa-Kah)	𐤇𐤊𐤄
Walk, Go (Ha-Lak)	𐤄𐤋𐤊
Want (Ra-Tazah)	𐤓𐤑𐤄
Warrior (Ga-Bar)	𐤂𐤁𐤓
Was (Ha-Ya-Tha)	𐤄𐤉𐤕
Waste (Tha-Haw)	𐤕𐤄𐤅
Watch (Sha-Mar)	𐤔𐤌𐤓
Water (Ma-Yam)	𐤌𐤉𐤌
Wave (Na-Yap)	𐤍𐤉𐤐
Way (Da-Rak)	𐤃𐤓𐤊
Weapon (Za-Yan)	𐤆𐤉𐤍
Week (Sha-Ba-Wi)	𐤔𐤁𐤅𐤏
Weight, Talent (Ka-Kar)	𐤊𐤊𐤓
Well, good (Ha-Ya-Tab)	𐤄𐤉𐤈𐤁
Well of Water (Ba-Ar)	𐤁𐤀𐤓

THE TRUTH

West (Ma-I-Rab)	𐤌𐤏𐤓𐤁	Wise (Chaa-Kam)	𐤇𐤊𐤌	
What (Mah)	𐤌𐤄	With (Ath)	𐤀𐤕	
When (Math-Ya)	𐤌𐤕𐤉	Woman (Ah-Ya-Shah)	𐤀𐤉𐤔𐤄	
Where (Ah-Yah)	𐤀𐤉𐤄	Wood, Forest (Ya-Ir)	𐤉𐤏𐤓	
Which (Ah-Sha-Ra)	𐤀𐤔𐤓	Write (Ka-Thab)	𐤊𐤕𐤁	
White (La-Ban)	𐤋𐤁𐤍	Year (Sha-Nah)	𐤔𐤍𐤄	
Who (Ma-Ya)	𐤌𐤉	Yellow (Taza-Hab)	𐤑𐤄𐤁	
Why (Ma-Da-Wi)	𐤌𐤃𐤅𐤏	Yes, So (Kan)	𐤊𐤍	
Window (Chaa-La-Wa)	𐤇𐤋𐤅𐤍	Yesterday (Ath-Ma-Wal)	𐤀𐤕𐤌𐤅𐤋	
Wine (Ya-Yan)	𐤉𐤉𐤍	Young (Taza-I-Yar)	𐤑𐤏𐤓	
Winter (Chaa-Rap)	𐤇𐤓𐤐	Youth (m) (Na-Ir)	𐤍𐤏𐤓	

THE TRUTH

The Israelite Network Service Request Form

What price is your freedom worth?

Welcome to the Israelite Network. Thank you for joining with us. Fear and ignorance are the chains of slavery. Add more honors to your life by getting involved. It is time to stop living on your knees. We fight for your liberation and your support is no longer an option, it is a necessity. We are dedicated to revealing the truth according to the Biblical facts, and to provide you with community support.

You may use this form to make contributions and to order any of our products and services. You can also submit this form through the Internet at our web site, **http//www.israelite.net**. Feel free to call us at (212) 586-5969, or mail the form to: THE ISRAELITE NETWORK, P.O. BOX 1747, NYC, NY 10101.

Name: **Organization:**

Address: **City:**   **State/Province:**

Zip/Postal: **Country:**   **Tel:**   **Fax:**   **E-mail:**

Please make Your Selection (s) note any quantity numbers:

- ❑ Ordering book - **THE TRUTH: Identity, Wisdom and Destiny of the descendents of the twelve tribes of Israel, the genealogy of the nations, and other secret bible mysteries... $24.95**
- ❑ Ordering book - **THE TORAH - In Ancient Hebrew: $45**
- ❑ Ordering book - **THE TANACH - In Ancient Hebrew Volume One: $45**
- ❑ Ordering book - **THE TANACH - In Ancient Hebrew Volume Two: $45**
- ❑ Ordering book - **ANCIENT HEBREW - ENGLISH DICTIONARY: $45**
- ❑ Ordering Newsletter, Holy Calendar, pins and flags
- ❑ Annual Membership Donation
- ❑ Paying tithes
- ❑ Making a freewill offering
- ❑ Donation to the missionary Program
- ❑ Offering / Requesting Goods and Services
- ❑ Volunteering
- ❑ Becoming a Distributor of the books
- ❑ Setting up an Israelite Network Sanctuary

Note Comments, instructions, and prayer requests here:

Enter your Classified Advertisement, with the location and details.
What positions are you trying to fill/find or goods/services you are offering? It will be published on http://iraelite.net:

I pledge a donation of $ **and request:**   **pins,**   **flags,**   **Newsletter,**   **Holy Days Calendar.**

We are fighting for your freedom and you need to take an active role now. The time is very short. Listen to your conscience. Put your money where you mind is. If you appreciate our work lets heart it with a pledge. If you will benefit from our services and efforts you should contribute your share, so that we can continue to service a world in need of the truth, love and salvation. Thank you and welcome to the Israelite Network.

Printed in the United States
3746